SELECTIONS AND ESSAYS

BY

JOHN RUSKIN

THE MODERN
STUDENT'S LIBRARY

EACH VOLUME EDITED BY A LEADING
AMERICAN AUTHORITY

This series is composed of such works as
are conspicuous in the province of literature
for their enduring influence. Every volume
is recognized as essential to a liberal education and will tend to infuse a love for true
literature and an appreciation of the qualities which cause it to endure.

*A descriptive list of the volumes published in
this series appears in the last pages
of this volume*

CHARLES SCRIBNER'S SONS

SELECTIONS AND ESSAYS

BY

JOHN RUSKIN

EDITED, WITH AN INTRODUCTION

BY

FREDERICK WILLIAM ROE

ASSISTANT PROFESSOR OF ENGLISH, UNIVERSITY OF WISCONSIN

CHARLES SCRIBNER'S SONS

NEW YORK   CHICAGO   BOSTON   ATLANTA
SAN FRANCISCO   DALLAS

CONTENTS

III. ART *all of*

IV. ART AND SOCIETY

CONTENTS

INTRODUCTION

The life of John Ruskin, like that of his master Carlyle, stretched nearly across the nineteenth century. Born in 1819, before the industrial revolution had fairly begun, he lived to see England transformed, by the application of steam and electricity, into the England of to-day, for he died as late as 1900, at the age of eighty-one. Considering the great range and abundance of his work, considering his distinction as a writer of prose, as an art-critic, and as a social reformer, Ruskin's career was extraordinary even in an age of great men. His first printed book appeared in 1830, when he was a boy of eleven, his last in 1889, fifty-nine years later. As his latest biographer, Sir E. T. Cook, says: "the world in which he lived and moved and had his being was from his earliest years the world of art and letters." For more than half a century, he wrote, lectured, and talked on mountains, waves, leaves, and clouds; rocks, minerals, birds, and flowers; painting, architecture, sculpture, engraving, and drawing; political economy, social reform, education, and ethics; myths, literature, and religion. These discursive writings, recently gathered into the *Library Edition*, number thirty-seven volumes,—a splendid monument of life-long devotion to truth, beauty, and justice. No literary reputation and influence could be more stormy than his. In the days when his position as an art-critic was at its height, he was hailed by William Morris and Burne-Jones as a "Luther of the Arts." Even the cool rationalist, John Stuart Mill, recorded in his diary that whereas most men were but commentators, "Ruskin was one of those two men in Europe who seemed to draw what he said from a source within himself." Then came a change. "From 1845 to 1860," said Ruskin, "I went on with more or less of public applause; and then in 1860 people saw a change come over me which they highly disapproved, and I went on from 1860 to 1875 under the weight of continuously increasing public recusancy and reprobation." The transition was from art to political economy, and with it his reputation for a time collapsed. The reviews railed at him as a quixotic sentimentalist suddenly gone mad. Friends withdrew in disgust. When *Unto This Last* appeared, Rossetti called it "bosh" and declared that Ruskin talked "awful rubbish." Ruskin himself wrote that people were now accustomed to hear him spoken of by artists as a "superannuated enthusiast," and by philosophers and practical people as a "delirious visionary." Out of the darkness of these later years one of the few voices of encouragement was the voice of Carlyle, the old crabbed prophet of his age, who rejoiced to see the "fierce lightning-bolts" that Ruskin was "copiously and desperately pouring into the black world of anarchy all around him." But time has wrought its revenges. To-day Ruskin ranks securely among the major Victorians, a writer whose message has immensely quickened our sense of beauty in the world of nature and our sense of justice in the world of men:—"one of the greatest English writers, and one of the greatest writers of our age," said Tolstoi; one of "the six authors in whom the stateliest English prose was to be found," according to Tennyson.

Ruskin's fame began with the publication of the first volume of *Modern Painters* in 1843, a book which came from the press as the anonymous work of a "Graduate of Oxford," then twenty-four years of age, who feared that he might not obtain a fair hearing with his readers if they knew his youth. The volume won a place for itself almost instantly, and its authorship was soon a matter of common knowledge. Ruskin was heralded as the apostle of a new revelation of beauty. "It is evidently not the work of a critic only," said one reviewer, "but of a painter and poet." "The grand doctrines of truth and sincerity in art, and the nobleness and solemnity of our human life, which he teaches with the inspiration of a Hebrew prophet," wrote George Eliot, "must be stirring up young minds in a promising way." The younger

artists of the time were indeed captivated. Holman Hunt
sat up most of the night "more than once," reading a borrowed copy until the echo of its words remained an enchantment to his ears. To groups of Oxford undergraduates William Morris spouted passages of its wonderful prose in a
voice that fired his listeners with rapturous admiration.
When the young Pre-Raphaelites were attacked in 1850
and 1851, Millais, in anger and despair, went for help to
Ruskin, who at once wrote a letter to *The Times* that turned
the tide of opinion in favor of the brotherhood. Men might
pardonably envy, as Swinburne said, "the authority and
the eloquence which gave such weight and effect to praise."

Modern Painters was begun as a defense of Turner, then
as now the first of English landscape-painters. In 1843, the
artist was a member of the Royal Academy and had made
a fortune from his pictures, and he was now turning out can-
vases in his later manner, which the reviews were violently
attacking as meaningless and absurd, as a series of incoherent
dreams evoked by a senescent imagination. To Ruskin this
assault was little short of blasphemous, and he rushed to
the defense of his idol with the ardor of a romantic knight
upon an adventure. Young as he was, his enthusiasm for
Turner was even then old. At thirteen he had received as
a birthday gift Roger's *Italy*, illustrated with the painter's
vignettes. At fourteen he had begun to copy Turner's drawings, and at seventeen he had flung off his first reply to *Black-
wood's* criticism of the painter, in which he had described
Turner's art as "embodied enchantment, delineated magic,"
and as "seizing the soul and essence of truth." Before he
was twenty-one, his father had given him two Turners, and
when he was of age, he had begun collecting for himself, until
the Ruskin home contained one of the choicest collections
in England, numbering by 1860, says Cook, "two oil pictures and more than a hundred drawings and sketches."
Turner's works were to him a symbol of all beauty in landscape and of all mystery and tragedy in man,—"studied
melodies of exquisite color, and deeply-toned poems." To
fight for them was to fight for all that Ruskin best loved in
nature and most revered in art. Like Scott in the famous

"Liddesdale Raids," he had in fact been unconsciously preparing himself all during his youth for the career upon which he was now so suddenly launched. He has described those early years with great fulness and charm in *Praeterita*, the book that to many readers is the most delightful of his writings. Here we learn of the favoring circumstances in the boyhood of the future apostle of beauty:—the initiation into art and literature by a liberal-minded father, an English merchant of the old school; the steady discipline in biblical reading and fundamental pieties from a devoted, if narrow-minded, mother; the quiet and sure expansion of natural aptitudes in the midst of the "monastic severities and aristocratic dignities" of Herne Hill; and, perhaps most fortunate of all, the coaching-tours about England, Scotland, and Wales, when in the most charming and leisurely of ways the boy Ruskin saw all that was best worth seeing of natural, architectural, or historical interest, until he was stirred to passionate happiness before the "panoramic apocalypse of a lovely world." Thus awakened, the most innate elements of his genius were not afterward misdirected by school or college, and were in fact subsequently much strengthened by regular drawing lessons and continental tours. Ruskin came to the defense of Turner, therefore, fortified by a prolonged cultivation of those capacities which were to be of greatest use to him as a critic of art,—the most important of which he considered to be the "habit of fixed attention with both eyes and mind," and the development of which, he says, "rendered the power of greater art over me, when I first saw it, as intense as that of magic, so that it appealed to me like a vision out of another world."

Ruskin's work in the field of art was the main occupation of his life up to 1860, when the fifth and last volume of *Modern Painters* was published. To this earlier period of his career, belong also the two major works on architecture, *The Seven Lamps of Architecture* (1849) and *The Stones of Venice* (3 vols. 1851–1853). Taken together these nine volumes contain probably the most inspiring exposition of the principles of painting and architecture yet written in English, and include that part of Ruskin's literary work which posterity seems likely to regard as most enduring. The spirit revealed in them is not the spirit of the critic so much as that of the poet,—the temper in other words of the inspired interpreter, dogmatic, paradoxical, and capricious if the reader will, but yet unafraid of his enthusiasms and his visions, and in command repeatedly, though not uniformly, of a style of incomparable sweep and beauty. Ruskin came upon a dull world of conventionalists and connoisseurs to proclaim the gospel that art was not a mere matter of technicalities and studio jargon, nor a pretty plaything of aristocratic society, but something large and noble, with a deep rootage in the healthy soil of our common humanity. As William Morris said, he "let a flood of daylight into the cloud of sham-twaddle which was once the whole substance of art-criticism, and is still the staple." It was indeed a central aim of his art-teaching, as it was of Morris's, to declare that a thing of beauty was not a joy forever unless it could be a joy for all. And underneath all the "oscillations of temper and progressions of discovery" in Ruskin's books on art, accordingly, there will be found a few simple principles which supply a clue to the main purposes of his life. They may be stated as follows:

(1) Art is the expression of the passionate joy of the artist in the beautiful things of the world of man or nature. (Ruskin's "ideas" of truth and beauty.)

(2) Art is the selection and re-creation of these beautiful objects by the artist's imagination into new wholes. (Ruskin's "ideas of relation.")

(3) Art is thus an expression of the mind of the artist; and the nobility ("integrity," "virtue") of his mind is the measure of its greatness.

(4) Great art, therefore, demands not only technical mastery ("the first morality of a painter"), but an essentially sound life; and a sound life is the foundation of great art, whether of the individual, nation, or race.

True art, in summary, is the re-creation of beautiful objects into new wholes by a person or a people, who are sufficiently free and alive to contemplate them with passionate pleasure.

This artistic faith is the root from which springs Ruskin's social and economic philosophy. Beginning with nature, continuing with Turner and landscape art, proceeding onward into Italian painting and sculpture, rushing headlong into the intricacies of architecture, he was almost insensibly drawn into digressions upon moral, social, and educational questions; because as the scope of his studies widened he saw in clearer light the dependence of great art upon sound life. "I am forced," he said, "by precisely the same instinct to the consideration of political questions that urges me to examine the laws of architectural or mountain forms." And when Ruskin took up the study of architecture, pre-eminently the art of a people, his faiths and formulas almost immediately received larger and more luminous illustration. "The book I called The Seven Lamps," he said, "was to show that certain right states of temper and moral feeling were the magic powers by which all good architecture, without exception, has been produced. *The Stones of Venice* had, from beginning to end, no other aim than to show that the Gothic architecture of Venice had arisen out of, and indicated in all its features, a state of pure national faith, and of domestic virtue; and that its Renaissance architecture had arisen out of, and in all its features indicated, a state of concealed national infidelity, and of domestic corruption." Again in the final volume of *Modern Painters* Ruskin states his position with an even clearer emphasis: "In these books of mine, their distinctive character, as essays on art, is their bringing everything to a root in human passion or human hope. Arising first not in any desire to explain the principles of art, but in the endeavor to defend an individual painter from injustice, they have been colored throughout,— nay, continually altered in shape, and even warped and broken, by digressions respecting social questions, which had for me an interest tenfold greater than the work I had been forced into undertaking. Every principle of painting which I have stated is traced to some vital or spiritual fact; and in my works on architecture the preference accorded finally to one school over another, is founded on a comparison of their influences on the life of the workman—a ques-

dividualistic creed of Adam Smith, Bentham, Malthus, and Ricardo, founders of the "dismal science," as Carlyle contemptuously called it. Upholding a gospel of enlightened selfishness, these men preached the dogmas of laizzez-faire, competition, and self-interest, and they systematically opposed every kind of governmental regulation as subversive of individual liberty and initiative. Their political economy aimed to be impersonal and scientific, a system of laws immutable and universal. To Ruskin these doctrines were as false as they were soulless. The science of political economy, he said, "is a Lie"; it is a "carnivorous political economy"; "it founds an ossificant theory of progress on the negation of a soul." With characteristic vehemence and audacity, he flung challenge upon challenge into the fortified camp of the enemy. When they proclaimed that labor depended for its value upon the law of supply and demand, he asked: "What does demand depend upon, and what does supply depend upon?" To the assertion that "the intrinsic value of commodities is a question outside of political economy," he replied that value is the life-giving principle of a thing and therefore of immense consequence in the commercial affairs of men. Against the dogma of Jevons's that pleasure and pain "are the ultimate objects of the calculus of political economy," he shot the counter dogma that "there is a swine's pleasure, and dove's; villain's pleasure, and gentleman's, to be arranged." The great error of the press and of the chancellor of the exchequer, he declared, "is the quite infinitely and diabolically stupid habit of thinking that increase of *money* is the increase of prosperity. . . . Nothing that I yet know of, in the records of human stupidity, equals the saying of Bright, in the House, that 'in a common sense mercantile community the adulteration of food can only be considered a form of competition.'"

Ruskin was determined to explode these popular orthodoxies with certain dynamic heresies of his own. "All common political economy," he wrote to Norton, "is founded on the axiom, 'Man is a beast of prey.' (It was so stated in these words by Mr. Mill at a social science meeting.) My

tion by all other writers on the subject of architecture wholly forgotten or despised." Thus it was in Gothic architecture, that "magnificently human" art of the twelfth and thirteenth centuries, when the religion and poetry of an epoch were wrought into stone, when guildsmen joined hands with burgher and bishop to put beauty alike into shop and cottage, palace and cathedral,—it was in this superb communal art of the Middle Age that Ruskin discovered the thread that guided him through the labyrinth of modern life. For here the humblest craftsman, as well as the master builder, each according to his capacity, realized the joy of creative effort; since each was left free within his own field to put himself into his work. Here was demonstrated on a large scale and throughout a period the truth of Ruskin's faith that the laws which regulate the finest industries, such as architecture and painting, should furnish the clue to the laws that must regulate all industries. What we have to do with all our workers, he declared, is "to look for the *thoughtful* part of them, and get that out of them, whatever we lose for it, whatever faults and errors we are obliged to take with it." This creed, underlying both art-teaching and social philosophy, is epitomized in one of his most brilliant aphorisms: "Life without industry is guilt, and industry without art is brutality."

The creation of art, as understood in this wider sense and as intended for all, depends, however, upon a beautiful environment and a sound, co-operative life alike for the individual and for the nation. "The beginning of all ideal art," said Ruskin, "must be for us in the realistic art of bestowing health and happiness. The first schools of beauty must be the streets of your cities, and the chief of our fair designs must be to keep the living creatures round us clean, and in human comfort." But what did this enchanted worshipper of the beautiful see about him when in middle age he began to read the signs of the times as before he had read the appearances of mountains and sky? He saw with horror the young giant of industrialism, advancing across the face of the land, treading down the older order, and leaving in his path wreck and confusion, grime, squalor, and noise.

He saw mills and tenements springing up on all sides, and swarming with an army of unhappy toilers, a dirty, over-worked, underpaid, unhappy multitude. He saw men degraded into machines, cut up into "cogs and compasses" of themselves, personified negations of the very principle that he had come to regard as most sacred. The picture is familiar to us to-day. To Ruskin it was new and appalling. "The vastness of the horror of this world's blindness and misery," he wrote to Charles Eliot Norton in 1862, "opens upon me." With a sense of indignation that "burned in him continually," with a discontent that he likened to the discontent of Virgil and Dante, he threw himself into the struggle, writing not now the long-drawn cadences that had delighted his earliest readers, but henceforth commanding a style that sometimes rose to the trenchant literalness of Swift and sometimes to the graphic and atrabilian exaggeration of Carlyle, without Carlyle's Teufelsdröckhian humor. He went out, as Henley suggests, not with a lyre to sing, but with a sword to slay. "It is the vainest of affectations," Ruskin insisted, "to try and put beauty into shadows, while all real things that cast them are in deformity and pain. . . . *You cannot have a landscape by Turner without a country for him to paint; you cannot have a portrait by Titian without a man to be pourtrayed. . . . The beginning of art is in getting our country clean, and our people beautiful. . . .* Beautiful art can only be produced by people who have beautiful things about them, and leisure to look at them."

As Ruskin looked out upon this modern world, he saw with prophetic insight the evils that were and that were to be,—the increase of crime, the growth of capitalism, the spread of landlordism, the taxation of labor, the widening separation between masters and men, the growing unrest of the overworked and the growing luxury of the under-worked. "During the last eight hundred years," he said, "the upper-classes of Europe have been one large Picnic Party." They had not done the work but they had taken the wages. With great clearness he could discern the approaching struggle between a feudalistic and a democratic social order, and though he beheld coming events with alarm,

he knew that a society founded upon injustice could not endure. The upper-classes were losing their power to govern; the populace was losing respect for its rulers and was pressing blindly forward along a road that led it knew not where. "We are on the eve of a great political crisis, if not of political change," he wrote in 1869. "A struggle is approaching between the newly-risen power of democracy and the apparently departing power of feudalism; and another struggle, no less imminent, and far more dangerous, between wealth and pauperism." And so after 1860 Ruskin turned to political economy and the laws by which men live and toil. His works on political economy are *Unto This Last* (1862); *Munera Pulveris* (1862–1863 in magazine, 1872 in book); and *Time and Tide* (1867). The first is a collection of four papers written in the solitude of the Alps and published in the *Cornhill Magazine*, of which Thackeray was then editor. The series was abruptly stopped with the fourth number, owing to the storm of protest from the reading public. A like fate awaited *Munera Pulveris*, a series of articles which Froude was bold enough to admit into *Fraser's*, but which the publishers suppressed after the fourth number. *Time and Tide* is the title attached to twenty-five letters written to Thomas Dixon, a cork-cutter of Sunderland. They appeared in the *Manchester Examiner* and the *Leeds Guardian*, and contained the fullest statement that Ruskin had yet made concerning Social reform. With these works should also be included *Sesame and Lilies* (1865), *Ethics of the Dust*, and *Crown of Wild Olive* (1866), most of which were first presented to the public as lectures; together with *Fors Clavigera*, an amazing congeries of Ruskiniana in ninety-six letters addressed "to the workmen and laborers of Great Britain." The first was dated January 1, 1871, and the last, Christmas, 1884,—the whole containing amid a mass of irrelevant personalia a succession of jeremiads on the shams and corruptions in modern life, besides many schemes and brilliant suggestions of social reconstruction.

"Mr. Ruskin's first claim as a social reformer," says Professor Hobson, "is that he reformed political economy." What Ruskin undertook to reform was the orthodox in-political economy is based on the axiom, 'Man is an animal whose physical power depends on its social faiths and affections.' . . . The economy I have taught, in opposition to the popular view, is the science which not merely ascertains the relation of existing supply and demand, but determines what *ought* to be demanded and what *can* be supplied." Considered in their entirety Ruskin's teachings have not much commended themselves to the excathedra professors of economic science, less perhaps because of their revolutionary character than because they are so largely intermingled with alien material,—with fantastic notions on marriage and money, interest and machinery, etymology and mythology, besides a good deal that is merely reiterated and angry preaching. But at the heart of them there is nothing either sentimental or utopian. There is nothing more heretical than one or two eternal truths, driven home by brilliant audacities and paradoxes, intended rather to blow up old dogmas of contemporary economists than to exploit new ones. Reduced to its simplest terms Ruskin's social and political creed was a bold declaration that in our industrial enterprises, big and little, we must not leave out of account the human factor. Political economy is impossible, he contended, except "under certain conditions of moral culture. Which is only to say, that industry, frugality, and discretion, the three foundations of economy, are moral qualities. . . . All effort in social improvement is paralyzed, because no one has been bold or clear-sighted enough to put and press home this radical question: 'What is indeed the noblest tone and reach of life for men; and how can the possibility of it be extended to the greatest numbers?' It is answered, broadly and rashly, that wealth is good; that knowledge is good; that art is good; that luxury is good. Whereas some of them are good in the abstract, but good if only rightly received. Nor have any steps whatever been yet securely taken, nor otherwise than in the resultless rhapsody of moralists,—to ascertain what luxuries and what learning it is either kind to bestow, or wise to desire. . . . My principles of Political Economy were all involved in a single phrase spoken three years ago (1857) at Manchester:

'Soldiers of the Ploughshare as well as Soldiers of the Sword': and they were all summed in a single sentence in the last volume of *Modern Painters*—'Government and Co-operation are in all things the Law of Life; Anarchy and Competition the Laws of Death.'"

A full exposition of Ruskin's ideals of social reconstruction based upon the foregoing principles is a chapter by itself. But the central motive of every scheme and every dream of a new order is contained in the chapter on the Nature of Gothic in *Stones of Venice*,—one of the most eloquent and most convincing manifestoes written in the nineteenth century. "To some of us when we first read it, now many years ago," said William Morris, "it seemed to point out a new road on which the world should travel." "It set fire to his enthusiasm," says Professor Mackail, Morris's biographer, "and kindled the belief of his whole life." Here, as we have seen, in the Gothic of the medieval builders Ruskin discovered a way out of the tangled troubles of his age. Like Carlyle, he went back to an older century for a light to guide him in his own; for both these prophets believed in an aristocratic, not to say a feudal, form of society, with people organized into classes according to their station and work, the rich and gifted bearing the responsibility of stewardship and leadership. Many of the most fruitful of Ruskin's social ideals indeed found expression in his various schemes for a re-establishment of the medieval guilds, adapted to modern conditions. A part of his teaching in this connection is fantastic, but much of it forecasts the form that society will inevitably take as time goes on. "I believe most firmly," he said, "that as the laws of national prosperity get familiar to us, we shall more and more cast our toil into social and communicative systems; and that one of the first means of our doing so, will be the re-establishing guilds of every important trade in a vital, not formal, condition;— that there will be a great council or government house for members of every trade, built in whatever town of the Kingdom occupies itself principally in such trade, with minor council-halls in other cities; and to each council-hall, officers attached, whose first business may be to examine into the circumstances of every operative, in that trade, who chooses to report himself to them when out of work, and to set him to work, if he is indeed able and willing, at a fixed rate of wages, determined at regular periods in the council-meetings; and whose next duty may be to bring reports before the council of all improvements made in the business, and means of its extension: not allowing private patents of any kind, but making all improvements available to every member of the guild, only alloting, after successful trial of them, a certain reward to the inventors. . . . Sooner or later, we shall have to register our people, and to know how they live; and to make sure, if they are capable of work, that right work is given them to do. The different classes of work for which bodies of men could be consistently organized, might ultimately become numerous";—such as road-making, bringing in of waste land, harbor-making, porterage, repair of buildings, dress-making, works of art. What Ruskin pleaded for in this program was: co-operation among masters and contentment among operatives; fixed standard of product; fixed wages, at least for determined periods; annually fixed prices and warranted articles; limitation of income for masters, who are not to take all the profits; reduction of servile work to the minimum; efficiency and permanency in chosen employment; always as much art in work as possible. To these proposals others were added from time to time, such as, income tax, reformation of criminals by active employment, forced work for the idle, healthy and comfortable homes for workmen, shorter hours with more leisure for self-development, homes for the aged and destitute.

In the furtherance of these ends government and education must play the largest part. Ruskin was a pioneer in his contention that the function of the state is to educate, guide, control, and care for its people, rather than to prohibit, punish, and repress them. As early as 1863 he advocated state control of railroads. He favored government establishments for trades, where standards might be exhibited of the best in labor conditions and the best in products. He believed in government schools of trial, where young men might engage in various kinds of work by turns, in order to show what they were fit for and how they might subsequently be employed to the best advantage both for themselves and for the state. Interesting in this connection are his experiments in social reform;—his Guild of St. George; the Hinksey Diggers; the weaving industry at Laxey; the renting scheme at Barmouth; housing, tea-shop, and road-sweeping in London; together with teaching at the first Working Men's College established in London, the beginning of social-centre movements everywhere. Ruskin entered into these projects with the unspoiled zest of a youthful reformer, because of his profound belief in teaching by example, because of his equally profound belief in education. There must be education for all, he steadily maintained, just as there must be art for all. But it must be education for work, in the first place, and, in the second, it must recognize the eternal differences in human nature. "The cry for the education of the lower classes, which is heard every day more loudly and widely," he said, "is a wise and sacred cry, provided it be extended into one for the education of *all* classes, with definite respect to the work each man has to do, and the substance of which he is made." Ruskin's entire body of economic and social teaching, saturated with ethical ideals as it is, rests finally upon the faith that human nature can be changed; that it can and must be educated in the heart as well as in the head; that a sense of human values must be awakened in the body politic; that people must be trained not only to do original and good work, but to be good judges of the same; that they must be taught to control their desire for luxuries and to have a proper regard for the claims of the poor and the dependent. "I take Wordsworth's single line, 'We live by admiration, hope, and love,'" said he, "for my literal guide in all education."

To the men of his own time Ruskin's social creed was the dream of a sentimental lover of beauty, who had lost his way in an alien world where confusion and ugliness had so wrought upon his sensibilities that he could not be trusted to see things as they were, in their right relations and in their proper places. Much of it is vision still; but so, too, is the

divine kingdom of Plato, and the still more divine kingdom
of the prophet of Galilee. Ruskin well knew that this was
so. He knew that generations of mankind must go and come
before the world should see the realization of his ideals. He
knew that his experiments in reorganization were "forward,
not permanent," and that the giant forces of commerce and
industry would stride on unheeding for long years yet to
be. But with undiminished faith to the end, he sought to
convince his contemporaries of the sincerity of his convic-
tions and of the truth and practicability of his dreams. Most
of all, he meant to prove to them that the spirit of all his
teaching was love, and the goal of all his striving, justice.

FREDERICK W. ROE.

RUSKIN'S ESSAYS

I. AUTOBIOGRAPHY

THE SPRINGS OF WANDEL

[Præterita, Vol. I, Ch. 1.]

I AM, and my father was before me, a violent Tory of
the old school;—Walter Scott's school, that is to say, and
Homer's. I name these two out of the numberless great
Tory writers, because they were my own two masters. I
had Walter Scott's novels, and the *Iliad* (Pope's translation), for constant reading when I was a child, on week-
days: on Sunday, their effect was tempered by *Robinson
Crusoe* and the *Pilgrim's Progress;* my mother having it
deeply in her heart to make an evangelical clergyman of
me. Fortunately, I had an aunt more evangelical than
my mother; and my aunt gave me cold mutton for Sunday's dinner, which—as I much preferred it hot—greatly
diminished the influence of the *Pilgrim's Progress;* and
the end of the matter was, that I got all the noble imaginative teaching of Defoe and Bunyan, and yet—am not
an evangelical clergyman.

I had, however, still better teaching than theirs, and
that compulsorily, and every day of the week.

Walter Scott and Pope's Homer were reading of my
own election, and my mother forced me, by steady daily
toil, to learn long chapters of the Bible by heart; as well
as to read it every syllable through, aloud, hard names
and all, from Genesis to the Apocalypse, about once a
year: and to that discipline—patient, accurate, and resolute—I owe, not only a knowledge of the book, which I
find occasionally serviceable, but much of my general
power of taking pains, and the best part of my taste in

literature. From Walter Scott's novels I might easily, as I grew older, have fallen to other people's novels; and Pope might, perhaps, have led me to take Johnson's English, or Gibbon's, as types of language; but once knowing the 32nd of Deuteronomy, the 119th Psalm, the 15th of 1st Corinthians, the Sermon on the Mount, and most of the Apocalypse, every syllable by heart, and having always a way of thinking with myself what words meant, it was not possible for me, even in the foolishest times of youth, to write entirely superficial or formal English; and the affectation of trying to write like Hooker and George Herbert was the most innocent I could have fallen into.

From my own chosen masters, then, Scott and Homer, I learned the Toryism which my best after-thought has only served to confirm.

That is to say, a most sincere love of kings, and dislike of everybody who attempted to disobey them. Only, both by Homer and Scott, I was taught strange ideas about kings, which I find for the present much obsolete; for, I perceived that both the author of the *Iliad* and the author of *Waverley* made their kings, or king-loving persons, do harder work than anybody else. Tydides or Idomeneus always killed twenty Trojans to other people's one, and Redgauntlet speared more salmon than any of the Solway fishermen; and — which was particularly a subject of admiration to me—I observed that they not only did more, but in proportion to their doings *got* less, than other people—nay, that the best of them were even ready to govern for nothing! and let their followers divide any quantity of spoil or profit. Of late it has seemed to me that the idea of a king has become exactly the contrary of this, and that it has been supposed the duty of superior persons generally to govern less, and get more, than anybody else. So that it was, perhaps, quite as well that in those early days my contemplation of existent kingship was a very distant one.

The aunt who gave me cold mutton on Sundays was my father's sister: she lived at Bridge-end, in the town of Perth, and had a garden full of gooseberry-bushes, sloping down to the Tay, with a door opening to the water, which ran past it, clear-brown over the pebbles three or four feet deep; swift-eddying,—an infinite thing for a child to look down into.

My father began business as a wine-merchant, with no capital, and a considerable amount of debts bequeathed him by my grandfather. He accepted the bequest, and paid them all before he began to lay by anything for himself,—for which his best friends called him a fool, and I, without expressing any opinion as to his wisdom, which I knew in such matters to be at least equal to mine, have written on the granite slab over his grave that he was "an entirely honest merchant." As days went on he was able to take a house in Hunter Street, Brunswick Square, No. 54 (the windows of it, fortunately for me, commanded a view of a marvellous iron post, out of which the water-carts were filled through beautiful little trap-doors, by pipes like boa-constrictors; and I was never weary of contemplating that mystery, and the delicious dripping consequent); and as years went on, and I came to be four or five years old, he could command a post-chaise and pair for two months in the summer, by help of which, with my mother and me, he went the round of his country customers (who liked to see the principal of the house his own traveller); so that, at a jog-trot pace, and through the panoramic opening of the four windows of a postchaise, made more panoramic still to me because my seat was a little bracket in front (for we used to hire the chaise regularly for the two months out of Long Acre, and so could have it bracketed and pocketed as we liked), I saw all the high-roads, and most of the cross ones, of England and Wales; and great part of lowland Scotland, as far as Perth, where every other year we spent the whole summer: and I used to read the *Abbot* at Kinross, and the *Monastery* in Glen Farg, which I confused with "Glendearg," and thought that the White Lady had as certainly lived by the streamlet in that glen of the Ochils, as the Queen of Scots in the island of Loch Leven.

To my farther great benefit, as I grew older, I thus saw nearly all the noblemen's houses in England; in reverent and healthy delight of uncovetous admiration,—perceiving, as soon as I could perceive any political truth at all, that it was probably much happier to live in a small house, and have Warwick Castle to be astonished at, than to live in Warwick Castle and have nothing to be astonished at; but that, at all events, it would not make Brunswick Square in the least more pleasantly habitable, to pull Warwick Castle down. And at this day, though I have kind invitations enough to visit America, I could not, even for a couple of months, live in a country so miserable as to possess no castles.

Nevertheless, having formed my notion of kinghood chiefly from the FitzJames of the *Lady of the Lake,* and of noblesse from the Douglas there, and the Douglas in *Marmion,* a painful wonder soon arose in my child-mind, why the castles should now be always empty. Tantallon was there; but no Archibald of Angus:—Stirling, but no Knight of Snowdoun. The galleries and gardens of England were beautiful to see—but his Lordship and her Ladyship were always in town,• said the housekeepers and gardeners. Deep yearning took hold of me for a kind of "Restoration," which I began slowly to feel that Charles the Second had not altogether effected, though I always wore a gilded oak-apple very piously in my button-hole on the 29th of May. It seemed to me that Charles the Second's Restoration had been, as compared with the Restoration I wanted, much as that gilded oak-apple to a real apple. And as I grew wiser, the desire for sweet pippins instead of bitter ones, and Living Kings instead of dead ones, appeared to me rational as well as romantic; and gradually it has become the main purpose of my life to grow pippins, and its chief hope, to see Kings.

HERNE-HILL ALMOND BLOSSOMS

[*Præterita,* Vol. I, Ch. 2.]

WHEN I was about four years old my father found himself able to buy the lease of a house on Herne Hill, a rustic eminence four miles south of the "Standard in Cornhill"; of which the leafy seclusion remains, in all essential points of character, unchanged to this day: certain Gothic splendors, lately indulged in by our wealthier neighbors, being the only serious innovations; and these are so graciously concealed by the fine trees of their grounds, that the passing viator remains unappalled by them; and I can still walk up and down the piece of road between the Fox tavern and the Herne Hill station, imagining myself four years old.

Our house was the northernmost of a group which stand accurately on the top or dome of the hill, where the ground is for a small space level, as the snows are (I understand), on the dome of Mont Blanc; presently falling, however, in what may be, in the London clay formation, considered a precipitous slope, to our valley of Chamouni (or of Dulwich) on the east; and with a softer descent into Cold Harbour-lane on the west: on the south, no less beautifully declining to the dale of the Effra (doubtless shortened from Effrena, signifying the "Unbridled" river; recently, I regret to say, bricked over for the convenience of Mr. Biffin, chemist, and others); while on the north, prolonged indeed with slight depression some half mile or so, and receiving, in the parish of Lambeth, the chivalric title of "Champion Hill," it plunges down at last to efface itself in the plains of Peckham, and the rural barbarism of Goose Green.

The group, of which our house was the quarter, consisted of two precisely similar partner-couples of houses, gardens and all to match; still the two highest blocks of buildings seen from Norwood on the crest of the ridge; so that the house itself, three-storied, with garrets above, commanded, in those comparatively smokeless days, a very notable view from its garret windows, of the Norwood hills on one side, and the winter sunrise over them; and of the valley of the Thames on the other, with Windsor telescopically clear in the distance, and Harrow, conspicuous always in fine weather to open vision against the summer sunset. It had front and back garden in sufficient proportion to its size; the front, richly set with old evergreens, and well-grown lilac and laburnum; the back, seventy yards long by twenty wide, renowned over all the hill for its pears and apples, which had been chosen with extreme care by our predecessor (shame on me to forget the name of a man to whom I owe so much!)— and possessing also a strong old mulberry tree, a tall white-heart cherry tree, a black Kentish one, and an almost unbroken hedge, all round, of alternate gooseberry and currant bush; decked, in due season, (for the ground was wholly beneficent,) with magical splendor of abundant fruit: fresh green, soft amber, and rough-bristled crimson bending the spinous branches; clustered pearl and pendent ruby joyfully discoverable under the large leaves that looked like vine.

The differences of primal importance which I observed between the nature of this garden, and that of Eden, as I had imagined it, were, that, in this one, *all* the fruit was forbidden; and there were no companionable beasts: in other respects the little domain answered every purpose of Paradise to me; and the climate, in that cycle of our years, allowed me to pass most of my life in it. My mother never gave me more to learn than she knew I could easily get learned, if I set myself honestly to work, by twelve o'clock. She never allowed anything to disturb me when my task was set; if it was not said rightly by twelve o'clock, I was kept in till I knew it, and in general, even when Latin Grammar came to supplement the Psalms, I was my own master for at least an hour before half-past one dinner, and for the rest of the afternoon.

My mother, herself finding her chief personal pleasure in her flowers, was often planting or pruning beside me, at least if I chose to stay beside *her*. I never thought of doing anything behind her back which I would not have done before her face; and her presence was therefore no restraint to me; but, also, no particular pleasure, for, from having always been left so much alone, I had generally my own little affairs to see after; and, on the whole, by the time I was seven years old, was already getting too independent, mentally, even of my father and mother; and, having nobody else to be dependent upon, began to lead a very small, perky, contented, conceited, Cock-Robinson-Crusoe sort of life, in the central point which it appeared to me, (as it must naturally appear to geometrical animals,) that I occupied in the universe.

This was partly the fault of my father's modesty; and partly of his pride. He had so much more confidence in my mother's judgment as to such matters than in his own, that he never ventured even to help, much less to cross her, in the conduct of my education; on the other hand, in the fixed purpose of making an ecclesiastical gentleman of me, with the superfinest of manners, and access to the highest circles of fleshly and spiritual society, the visits to Croydon, where I entirely loved my aunt, and young baker-cousins, became rarer and more rare: the society of our neighbors on the hill could not be had without breaking up our regular and sweetly selfish manner of living; and on the whole, I had nothing animate to care for, in a childish way, but myself, some nests of ants, which the gardener would never leave undisturbed for me, and a sociable bird or two; though I never had the sense or perseverance to make one really tame. But that was partly because, if ever I managed to bring one to be the least trustful of me, the cats got it.

Under these circumstances, what powers of imagination I possessed, either fastened themselves on inanimate things,—the sky, the leaves, and pebbles, observable within the walls of Eden,—or caught at any opportunity of flight into regions of romance, compatible with the objective realities of existence in the nineteenth century, within a mile and a quarter of Camberwell Green.

Herein my father, happily, though with no definite intention other than of pleasing me, when he found he could do so without infringing any of my mother's rules, became my guide. I was particularly fond of watching him shave; and was always allowed to come into his room in the morning (under the one in which I am now writing), to be the motionless witness of that operation. Over his dressing-table hung one of his own water-color drawings, made under the teaching of the elder Nasmyth; I believe, at the High School of Edinburgh. It was done in the early manner of tinting, which, just about the time when my father was at the High School, Dr. Munro was teaching Turner; namely, in gray under-tints of Prussian blue and British ink, washed with warm color afterward on the lights. It represented Conway Castle, with its Frith, and, in the foreground, a cottage, a fisherman, and a boat at the water's edge.

When my father had finished shaving, he always told me a story about this picture. The custom began without any initial purpose of his, in consequence of my troublesome curiosity whether the fisherman lived in the cottage, and where he was going to in the boat. It being settled, for peace' sake, that he *did* live in the cottage, and was going in the boat to fish near the castle, the plot of the drama afterward gradually thickened; and became, I believe, involved with that of the tragedy of *Douglas,* and of the *Castle Spectre,* in both of which pieces my father had performed in private theatricals, before my mother, and a select Edinburgh audience, when he was a boy of sixteen, and she, at grave twenty, a model housekeeper, and very scornful and religiously suspicious of theatricals. But she was never weary of telling me, in later years, how beautiful my father looked in his Highland dress, with the high black feathers.

In the afternoons, when my father returned (always punctually) from his business, he dined, at half-past four, in the front parlor, my mother sitting beside him to hear the events of the day, and give counsel and encouragement with respect to the same;—chiefly the last, for my father was apt to be vexed if orders for sherry fell the least short of their due standard, even for a day or two. I was never present at this time, however, and only avouch what I relate by hearsay and probable conjecture; for between four and six it would have been a grave misdemeanor in me if I so much as approached the parlor door. After that, in summer time, we were all in the garden as long as the day lasted; tea under the whiteheart cherry tree; or in winter and rough weather, at six o'clock in the drawing-room,—I having my cup of milk, and slice of bread-and-butter, in a little recess, with a table in front of it, wholly sacred to me; and in which I remained in the evenings as an Idol in a niche, while my mother knitted, and my father read to her,—and to me, so far as I chose to listen.

The series of the Waverley novels, then drawing toward its close, was still the chief source of delight in all households caring for literature; and I can no more recollect the time when I did not know them than when I did not know the Bible; but I have still a vivid remembrance of my father's intense expression of sorrow mixed with scorn, as he threw down *Count Robert of Paris,* after reading three or four pages; and knew that the life of Scott was ended: the scorn being a very complex and bitter feeling in him,—partly, indeed, of the book itself, but chiefly of the wretches who were tormenting and selling the wrecked intellect, and not a little, deep down, of the subtle dishonesty which had essentially caused the ruin. My father never could forgive Scott his concealment of the Ballantyne partnership.

Such being the salutary pleasures of Herne Hill, I have next with deeper gratitude to chronicle what I owe to my mother for the resolutely consistent lessons which so exercised me in the Scriptures as to make every word of them familiar to my ear in habitual music,—yet in that familiarity reverenced, as transcending all thought, and ordaining all conduct.

This she effected, not by her own sayings or personal authority; but simply by compelling me to read the book thoroughly, for myself. As soon as I was able to read with fluency, she began a course of Bible work with me, which never ceased till I went to Oxford. She read alternate verses with me, watching, at first, every intonation of my voice, and correcting the false ones, till she made me understand the verse, if within my reach, rightly, and energetically. It might be beyond me altogether; that she did not care about; but she made sure that as soon as I got hold of it at all, I should get hold of it by the right end.

In this way she began with the first verse of Genesis, and went straight through, to the last verse of the Apocalypse; hard names, numbers, Levitical law, and all; and began again at Genesis the next day. If a name was hard, the better the exercise in pronunciation,—if the chapter was tiresome, the better lesson in patience,—if loathsome, the better lesson in faith that there was some use in its being so outspoken. After our chapters, (from two to three a day, according to their length, the first thing after breakfast, and no interruption from servants allowed,—none from visitors, who either joined in the reading or had to stay upstairs,—and none from any visitings or excursions, except real travelling,) I had to learn a few verses by heart, or repeat, to make sure I had not lost, something of what was already known; and, with the chapters thus gradually possessed from the first word to the last, I had to learn the whole body of the fine old Scottish paraphrases, which are good, melodious, and forceful verse; and to which, together with the Bible itself, I owe the first cultivation of my ear in sound.

It is strange that of all the pieces of the Bible which my mother thus taught me, that which cost me most to learn, and which was, to my child's mind, chiefly repulsive —the 119th Psalm—has now become of all the most precious to me, in its overflowing and glorious passion of love for the Law of God, in opposition to the abuse of it by modern preachers of what they imagine to be His gospel.

But it is only by deliberate effort that I recall the long morning hours of toil, as regular as sunrise,—toil on both sides equal—by which, year after year, my mother forced me to learn these paraphrases, and chapters, (the eighth of 1st Kings being one—try it, good reader, in a leisure hour!) allowing not so much as a syllable to be missed or misplaced; while every sentence was required to be said over and over again till she was satisfied with the accent of it. I recollect a struggle between us of about three weeks, concerning the accent of the "of" in the lines

> "Shall any following spring revive
> The ashes of the urn?"—

I insisting, partly in childish obstinacy, and partly in true instinct for rhythm, (being wholly careless on the subject both of urns and their contents,) on reciting it with an accented *of*. It was not, I say, till after three weeks' labor, that my mother got the accent lightened on the "of" and laid on the ashes, to her mind. But had it taken three years she would have done it, having once undertaken to do it. And, assuredly, had she not done it,—well, there's no knowing what would have happened; but I'm very thankful she *did*.

I have just opened my oldest (in use) Bible,—a small, closely, and very neatly printed volume it is, printed in Edinburgh by Sir D. Hunter Blair and J. Bruce, Printers to the King's Most Excellent Majesty, in 1816. Yellow, now, with age; and flexible, but not unclean, with much use; except that the lower corners of the pages at 8th of 1st Kings, and 32d Deuteronomy, are worn somewhat thin and dark, the learning of these two chapters having cost me much pains. My mother's list of the chapters with which, thus learned, she established my soul in life, has just fallen out of it. I will take what indulgence the incurious reader can give me, for printing the list thus accidentally occurrent:—

Exodus,	chapters	15th and 20th.
2 Samuel,	"	1st, from 17th verse to end.
1 Kings,	"	8th.
Psalms,	"	23d, 32d, 90th, 91st, 103d, 112th, 119th, 139th.
Proverbs,	"	2d, 3d, 8th, 12th.
Isaiah,	"	58th.
Matthew,	"	5th, 6th, 7th.
Acts,	"	26th.
1 Corinthians,	"	13th, 15th.
James,	"	4th.
Revelation,	"	5th, 6th.

And, truly, though I have picked up the elements of a little further knowledge—in mathematics, meteorology, and the like, in after life,—and owe not a little to the teaching of many people, this maternal installation of my mind in that property of chapters I count very confidently the most precious, and, on the whole, the one *essential* part of all my education.

And it is perhaps already time to mark what advantage and mischief, by the chances of life up to seven years old, had been irrevocably determined for me.

I will first count my blessings (as a not unwise friend once recommended me to do, continually; whereas I have a bad trick of always numbering the thorns in my fingers and not the bones in them).

And for best and truest beginning of all blessings, I had been taught the perfect meaning of Peace, in thought, act, and word.

I never had heard my father's or mother's voice once

raised in any question with each other; nor seen an angry, or even slightly hurt or offended, glance in the eyes of either. I had never heard a servant scolded; nor even suddenly, passionately, or in any severe manner, blamed. I had never seen a moment's trouble or disorder in any household matter; nor anything whatever either done in a hurry, or undone in due time. I had no conception of such a feeling as anxiety; my father's occasional vexation in the afternoons, when he had only got an order for twelve butts after expecting one for fifteen, as I have just stated, was never manifested to *me;* and itself related only to the question whether his name would be a step higher or lower in the year's list of sherry exporters; for he never spent more than half his income, and therefore found himself little incommoded by occasional variations in the total of it. I had never done any wrong that I knew of—beyond occasionally delaying the commitment to heart of some improving sentence, that I might watch a wasp on the window-pane, or a bird in the cherry tree; and I had never seen any grief.

Next to this quite priceless gift of Peace, I had received the perfect understanding of the natures of Obedience and Faith. I obeyed word, or lifted finger, of father or mother, simply as a ship her helm; not only without idea of resistance, but receiving the direction as a part of my own life and force, and helpful law, as necessary to me in every moral action as the law of gravity in leaping. And my practice in Faith was soon complete: nothing was ever promised me that was not given; nothing ever threatened me that was not inflicted, and nothing ever told me that was not true.

Peace, obedience, faith; these three for chief good; next to these, the habit of fixed attention with both eyes and mind—on which I will not further enlarge at this moment, this being the main practical faculty of my life, causing Mazzini to say of me, in conversation authentically reported, a year or two before his death, that I had "the most analytic mind in Europe." An opinion in which, so far as I am acquainted with Europe, I am myself entirely disposed to concur.

Lastly, an extreme perfection in palate and all other

bodily senses, given by the utter prohibition of cake, wine, comfits, or, except in carefullest restriction, fruit; and by fine preparation of what food was given me. Such I esteem the main blessings of my childhood;—next, let me count the equally dominant calamities.

First, that I had nothing to love.

My parents were—in a sort—visible powers of nature to me, no more loved than the sun and the moon: only I should have been annoyed and puzzled if either of them had gone out; (how much, now, when both are darkened!) —still less did I love God; not that I had any quarrel with Him, or fear of Him; but simply found what people told me was His service, disagreeable; and what people told me was His book, not entertaining. I had no companions to quarrel with, neither; nobody to assist, and nobody to thank. Not a servant was ever allowed to do anything for me, but what it was their duty to do; and why should I have been grateful to the cook for cooking, or the gardener for gardening,—when the one dared not give me a baked potato without asking leave, and the other would not let my ants' nests alone, because they made the walks untidy? The evil consequence of all this was not, however, what might perhaps have been expected, that I grew up selfish or unaffectionate; but that, when affection did come, it came with violence utterly rampant and unmanageable, at least by me, who never before had anything to manage.

For (second of chief calamities) I had nothing to endure. Danger or pain of any kind I knew not: my strength was never exercised, my patience never tried, and my courage never fortified. Not that I was ever afraid of anything,—either ghosts, thunder, or beasts; and one of the nearest approaches to insubordination which I was ever tempted into as a child, was in passionate effort to get leave to play with the lion's cubs in Wombwell's menagerie.

Thirdly. I was taught no precision nor etiquette of manners; it was enough if, in the little society we saw, I remained unobtrusive, and replied to a question without shyness: but the shyness came later, and increased as I grew conscious of the rudeness arising from the want of social discipline, and found it impossible to acquire, in advanced life, dexterity in any bodily exercise, skill in any pleasing accomplishment, or ease and tact in ordinary behavior.

Lastly, and chief of evils. My judgment of right and wrong, and powers of independent action, were left entirely undeveloped; because the bridle and blinkers were never taken off me. Children should have their times of being off duty, like soldiers; and when once the obedience, if required, is certain, the little creature should be very early put for periods of practice in complete command of itself; set on the bareback horse of its own will, and left to break it by its own strength. But the ceaseless authority exercised over my youth left me, when cast out at last into the world, unable for some time to do more than drift with its vortices.

My present verdict, therefore, on the general tenor of my education at that time, must be, that it was at once too formal and too luxurious; leaving my character, at the most important moment for its construction, cramped indeed, but not disciplined; and only by protection innocent, instead of by practice virtuous.

SCHAFFHAUSEN AND MILAN

[*Præterita*, Vol. I, Ch. 6.]

THE poor modern slaves and simpletons who let themselves be dragged like cattle, or felled timber, through the countries they imagine themselves visiting, can have no conception whatever of the complex joys, and ingenious hopes, connected with the choice and arrangement of the travelling carriage in old times. The mechanical questions first, of strength—easy rolling—steady and safe poise of persons and luggage; the general stateliness of effect to be obtained for the abashing of plebeian beholders; the cunning design and distribution of store-cellars under the seats, secret drawers under front windows, invisible pockets under padded lining, safe from dust, and accessible only by insidious slits, or necromantic valves like Aladdin's trap-door; the fitting of cushions where they would not slip, the rounding of corners for more delicate repose; the prudent attachments and springs of blinds; the perfect fitting of windows, on which one-half the comfort of a travelling carriage really depends; and the adaptation of all these concentrated luxuries to the probabilities of who would sit where, in the little apartment which was to be virtually one's home for five or six months;—all this was an imaginary journey in itself, with every pleasure, and none of the discomfort, of practical travelling.

On the grand occasion of our first continental journey —which was meant to be half a year long—the carriage was chosen with, or in addition fitted with, a front seat outside for my father and Mary, a dickey, unusually large, for Anne and the courier, and four inside seats, though those in front very small, that papa and Mary might be received inside in stress of weather. I recollect, when we had finally settled which carriage we would have, the polite Mr. Hopkinson, advised of my dawning literary reputation, asking me (to the joy of my father) if I could translate the motto of the former possessor, under his painted arms,—*"Vix ea nostra voco,"*—which I accomplishing successfully, farther wittily observed that however by right belonging to the former possessor, the motto was with greater propriety applicable to *us*.

For a family carriage of this solid construction, with its luggage, and load of six or more persons, four horses were of course necessary to get any sufficient way on it; and half-a-dozen such teams were kept at every posthouse. The modern reader may perhaps have as much difficulty in realizing these savagely and clumsily locomotive periods, though so recent, as any aspects of migratory Saxon or Goth; and may not think me vainly garrulous in their description.

The French horses, and more or less those on all the great lines of European travelling, were properly stout trotting cart-horses, well up to their work and over it; untrimmed, long-tailed, good-humoredly licentious, whinnying and frolicking with each other when they had a chance; sagaciously steady to their work; obedient to the voice mostly, to the rein only for more explicitness; never

touched by the whip, which was used merely to express
the driver's exultation in himself and them,—signal ob-
structive vehicles in front out of the way, and advise all
the inhabitants of the villages and towns traversed on
the day's journey, that persons of distinction were honoring them by their transitory presence. If everything was
right, the four horses were driven by one postilion riding
the shaft horse; but if the horses were young, or the
riders unpracticed, there was a postilion for the leaders
also. As a rule, there were four steady horses and a good
driver, rarely drunk, often very young, the men of
stronger build being more useful for other work, and any
clever young rider able to manage the well-trained and
merry-minded beasts, besides being lighter on their backs.
Half the weight of the cavalier, in such cases, was in his
boots, which were often brought out slung from the sad-
dle like two buckets, the postilion, after the horses were
harnessed, walking along the pole and getting into them.

Scarcely less official, for a travelling carriage of good
class, than its postilions, was the courier, or properly,
avant-courier, whose primary office it was to ride in advance at a steady gallop, and order the horses at each
post-house to be harnessed and ready waiting, so that no
time might be lost between stages. His higher function
was to make all bargains and pay all bills, so as to save
the family unbecoming cares and mean anxieties, besides the trouble and disgrace of trying to speak French
or any other foreign language. He, farther, knew the
good inns in each town, and all the good rooms in each
inn, so that he could write beforehand to secure those
suited to his family. He was also, if an intelligent man
and high-class courier, well acquainted with the proper
sights to be seen in each town, and with all the occult
means to be used for getting sight of those that weren't
to be seen by the vulgar. Murray, the reader will remember, did not exist in those days; the courier was a
private Murray, who knew, if he had any wit, not the
things to be seen only, but those you would yourself best
like to see, and gave instructions to your valet-de-place
accordingly, interfering only as a higher power in cases
of difficulty needing to be overcome by money or tact. He

invariably attended the ladies in their shopping expeditions, took them to the fashionable shops, and arranged as he thought proper the prices of articles. Lastly, he knew, of course, all the other high-class couriers on the road, and told you, if you wished to know, all the people of consideration who chanced to be with you in the inn.

My father would have considered it an insolent and revolutionary trespass on the privileges of the nobility to have mounted his courier to ride in advance of us; besides that, wisely liberal of his money for comfort and pleasure, he never would have paid the cost of an extra horse for show. The horses were, therefore, ordered in advance, when possible, by the postilions of any preceding carriage (or, otherwise, we did not mind waiting till they were harnessed), and we carried our courier behind us in the dickey with Anne, being in all his other functions and accomplishments an indispensable luxury to us. Indispensable, first, because none of us could speak anything but French, and that only enough to ask our way in; for all specialties of bargaining, or details of information, we were helpless, even in France,—and might as well have been migratory sheep, or geese, in Switzerland or Italy. Indispensable, secondly, to my father's peace of mind, because, with perfect liberality of temper, he had a great dislike to being over-reached. He perfectly well knew that his courier would have his commission, and allowed it without question; but he knew also that his courier would not be cheated by other people, and was content in his representative. Not for ostentation, but for real enjoyment and change of sensation from his suburban life, my father liked large rooms; and my mother, in mere continuance of her ordinary and essential habits, liked clean ones; clean, and large, means a good inn and a first floor. Also my father liked a view from his windows, and reasonably said, "Why should we travel to see less than we may?"—so that meant first floor *front*. Also my father liked delicate cookery, just because he was one of the smallest and rarest eaters; and my mother liked good meat. That meant, dinner without limiting price, in reason. Also, though my father never went into society, he all the more enjoyed getting a glimpse, reverentially, of fashionable people—I mean, people of rank—he scorned fashion,—and it was a great thing to him to feel that Lord and Lady —— were on the opposite landing, and that, at any moment, he might conceivably meet and pass them on the stairs. Salvador, duly advised, or penetratively perceptive of these dispositions of my father, entirely pleasing and admirable to the courier mind, had carte-blanche in all administrative functions and bargains. We found our pleasant rooms always ready, our good horses always waiting, everybody took their hats off when we arrived and departed. Salvador presented his accounts weekly, and they were settled without a word of demur.

To all these conditions of luxury and felicity, can the modern steam-puffed tourist conceive the added ruling and culminating one—that we were never in a hurry? coupled with the correlative power of always starting at the hour we chose, and that if we weren't ready, the horses would wait? As a rule, we breakfasted at our own home time—eight; the horses were pawing and neighing at the door (under the archway, I should have said) by nine. Between nine and three,—reckoning seven miles an hour, including stoppages, for minimum pace,—we had done our forty to fifty miles of journey, sat down to dinner at four,—and I had two hours of delicious exploring by myself in the evening; ordered in punctually at seven to tea, and finishing my sketches till half-past nine,—bedtime.

On longer days or journey we started at six, and did twenty miles before breakfast, coming in for four o'clock dinner as usual. In a quite long day we made a second stop, dining at any nice village hostelry, and coming in for late tea, after doing our eighty or ninety miles. But these pushes were seldom made unless to get to some pleasant cathedral town for Sunday, or pleasant Alpine village. We never travelled on Sunday; my father and I nearly always went—as philosophers—to mass, in the morning, and my mother, in pure good-nature to us (I scarcely ever saw in her a trace of feminine curiosity), would join with us in some such profanity as a drive on the Corso, or the like, in the afternoon. But we all, even my father, liked a walk in the fields better, round an Alpine châlet village.

At page 81 I threatened more accurate note of my first impressions of Switzerland and Italy in 1833. Of customary Calais I have something to say later on,—here I note only our going up Rhine to Strasburg, where, with all its miracles of building, I was already wise enough to feel the cathedral stiff and iron-worky; but was greatly excited and impressed by the high roofs and rich fronts of the wooden houses, in their sudden indication of nearness to Switzerland; and especially by finding the scene so admirably expressed by Prout in the 36th plate of his *Flanders and Germany,* still uninjured. And then, with Salvador was held council in the inn-parlor of Strasburg, whether—it was then the Friday afternoon—we should push on to-morrow for our Sunday's rest to Basle, or to Schaffhausen.

How much depended—if ever anything "depends" on anything else,—on the issue of that debate! Salvador inclined to the straight and level Rhine-side road, with the luxury of the "Three Kings" attainable by sunset. But at Basle, it had to be admitted, there were no Alps in sight, no cataract within hearing, and Salvador honorably laid before us the splendid alternative possibility of reaching, by traverse of the hilly road of the Black Forest, the gates of Schaffhausen itself, before they closed for the night.

The Black Forest! The fall of Schaffhausen! The chain of the Alps! within one's grasp for Sunday! What a Sunday, instead of customary Walworth and the Dulwich fields! My impassioned petition at last carried it, and the earliest morning saw us trotting over the bridge of boats to Kehl, and in the eastern light I well remember watching the line of the Black Forest hills enlarge and rise, as we crossed the plain of the Rhine. "Gates of the hills"; opening for me to a new life—to cease no more, except at the Gates of the Hills whence one returns not.

And so, we reached the base of the Schwarzwald, and entered an ascending dingle; and scarcely, I think, a quarter of an hour after entering, saw our first "Swiss cottage." How much it meant to all of us,—how much prophesied to me, no modern traveller could the least conceive, if I spent days in trying to tell him. A sort of triumphant shriek—like all the railway whistles going off at once at Clapham Junction—has gone up from the Fooldom of Europe at the destruction of the myth of William Tell. To us, every word of it was true—but mythically luminous with more than mortal truth; and here, under the black woods, glowed the visible, beautiful, tangible testimony to it in the purple larch timber, carved to exquisiteness by the joy of peasant life, continuous, motionless there in the pine shadow on its ancestral turf,—unassailed and unassailing, in the blessedness of righteous poverty, of religious peace.

The myth of William Tell is destroyed forsooth? and you have tunnelled Gothard, and filled, it may be, the Bay of Uri;—and it was all for you and your sake that the grapes dropped blood from the press of St. Jacob, and the pine club struck down horse and helm in Morgarten Glen?

Difficult enough for you to imagine, that old travellers' time when Switzerland was yet the land of the Swiss, and the Alps had never been trod by foot of man. Steam, never heard of yet, but for short fair weather crossing at sea (were there paddle-packets across Atlantic? I forget). Any way, the roads by land were safe; and entered once into this mountain Paradise, we wound on through its balmy glens, past cottage after cottage on their lawns, still glistering in the dew.

The road got into more barren heights by the mid-day, the hills arduous; once or twice we had to wait for horses, and we were still twenty miles from Schaffhausen at sunset; it was past midnight when we reached her closed gates. The disturbed porter had the grace to open them —not quite wide enough; we carried away one of our lamps in collision with the slanting bar as we drove through the arch. How much happier the privilege of dreamily entering a mediæval city, though with the loss of a lamp, than the free ingress of being jammed between a dray and a tramcar at a railroad station!

It is strange that I but dimly recollect the following

morning; I fancy we must have gone to some sort of church or other; and certainly, part of the day went in admiring the bow-windows projecting into the clean streets. None of us seem to have thought the Alps would be visible without profane exertion in climbing hills. We dined at four, as usual, and the evening being entirely fine, went out to walk, all of us,—my father and mother and Mary and I.

We must have still spent some time in town-seeing, for it was drawing toward sunset, when we got up to some sort of garden promenade—west of the town, I believe; and high above the Rhine, so as to command the open country across it to the south and west. At which open country of low undulation, far into blue,—gazing as at one of our own distances from Malvern of Worcestershire, or Dorking of Kent,—suddenly—behold—beyond!

There was no thought in any of us for a moment of their being clouds. They were clear as crystal, sharp on the pure horizon sky, and already tinged with rose by the sinking sun. Infinitely beyond all that we had ever thought or dreamed,—the seen walls of lost Eden could not have been more beautiful to us; not more awful, round heaven, the walls of sacred Death.

It is not possible to imagine, in any time of the world, a more blessed entrance into life, for a child of such a temperament as mine. True, the temperament belonged to the age: a very few years,—within the hundred,—before that, no child could have been born to care for mountains, or for the men that lived among them, in that way. Till Rousseau's time, there had been no "sentimental" love of nature; and till Scott's, no such apprehensive love of "all sorts and conditions of men," not in the soul merely, but in the flesh. St. Bernard of La Fontaine, looking out to Mont Blanc with his child's eyes, sees above Mont Blanc the Madonna; St. Bernard of Talloires, not the Lake of Annecy, but the dead between Martigny and Aosta. But for me, the Alps and their people were alike beautiful in their snow, and their humanity; and I wanted, neither for them nor myself, sight of any thrones in heaven but the rocks, or of any spirits in heaven but the clouds.

Thus, in perfect health of life and fire of heart, not wanting to be anything but the boy I was, not wanting to have anything more than I had; knowing of sorrow only just so much as to make life serious to me, not enough to slacken in the least its sinews; and with so much of science mixed with feeling as to make the sight of the Alps not only the revelation of the beauty of the earth, but the opening of the first page of its volume,—I went down that evening from the garden-terrace of Schaff-hausen with my destiny fixed in all of it that was to be sacred and useful. To that terrace, and the shore of the Lake of Geneva, my heart and faith return to this day, in every impulse that is yet nobly alive in them, and every thought that has in it help or peace.

The morning after that Sunday's eve at Schaffhausen was also cloudless, and we drove early to the falls, seeing again the chain of the Alps by morning light, and learn-ing, at Lauffen, what an Alpine river was. Coming out of the gorge of Balsthal, I got another ever memorable sight of the chain of the Alps, and these distant views, never seen by the modern traveller, taught me, and made me feel, more than the close marvels of Thun and Inter-lachen. It was again fortunate that we took the grandest pass into Italy,—that the first ravine of the main Alps I saw was the Via Mala, and the first lake of Italy, Como.

We took boat on the little recessed lake of Chiavenna, and rowed down the whole way of waters, passing another Sunday at Cadenabbia, and then, from villa to villa, across the lake, and across, to Como, and so to Milan by Monza.

It was then full, though early, summer time; and the first impression of Italy always ought to be in her sum-mer. It was also well that, though my heart was with the Swiss cottager, the artificial taste in me had been mainly formed by Turner's rendering of those very scenes, in Rogers's *Italy*. The "Lake of Como," the two moon-light villas, and the "Farewell," had prepared me for all that was beautiful and right in the terraced gardens, proportioned arcades, and white spaces of sunny wall, which have in general no honest charm for the English mind. But to me, they were almost native through

Turner,—familiar at once, and revered. I had no idea then of the Renaissance evil in them; they were associated only with what I had been told of the "divine art" of Raphael and Lionardo, and, by my ignorance of dates, associated with the stories of Shakespeare. Portia's villa, —Juliet's palace,—I thought to have been like these.

Also, as noticed in the preface to reprint of Vol. II of *Modern Painters,* I had always a quite true perception of size, whether in mountains or buildings, and with the perception, joy in it; so that the vastness of scale in the Milanese palaces, and the "mount of marble, a hundred spires," of the duomo, impressed me to the full at once: and not having yet the taste to discern good Gothic from bad, the mere richness and fineness of lace-like tracery against the sky was a consummate rapture to me—how much more getting up to it and climbing among it, with the Monte Rosa seen between its pinnacles across the plain!

I had been partly prepared for this view by the admirable presentment of it in London, a year or two before, in an exhibition, of which the vanishing has been in later life a greatly felt loss to me,—Burford's panorama in Leicester Square, which was an educational institution of the highest and purest value, and ought to have been supported by the Government as one of the most beneficial school instruments in London. There I had seen, exquisitely painted, the view from the roof of Milan Cathedral, when I had no hope of ever seeing the reality, but with a joy and wonder of the deepest;—and now to be there, indeed, made deep wonder become fathomless.

Again, most fortunately, the weather was clear and cloudless all day long, and as the sun drew westward, we were able to drive to the Corso, where, at that time, the higher Milanese were happy and proud as ours in their park, and whence, no railway station intervening, the whole chain of the Alps was visible on one side, and the beautiful city with its dominant frost-crystalline Duomo on the other. Then the drive home in the open carriage through the quiet twilight, up the long streets, and round the base of the Duomo, the smooth pavement under the wheels adding with its silentness to the sense

of dream wonder in it all,—the perfect air in absolute
calm, the just seen majesty of encompassing Alps, the
perfectness—so it seemed to me—and purity, of the sweet,
stately, stainless marble against the sky. What more,
what else, could be asked of seemingly immutable good
in this mutable world?

I wish in general to avoid interference with the reader's
judgment on the matters which I endeavor serenely to
narrate; but may, I think, here be pardoned for observing to him the advantage, in a certain way, of the contemplative abstraction from the world which, during this
early continental travelling, was partly enforced by our
ignorance, and partly secured by our love of comfort.
There is something peculiarly delightful—nay, delightful
inconceivably by the modern German-plated and French-
polished tourist, in passing through the streets of a foreign city without understanding a word that anybody
says! One's ear for all sound of voices then becomes
entirely impartial; one is not diverted by the meaning
of syllables from recognizing the absolute guttural, liquid,
or honeyed quality of them: while the gesture of the body
and the expression of the face have the same value for
you that they have in a pantomime; every scene becomes
a melodious opera to you, or a picturesquely inarticulate
Punch. Consider, also, the gain in so consistent tran-
quillity. Most young people nowadays, or even lively old
ones, travel more in search of adventures than of information. One of my most valued records of recent wandering is a series of sketches by an amiable and extremely
clever girl, of the things that happened to her people
and herself every day that they were abroad. Here it is
brother Harry, and there it is mamma, and now pater-
familias, and now her little graceful self, and anon her
merry or remonstrant sisterhood, who meet with enchant-
ing hardships, and enviable misadventures; bind themselves with fetters of friendship, and glance into spark-
lings of amourette, with any sort of people in conical
hats and fringy caps: and it is all very delightful and
condescending; and, of course, things are learned about
the country that way which can be learned in no other
way, but only about that part of it which interests itself

in you, or which you have pleasure in being acquainted with. Virtually, you are thinking of yourself all the time; you necessarily talk to the cheerful people, not to the sad ones; and your head is for the most part vividly taken up with very little things. I don't say that our isolation was meritorious, or that people in general should know no language but their own. Yet the meek ignorance has these advantages. We did not travel for adventures, nor for company, but to see with our eyes, and to measure with our hearts. If you have sympathy, the aspect of humanity is more true to the depths of it than its words; and even in my own land, the things in which I have been least deceived are those which I have learned as their Spectator.

INFLUENCE OF NATURE

[Modern Painters, Vol. III, Ch. 17.]

THE first thing which I remember, as an event in life, was being taken by my nurse to the brow of Friar's Crag on Derwent Water; the intense joy, mingled with awe, that I had in looking through the hollows in the mossy roots, over the crag, into the dark lake, has associated itself more or less with all twining roots of trees ever since. Two other things I remember as, in a sort, beginnings of life;—crossing Shapfells (being let out of the chaise to run up the hills), and going through Glenfarg, near Kinross, in a winter's morning, when the rocks were hung with icicles; these being culminating points in an early life of more travelling than is usually indulged to a child. In such journeyings, whenever they brought me near hills, and in all mountain ground and scenery, I had a pleasure, as early as I can remember, and continuing till I was eighteen or twenty, infinitely greater than any which has been since possible to me in anything; comparable for intensity only to the joy of a lover in being near a noble and kind mistress, but no more explicable or definable than that feeling of love itself. Only thus much I can remember, respecting it, which is important to our present subject.

First: it was never independent of associated thought. Almost as soon as I could see or hear, I had got reading enough to give me associations with all kinds of scenery; and mountains, in particular, were always partly confused with those of my favorite book, Scott's *Monastery;* so that Glenfarg and all other glens were more or less enchanted to me, filled with forms of hesitating creed about Christie of the Clint Hill, and the monk Eustace; and with a general presence of White Lady everywhere. I also generally knew, or was told by my father and mother, such simple facts of history as were necessary to give more definite and justifiable association to other scenes which chiefly interested me, such as the ruins of Lochleven and Kenilworth; and thus my pleasure in mountains or ruins was never, even in earliest childhood, free from a certain awe and melancholy, and general sense of the meaning of death, though, in its principal influence, entirely exhilarating and gladdening.

Secondly, it was partly dependent on contrast with a very simple and unamused mode of general life; I was born in London, and accustomed, for two or three years, to no other prospect than that of the brick walls over the way; had no brothers nor sisters, nor companions; and though I could always make myself happy in a quiet way, the beauty of the mountains had an additional charm of change and adventure which a country-bred child would not have felt.

Thirdly: there was no definite religious feeling mingled with it. I partly believed in ghosts and fairies; but supposed that angels belonged entirely to the Mosaic dispensation, and cannot remember any single thought or feeling connected with them. I believed that God was in heaven, and could hear me and see me; but this gave me neither pleasure nor pain, and I seldom thought of it at all. I never thought of nature as God's work, but as a separate fact or existence.

Fourthly: it was entirely unaccompanied by powers of reflection or invention. Every fancy that I had about nature was put into my head by some book; and I never reflected about anything till I grew older; and then, the more I reflected, the less nature was precious to me: I could then make myself happy, by thinking, in the dark, or in the dullest scenery; and the beautiful scenery became less essential to my pleasure.

Fifthly: it was, according to its strength, inconsistent with every evil feeling, with spite, anger, covetousness, discontent, and every other hateful passion; but would associate itself deeply with every just and noble sorrow, joy, or affection. It had not, however, always the power to repress what was inconsistent with it; and, though only after stout contention, might at last be crushed by what it had partly repressed. And as it only acted by setting one impulse against another, though it had much power in moulding the character, it had hardly any in strengthening it; it formed temperament but never instilled principle; it kept me generally good-humored and kindly, but could not teach me perseverance or self-denial: what firmness or principle I had was quite independent of it; and it came itself nearly as often in the form of a temptation as of a safeguard, leading me to ramble over hills when I should have been learning lessons, and lose days in reveries which I might have spent in doing kindnesses.

Lastly: although there was no definite religious sentiment mingled with it, there was a continual perception of Sanctity in the whole of nature, from the slightest thing to the vastest;—an instinctive awe, mixed with delight; an indefinable thrill, such as we sometimes imagine to indicate the presence of a disembodied spirit. I could only feel this perfectly when I was alone; and then it would often make me shiver from head to foot with the joy and fear of it, when after being some time away from hills, I first got to the shore of a mountain river, where the brown water circled among the pebbles, or when I first saw the swell of distant land against the sunset, or the first low broken wall, covered with mountain moss. I cannot in the least *describe* the feeling; but I do not think this is my fault, nor that of the English language, for I am afraid, no feeling *is* describable. If we had to explain even the sense of bodily hunger to a person who had never felt it, we should be hard put to it for words; and the joy in nature seemed to me to come of a sort of heart-hunger, satisfied with the presence of a Great and Holy Spirit. These feelings remained in their full intensity till I was eighteen or twenty, and then, as the reflective and practical power increased, and the "cares of this world" gained upon me, faded gradually away, in the manner described by Wordsworth in his *Intimations of Immortality.*

I cannot, of course, tell how far I am justified in supposing that these sensations may be reasoned upon as common to children in general. In the same degree they are not of course common, otherwise children would be, most of them, very different from what they are in their choice of pleasures. But, as far as such feelings exist, I apprehend they are more or less similar in their nature and influence; only producing different characters according to the elements with which they are mingled. Thus, a very religious child may give up many pleasures to which its instincts lead it, for the sake of irksome duties; and an inventive child would mingle its love of nature with watchfulness of human sayings and doings; but I believe the feelings I have endeavored to describe are the pure landscape-instinct; and the likelihoods of good or evil resulting from them may be reasoned upon as generally indicating the usefulness or danger of the modern love and study of landscape.

II. NATURE

THE SPLENDORS OF SUNSET

[*Modern Painters,* Vol. I, Pt. 2, § 2, Ch. 2.]

WE have been speaking hitherto of what is constant and necessary in nature, of the ordinary effects of daylight on ordinary colors, and we repeat again, that no gorgeousness of the pallet can reach even these. But it is a widely different thing when nature herself takes a coloring fit, and does something extraordinary, something really to exhibit her power. She has a thousand ways and means of rising above herself, but incomparably the noblest manifestations of her capability of color are in these sunsets among the high clouds. I speak especially of the moment before the sun sinks, when his light turns pure rose-color, and when this light falls upon a zenith covered with countless cloud-forms of inconceivable delicacy, threads and flakes of vapor, which would in common daylight be pure snow-white, and which give therefore fair field to the tone of light. There is then no limit to the multitude, and no check to the intensity, of the hues assumed. The whole sky from the zenith to the horizon becomes one molten mantling sea of color and fire; every black bar turns into massy gold, every ripple and wave into unsullied shadowless crimson, and purple, and scarlet, and colors for which there are no words in language, and no ideas in the mind,—things which can only be conceived while they are visible; the intense hollow blue of the upper sky melting through it all, showing here deep, and pure, and lightless; there, modulated by the filmy formless body of the transparent vapor, till it is lost imperceptibly in its crimson and gold. . . . The concurrence of circumstances necessary to produce the sunsets of which I speak does not take place above five or six times in the summer, and then only for a space of from five to ten minutes, just as the sun reaches the horizon. Considering how seldom people think of looking for sunset at all, and how seldom, if they do, they are in a position from which it can be fully seen, the chances that their attention should be awake, and their position favorable, during these few flying instants of the year, are almost as nothing. What can the citizen, who can see only the red light on the canvas of the wagon at the end of the street, and the crimson color of the bricks of his neighbor's chimney, know of the flood of fire which deluges the sky from the horizon to the zenith? What can even the quiet inhabitant of the English lowlands, whose scene for the manifestation of the fire of heaven is limited to the tops of hayricks, and the rooks' nests in the old elm trees, know of the mighty passages of splendor which are tossed from Alp to Alp over the azure of a thousand miles of champaign? Even granting the constant vigor of observation, and supposing the possession of such impossible knowledge, it needs but a moment's reflection to prove how incapable the memory is of retaining for any time the distinct image of the sources even of its most vivid impressions. What recollection have we of the sunsets which delighted us last year? We may know that they were magnificent, or glowing, but no distinct image of color or form is retained— nothing of whose *degree* (for the great difficulty with the memory is to retain, not facts, but *degrees* of fact) we could be so certain as to say of anything now presented to us, that it is like it. If we did say so, we should be wrong; for we may be quite certain that the energy of an impression fades from the memory, and becomes more and more indistinct every day; and thus we compare a faded and indistinct image with the decision and certainty of one present to the senses. How constantly do we affirm that the thunderstorm of last week was the most terrible one we ever saw in our lives, because we compare it, not with the thunderstorm of last year, but with the faded and feeble recollection of it!

THE OPEN SKY

[*Modern Painters,* Vol. I, Pt. 2, § 3, Ch. 1.]

IT is a strange thing how little in general people know about the sky. It is the part of creation in which nature has done more for the sake of pleasing man, more for the sole and evident purpose of talking to him and teaching him, than in any other of her works, and it is just the part in which we least attend to her. There are not many of her other works in which some more material or essential purpose than the mere pleasing of man is not answered by every part of their organization; but every essential purpose of the sky might, so far as we know, be answered, if once in three days, or thereabouts, a great, ugly, black rain-cloud were brought up over the blue, and everything well watered, and so all left blue again till next time, with perhaps a film of morning and evening mist for dew. And instead of this, there is not a moment of any day of our lives, when nature is not producing scene after scene, picture after picture, glory after glory, and working still upon such exquisite and constant principles of the most perfect beauty, that it is quite certain it is all done for us, and intended for our perpetual pleasure. And every man, wherever placed, however far from other sources of interest or of beauty, has this doing for him constantly. The noblest scenes of the earth can be seen and known but by few; it is not intended that man should live always in the midst of them: he injures them by his presence, he ceases to feel them if he be always with them: but the sky is for all; bright as it is, it is not

> "Too bright nor good
> For human nature's daily food;"

it is fitted in all its functions for the perpetual comfort and exalting of the heart, for soothing it and purifying it from its dross and dust. Sometimes gentle, sometimes capricious, sometimes awful, never the same for two moments together; almost human in its passions, almost spiritual in its tenderness, almost divine in its infinity, its appeal to what is immortal in us is as distinct as its ministry of chastisement or of blessing to what is mortal is essential. And yet we never attend to it, we never make it a subject of thought, but as it has to do with our animal sensations: we look upon all by which it speaks to us more clearly than to brutes, upon all which bears witness to the intention of the Supreme that we are to receive more from the covering vault than the light and the dew which we share with the weed and the worm, only as a succession of meaningless and monotonous accident, too common and too vain to be worthy of a moment of watchfulness, or a glance of admiration. If in our moments of utter idleness and insipidity, we turn to the sky as a last resource, which of its phenomena do we speak of? One says it has been wet, and another, it has been windy; and another, it has been warm. Who, among the whole chattering crowd, can tell me of the forms and the precipices of the chain of tall white mountains that girded the horizon at noon yesterday? Who saw the narrow sunbeam that came out of the south and smote upon their summits until they melted and mouldered away in a dust of blue rain? Who saw the dance of the dead clouds when the sunlight left them last night, and the west wind blew them before it like withered leaves? All has passed, unregretted as unseen; or if the apathy be ever shaken off, even for an instant, it is only by what is gross, or what is extraordinary; and yet it is not in the broad and fierce manifestations of the elemental energies, not in the clash of the hail, nor the drift of the whirlwind, that the highest characters of the sublime are developed. God is not in the earthquake, nor in the fire, but in the still, small voice. They are but the blunt and the low faculties of our nature, which can only be addressed through lamp-black and lightning. It is in quiet and subdued passages of unobtrusive majesty, the deep, and the calm, and the perpetual; that which must be sought ere it is seen, and loved ere it is understood; things which the angels work out for us daily, and yet vary eternally: which are never wanting, and never repeated; which are to be found always, yet each one found but once; it is through these that the lesson of devotion is chiefly taught, and the blessing of beauty given. These are what the artist of highest aim must study; it is these, by the combination of which his ideal is to be created; these, of which so little notice is ordinarily taken by common observers, that I fully believe, little as people in general are concerned with art, more of their ideas of sky are derived from pictures than from reality; and that if we could examine the conception formed in the minds of most educated persons when we talk of clouds, it would frequently be found composed of fragments of blue and white reminiscences of the old masters.

THE SKIES OF NATURE, MORNING, NOON, SUNSET, SUNRISE

[Modern Painters, Vol. I, Pt. 2, § 3, Ch. 4.]

STAND upon the peak of some isolated mountain at daybreak, when the night mists first rise from off the plains, and watch their white and lake-like fields, as they float in level bays and winding gulfs about the islanded summits of the lower hills, untouched yet by more than dawn, colder and more quiet than a windless sea under the moon of midnight; watch when the first sunbeam is sent upon the silver channels, how the foam of their undulating surface parts and passes away, and down under their depths the glittering city and green pasture lie like Atlantis, between the white paths of winding rivers; the flakes of light falling every moment faster and broader among the starry spires, as the wreathed surges break and vanish above them, and the confused crests and ridges of the dark hills shorten their gray shadows upon the plain. . . . Wait a little longer, and you shall see those scattered mists rallying in the ravines, and floating up toward you, along the winding valleys, till they couch in quiet masses, iridescent with the morning light, upon the broad breasts of the higher hills, whose leagues of massy undulation will melt back and back into that robe of material light, until they fade away, lost in its lustre, to appear again above, in the serene heaven, like a wild, bright, impossible dream, foundationless and inaccessible, their very bases vanishing in the unsubstantial and mocking blue of the deep lake below. . . . Wait yet a little longer, and you shall see those mists gather themselves into white towers, and stand like fortresses along the promontories, massy and motionless, only piled with every instant higher and higher into the sky, and casting longer shadows athwart the rocks; and out of the pale blue of the horizon you will see forming and advancing a troop of narrow, dark, pointed vapors, which will cover the sky, inch by inch, with their gray network, and take the light off the landscape with an eclipse which will stop the singing of the birds and the motion of the leaves, together; and then you will see horizontal bars of black shadow forming under them, and lurid wreathes create themselves, you know not how, along the shoulders of the hills; you never see them form, but when you look back to a place which was clear an instant ago, there is a cloud on it, hanging by the precipices, as a hawk pauses over his prey. . . . And then you will hear the sudden rush of the awakened wind, and you will see those watch-towers of vapor swept away from their foundations, and waving curtains of opaque rain let down to the valleys, swinging from the burdened clouds in black bending fringes, or

pacing in pale columns along the lake level, grazing its
surface into foam as they go. And then, as the sun
sinks, you shall see the storm drift for an instant from
off the hills, leaving their broad sides smoking, and
loaded yet with snow-white, torn, steam-like rags of capricious vapor, now gone, now gathered again; while the
smoldering sun, seeming not far away, but burning like
a red-hot ball beside you, and as if you could reach it,
plunges through the rushing wind and rolling cloud with
headlong fall, as if it meant to rise no more, dyeing all
the air about it with blood. . . . And then you shall hear
the fainting tempest die in the hollow of the night, and
you shall see a green halo kindling on the summit of the
eastern hills, brighter—brighter yet, till the large white
circle of the slow moon is lifted up among the barred
clouds, step by step, line by line; star after star she
quenches with her kindling light, setting in their stead
an army of pale, penetrable, fleecy wreaths in the heaven,
to give light upon the earth, which move together, hand
in hand, company by company, troop by troop, so measured in their unity of motion, that the whole heaven
seems to roll with them, and the earth to reel under them.
. . . And then wait yet for one hour until the east again
becomes purple, and the heaving mountains, rolling against
it in darkness, like waves of a wild sea, are drowned one
by one in the glory of its burning: watch the white
glaciers blaze in their winding paths about the mountains,
like mighty serpents with scales of fire: watch the col-
umnar peaks of solitary snow, kindling downward, chasm
by chasm, each in itself a new morning; their long ava-
lanches cast down in keen streams brighter than the
lightning, sending each his tribute of driven snow, like
altar-smoke, up to the heaven; the rose-light of their
silent domes flushing that heaven about them and above
them, piercing with purer light through its purple lines
of lifted cloud, casting a new glory on every wreath as it
passes by, until the whole heaven, one scarlet canopy, is
interwoven with a roof of waving flame, and tossing, vault
beyond vault, as with the drifted wings of many companies of angels: and then, when you can look no more

for gladness, and when you are bowed down with fear
and love of the Maker and Doer of this, tell me who
has best delivered this His message unto men!

WATER

[Modern Painters, Vol. I, Pt. 2, § 5, Chs. 1, 2, 3.]

(a) OF all inorganic substances, acting in their own
proper nature, and without assistance or combination,
water is the most wonderful. If we think of it as the
source of all the changefulness and beauty which we
have seen in clouds; then as the instrument by which
the earth we have contemplated was modelled into symmetry, and its crags chiselled into grace; then as, in
the form of snow, it robes the mountains it has made
with that transcendent light which we could not have
conceived if we had not seen; then as it exists in the
foam of the torrent, in the iris which spans it, in the
morning mist which rises from it, in the deep crystalline
pools which mirror its hanging shore, in the broad lake
and glancing river; finally, in that which is to all human
minds the best emblem of unwearied unconquerable
power, the wild, various, fantastic, tameless unity of the
sea; what shall we compare to this mighty, this universal
element, for glory and for beauty? or how shall we follow
its eternal changefulness of feeling? It is like trying to
paint a soul.

To suggest the ordinary appearance of calm water, to
lay on canvas as much evidence of surface and reflection
as may make us understand that water is meant, is, perhaps, the easiest task of art; and even ordinary running
or falling water may be sufficiently rendered, by observing careful curves of projection with a dark ground, and
breaking a little white over it, as we see done with judgment and truth by Ruysdael. But to paint the actual
play of hue on the reflective surface, or to give the forms
and fury of water when it begins to show itself; to give
the flashing and rocket-like velocity of a noble cataract,
or the precision and grace of the sea wave, so exquisitely
modelled, though so mockingly transient, so mountainous
in its form, yet so cloud-like in its motion, with its

variety and delicacy of color, when every ripple and wreath has some peculiar passage of reflection upon itself alone, and the radiating and scintillating sunbeams are mixed with the dim hues of transparent depth and dark rock below; to do this perfectly is beyond the power of man; to do it even partially has been granted to but one or two, even of those few who have dared to attempt it. . . .

Now, the fact is, that there is hardly a road-side pond or pool which has not as much landscape *in* it as above it. It is not the brown, muddy, dull thing we suppose it to be; it has a heart like ourselves, and in the bottom of that there are the boughs of the tall trees, and the blades of the shaking grass, and all manner of hues of variable pleasant light out of the sky. Nay, the ugly gutter, that stagnates over the drain-bars in the heart of the foul city, is not altogether base; down in that, if you will look deep enough, you may see the dark serious blue of far-off sky, and the passing of pure clouds. It is at your own will that you see in that despised stream, either the refuse of the street, or the image of the sky. So it is with almost all other things that we unkindly despise.

. . . . . .

(b) Stand for half an hour beside the Fall of Schaffhausen, on the north side where the rapids are long, and watch how the vault of water first bends, unbroken, in pure polished velocity, over the arching rocks at the brow of the cataract, covering them with a dome of crystal twenty feet thick, so swift that its motion is unseen except when a foam-globe from above darts over it like a falling star; and how the trees are lighted above it under all their leaves, at the instant that it breaks into foam; and how all the hollows of that foam burn with green fire like so much shattering chrysoprase; and how, ever and anon, startling you with its white flash, a jet of spray leaps hissing out of the fall, like a rocket, bursting in the wind and driven away in dust, filling the air with light; and how, through the curdling wreaths of the restless crashing abyss below, the blue of the water, paled by the foam in its body, shows purer than the sky through white rain-cloud; while the shuddering iris stoops in tremulous stillness over all, fading and flushing alternately through the choking spray and shattered sunshine, hiding itself at last among the thick golden leaves which toss to and fro in sympathy with the wild water; their dripping masses lifted at intervals, like sheaves of loaded corn, by some stronger gush from the cataract, and bowed again upon the mossy rocks as its roar dies away; the dew gushing from their thick branches through drooping clusters of emerald herbage, and sparkling in white threads along the dark rocks of the shore, feeding the lichens which chase and checker them with purple and silver.

.   .   .   .   .   .

(c) As the right rendering of the Alps depends on power of drawing snow, so the right painting of the sea must depend, at least in all coast scenery, in no small measure on the power of drawing foam. Yet there are two conditions of foam of invariable occurrence on breaking waves, of which I have never seen the slightest record attempted; first, the thick, creamy, curdling, overlapping, massy foam, which remains for a moment only after the fall of the wave, and is seen in perfection in its running up the beach; and, secondly, the thin white coating into which this subsides, which opens into oval gaps and clefts, marbling the waves over their whole surface, and connecting the breakers on a flat shore by long dragging streams of white.

It is evident that the difficulty of expressing either of these two conditions must be immense. The lapping and curdling foam is difficult enough to catch, even when the lines of its undulation alone are considered; but the lips, so to speak, which lie along these lines, are full, projecting, and marked by beautiful light and shade; each has its high light, a gradation into shadow of indescribable delicacy, a bright reflected light, and a dark cast shadow: to draw all this requires labor and care, and firmness of work, which, as I imagine, must always, however skilfully bestowed, destroy all impressions of wildness, accidentalism, and evanescence, and so kill the sea. Again, the openings in the thin subsided foam, in their irregular modifications of circular and oval shapes dragged hither and thither, would be hard enough to draw, even if they could be seen on a flat surface; instead of which, every one of the openings is seen in undulation on a tossing surface, broken up over small surges and ripples, and so thrown into perspectives of the most hopeless intricacy. Now it is not easy to express the fall of a pattern with oval openings on the folds of drapery. I do not know that anyone under the mark of Veronese or Titian could even do this as it ought to be done, yet in drapery much stiffness and error may be overlooked: not so in sea; the slightest inaccuracy, the slightest want of flow and freedom in the line, is attached by the eye, in a moment, of high treason, and I believe success to be impossible.

Yet there is not a wave, nor any violently agitated sea, on which both these forms do not appear; the latter especially, after some time of storm, extends over their whole surfaces: the reader sees, therefore, why I said that sea could only be painted by means of more or less dexterous conventionalism, since two of its most enduring phenomena cannot be represented at all.

Again, as respects the form of breakers on an even shore, there is difficulty of no less formidable kind. There is in them an irreconcilable mixture of fury and formalism. Their hollow surface is marked by parallel lines, like those of a smooth mill-weir, and graduated by reflected and transmitted lights of the most wonderful intricacy, its curve being at the same time necessarily of mathematical purity and precision; yet at the top of this curve, when it nods over, there is a sudden laxity and giving way, the water swings and jumps along the ridge like a shaken chain, and the motion runs from part to part as it does through a serpent's body. Then the wind is at work on the extreme edge, and instead of letting it fling itself off naturally, it supports it, and drives it back, or scrapes it off and carries it bodily away; so that the spray at the top is in a continual transition between forms projected by their own weight, and forms blown and carried off with their weight overcome. Then at last, when it has come down, who shall say what shape that may be called, which "shape has none," of the great crash where it touches the beach. . . .

Seen from the land, the curl of the breakers, even in nature, is somewhat uniform and monotonous; the size of the waves out at sea is uncomprehended; and those nearer the eye seem to succeed and resemble each other, to move slowly to the beach, and to break in the same lines and forms.

Afloat even twenty yards from the shore, we receive a totally different impression. Every wave around us appears vast, every one different from all the rest; and the breakers present, now that we see them with their backs toward us, the grand, extended, and varied lines of long curvature which are peculiarly expressive both of velocity and power. Recklessness, before unfelt, is manifested in the mad, perpetual, changeful, undirected motion, not of wave after wave, as it appears from the shore, but of the very same water rising and falling. Of waves that successively approach and break, each appears to the mind a separate individual, whose part being performed, it perishes, and is succeeded by another; and there is nothing in this to impress us with the idea of restlessness, any more than in any successive and continuous functions of life and death. But it is when we perceive that it is no succession of wave, but the same water, constantly rising, and crashing, and recoiling, and rolling in again in new forms and with fresh fury, that we perceive the perturbed spirit, and feel the intensity of its unwearied rage. The sensation of power is also trebled; for not only is the vastness of apparent size much increased, but the whole action is different; it is not a passive wave, rolling sleepily forward until it tumbles heavily, prostrated upon the beach; but a sweeping exertion of tremendous and living strength, which does not now appear to *fall,* but to *burst* upon the shore; which never perishes but recoils and recovers.

.   .   .   .   .

(d) The noblest sea that Turner has ever painted, and, if so, the noblest certainly ever painted by man, is that of the Slave Ship, the chief Academy picture of the Exhibition of 1840. It is a sunset on the Atlantic, after prolonged storm; but the storm is partially lulled, and the torn and streaming rain-clouds are moving in scarlet lines to lose themselves in the hollow of the night. The whole surface of sea included in the picture is divided into two ridges of enormous swell, not high, nor local, but a low broad heaving of the whole ocean, like the lifting of its bosom by deep-drawn breath after the torture of the storm. Between these two ridges the fire of the sunset falls along the trough of the sea, dyeing it with an awful but glorious light, the intense and lurid splendor which burns like gold, and bathes like blood. Along this fiery path and valley, the tossing waves by which the swell of the sea is restlessly divided, lift themselves in dark, indefinite, fantastic forms, each casting a faint and ghastly shadow behind it along the illumined foam. They do not rise everywhere, but three or four together in wild groups, fitfully and furiously, as the under strength of the swell compels or permits them; leaving between them treacherous spaces of level and whirling water, now lighted with green and lamplike fire, now flashing back the gold of the declining sun, now fearfully dyed from above with the undistinguishable images of the burning clouds, which fall upon them in flakes of crimson and scarlet, and give to the reckless waves the added motion of their own fiery flying. Purple and blue, the lurid shadows of the hollow breakers are cast upon the mist of night, which gathers cold and low, advancing like the shadow of death upon the guilty* ship as it labors amidst the lightning of the sea, its thin masts written upon the sky in lines of blood, girded with condemnation in that fearful hue which signs the sky with horror, and mixes its flaming flood with the sunlight, and, cast far along the desolate heave of the sepulchral waves, incarnadines the multitudinous sea.

LEAFAGE OF TREES

[*Modern Painters,* Vol. I, Pt. 2, § 6, Ch. 1.]

ONE of the most remarkable characters of natural leafage is the constancy with which, while the leaves are arranged on the spray with exquisite regularity, that

---

* She is a slaver, throwing her slaves overboard. The near sea is encumbered with corpses. [Ruskin's note.]

regularity is modified in their actual effect. For as in every group of leaves some are seen sideways, forming merely long lines, some foreshortened, some crossing each other, every one differently turned and placed from all the others, the forms of the leaves, though in themselves similar, give rise to a thousand strange and differing forms in the group; and the shadows of some, passing over the others, still farther disguise and confuse the mass, until the eye can distinguish nothing but a graceful and flexible disorder of innumerable forms, with here and there a perfect leaf on the extremity, or a symmetrical association of one or two, just enough to mark the specific character and to give unity and grace, but never enough to repeat in one group what was done in another, never enough to prevent the eye from feeling that, however regular and mathematical may be the structure of parts, what is composed out of them is as various and infinite as any other part of nature. Nor does this take place in general effect only. Break off an elm bough three feet long, in full leaf, and lay it on the table before you, and try to draw it, leaf for leaf. It is ten to one if in the whole bough (provided you do not twist it about as you work) you find one form of a leaf exactly like another; perhaps you will not even have *one* complete. Every leaf will be oblique, or foreshortened, or curled, or crossed by another, or shaded by another, or have something or other the matter with it; and though the whole bough will look graceful and symmetrical, you will scarcely be able to tell how or why it does so, since there is not one line of it like another.

But if nature is so various when you have a bough on the table before you, what must she be when she retires from you, and gives you her whole mass and multitude? The leaves then at the extremities become as fine as dust, a mere confusion of points and lines between you and the sky, a confusion which, you might as well hope to draw sea-sand particle by particle, as to imitate leaf for leaf. This, as it comes down into the body of the tree, gets closer, but never opaque; it is always transparent with crumbling lights in it letting you through to the sky: then out of this come, heavier and heavier, the masses of illumined foliage, all dazzling and inextricable, save here and there a single leaf on the extremities: then, under these, you get deep passages of broken irregular gloom, passing into transparent, green-lighted, misty hollows; the twisted stems glancing through them in their pale and entangled infinity, and the shafted sunbeams, rained from above, running along the lustrous leaves for an instant; then lost, then caught again on some emerald bank or knotted root, to be sent up again with a faint reflex on the white under-sides of dim groups of drooping foliage, the shadows of the upper boughs running in gray network down the glossy stems, and resting in quiet checkers upon the glittering earth; but all penetrable and transparent, and, in proportion, inextricable and incomprehensible, except where across the labyrinth and the mystery of the dazzling light and dreamlike shadow, falls close to us, some solitary spray, some wreath of two or three motionless large leaves, the type and embodying of all that in the rest we feel and imagine, but can never see.

GRASS

[Modern Painters, Vol. III, Pt. 4, Ch. 14.]

GATHER a single blade of grass, and examine for a minute, quietly, its narrow sword-shaped strip of fluted green. Nothing, as it seems there, of notable goodness or beauty. A very little strength, and a very little tallness, and a few delicate long lines meeting in a point,— not a perfect point, neither, but blunt and unfinished, by no means a creditable or apparently much cared-for example of Nature's workmanship; made, as it seems, only to be trodden on to-day, and to-morrow to be cast into the oven; and a little pale and hollow stalk, feeble and flaccid, leading down to the dull brown fibres of roots. And yet, think of it well, and judge whether of all the gorgeous flowers that beam in summer air, and of all strong and goodly trees, pleasant to the eyes or good for food,—stately palm and pine, strong ash and oak, scented citron, burdened vine,—there be any by man so deeply loved, by God so highly graced, as that narrow point of feeble green. It seems to me not to have been without a peculiar significance, that our Lord, when about to work the miracle which, of all that He showed, appears to have been felt by the multitude as the most impressive,—the miracle of the loaves,—commanded the people to sit down by companies "upon the green grass." He was about to feed them with the principal produce of earth and the sea, the simplest representations of the food of mankind. He gave them the *seed* of the herb; He bade them sit down upon the herb itself, which was as great a gift, in its fitness for their joy and rest, as its perfect fruit, for their sustenance; thus, in this single order and act, when rightly understood, indicating for evermore how the Creator had entrusted the comfort, consolation, and sustenance of man, to the simplest and most despised of all the leafy families of the earth. And well does it fulfil its mission. Consider what we owe merely to the meadow grass, to the covering of the dark ground by that glorious enamel, by the companies of those soft, and countless, and peaceful spears. The fields! Follow but forth for a little time the thoughts of all that we ought to recognize in those words. All spring and summer is in them, —the walks by silent, scented paths,—the rests in noonday heat,—the joy of herds and flocks,—the power of all shepherd life and meditation,—the life of sunlight upon the world, falling in emerald streaks, and failing in soft blue shadows, where else it would have struck upon the dark mould, or scorching dust,—pastures beside the pacing brooks,—soft banks and knolls of lowly hills,—thymy slopes of down overlooked by the blue line of lifted sea, —crisp lawns all dim with early dew, or smooth in evening warmth of barred sunshine, dinted by happy feet, and softening in their fall the sound of loving voices; all these are summed in those simple words; and these are not all. We may not measure to the full the depth of this heavenly gift in our own land; though still, as we think of it longer, the infinite of that meadow sweetness, Shakspere's peculiar joy, would open on us more and more, yet we have it but in part. Go out, in the springtime, among the meadows that slope from the shores of the Swiss lakes to the roots of their lower mountains.

There, mingled with the taller gentians and the while narcissus, the grass grows deep and free; and as you follow the winding mountain paths, beneath arching boughs all veiled and dim with blossom,—paths that forever droop and rise over the green banks and mounds sweeping down in scented undulation, steep to the blue water, studded here and there with new-mown heaps, filling all the air with fainter sweetness,—look up toward the higher hills, where the waves of everlasting green roll silently into their long inlets among the shadows of the pines; and we may, perhaps, at last know the meaning of those quiet words of the 147th Psalm, "He maketh grass to grow upon the mountains."

There are also several lessons symbolically connected with this subject, which we must not allow to escape us. Observe, the peculiar characters of the grass, which adapt it especially for the service of man, are its apparent *humility,* and *cheerfulness.* Its humility, in that it seems created only for lowest service,—appointed to be trodden on, and fed upon. Its cheerfulness, in that it seems to exult under all kinds of violence and suffering. You roll it, and it is stronger the next day; you mow it, and it multiplies its shoots, as if it were grateful; you tread upon it, and it only sends up richer perfume. Spring comes, and it rejoices with all the earth,—glowing with variegated flame of flowers,—waving in soft depth of fruitful strength. Winter comes, and though it will not mock its fellow plants by growing then, it will not pine and mourn, and turn colorless and leafless as they. It is always green; and is only the brighter and gayer for the hoarfrost.

LICHEN

[*Modern Painters,* Vol. V, Pt. 6, Ch. 10.]

LICHEN, and mosses (though these last in their luxuriance are deep and rich as herbage, yet both for the most part humblest of the green things that live),—how of these? Meek creatures! the first mercy of the earth, veiling with hushed softness its dintless rocks; creatures full of pity, covering with strange and tender honor the scarred disgrace of ruin,—laying quiet finger on the trembling stones, to teach them rest. No words, that I know of, will say what these mosses are. None are delicate enough, none perfect enough, none rich enough. How is one to tell of the rounded bosses of furred and beaming green,—the starred divisions of rubied bloom, fine-filmed, as if the Rock Spirits could spin porphyry as we do glass,—the traceries of intricate silver, and fringes of amber, lustrous, arborescent, burnished through every fibre into fitful brightness and glossy traverses of silken change, yet all subdued and pensive, and framed for simplest, sweetest offices of grace? They will not be gathered, like the flowers, for chaplet or love-token; but of these the wild bird will make its nest, and the wearied child his pillow.

And, as the earth's first mercy, so they are its last gift to us. When all other service is vain, from plant and tree, the soft mosses and gray lichen take up their watch by the head-stone. The woods, the blossoms, the gift-bearing grasses, have done their parts for a time, but these do service forever. Trees for the builder's yard, flowers for the bride's chamber, corn for the granary, moss for the grave.

Yet as in one sense the humblest, in another they are the most honored of the earth-children. Unfading, as motionless, the worm frets them not, and the autumn wastes not. Strong in lowliness, they neither blanch in heat nor pine in frost. To them, slow-fingered, constant-hearted, is entrusted the weaving of the dark, eternal tapestries of the hills; to them, slow-pencilled, iris-dyed, the tender framing of their endless imagery. Sharing the stillness of the unimpassioned rock, they share also its endurance; and while the winds of departing spring scatter the white hawthorn blossom like drifted snow, and summer dims on the parched meadow the drooping of its cowslip-gold,—far above, among the mountains, the silver lichen-spots rest, star-like, on the stone; and the gathering orange stain upon the edge of yonder western peak reflects the sunsets of a thousand years.

The Bird and the Serpent

[*Queen of the Air,* Lecture 2.]

Now we have two orders of animals to take some note
of in connection with Athena, and one vast order of
plants, which will illustrate this matter very sufficiently
for us.

The two orders of animals are the serpent and the bird;
the serpent, in which the breath, or spirit, is less than in
any other creature, and the earth-power greatest:—the
bird, in which the breath, or spirit, is more full than in
any other creature, and the earth-power least.

We will take the bird first. It is little more than a
drift of the air brought into form by plumes; the air is
in all its quills, it breathes through its whole frame and
flesh, and glows with air in its flying, like a blown flame:
it rests upon the air, subdues it, surpasses it, outraces
it;—*is* the air, conscious of itself, conquering itself, ruling itself.

Also, into the throat of the bird is given the voice of
the air. All that in the wind itself is weak, wild, useless
in sweetness, is knit together in its song. As we may
imagine the wild form of the cloud closed into the perfect form of the bird's wings, so the wild voice of the
cloud into its ordered and commanded voice; unwearied,
rippling through the clear heaven in its gladness, in-
terpreting all intense passion through the soft spring
nights, bursting into acclaim and rapture of choir at daybreak, or lisping and twittering among the boughs and
hedges through heat of day, like little winds that only
make the cowslip bells shake, and ruffle the petals of the
wild rose.

Also, upon the plumes of the bird are put the colors
of the air: on these the gold of the cloud, that cannot be
gathered by any covetousness; the rubies of the clouds,
that are not the price of Athena, but *are* Athena; the
vermilion of the cloud-bar, and the flame of the cloud-
crest, and the snow of the cloud, and its shadow, and the
melted blue of the deep wells of the sky—all these, seized
by the creating spirit, and woven by Athena herself into

films and threads of plume; with wave on wave following and fading along breast, and throat, and opened wings, infinite as the dividing of the foam and the sifting of the sea-sand;—even the white down of the cloud seeming to flutter up between the stronger plumes, seen, but too soft for touch.

And so the Spirit of the Air is put into, and upon, this created form; and it becomes, through twenty centuries, the symbol of Divine help, descending, as the Fire, to speak, but as the Dove, to bless.

Next, in the serpent we approach the source of a group of myths, world-wide, founded on great and common human instincts, respecting which I must note one or two points which bear intimately on all our subject. For it seems to me that the scholars who are at present occupied in interpretation of human myths have most of them forgotten that there are any such things as natural myths; and that the dark sayings of men may be both difficult to read, and not always worth reading; but the dark sayings of nature will probably become clearer for the looking into, and will very certainly be worth reading. And, indeed, all guidance to the right sense of the human and variable myths will probably depend on our first getting at the sense of the natural invariable ones. The dead hieroglyph may have meant this or that — the living hieroglyph means always the same; but remember, it is just as much a hieroglyph as the other; nay, more,—a "sacred or reserved sculpture," a thing with an inner language. The serpent crest of the king's crown, or of the god's, on the pillars of Egypt, is a mystery; but the serpent itself, gliding past the pillar's foot, is it less a mystery? Is there, indeed, no tongue, except the mute forked flash from its lips, in that running brook of horror on the ground?

Why that horror? We all feel it, yet how imaginative it is, how disproportioned to the real strength of the creature! There is more poison in an ill-kept drain,—in a pool of dish-washings at a cottage door,—than in the deadliest asp of Nile. Every back-yard which you look down into from the railway, as it carries you out by Vauxhall or Deptford, holds its coiled serpent: all the

walls of those ghastly suburbs are enclosures of tank
temples for serpent worship; yet you feel no horror in
looking down into them, as you would if you saw the
livid scales and lifted head. There is more venom, mortal, inevitable, in a single word sometimes, or in the
gliding entrance of a worldless thought, than ever "vanti
Libia con sua rena." But that horror is of the myth,
not of the creature. There are myriads lower than this,
and more loathsome, in the scale of being; the links between dead matter and animation drift everywhere unseen. But it is the strength of the base element that is
so dreadful in the serpent; it is the very omnipotence of
the earth. That rivulet of smooth river—how does it
flow, think you? It literally rows on the earth, with
every scale for an oar; it bites the dust with the ridges
of its body. Watch it, when it moves slowly:—A wave,
but without wind! a current, but with no fall! all the
body moving at the same instant, yet some of it to one
side, some to another, or some forward, and the rest of
the coil backward; but all with the same calm will and
equal way—no contraction, no extension; one sound-
less, causeless march of sequent rings, and spectral procession of spotted dust, with dissolution in its fangs, dis-
location in its coils. Startle it;—the winding stream
will become a twisted arrow;—the wave of poisoned life
will lash through the grass like a cast lance.* It scarcely
breathes with its one lung (the other shrivelled and
abortive); it is passive to the sun and shade, and is cold
or hot like a stone; yet, "it can outclimb the monkey,
outswim the fish, outleap the jerboa, outwrestle the ath-
lete, and crush the tiger." It is a divine hieroglyph of

---

* I cannot understand this swift forward motion of serpents. The
seizure of prey by the constrictor, though invisibly swift, is quite simple
in mechanism; it is simply the return to its coil of an opened watch-
spring, and is just as instantaneous. But the steady and continuous
motion, without a visible fulcrum (for the whole body moves at the
same instant, and I have often seen even small snakes glide as fast
as I could walk), seems to involve a vibration of the scales quite too
rapid to be conceived. The motion of the crest and dorsal fin of the
hippocampus, which is one of the intermediate types between serpent and
fish, perhaps gives some resemblance of it, dimly visible, for the quivering turns the fin into a mere mist. The entrance of the two barbs
of a bee's sting by alternate motion, "the teeth of one barb acting as
a fulcrum for the other," must be something like the serpent motion
on a small scale. [Ruskin's note.]

the demoniac power of the earth,—of the entire earthly
nature. As the bird is the clothed power of the air, so
this is the clothed power of the dust; as the bird the symbol of the spirit of life, so this of the grasp and sting
of death.

THE RHONE

[Præterita, Vol. II, Ch. 5.]

FOR all other rivers there is a surface, and an underneath, and a vaguely displeasing idea of the bottom. But
the Rhone flows like one lambent jewel; its surface is
nowhere, its ethereal self is everywhere, the iridescent
rush and translucent strength of it blue to the shore, and
radiant to the depth.

Fifteen feet thick, of not flowing, but flying water;
not water, neither,—melted glacier, rather, one should
call it; the force of the ice is with it, and the wreathing
of the clouds, the gladness of the sky, and the continuance of Time.

Waves of clear sea are, indeed, lovely to watch, but
they are always coming or gone, never in any taken shape
to be seen for a second. But here was one mighty wave
that was always itself, and every fluted swirl of it, constant as the wreathing of a shell. No wasting away of
the fallen foam, no pause for gathering of power, no
helpless ebb of discouraged recoil; but alike through
bright day and lulling night, the never-pausing plunge,
and never-fading flash, and never-hushing whisper, and,
while the sun was up, the ever-answering glow of un-
earthly aquamarine, ultramarine, violet-blue, gentian-
blue, peacock-blue, river-of-paradise blue, glass of a
painted window melted in the sun, and the witch of the
Alps flinging the spun tresses of it forever from her
snow.

The innocent way, too, in which the river used to stop
to look into every little corner. Great torrents always
seem angry, and great rivers too often sullen; but there
is no anger, no disdain, in the Rhone. It seemed as if
the mountain stream was in mere bliss at recovering itself again out of the lake-sleep, and raced because it re-

joiced in racing, fain yet to return and stay. There were
pieces of wave that danced all day as if Perdita were
looking on to learn; there were little streams that skipped
like lambs and leaped like chamois; there were pools that
shook the sunshine all through them, and were rippled in
layers of overlaid ripples, like crystal sand; there were
currents that twisted the light into golden braids, and
inlaid the threads with turquoise enamel; there were
strips of stream that had certainly above the lake been
millstreams, and were looking busily for mills to turn
again; there were shoots of stream that had once shot
fearfully into the air, and now sprang up again laughing
that they had only fallen a foot or two;—and in the midst
of all the gay glittering and eddied lingering, the noble
bearing by of the midmost depth, so mighty, yet so ter-
rorless and harmless, with its swallows skimming instead
of petrels, and the dear old decrepit town as safe in the
embracing sweep of it as if it were set in a brooch of
sapphire.

The Mountain Glory

[Modern Painters, Vol. IV, Ch. 20]

I HAVE dwelt, in the foregoing chapter, on the sadness
of the hills with the greater insistence that I feared my
own excessive love for them might lead me into too
favorable interpretation of their influences over the human heart; or, at least, that the reader might accuse me
of fond prejudice, in the conclusions to which, finally, I
desire to lead him concerning them. For, to myself,
mountains are the beginning and the end of all natural
scenery; in them, and in the forms of inferior landscape
that lead to them, my affections are wholly bound up;
and though I can look with happy admiration at the lowland flowers, and woods, and open skies, the happiness is
tranquil and cold, like that of examining detached flowers in a conservatory, or reading a pleasant book; and if
the scenery be resolutely level, insisting upon the declaration of its own flatness in all the detail of it, as in Hol-
land, or Lincolnshire, or Central Lombardy, it appears
to me like a prison, and I cannot long endure it. But

the slightest rise and fall in the road,—a mossy bank at the side of a crag of chalk, with brambles at its brow, overhanging it,—a ripple over three or four stones in the stream by the bridge,—above all, a wild bit of ferny ground under a fir or two, looking as if, possibly, one might see a hill if one got to the other side of the trees, will instantly give me intense delight, because the shadow, or the hope, of the hills, is in them.

And thus, although there are few districts of northern Europe, however apparently dull or tame, in which I cannot find pleasure, though the whole of northern France (except Champagne), dull as it seems to most travellers, is to me a perpetual Paradise; and, putting Lincolnshire, Leicestershire, and one or two such other perfectly flat districts aside, there is not an English county which I should not find entertainment in exploring the cross-roads of, foot by foot; yet all my best enjoyment would be owing to the imagination of the hills, coloring, with their far-away memories, every lowland stone and herb. The pleasant French coteau, green in the sunshine, delights me, either by what real mountain character it has in itself (for in extent and succession of promontory the flanks of the French valleys have quite the sublimity of true mountain distances), or by its broken ground and rugged steps among the vines, and rise of the leafage above, against the blue sky, as it might rise at Vevay or Como. There is not a wave of the Seine but is associated in my mind with the first rise of the sandstones and forest pines of Fontainebleau; and with the hope of the Alps, as one leaves Paris with the horses' heads to the southwest, the morning sun flashing on the bright waves at Charenton. If there be *no* hope or association of this kind, and if I cannot deceive myself into fancying that perhaps at the next rise of the road there may be seen the film of a blue hill in the gleam of sky at the horizon, the landscape, however beautiful, produces in me even a kind of sickness and pain; and the whole view from Richmond Hill or Windsor Terrace,—nay, the gardens of Alcinous, with their perpetual summer,—or of the Hesperides (if they were flat, and not close to Atlas), golden apples and all,—I

would give away in an instant, for one mossy granite
stone a foot broad, and two leaves of lady-fern.*

I know that this is in great part idiosyncrasy; and
that I must not trust to my own feelings, in this respect,
as representative of the modern landscape instinct: yet
I know it is not idiosyncrasy, in so far as there may be
proved to be indeed an increase of the absolute beauty
of all scenery in exact proportion to its mountainous
character, providing that character be *healthily* mountainous. I do not mean to take the Col de Bonhomme
as representative of hills, any more than I would take
Romney Marsh as representative of plains; but putting
Leicestershire or Staffordshire fairly beside Westmore-
land, and Lombardy or Champagne fairly beside the
Pays de Vaud or the Canton Berne, I find the increase
in the calculable sum of elements of beauty to be steadily in proportion to the increase of mountainous character; and that the best image which the world can give
of Paradise is in the slope of the meadows, orchards,
and corn-fields on the sides of a great Alp, with its purple rocks and eternal snows above; this excellence not
being in any wise a matter referable to feeling, or individual preferences, but demonstrable by calm enumeration of the number of lovely colors on the rocks, the
varied grouping of the trees, and quantity of noble incidents in stream, crag, or cloud, presented to the eye
at any given moment.

For consider, first, the difference produced in the
whole tone of landscape color by the introductions of
purple, violet, and deep ultramarine blue, which we owe

---

* In tracing the *whole* of the deep enjoyment to mountain association, I of course except whatever feelings are connected with the
observance of rural life, or with that of architecture. None of these
feelings arise out of the landscape, properly so called: the pleasure with
which we see a peasant's garden fairly kept, or a plowman doing his
work well, or a group of children playing at a cottage door, being
wholly separate from that which we find in the fields or commons
around them; and the beauty of architecture, or the associations connected with it, in like manner often ennobling the most tame scenery;—
yet not so but that we may always distinguish between the abstract
character of the unassisted landscape, and the charm which it derives
from the architecture. Much of the majesty of French landscape consists in its grand and gray village churches and turreted farmhouses,
not to speak of its cathedrals, castles, and beautifully placed cities.
[Ruskin's note.]

to mountains. In an ordinary lowland landscape we have the blue of the sky; the green of grass, which I will suppose (and this is an unnecessary concession to the lowlands) entirely fresh and bright; the green of trees; and certain elements of purple, far more rich and beautiful than we generally should think, in their bark and shadows (bare hedges and thickets, or tops of trees, in subdued afternoon sunshine, are nearly perfect purple, and of an exquisite tone), as well as in ploughed fields, and dark ground in general. But among mountains, in *addition* to all this, large unbroken spaces of pure violet and purple are introduced in their distances; and even near, by films of cloud passing over the darkness of ravines or forests, blues are produced of the most subtle tenderness; these azures and purples* passing into rose-color of otherwise wholly unattainable delicacy among the upper summits, the blue of the sky being at the same time purer and deeper than in the plains. Nay, in some sense, a person who has never seen the rose-color of the rays of dawn crossing a blue mountain twelve or fifteen miles away, can hardly be said to know what *tenderness* in color means at all; *bright* tenderness he may, indeed, see in the sky or in a flower, but this grave tenderness of the far-away hill-purples he cannot conceive.

Together with this great source of pre-eminence in *mass* of color, we have to estimate the influence of the finished inlaying and enamel-work of the color-jewellery on every stone; and that of the continual variety in species of flower; most of the mountain flowers being, besides, separately lovelier than the lowland ones. The wood hyacinth and wild rose are, indeed, the only *supreme* flowers that the lowlands can generally show; and the wild rose is also a mountaineer, and more fragrant in

---

* One of the principal reasons for the false supposition that Switzerland is not picturesque, is the error of most sketchers and painters in representing pine forest in middle distance as dark *green*, or gray green, whereas its true color is always purple, at distances of even two or three miles. Let any traveller coming down the Montanvert look for an aperture, three or four inches wide, between the near pine branches, through which, standing eight or ten feet from it, he can see the opposite forests on the Breven or Flégère. Those forests are not above two or two and a half miles from him; but he will find the aperture filled by a tint of nearly pure azure or purple, not by green. [Ruskin's note.]

the hills, while the wood hyacinth, or grape hyacinth, at its best, cannot match even the dark bell-gentian, leaving the light-blue star-gentian in its uncontested queenliness, and the Alpine rose and Highland heather wholly without similitude. The violet, lily of the valley, crocus, and wood anemone are, I suppose, claimable partly by the plains as well as the hills; but the large orange lily and narcissus I have never seen but on hill pastures, and the exquisite oxalis is pre-eminently a mountaineer.

To this supremacy in mosses and flowers we have next to add an inestimable gain in the continual presence and power of water. Neither in its clearness, its color, its fantasy of motion, its calmness of space, depth, and reflection, or its wrath, can water be conceived by a lowlander, out of sight of sea. A sea wave is far grander than any torrent—but of the sea and its influences we are not now speaking; and the sea itself, though it *can* be clear, is never calm, among our shores, in the sense that a mountain lake can be calm. The sea seems only to pause; the mountain lake to sleep, and to dream. Out of sight of the ocean a lowlander cannot be considered ever to have seen water at all. The mantling of the pools in the rock shadows, with the golden flakes of light sinking down through them like falling leaves, the ringing of the thin currents among the shallows, the flash and the cloud of the· cascade, the earthquake and foam-fire of the cataract, the long lines of alternate mirror and mist that lull the imagery of the hills reversed in the blue of morning,—all these things belong to those hills as their undivided inheritance.

To this supremacy in wave and stream is joined a no less manifest pre-eminence in the character of trees. It is possible among plains, in the species of trees which properly belong to them, the poplars of Amiens, for instance, to obtain a serene simplicity of grace, which, as I said, is a better help to the study of gracefulness, as such, than any of the wilder groupings of the hills; so, also, there are certain conditions of symmetrical luxuriance developed in the park and avenue, rarely rivalled in their way among mountains; and yet the mountain superiority in foliage is, on the whole, nearly as complete as it is in water: for exactly as there are some expressions in the broad reaches of a navigable lowland river, such as the Loire or Thames, not, in their way, to be matched among the rock rivers, and yet for all that a lowlander cannot be said to have truly seen the element of water at all; so even in the richest parks and avenues he cannot be said to have truly seen trees. For the resources of trees are not developed until they have difficulty to contend with; neither their tenderness of brotherly love and harmony, till they are forced to choose their ways of various life where there is contracted room for them, talking to each other with their restrained branches. The various action of trees rooting themselves in inhospitable rocks, stooping to look into ravines, hiding from the search of glacier winds, reaching forth to the rays of rare sunshine, crowding down together to drink at sweetest streams, climbing hand in hand among the difficult slopes, opening in sudden dances round the mossy knolls, gathering into companies at rest among the fragrant fields, gliding in grave procession over the heavenward ridges—nothing of this can be conceived among the unvexed and unvaried felicities of the lowland forest: while to all these direct sources of greater beauty are added, first the power of redundance,—the mere quantity of foliage visible in the folds and on the promontories of a single Alp being greater than that of an entire lowland landscape (unless a view from some cathedral tower); and to this charm of redundance, that of clearer *visibility,*—tree after tree being constantly shown in successive height, one behind another, instead of the mere tops and flanks of masses, as in the plains; and the forms of multitudes of them continually defined against the clear sky, near and above, or against white clouds entangled among their branches, instead of being confused in dimness of distance.

Finally, to this supremacy in foliage we have to add the still less questionable supremacy in clouds. There is no effect of sky possible in the lowlands which may not in equal perfection be seen among the hills; but there are effects by tens of thousands, forever invisible and inconceivable to the inhabitant of the plains, manifested among the hills in the course of one day. The mere power of familiarity with the clouds, of walking with them and above them, alters and renders clear our whole conception of the baseless architecture of the sky; and for the beauty of it, there is more in a single wreath of early cloud, pacing its way up an avenue of pines, or pausing among the points of their fringes, than in all the white heaps that fill the arched sky of the plains from one horizon to the other. And of the nobler cloud manifestations,—the breaking of their troublous seas against the crags, their black spray sparkling with lightning; or the going forth of the morning along their pavements of moving marble, level-laid between dome and dome of snow;—of these things there can be as little imagination or understanding in an inhabitant of the plains as of the scenery of another planet than his own.

And, observe, all these superiorities are matters plainly measurable and calculable, not in any wise to be referred to estimate of *sensation*. Of the grandeur or expression of the hills I have not spoken; how far they are great, or strong, or terrible, I do not for the moment consider, because vastness, and strength, and terror, are not to all minds subjects of desired contemplation. It may make no difference to some men whether a natural object be large or small, whether it be strong or feeble. But loveliness of color, perfectness of form, endlessness of change, wonderfulness of structure, are precious to all undiseased human minds; and the superiority of the mountains in all these things to the lowland is, I repeat, as measurable as the richness of a painted window matched with a white one, or the wealth of a museum compared with that of a simply furnished chamber. They seem to have been built for the human race, as at once their schools and cathedrals; full of treasures of illuminated manuscript for the scholar, kindly in simple lessons to the worker, quiet in pale cloisters for the thinker, glorious in holiness for the worshipper. And of these great cathedrals of the earth, with their gates of rock, pavements of cloud, choirs of stream and stone, altars of snow, and vaults of purple traversed by the continual stars,—of these, as we have seen, it was written, nor long ago, by one of the best of the poor human race for whom they were built, wondering in himself for whom their Creator *could* have made them, and thinking to have entirely discerned the Divine intent in them—"They are inhabited by the Beasts."

Was it then indeed thus with us, and so lately? Had mankind offered no worship in their mountain churches? Was all that granite sculpture and floral painting done by the angels in vain?

Not so. It will need no prolonged thought to convince us that in the hills the purposes of their Maker have indeed been accomplished in such measure as, through the sin or folly of men, He ever permits them to be accomplished. It may not seem, from the general language held concerning them, or from any directly traceable results, that mountains have had serious influence on human intellect; but it will not, I think, be difficult to show that their occult influence has been both constant and essential to the progress of the race.

LA RICCIA—SUNLIGHT AFTER STORM

[Modern Painters, Vol. I, Pt. 2, § 2, Ch. 2.]

THERE is, in the first room of the National Gallery, a landscape attributed to Gaspar Poussin, called sometimes Aricia, sometimes Le or La Riccia, according to the fancy of catalogue printers. Whether it can be supposed to resemble the ancient Aricia, now La Riccia, close to Albano, I will not take upon me to determine, seeing that most of the towns of these old masters are quite as like one place as another; but, at any rate, it is a town on a hill, wooded with two-and-thirty bushes, of very uniform size, and possessing about the same number of leaves each. These bushes are all painted in with one dull opaque brown, becoming very slightly greenish toward the lights, and discover in one place a bit of rock, which of course would in nature have been cool and gray beside the lustrous hues of foliage, and which, therefore, being moreover completely in shade, is consistently and scientifically painted of a very clear, pretty, and positive brick red, the only thing like color in the picture. The foreground is a piece of road which, in order to make allowance for its greater nearness, for its being completely in light, and, it may be presumed, for the quantity of vegetation usually present on carriage-roads, is given in a very cool green gray; and the truth of the picture is completed by a number of dots in the sky on the right, with a stalk to them, of a sober and similar brown.

Not long ago, I was slowly descending this very bit of carriage-road, the first turn after you leave Albano, not a little impeded by the worthy successors of the ancient prototypes of Veiento. It had been wild weather when I left Rome, and all across the Campagna the clouds were sweeping in sulphurous blue, with a clap of thunder or two, and breaking gleams of sun along the Claudian aqueduct, lighting up the infinity of its arches like the bridge of chaos. But as I climbed the long slope of the Alban Mount, the storm swept finally to the north, and the noble outline of the domes of Albano, and graceful darkness of its ilex grove rose against pure streaks of alternate blue and amber; the upper sky gradually flushing through the last fragments of rain-cloud in deep palpitating azure, half æther and half dew. The noonday sun came slanting down the rocky slopes of La Riccia, and its masses of entangled and tall foliage, whose autumnal tints were mixed with the wet verdure of a thousand evergreens, were penetrated with it as with rain. I cannot call it color, it was conflagration. Purple, and crimson, and scarlet, like the curtains of God's tabernacle, the rejoicing trees sank into the valley in showers of light, every separate leaf quivering with buoyant and burning life; each, as it turned to reflect or to transmit the sunbeam, first a torch and then an emerald. Far up into the recesses of the valley, the green vistas arched like the hollows of mighty waves of some crystalline sea, with the arbutus flowers dashed along their flanks for foam, and silver flakes of orange spray tossed into the air around them, breaking over the gray walls of rock into a thousand separate stars, fading and kindling alternately as the weak wind lifted and let them fall. Every glade of grass burned like the golden floor of heaven, opening in sudden gleams as the foliage broke and closed above it, as sheet-lightning opens in a cloud at sunset; the motionless masses of dark rock—dark though flushed with scarlet lichen, casting their quiet shadows across its restless radiance, the fountain underneath them filling its marble hollow with blue mist and fitful sound; and over all, the multitudinous bars of amber and rose, the sacred clouds that have no darkness, and only exist to illumine, were seen in fathomless intervals between the solemn and orbed repose of the stone pines, passing to lose themselves in the last, white, blinding lustre of the measureless line where the Campagna melted into the blaze of the sea.

THE CAMPAGNA OF ROME

[Modern Painters, Vol. I, preface to 2nd edition.]

PERHAPS there is no more impressive scene on earth than the solitary extent of the Campagna of Rome under evening light. Let the reader imagine himself for a moment withdrawn from the sounds and motion of the living world, and sent forth alone into this wild and wasted plain. The earth yields and crumbles beneath his foot, tread he never so lightly, for its substance is white, hollow, and carious, like the dusty wreck of the bones of men.* The long knotted grass waves and tosses feebly in the evening wind, and the shadows of its motion shake feverishly along the banks of ruin that lift themselves to the sunlight. Hillocks of mouldering earth heave around him, as if the dead beneath were struggling in their sleep; scattered blocks of black stone, four-square, remnants of mighty edifices, not one left upon another, lie upon them to keep them down. A dull purple poisonous haze stretches level along the desert, veiling its spectral wrecks of massy ruins, on whose rents the red light rests, like dying fire on defiled altars. The blue ridge of the Alban Mount lifts itself against a solemn space of

---

* The vegetable soil of the Campagna is chiefly formed by decomposed lavas, and under it lies a bed of white pumice, exactly resembling remnants of bones. [Ruskin's Note.]

green, clear, quiet sky. Watch-towers of dark clouds stand steadfastly along the promontories of the Apennines. From the plain to the mountains, the shattered aqueducts, pier beyond pier, melt into the darkness, like shadowy and countless troops of funeral mourners, passing from a nation's grave.

III. ART

GREATNESS IN ART

[*Modern Painters,* Vol. I, Pt. 1, § 1, Ch. 2.]

In the 15th Lecture of Sir Joshua Reynolds, incidental notice is taken of the distinction between those excellences in the painter which belong to him *as such,* and those which belong to him in common with all men of intellect, the general and exalted powers of which art is the evidence and expression, not the subject. But the distinction is not there dwelt upon as it should be, for it is owing to the slight attention ordinarily paid to it, that criticism is open to every form of coxcombry, and liable to every phase of error. It is a distinction on which depend all sound judgment of the rank of the artist, and all just appreciation of the dignity of art.

Painting, or art generally, as such, with all its technicalities, difficulties, and particular ends, is nothing but a noble and expressive language, invaluable as the vehicle of thought, but by itself nothing. He who has learned what is commonly considered the whole art of painting, that is, the art of representing any natural object faithfully, has as yet only learned the language by which his thoughts are to be expressed. He has done just as much toward being that which we ought to respect as a great painter, as a man who has learned how to express himself grammatically and melodiously has toward being a great poet. The language is, indeed, more difficult of acquirement in the one case than in the other, and possesses more power of delighting the sense, while it speaks to the intellect; but it is, nevertheless, nothing more than language, and all those excellences which are peculiar to the painter as such, are merely what rhythm, melody, precision, and force are in the words of the orator and the poet, necessary to their greatness, but not the test of their greatness. It is not by the mode of representing and saying, but by what is represented and said, that the respective greatness either of the painter or the writer is to be finally determined.

Speaking with strict propriety, therefore, we should call a man a great painter only as he excelled in precision and force in the language of lines, and a great versifier, as he excelled in precision and force in the language of words. A great poet would then be a term strictly, and in precisely the same sense, applicable to both, if warranted by the character of the images or thoughts each in their respective languages conveyed.

Take, for instance, one of the most perfect poems or pictures (I used the words as synonymous) which modern times have seen:—the "Old Shepherd's Chief-mourner." Here the exquisite execution of the glossy and crisp hair of the dog, the bright sharp touching of the green bough beside it, the clear painting of the wood of the coffin and the folds of the blanket, are language—language clear and expressive in the highest degree. But the close pressure of the dog's breast against the wood, the convulsive clinging of the paws, which has dragged the blanket off the trestle, the total powerlessness of the head laid, close and motionless, upon its folds, the fixed and tearful fall of the eye in its utter hopelessness, the rigidity of repose which marks that there has been no motion nor change in the trance of agony since the last blow was struck on the coffin-lid, the quietness and gloom of the chamber, the spectacles marking the place where the Bible was last closed, indicating how lonely has been the life, how unwatched the departure of him who is now laid solitary in his sleep;—these are all thoughts—thoughts by which the picture is separated at once from hundreds of equal merit, as far as mere painting goes, by which it ranks as a work of high art, and stamps its author, not as the neat imitator of the texture of a skin, or the fold of a drapery, but as the Man of Mind.

It is not, however, always easy, either in painting or

literature, to determine where the influence of language stops, and where that of thought begins. Many thoughts are so dependent upon the language in which they are clothed, that they would lose half their beauty if otherwise expressed. But the highest thoughts are those which are least dependent on language, and the dignity of any composition, and praise to which it is entitled, are in exact proportion to its independency of language or expression. A composition is indeed usually most perfect, when to such intrinsic dignity is added all that expression can do to attract and adorn; but in every case of supreme excellence this all becomes as nothing. We are more gratified by the simplest lines or words which can suggest the idea in its own naked beauty, than by the robe and the gem which conceal while they decorate; we are better pleased to feel by their absence how little they could bestow, than by their presence how much they can destroy.

There is therefore a distinction to be made between what is ornamental in language and what is expressive. That part of it which is necessary to the embodying and conveying of the thought is worthy of respect and attention as necessary to excellence, though not the test of it. But that part of it which is decorative has little more to do with the intrinsic excellence of the picture than the frame or the varnishing of it. And this caution in distinguishing between the ornamental and the expressive is peculiarly necessary in painting; for in the language of words it is nearly impossible for that which is not expressive to be beautiful, except by mere rhythm or melody, any sacrifice to which is immediately stigmatized as error. But the beauty of mere language in painting is not only very attractive and entertaining to the spectator, but requires for its attainment no small exertion of mind and devotion of time by the artist. Hence, in art, men have frequently fancied that they were becoming rhetoricians and poets when they were only learning to speak melodiously, and the judge has over and over again advanced to the honor of authors those who were never more than ornamental writing-masters.

Most pictures of the Dutch school, for instance, excepting always those of Rubens, Vandyke, and Rembrandt, are ostentatious exhibitions of the artist's power of speech, the clear and vigorous elocution of useless and senseless words; while the early efforts of Cimabue and Giotto are the burning messages of prophecy, delivered by the stammering lips of infants. It is not by ranking the former as more than mechanics, or the latter as less than artists, that the taste of the multitude, always awake to the lowest pleasures which art can bestow, and blunt to the highest, is to be formed or elevated. It must be the part of the judicious critic carefully to distinguish what is language, and what is thought, and to rank and praise pictures chiefly for the latter, considering the former as a totally inferior excellence, and one which cannot be compared with nor weighed against thought in any way nor in any degree whatsoever. The picture which has the nobler and more numerous ideas, however awkwardly expressed, is a greater and a better picture than that which has the less noble and less numerous ideas, however beautifully expressed. No weight, nor mass, nor beauty of execution, can outweigh one grain or fragment of thought. Three penstrokes of Raffaelle are a greater and a better picture than the most finished work that ever Carlo Dolci polished into inanity. A finished work of a great artist is only better than its sketch, if the sources of pleasure belonging to color and realization—valuable in themselves—are so employed as to increase the impressiveness of the thought. But if one atom of thought has vanished, all color, all finish, all execution, all ornament, are too dearly bought. Nothing but thought can pay for thought, and the instant that the increasing refinement or finish of the picture begins to be paid for by the loss of the faintest shadow of an idea, that instant all refinement or finish is an excrescence and a deformity.

Yet although in all our speculations on art, language is thus to be distinguished from, and held subordinate to, that which it conveys, we must still remember that there are certain ideas inherent in language itself, and that, strictly speaking, every pleasure connected with art has in it some reference to the intellect. The mere sensual pleasure of the eye, received from the most brilliant piece of coloring, is as nothing to that which it receives from a crystal prism, except as it depends on our perception of a certain meaning and intended arrangement of color, which has been the subject of intellect. Nay, the term idea, according to Locke's definition of it, will extend even to the sensual impressions themselves as far as they are "things which the mind occupies itself about in thinking"; that is, not as they are felt by the eye only, but as they are received by the mind through the eye. So that, if I say that the greatest picture is that which conveys to the mind of the spectator the greatest number of the greatest ideas, I have a definition which will include as subjects of comparison every pleasure which art is capable of conveying. If I were to say, on the contrary, that the best picture was that which most closely imitated nature, I should assume that art could only please by imitating nature; and I should cast out of the pale of criticism those parts of works of art which are not imitative, that is to say, intrinsic beauties of color and form, and those works of art wholly, which, like the Arabesques of Raffaelle in the Loggias, are not imitative at all. Now, I want a definition of art wide enough to include all its varieties of aim. I do not say, therefore, that the art is greatest which gives most pleasure, because perhaps there is some art whose end is to teach, and not to please. I do not say that the art is greatest which teaches us most, because perhaps there is some art whose end is to please, and not to teach. I do not say that the art is greatest which imitates best, because perhaps there is some art whose end is to create and not to imitate. But I say that the art is greatest which conveys to the mind of the spectator, by any means whatsoever, the greatest number of the greatest ideas; and I call an idea great in proportion as it is received by a higher faculty of the mind, and as it more fully occupies, and in occupying, exercises and exalts, the faculty by which it is received.

If this, then, be the definition of great art, that of a great artist naturally follows. He is the greatest artist who has embodied, in the sum of his works, the greatest number of the greatest ideas.

IDEAS OF TRUTH, BEAUTY, AND RELATION

[*Modern Painters,* Vol. I, Pt. 2, § 1, Chs. 5, 6, 7.]

(a) *Ideas of Truth:* The word Truth, as applied to art, signifies the faithful statement, either to the mind or senses, of any fact of nature.

We receive an idea of truth, then, when we perceive the faithfulness of such a statement.

The difference between ideas of truth and of imitation lies chiefly in the following points:

First,—Imitation can only be of something material, but truth has reference to statements both of the qualities of material things, and of emotions, impressions, and thoughts. There is a moral as well as material truth,— a truth of impression as well as of form,—of thought as well as of matter; and the truth of impression and thought is a thousand times the more important of the two. Hence, truth is a term of universal application, but imitation is limited to that narrow field of art which takes cognizance only of material things.

Secondly,—Truth may be stated by any signs or symbols which have a definite signification in the minds of those to whom they are addressed, although such signs be themselves no image nor likeness of anything. Whatever can excite in the mind the conception of certain facts, can give ideas of truth, though it be in no degree the imitation or resemblance of those facts. If there be— we do not say there is,—but if there be in painting anything which operates, as words do, not by resembling anything, but by being taken as a symbol and substitute for it, and thus inducing the effect of it, then this channel of communication can convey uncorrupted truth, though it do not in any degree resemble the facts whose conception it induces. But ideas of imitation, of course, require the likeness of the object. They speak to the perceptive faculties only: truth to the conceptive.

Thirdly, and in consequence of what is above stated, an idea of truth exists in the statement of *one* attribute of anything, but an idea of imitation requires the resemblance of as many attributes as we are usually cognizant of in its real presence. A pencil outline of the bough of a tree on white paper is a statement of a certain number of facts of form. It does not yet amount to the imitation of anything. The idea of that form is not given in nature by lines at all, still less by black lines with a white space between them. But those lines convey to the mind a distinct impression of a certain number of facts, which it recognizes as agreeable with its previous impressions of the bough of a tree; and it receives, therefore, an idea of truth. If, instead of two lines, we give a dark form with the brush, we convey information of a certain relation of shade between the bough and sky, recognizable for another idea of truth; but we have still no imitation, for the white paper is not the least like air, nor the black shadow like wood. It is not until after a certain number of ideas of truth have been collected together, that we arrive at an idea of imitation.

Hence it might at first sight appear, that an idea of imitation, inasmuch as several ideas of truth are united in it, is nobler than a simple idea of truth. And if it were necessary that the ideas of truth should be perfect, or should be subjects of contemplation *as such*, it would be so. But, observe, we require to produce the effect of imitation only so many and such ideas of truth as the *senses* are usually cognizant of. Now the senses are not usually, nor unless they be especially devoted to the service, cognizant, with accuracy, of any truths but those of space and projection. It requires long study and attention before they give certain evidence of even the simplest truths of form. For instance, the quay on which the figure is sitting, with his hand at his eyes, in Claude's "Seaport," No. 14 in the National Gallery, is egregiously out of perspective. The eye of this artist, with all his study, had thus not acquired the power of taking cognizance of the apparent form even of a simple parallelopiped: how much less of the complicated forms of boughs, leaves, or limbs? Although, therefore, something resembling the real form is necessary to deception, this something is not to be called a *truth* of form; for, strictly speaking, there are no degrees of truth, there are only degrees of approach to it; and an approach to it, whose feebleness and imperfection would instantly offend and give pain to a mind really capable of distinguishing truth, is yet quite sufficient for all the purposes of deceptive imitation. It is the same with regard to color. If we were to paint a tree sky-blue, or a dog rose-pink, the discernment of the public would be keen enough to discover the falsehood; but, so that there be just so much approach to truth of color as may come up to the common idea of it in men's minds, that is to say, if the trees be all bright green, and flesh unbroken buff, and ground unbroken brown, though all the real and refined truths of color be wholly omitted, or rather defied and contradicted, there is yet quite enough for all purposes of imitation. The only facts, then, which we are usually and certainly cognizant of, are those of distance and projection; and if these be tolerably given, with something like truth of form and color to assist them, the idea of imitation is complete. I would undertake to paint an arm, with every muscle out of its place, and every bone of false form and dislocated articulation, and yet to observe certain coarse and broad resemblances of true outline, which, with careful shading, would induce deception, and draw down the praise and delight of the discerning public. The other day at Bruges, while I was endeavoring to set down in my note-book something of the ineffable expression of the Madonna in the Cathedral, a French amateur came up to me, to inquire if I had seen the modern French pictures in a neighboring church. I had not, but felt little inclined to leave my marble for all the canvas that ever suffered from French brushes. My apathy was attacked with gradually increasing energy of praise. Rubens never executed—Titian never colored anything like them. I thought this highly probable, and still sat quiet. The voice continued at my ear. "Parbleu, Monsieur, Michel Ange n'a rien produit de plus beau!" "De plus *beau?*" repeated I, wishing to know what particular excellences of Michael Angelo were to be intimated by this expression. "Monsieur, on ne peut plus—c'est un tableau admirable—inconceivable; Monsieur," said the Frenchman, lifting up his hands to heaven, as he concentrated in one conclusive and overwhelming proposition the qualities

which were to outshine Rubens and overpower Buonaroti,
—"Monsieur, IL SORT!"

This gentleman could only perceive two truths—flesh
color and projection. These constituted his notion of
the perfection of painting; because they unite all that is
necessary for deception. He was not therefore cognizant
of many ideas of truth, though perfectly cognizant of
ideas of imitation.

We shall see, in the course of our investigation of ideas
of truth, that ideas of imitation not only do not imply
their presence, but even are inconsistent with it; and that
pictures which imitate so as to deceive, are never true.
But this is not the place for the proof of this; at present
we have only to insist on the last and greatest distinction between ideas of truth and of imitation—that the
mind, in receiving one of the former, dwells upon its own
conception of the fact, or form, or feeling stated, and is
occupied only with the qualities and character of that
fact or form, considering it as real and existing, being all
the while totally regardless of the signs or symbols by
which the notion of it has been conveyed. These signs
have no pretence, nor hypocrisy, nor legerdemain about
them;—there is nothing to be found out, or sifted, or
surprised in them;—they bear their message simply and
clearly, and it is that message which the mind takes from
them and dwells upon, regardless of the language in which
it is delivered. But the mind, in receiving an idea of
imitation, is wholly occupied in finding out that what has
been suggested to it is not what it appears to be: it does
not dwell on the suggestion, but on the perception that it
is a false suggesion: it derives its pleasure, not from the
contemplation of a truth, but from the discovery of a
falsehood. So that the moment ideas of truth are grouped
together, so as to give rise to an idea of imitation, they
change their very nature—lose their essence as ideas of
truth—and are corrupted and degraded, so as to share
in the treachery of what they have produced. Hence,
finally, ideas of truth are the foundation, and ideas of
imitation, the destruction, of all art. We shall be better
able to appreciate their relative dignity after the investigation which we propose of the functions of the former;

but we may as well now express the conclusion to which
we shall then be led—that no picture can be good which
deceives by its imitation, for the very reason that nothing
can be beautiful which is not true.

·　　·　　·　　·　　·　　·

(b) *Of Ideas of Beauty:* Any material object which
can give us pleasure in the simple contemplation of its
outward qualities without any direct and definite exertion of the intellect, I call in some way, or in some
degree, beautiful. Why we receive pleasure from some
forms and colors, and not from others, is no more to be
asked or answered than why we like sugar and dislike
wormwood. The utmost subtilty of investigation will
only lead us to ultimate instincts and principles of human
nature, for which no farther reason can be given than
the simple will of the Deity that we should be so created.
We may indeed perceive, as far as we are acquainted with
His nature, that we have been so constructed as, when
in a healthy and cultivated state of mind, to derive
pleasure from whatever things are illustrative of that
nature; but we do not receive pleasure from them *because*
they are illustrative of it, nor from any perception that
they are illustrative of it, but instinctively and necessarily, as we derive sensual pleasure from the scent of a
rose. On these primary principles of our nature, education and accident operate to an unlimited extent; they
may be cultivated or checked, directed or diverted, gifted
by right guidance with the most acute and faultless sense,
or subjected by neglect to every phase of error and disease. He who has followed up these natural laws of
aversion and desire, rendering them more and more authoritative by constant obedience, so as to derive pleasure
always from that which God originally intended should
give him pleasure, and who derives the greatest possible
sum of pleasure from any given object, is a man of
taste.

This, then, is the real meaning of this disputed word.
Perfect taste is the faculty of receiving the greatest possible pleasure from those material sources which are attractive to our moral nature in its purity and perfection.

He who receives little pleasure from these sources wants taste; he who receives pleasure from any other sources, has false or bad taste.

And it is thus that the term "taste" is to be distinguished from that of "judgment," with which it is constantly confounded. Judgment is a general term, expressing definite action of the intellect, and applicable to every kind of subject which can be submitted to it. There may be judgment of congruity, judgment of truth, judgment of justice, and judgment of difficulty and excellence. But all these exertions of the intellect are totally distinct from taste, properly so called, which is the instinctive and instant preferring of one material object to another without any obvious reason, except that it is proper to human nature in its perfection so to do.

Observe, however, I do not mean by excluding direct exertion of the intellect from ideas of beauty, to assert that beauty has no effect upon, nor connection with the intellect. All our moral feelings are so inwoven with our intellectual powers, that we cannot affect the one without in some degree addressing the other; and in all high ideas of beauty, it is more than probable that much of the pleasure depends on delicate and untraceable perceptions of fitness, propriety, and relation, which are purely intellectual, and through which we arrive at our noblest ideas of what is commonly and rightly called "intellectual beauty." But there is yet no immediate *exertion* of the intellect; that is to say, if a person receiving even the noblest ideas of simple beauty be asked *why* he likes the object exciting them, he will not be able to give any distinct reason, nor to trace in his mind any formed thought, to which he can appeal as a source of pleasure. He will say that the thing gratifies, fills, hallows, exalts his mind, but he will not be able to say why, or how. If he can, and if he can show that he perceives in the object any expression of distinct thought, he has received more than an idea of beauty—it is an idea of relation.

Ideas of beauty are among the noblest which can be presented to the human mind, invariably exalting and purifying it according to their degree; and it would appear that we are intended by the Deity to be constantly under their influence, because there is not one single object in nature which is not capable of conveying them, and which, to the rightly perceiving mind, does not present an incalculably greater number of beautiful than of deformed parts; there being in fact scarcely anything, in pure undiseased nature, like positive deformity, but only degrees of beauty, or such slight and rare points of permitted contrast as may render all around them more valuable by their opposition—spots of blackness in creation, to make its colors felt.

But although everything in nature is more or less beautiful, every species of object has its own kind and degree of beauty; some being in their own nature more beautiful than others, and few, if any, individuals possessing the utmost degree of beauty of which the species is capable. This utmost degree of specific beauty, necessarily coexistent with the utmost perfection of the object in other respects, is the ideal of the object.

Ideas of beauty, then, be it remembered, are the subjects of moral, but not of intellectual perception. By the investigation of them we shall be led to the knowledge of the ideal subjects of art.

. . . .

(c) *Of Ideas of Relation:* I use this term rather as one of convenience than as adequately expressive of the vast class of ideas which I wish to be comprehended under it, namely, all those conveyable by art, which are the subjects of distinct intellectual perception and action, and which are therefore worthy of the name of thoughts. But as every thought, or definite exertion of intellect, implies two subjects, and some connection or relation inferred between them, the term "ideas of relation" is not incorrect, though it is inexpressive.

Under this head must be arranged everything productive of expression, sentiment, and character, whether in figures or landscapes, (for there may be as much definite expression and marked carrying out of particular thoughts in the treatment of inanimate as of animate nature,) everything relating to the conception of the subject and

to the congruity and relation of its parts; not as they
enhance each other's beauty by known and constant laws
of composition, but as they give each other expression
and meaning, by particular application, requiring distinct thought to discover or to enjoy; the choice, for
instance, of a particular lurid or appalling light to illustrate an incident in itself terrible, or of a particular tone
of pure color to prepare the mind for the expression of
refined and delicate feeling; and, in a still higher sense,
the invention of such incidents and thoughts as can be
expressed in words as well as on canvas, and are totally
independent of any means of art but such as may serve
for the bare suggestion of them.   The principal object
in the foreground of Turner's "Building of Carthage" is
a group of children sailing toy boats.   The exquisite
choice of this incident, as expressive of the ruling passion which was to be the source of future greatness, in
preference to the tumult of busy stonemasons or arming
soldiers, is quite as appreciable when it is told as when
it is seen,—it has nothing to do with the technicalities
of painting; a scratch of the pen would have conveyed
the idea and spoken to the intellect as much as the
elaborate realizations of color.   Such a thought as this
is something far above all art; it is epic poetry of the
highest order.   Claude, in subjects of the same kind,
commonly introduces people carrying red trunks with iron
locks about, and dwells, with infantine delight, on the
lustre of the leather and the ornaments of the iron.   The
intellect can have no occupation here; we must look to
the imitation or to nothing.   Consequently, Turner rises
above Claude in the very first instant of the conception
of his picture, and acquires an intellectual superiority
which no powers of the draughtsman or the artist (supposing that such existed in his antagonist) could ever
wrest from him.

Such are the function and force of ideas of relation.
They are what I have asserted in the second chapter of
this section to be the noblest subjects of art.   Dependent
upon it only for expression, they cause all the rest of its
complicated sources of pleasure to take, in comparison
with them, the place of mere language or decoration;

nay, even the noblest ideas of beauty sink at once beside these into subordination and subjection. It would add little to the influence of Landseer's picture above instanced, Chap. II, § 4, that the form of the dog should be conceived with every perfection of curve and color which its nature was capable of, and that the ideal lines should be carried out with the science of a Praxiteles; nay, the instant that the beauty so obtained interfered with the impression of agony and desolation, and drew the mind away from the feeling of the animal to its outward form, that instant would the picture become monstrous and degraded. The utmost glory of the human body is a mean subject of contemplation, compared to the emotion, exertion, and character of that which animates it; the lustre of the limbs of the Aphrodite is faint beside that of the brow of the Madonna; and the divine form of the Greek god, except as it is the incarnation and expression of divine mind, is degraded beside the passion and the prophecy of the vaults of the Sistine.

Ideas of relation are, of course, with respect to art generally, the most extensive as the most important source of pleasure; and if we proposed entering upon the criticism of historical works, it would be absurd to attempt to do so without further subdivision and arrangement. But the old landscape painters got over so much canvas without either exercise of, or appeal to, the intellect, that we shall be little troubled with the subjects as far as they are concerned; and whatever subdivision we may adopt, as it will therefore have particular reference to the works of modern artists, will be better understood when we have obtained some knowledge of them in less important points.

By the term "ideas of relation," then, I mean in future to express all those sources of pleasure, which involve and require, at the instant of their perception, active exertion of the intellectual powers.

Truth in art is not in fleshly immitation of the material, but in how Truly that art conveys the that an emotion. Those truly beautiful wks will attract our moral sense & not our intellect

The Theoretic Faculty

[Modern Painters, Vol. II, Pt. 3, § 1, Ch. 2.]

I proceed, therefore, first to examine the nature of what I have called the Theoretic faculty, and to justify my substitution of the term "Theoretic" for "Æsthetic," which is the one commonly now employed with reference to it.

Now, the term "æsthesis" properly signifies mere sensual perception of the outward qualities and necessary effects of bodies; in which sense only, if we would arrive at any accurate conclusions on this difficult subject, it should always be used. But I wholly deny that the impressions of beauty are in any way sensual; they are neither sensual nor intellectual, but moral: and for the faculty receiving them, whose difference from mere perception I shall immediately endeavor to explain, no term can be more accurate or convenient than that employed by the Greeks, "Theoretic," which I pray permission, therefore, always to use, and to call the operation of the faculty itself Theoria.

Let us begin at the lowest point, and observe, first, what differences of dignity may exist between different kinds of æsthetic or sensual pleasure, properly so called.

Now it is evident that the being common to brutes, or peculiar to man, can alone be no rational test of inferiority or dignity in pleasures. We must not assume that man is the nobler animal, and then deduce the nobleness of his delights; but we must prove the nobleness of the delights, and thence the nobleness of the animal. The dignity of affection is no way lessened, because a large measure of it may be found in lower animals; neither is the vileness of gluttony and lust abated, because they are common to men. It is clear, therefore, that there is a standard of dignity in the pleasures and passions themselves, by which we also class the creatures capable of, or suffering them.

The first great distinction, we observe, is that noted by Aristotle, that men are called temperate and intemperate with regard to some, and not so with respect to others; and that those with respect to which they are so called are, by common consent, held to be the vilest. But Aristotle, though exquisitely subtle in his notation of facts, does not frequently give us satisfactory account of, or reason for them. Content with stating the fact of these pleasures being held the lowest, he shows not why this estimation of them is just, and confuses the reader by observing casually respecting the higher pleasures, what is indeed true, but appears at first opposed to his own position, namely, that "in these also men may be conceived as taking pleasure either rightly, or more or less than is right." Which being so, and evident capability of excess or defect existing in pleasures of this higher order, let us consider how it happens that men are not called intemperate when they indulge in excess of this kind; and what is that difference in nature of the pleasure, which diminishes the criminality of its excess.

Men are held intemperate, only when their desires *overcome or prevent the action of their reason;* and they are indeed intemperate in the exact degree in which such prevention or interference takes place, and therefore in many instances and acts which do not lower the world's estimation of their temperance. For so long as it can be supposed that the reason has acted imperfectly, owing to *its own* imperfection, or to the imperfection of the premises submitted to it,—as when men give an inordinate preference to their own pursuits, because they cannot, in the nature of things, have sufficiently experienced the goodness and benefit of others;—and so long as it may be presumed that men have referred to reason in what they do, and have not suffered its orders to be disobeyed through mere impulse and desire, though those orders may be full of error owing to the reason's own feebleness; so long, men are not held intemperate. But when it is palpably evident that the reason cannot have erred, but that its voice has been deadened or disobeyed; and that the reasonable creature has been dragged dead round the walls of his own citadel by mere passion, then, and then only, men are of all held intemperate. And this is evidently the case with respect to inordinate indulgence in pleasures of touch and taste; for these, being destructive in their continuance not only of all other pleasures, but of the very sensibilities by which they themselves are received, and this penalty being actually known and experienced by those indulging in them, so that the reason cannot but pronounce right respecting their perilousness, there is no palliation of the wrong choice; and the man, as utterly incapable of Will, is called intemperate, or ἀκόλαστος.

It would be well if the reader would for himself follow out this subject, which it would be irrelevant here to pursue farther, observing how a certain degree of intemperance is suspected and attributed to men with respect to higher impulses; as, for instance, in the case of anger, or any other passion criminally indulged; and yet is not so attributed as in the case of sensual pleasures: because in anger the reason is supposed not to have had time to operate, and to be itself affected by the presence of the passion, which seizes the man involuntarily and before he is aware; whereas, in the case of the sensual pleasures, the act is deliberate, and determined on beforehand, in direct defiance of reason. Nevertheless, if no precaution be taken against immoderate anger, and the passions gain upon the man, so as to be evidently wilful and unrestrained, and admitted contrary to all reason, we begin to look upon him as, in the real sense of the word, intemperate; and, in consequence, assign to him his place, for the time, among the beasts, as definitely as if he had yielded to the pleasurable temptations of touch or taste.

We see, then, that the primal ground of inferiority in these pleasures is that which *proves* their indulgence to be contrary to reason; namely, their destructiveness upon prolongation, and their incapability of coexisting continually with the better delights and true perfections of human nature.

And this incapability of continuance directs us to the second cause of their inferiority; namely, that they are given to us as subservient to life, as instruments of our preservation, compelling us to seek the things necessary to our being, and that, therefore, when this their function is fully performed, they ought to have an end; and can be only artificially, and under high penalty, prolonged.

But the pleasures of sight and hearing are given as gifts. They answer not any purposes of mere existence; for the distinction of all that is useful or dangerous to us might be made, and often is made, by the eye, without its receiving the slightest pleasure of sight. We might have learned to distinguish fruits and grain from flowers, without having any superior pleasure in the aspect of the latter; and the ear might have learned to distinguish the sounds that communicate ideas, or to recognize intimations of elemental danger, without perceiving either melody in the voice, or majesty in the thunder. And as these pleasures have no function to perform, so there is no limit to their continuance in the accomplishment of their end, for they are an end in themselves, and so may be perpetual with all of us; being in no way destructive, but rather increasing in exquisiteness by repetition.

Herein, then, we find very sufficient ground for the higher estimation of these delights; first, in their being eternal and inexhaustible, and, secondly, in their being evidently no means or instrument of life, but an object of life. Now, in whatever is an object of life, in whatever may be infinitely and for itself desired, we may be sure there is something of divine; for God will not make anything an object of life to His creatures which does not point to, or partake of, Himself. And so, though we were to regard the pleasures of sight merely as the highest of sensual pleasures, and though they were of rare occurrence, and, when occurring, isolated and imperfect, there would still be a supernatural character about them, owing to their self-sufficiency. But when, instead of being scattered, interrupted, or chance-distributed, they are gathered together, and so arranged to enhance each other as by chance they could not be, there is caused by them not only a feeling of strong affection toward the object in which they exist, but a perception of purpose and adaptation of it to our desires; a perception, therefore, of the immediate operation of the Intelligence which so formed us, and so feeds us.

Out of which perception arise Joy, Admiration, and Gratitude.

Now the mere animal consciousness of the pleasantness I call Æsthesis; but the exulting, reverent, and grateful perception of it I call Theoria. For this, and this only, is the full comprehension and contemplation of the Beautiful as a gift of God; a gift not necessary to our being, but added to, and elevating it, and twofold: first of the desire, and secondly of the thing desired.

And that this joyfulness and reverence are a necessary part of Theoretic pleasure, is very evident, when we consider that, by the presence of these feelings, even the lower and more sensual pleasures may be rendered Theoretic. Thus Aristotle has subtly noted that "we call not men intemperate so much with respect to the scents of roses or herb-perfumes as of ointments and of condiments," though the reason that he gives for this be futile enough. For the fact is, that of scents artificially prepared the extreme desire is intemperance; but of natural and God-given scents, which take their part in the harmony and pleasantness of creation, there can hardly be intemperance: not that there is any absolute difference between the two kinds, but that these are likely to be received with gratitude and joyfulness rather than those; so that we despise the seeking of essences and unguents, but not the sowing of violets along our garden banks. But all things may be elevated by affection, as the spikenard of Mary, and in the Song of Solomon the myrrh upon the handles of the lock, and the sense of Isaac of the field-fragrance upon his son. And the general law for all these pleasures is, that, when sought in the abstract and ardently, they are foul things; but when received with thankfulness and with reference to God's glory, they become Theoretic: and so we may find something divine in the sweetness of wild fruits, as well as in the pleasantness of the pure air, and the tenderness of its natural perfumes that come and go as they list.

It will now be understood why it was formerly said in the chapter respecting ideas of beauty, that those ideas were the subject of moral, and not of intellectual, nor altogether of sensual perception; and why I spoke of the pleasures connected with them as derived from "those material sources which are agreeable to our moral nature in its purity and perfection." For, as it is necessary to the existence of an idea of beauty, that the sensual pleasure which may be its basis should be accompanied first with joy, then with love of the object, then with the perception of kindness in a superior intelligence, finally with thankfulness and veneration toward that intelligence itself; and as no idea can be at all considered as in any way an idea of beauty, until it be made up of these emotions, any more than we can be said to have an idea of a letter of which we perceive the perfume and the fair writing, without understanding the contents of it, or intent of it; and as these emotions are in no way resultant from, nor obtainable by, any operation of the Intellect; it is evident that the sensation of beauty is not sensual on the one hand, nor is it intellectual on the other, but is dependent on a pure, right, and open state of the heart. Dependent both for its truth and for its intensity, insomuch that even the right after-action of the Intellect upon facts of beauty so apprehended, is dependent on the acuteness of the heart-feeling about them. And thus the Apostolic words come true, in this minor respect, as in all others, that men are "alienated from the life of God through the ignorance that is in them, having the *Understanding* darkened because of the hardness of their *hearts,* and so, being past feeling, give themselves up to lasciviousness." For we do indeed see constantly that men having naturally acute perceptions of the beautiful, yet not receiving it with a pure heart, nor into their hearts at all, never comprehend it, nor receive good from it; but make it a mere minister to their desires, and accompaniment and seasoning of lower sensual pleasures, until all their emotions take the same earthly stamp, and the sense of beauty sinks into the servant of lust.

Nor is what the world commonly understands by the cultivation of "taste," anything more or better than this; at least in times of corrupt and over-pampered civilization, when men build palaces, plant groves, and gather luxuries, that they and their devices may hang in the corners of the world like fine-spun cobwebs, with greedy, puffed-up, spider-like lusts in the middle. And this, which in Christian times is the abuse and corruption of the

sense of beauty, was in that Pagan life of which St.
Paul speaks, little less than the essence of it, and the
best they had. I do not know that of the expressions
of affection toward external nature to be found among
Heathen writers, there are any of which the leading
thought leans not toward the sensual parts of her. Her
beneficence they sought, and her power they shunned; her
teaching through both they understood never. The pleasant influences of soft winds, and ringing streamlets, and
shady coverts, of the violet couch and plane-tree shade,
they received, perhaps, in a more noble way than we; but
they found not anything, except fear, upon the bare
mountain, or in the ghostly glen. They loved the Hybla
heather more for its sweet hives than its purple hues.
But the Christian Theoria seeks not, though it accepts
and touches with its own purity, what the Epicurean
sought; but finds its food and the objects of its love
everywhere, in what is harsh and fearful as well as in
what is kind: nay, even in all that seems coarse and
commonplace, seizing that which is good; and sometimes
delighting more at finding its table spread in strange
places, and in the presence of its enemies, and its honey
coming out of the rock, than if all were harmonized into
a less wondrous pleasure; hating only what is· self-sighted
and insolent of men's work, despising all that is not of
God, unless reminding it of God, yet able to find evidence
of Him still where all seems forgetful of Him, and to
turn that into a witness of His working which was meant
to obscure it; and so with clear and unoffended sight
beholding Him for ever, according to the written promise, "Blessed are the pure in *heart,* for they shall see
God."

Accuracy and Inaccuracy in Impressions of Sense

[*Modern Painters,* Vol. II, Pt. 3, § 1, Ch. 3.]

Hitherto we have observed only the distinctions of dignity among pleasures of sense, considered merely as such,
and the way in which *any* of them may become theoretic
in being received with right feeling.

But as we go farther, and examine the distinctive nature of ideas of beauty, we shall, I believe, perceive something in them besides æsthetic pleasure, something which attests a more important function belonging to them than attaches to other sensual ideas, and exhibits a more exalted character in the faculty by which they are received. And this was what I alluded to when I said in the chapter already referred to that "we may indeed perceive, as far as we are acquainted with the nature of God, that we have been so constructed as in a healthy state of mind to derive pleasure from whatever things are illustrative of that nature."

This point it is necessary now farther to develop.

Our first inquiry must evidently be, how we are authorized to affirm of any man's mind, that it is in a healthy state or otherwise, respecting impressions of sight; and what canon or test there is by which we may determine of these impressions that they are or are not *rightly* esteemed beautiful. For it does not at first appear easy to prove that men ought to like one thing rather than another; and although this is granted generally by men's speaking of "bad" or "good" taste, yet the right of individual opinion (sometimes claimed even in moral matters, though then palpably without foundation) does not appear altogether irrational in matters æsthetic, wherein little operation of voluntary choice is supposed possible. It would appear strange, for instance, to assert, respecting a particular person who preferred the scent of violets to that of roses, that he had no right to do so. And yet, while I have said that the sensation of beauty is intuitive and necessary, as men derive pleasure from the scent of a rose, I have assumed that there are some sources from which it is rightly derived, and others from which it is wrongly derived; in other words, that men have no right to think some things beautiful and no right to remain apathetic with regard to others.

Hence then arise two questions, according to the sense in which the word *right* is taken: the first, in what way an impression of sense may be *deceptive*, and therefore a conclusion respecting it untrue; and the second, in what way an impression of sense, or the preference of one, may

be a subject of *will,* and therefore of moral duty or
delinquency.

To the first of these questions I answer, that we cannot
speak of the immediate impression of sense as false, nor
of its preference to others as mistaken: for no one can
be deceived respecting the actual sensation he perceives
or prefers.* But falsity may attach to his assertion or
supposition, that what he himself perceives is from the
same object perceived by others, or is always to be by
himself perceived, or is always to be by himself preferred;
and when we speak of a man as wrong in his impressions
of sense, we either mean that he feels differently from all,
or from a majority, respecting a certain object, or that
he prefers at present those of his impressions which ultimately he will not prefer.

To the second I answer, that over immediate impressions and immediate preferences we have no power, but
over *ultimate* impressions, and especially ultimate preferences, we have; and that, though we can neither at once
choose whether we shall see an object red, green, or blue,
nor determine to like the red better than the blue, or the
blue better than the red, yet we can, if we choose, make
ourselves ultimately susceptible of such impressions in
other degrees, and capable of pleasure in them in different measure. And seeing that wherever power of any
kind is given there is responsibility attached, it is the
duty of men to prefer certain impressions of sense to
others, *because* they have the power of doing so. And
this is precisely analogous to the law of the moral world,
whereby men are supposed not only capable of governing their likes and dislikes, but ·the whole culpability or

---

* I have not sufficiently carried out the analysis here. No note is
taken in the passage of diseased conditions of the organs; or imperfect
ones; jaundice or color-blindness is not thought of as affecting the
argument. But it is supposed that there may not be exact similarity in
sensations, even among healthy and well-organized persons, and that
when we say that we dislike, or like, peppermint or aniseed, it is conceivable that peppermint to some noses may not be exactly the same
thing as peppermint to others. It is, however, most rational and simple
to assume what is certainly the clearest probability, that the general
sensations of humanity are approximately alike; that a taste for garlic
or aniseed is an artificially acquired one, and that one for castor oil
or asafœtida would only be acquired by great perseverance. [Ruskin's
Note, 1883.]

propriety of actions is dependent upon this capability; so that men are guilty or otherwise, not for what they do, but for what they desire, the command being not Thou shalt obey, but Thou shalt love, the Lord thy God; a vain command if men were not capable of governing and directing their affections.

I assert, therefore, that even with respect to impressions of sense, we have a power of preference, and a corresponding duty; and I shall show first the nature of the power, and afterward the nature of the duty.

Let us take an instance from one of the lowest of the senses, and observe the kind of power we have over the impressions of lingual taste. On the first offering of two different things to the palate, it is not in our power to prevent or command the instinctive preference. One will be unavoidably and helplessly preferred to the other. But if the same two things be submitted to judgment frequently and attentively, it will be often found that their relations change. The palate, which at first perceived only the coarse and violent qualities of either, will, as it becomes more experienced, acquire greater subtlety of discrimination, perceiving in both characters at first unnoticed, which on continued experience will probably become more influential than the first impressions; and whatever this final verdict may be, it is felt by the person who gives it, and received by others, as a more correct one than the first.

So, then, the power we have over the preference of impressions of taste is not actual nor immediate, but only a power of testing and comparing them frequently and carefully, until that which is the more permanent, the more consistently agreeable, be determined. But when the instrument of taste is thus in some degree perfected and rendered subtle, by its being practised upon a single object, its conclusions will be more rapid with respect to others; and it will be able to distinguish more quickly in other things, and even to prefer at once those qualities which are calculated finally to give it most pleasure, though more capable with respect to those on which it is more frequently exercised; whence people are called "judges" with respect to this or that particular object of Taste.

Now, that verdicts of this kind are received as authoritative by others, proves another and more important fact; namely, that not only changes of opinion take place in consequence of experience, but that those changes are from *variation* of opinion to *unity* of opinion;—and that whatever may be the differences of estimate among unpractised or uncultivated tastes, there will be unity of taste among the experienced; and that, therefore, the result of repeated trial and experience is to arrive at principles of preference in some sort common to all, and which are a part of our nature.

I select the sense of taste for an instance, because it is the least favorable to the position I hold, since there is more latitude allowed, and more actual variety of verdict, in the case of this sense than of any other, and yet, however susceptible of variety even the ultimate approximations of its preferences may be, the authority of judges is distinctly allowed; and we hear every day the admission, by those of unpractised palate, that they are, or may be, wrong in their opinions respecting the real pleasureableness of things either to themselves or to others.

The sense, however, in which they thus use the word "wrong" is merely that of falseness or inaccuracy in conclusion, not of moral delinquency. But there is, as I have stated, a duty, more or less imperative, attached to every power we possess, and therefore to this power over the lower senses as well as to all others.

And this duty is, evidently, to bring every sense into that state of cultivation in which it shall form the truest conclusions respecting all that is submitted to it, and procure us the greatest amount of pleasure consistent with its due relation to other senses and functions. Which three constituents of perfection in sense, (1) true judgment, (2) maximum sensibility, and (3) right relation to others, are invariably coexistent and involved one by the other; for the true judgment is the result of the high sensibility, and the high sensibility of the right relation. Thus, for instance, with respect to pleasures of taste, it is our duty not to devote such inordinate attention to the discrimination of them as must be inconsistent with our pursuit, and destructive of our capacity, of higher and preferable pleasures, but to cultivate the sense of them in that way which is consistent with all other good; by temperance, namely, and by such attention as the mind, at certain resting moments, may fitly pay even to so ignoble a source of pleasure as this. By which discipline we shall bring the faculty of taste itself to its real maximum of sensibility; for it cannot be doubted that health, hunger, and such general refinement of bodily habits as shall make the body a perfect and fine instrument in all respects, are better promoters of actual enjoyment of taste, than the sickened, sluggish, hard-stimulated fastidiousness of Epicurism.

So also it will certainly be found with all the senses, that they individually receive the greatest and purest pleasure when they are in right condition and degree of subordination to all the rest; and that by the overcultivation of any one (for morbid sources of pleasure, and correspondent temptations to irrational indulgence, confessedly are attached to all) we shall add more to their power as instruments of punishment than of pleasure.

If then, as we find in this example of the lowest sense, the power we have over sensation depends mainly on the exercise of attention through certain prolonged periods; and if by this exercise we arrive at ultimate, constant, and common sources of agreeableness, casting off those which are external, accidental, and individual; that which is required in order to the attainment of accurate conclusions respecting the essence of the Beautiful is nothing more than earnest, loving, and unselfish attention to our impressions of it, by which those which are shallow, false, or peculiar to times and temperaments, may be distinguished from those that are eternal. And this dwelling upon and fond contemplation of them (the Anschauung of the Germans), is perhaps as much as was meant by the Greek Theoria: and it is indeed a very noble exercise of the souls of men, and one by which they are peculiarly distinguished from the anima of lower creatures, which cannot, I think, be proved to have any capacity of contemplation at all, but only a restless vividness of perception and conception, the "fancy" of Hooker (*Eccl. Pol.*, book i, chap. vi, 2).

But two very important points are to be observed respecting the direction and discipline of the attention in the early stages of judgment. The first, that, for beneficent purposes, the nature of man has been made reconcilable by custom to many things naturally painful to it, and even improper for it; and that therefore, though by continual experience, united with thought, we may discover that which is best of several, yet if we submit ourselves to authority or fashion, and close our eyes, we may be by custom made to tolerate, and even to love and long for, that which is naturally painful and pernicious to us; whence arise incalculable embarrassments on the subject of art.

The second, that, in order to the discovery of that which is better of two things, it is necessary that both should be equally submitted to the attention, and therefore that we should have so much faith in authority as shall make us repeatedly observe and attend to that which is said to be right, even though at present we may not feel it so. And in the right mingling of this faith with the openness of heart which proves all things, lies the great difficulty of the cultivation of the taste, as far as the spirit of the scholar is concerned; though, even when he has this spirit, he may be long retarded by having evil examples submitted to him by ignorant masters.

The temper, therefore, by which right taste is formed, is characteristically patient. It dwells upon what is submitted to it. It does not trample upon it, lest it should be pearls, even though it look like husks. It is a good ground, soft, penetrable, retentive; it does not send up thorns of unkind thoughts, to choke the weak seed; it is hungry and thirsty too, and drinks all the dew that falls on it. It is "an honest and good heart," that shows no too ready springing before the sun be up, but fails not afterward; it is distrustful of itself, so as to be ready to believe and to try all things, and yet so trustful of itself, that it will neither quit what it has tried, nor take anything without trying. And the pleasure which it has in things that it finds true and good is so great, that it cannot possibly be led aside by any tricks of fashion, or diseases of vanity; it cannot be cramped in its conclusions by partialities and hypocrisies; its visions and its delights are too penetrating, too living, for any whitewashed object or shallow fountain long to endure or supply. It clasps all that it loves so hard, that it crushes it if it be hollow.

Now, the conclusions of this disposition are sure to be eventually right; more and more right according to the general maturity of all the powers, but it is sure to come (*quite*) right at last, because its operation is in analogy to, and in harmony with, the whole spirit of the Christian moral system, and must ultimately love and rest in the great sources of happiness common to all the human race, and based on the relations they hold to their Creator.

These common and general sources of pleasure consist, I believe, in a certain seal, or impress of divine work and character, upon whatever God has wrought in all the world; only, it being necessary for the perception of them, that their contraries should also be set before us, these divine characteristics, though inseparable from all divine works, are yet suffered to exist in such varieties of degree, that their most limited manifestations shall, in opposition to their most abundant, act as a foil or contrary; just as we conceive of cold as contrary to heat, though the most extreme cold we can produce or conceive is not inconsistent with an unknown amount of heat in the body.

Our purity of taste, therefore, is best tested by its universality; for if we can only admire this thing or that, we may be sure that our cause for liking is of a finite and false nature. But if we can perceive beauty in everything of God's doing, we may argue that we have reached the true perception of its universal laws. Hence, false taste may be known by its fastidiousness, by its demands of pomp, splendor, and unusual combination, by its enjoyment only of particular styles and modes of things, and by its pride also: for it is for ever meddling, mending, accumulating, and self-exalting; its eye is always upon itself, and it tests all things round it by the way they fit it. But true taste is forever growing, learning, reading, worshipping, laying its hand upon its mouth because it is astonished, lamenting over itself, and testing itself by the way that it fits things. And it finds whereof to feed, and whereby to grow, in all things. The complaint so often heard from young artists, that they have not within their reach materials or subjects enough for their fancy, is utterly groundless, and the sign only of their own blindness and inefficiency; for there is that to be seen in every street and lane of every city,—that to be felt and found in every human heart and countenance,—that to be loved in every roadside weed and moss-grown wall which, in the hands of faithful men, may convey emotions of glory and sublimity continual and exalted.

Let therefore the young artist beware of the spirit of Choice; it is an insolent spirit at the best, and commonly a base and blind one too, checking all progress and blasting all power, encouraging weaknesses, pampering partialities, and teaching us to look to accidents of nature for the help and the joy which should come from our own hearts. He draws nothing well who thirsts not to draw *everything*; when a good painter shrinks, it is because he is humbled, not fastidious; when he stops, it is because he is surfeited, and not because he thinks Nature has given him unkindly food, or that he fears famine.

Hence, it becomes a more imperative duty to accustom ourselves to the enjoyment of those pleasures of sight which are most elevated in character, because these are not only the most acute, but the most easily, constantly, and unselfishly attainable. For had it been ordained by the Almighty that the highest pleasures of sight should be those of most difficult attainment, and that to arrive at them it should be necessary to accumulate gilded palaces, tower over tower, and pile artificial mountains around insinuated lakes, there would have been a direct contradiction between the unselfish duties and inherent desires of every individual. But no such contradiction exists in the system of Divine Providence; which, leaving it open to us if we will, as creatures in probation, to abuse this sense like every other, and pamper it with selfish and thoughtless vanities as we pamper the palate with deadly meats, until the appetite of tasteful cruelty is lost in its sickened satiety, incapable of pleasure, unless, Caligula like, it concentrate the labor of a million of lives into the sensation of an hour, leaves it also open to us, by humble and loving ways, to make ourselves susceptible of deep delight from the meanest objects of creation;—a delight which shall not separate us from our fellows, nor require the sacrifice of any duty or occupation, but which shall bind us closer to men and to God, and be with us always, harmonized with every action, consistent with every claim, unchanging and eternal.

Seeing then that these qualities of material objects which are calculated to give us this universal pleasure, are demonstrably constant in their address to human nature, they must belong in some measure to whatever has been esteemed beautiful throughout successive ages of the world, and they are also by their definition common to all the works of God. Therefore it is evident that it must be possible to reason them out, as well as to feel them out; possible to divest every object of that which makes it accidentally or temporarily pleasant, and to strip it bare of distinctive qualities, until we arrive at those which it has in common with all other beautiful things, which we may then safely affirm to be the cause of its ultimate and true delightfulness.

Now this process of reasoning will be that which I shall endeavor to employ in the succeeding investigations, a process perfectly safe, so long as we are quite sure that we are reasoning concerning objects which produce in us one and the same sensation, but not safe if the sensation produced be of a different nature, though it may be equally agreeable; for what produces a different sensation must be a different cause. And the difficulty of reasoning respecting Beauty arises chiefly from the ambiguity of the word, which stands in different people's minds for totally different sensations, for which there can be no common cause.

When, for instance, Mr. Alison endeavors to support his position, that "no man is sensible to beauty in those objects with regard to which he has not previous ideas," by the remark that "the beauty of a theory, or of a relic of antiquity, is unintelligible to a peasant," we see at once that it is hopeless to argue with a man who, under his general term Beauty, may, for anything we know, be sometimes speaking of mathematical demonstrability and sometimes of historical interest. While, even if we could succeed in limiting the term to the sense of external attractiveness, there would be still room for many phases of error; for though the beauty of a snowy mountain and of a human cheek or forehead, so far as both are considered as mere matter, is the same, and traceable to certain qualities of color and line, common to both, and by reason extricable; yet the flush of the cheek and moulding of the brow, as they express modesty, affection, or intellect, possess sources of agreeableness which are not common to the snowy mountain, and the interference of whose influence we must be cautious to prevent in our examination of those which are material or universal.

The first thing, then, that we have to do, is accurately to discriminate and define those appearances from which we are about to reason as belonging to beauty, properly so called, and to clear the ground of all the confused ideas and erroneous theories with which the misapprehension or metaphorical use of the term has encumbered it.

By the term Beauty, then, properly are signified two things. First, that external quality of bodies already so often spoken of, and which, whether it occur in a stone, flower, beast, or in man, is absolutely identical, which, as I have already asserted, may be shown to be in some sort typical of the Divine attributes, and which therefore I shall, for distinction's sake, call Typical Beauty: and, secondarily, the appearance of felicitous fulfilment of function in living things, more especially of the joyful and right exertion of perfect life in man; and this kind of beauty I shall call Vital Beauty.

Any application of the word Beautiful to other appearances or qualities than these is either false or metaphorical; as, for instance, to the splendor of a discovery, the fitness of a proportion, the coherence of a chain of reasoning, or the power of bestowing pleasure which objects receive from association, a power confessedly great, and interfering, as we shall presently find, in a most embarrassing way with the attractiveness of inherent beauty.

But in order that the mind of the reader may not be biassed at the outset by that which he may happen to have received of current theories respecting beauty, founded on the above metaphorical uses of the word (theories which are less to be reprobated as accounting falsely for the sensations of which they treat, than as confusing two or more pleasurable sensations together), I shall briefly glance at the four erroneous positions most frequently held upon this subject, before proceeding to examine those typical and vital properties of things, to which I conceive that all our original conceptions of beauty may be traced.

THE GRAND STYLE

[*Modern Painters,* Vol. III, Ch. 1.]

IN taking up the clue of an inquiry, now intermitted for nearly ten years, it may be well to do as a traveller would, who had to recommence an interrupted journey in a guideless country; and, ascending, as it were, some little hill beside our road, note how far we have already advanced, and what pleasantest ways we may choose for farther progress.

I endeavored, in the beginning of the first volume, to divide the sources of pleasure open to us in Art into certain groups, which might conveniently be studied in succession. After some preliminary discussion, it was concluded that these groups were, in the main, three; consisting, first, of the pleasures taken in perceiving simple resemblance to Nature (Ideas of Truth); secondly, of the pleasures taken in the beauty of the things chosen to be painted (Ideas of Beauty); and, lastly, of pleasures taken in the meanings and relations of these things (Ideas of Relation).

The first volume, treating of the ideas of Truth, was chiefly occupied with an inquiry into the various success with which different artists had represented the facts of Nature,—an inquiry necessarily conducted very imperfectly, owing to the want of pictorial illustration.

The second volume merely opened the inquiry into the nature of ideas of Beauty and Relation, by analyzing (as far as I was able to do so) the two faculties of the human mind which mainly seized such ideas; namely, the contemplative and imaginative faculties.

It remains for us to examine the various success of artists, especially of the great landscape-painter whose works have been throughout our principal subject, in addressing these faculties of the human mind, and to consider who among them has conveyed the noblest ideas of beauty, and touched the deepest sources of thought.

I do not intend, however, now to pursue the inquiry in a method so laboriously systematic; for the subject may, it seems to me, be more usefully treated by pursuing the different questions which rise out of it just as they occur to us, without too great scrupulousness in marking connections, or insisting on sequences. Much time is wasted by human beings, in general, on establishment of systems; and it often takes more labor to master the intricacies of an artificial connection, than to remember the separate facts which are so carefully connected. I suspect that system-makers, in general, are not of much more use, each in his own domain, than, in that of Pomona, the old women who tie cherries upon sticks, for the more convenient portableness of the same. To cultivate well, and choose well, your cherries, is of some importance; but if they can be had in their own wild way of clustering about their crabbed stalk, it is a better connection for them than any other; and, if they cannot, then, so that they be not bruised, it makes to a boy of a practical disposition not much difference whether he gets them by handfuls, or in beaded symmetry on the exalting stick. I purpose, therefore, henceforward to trouble myself little with sticks or twine, but to arrange my chapters with a view to convenient reference, rather than to any careful division of subjects, and to follow out, in any by-ways that may open, on right hand or left, whatever question it seems useful at any moment to settle.

And, in the outset, I find myself met by one which I ought to have touched upon before—one of especial in-

terest in the present state of the Arts. I have said that
the art is greatest which includes the greatest ideas; but
I have not endeavored to define the nature of this greatness in the ideas themselves. We speak of great truths,
of great beauties, great thoughts. What is it which
makes one truth greater than another, one thought
greater than another? This question is, I repeat, of peculiar importance at the present time; for, during a
period now of some hundred and fifty years, all writers
on Art who have pretended to eminence, have insisted
much on a supposed distinction between what they call
the Great and the Low Schools; using the terms "High
Art," "Great or Ideal Style," and other such, as descriptive of a certain noble manner of painting, which it was
desirable that all students of Art should be early led to
reverence and adopt; and characterizing as "vulgar," or
"low," or "realist," another manner of painting and conceiving, which it was equally necessary that all students
should be taught to avoid.

But lately this established teaching, never very intelligible, has been gravely called in question. The advocates and self-supposed practicers of "High Art" are beginning to be looked upon with doubt, and their peculiar
phraseology to be treated with even a certain degree of
ridicule. And other forms of Art are partly developed
among us, which do not pretend to be high, but rather
to be strong, healthy, and humble. This matter of "highness" in Art, therefore, deserves our most careful consideration. Has it been, or is it, a true highness, a true
princeliness, or only a show of it, consisting in courtly
manners and robes of state? Is it rocky height or cloudy
height, adamant or vapor, on which the sun of praise so
long has risen and set? It will be well at once to consider this.

And first, let us get, as quickly as may be, at the exact meaning with which the advocates of "High Art" use
that somewhat obscure and figurative· term.

I do not know that the principles in question are anywhere more distinctly expressed than in two papers in
the *Idler,* written by Sir Joshua Reynolds, of course
under the immediate sanction of Johnson; and which

may thus be considered as the utterance of the views
then held upon the subject by the artists of chief skill,
and critics of most sense, arranged in a form so brief
and clear as to admit of their being brought before the
public for a morning's entertainment. I cannot, therefore, it seems to me, do better than quote these two letters, or at least the important parts of them, examining
the exact meaning of each passage as it occurs. There
are, in all, in the *Idler* three letters on painting, Nos. 76,
79, and 82; of these, the first is directed only against
the impertinences of pretended connoisseurs, and is as
notable for its faithfulness as for its wit in the description of the several modes of criticism in an artificial and
ignorant state of society: it is only, therefore, in the two
last papers that we find the expression of the doctrines
which it is our business to examine.

No. 79 (Saturday, October 20, 1759) begins, after a
short preamble, with the following passage:—

"Amongst the Painters, and the writers on Painting,
there is one maxim universally admitted and continually inculcated. *Imitate nature* is the invariable rule;
but I know none who have explained in what manner
this rule is to be understood; the consequence of which
is, that everyone takes it in the most obvious sense—
that objects are represented naturally, when they have
such relief that they seem real. It may appear strange,
perhaps, to hear this sense of the rule disputed; but it
must be considered, that, if the excellency of a Painter
consisted only in this kind of imitation, Painting must
lose its rank, and be no longer considered as a liberal
art, and sister to Poetry: this imitation being merely
mechanical, in which the slowest intellect is always sure
to succeed best; for the Painter of genius cannot stoop
to drudgery, in which the understanding has no part;
and what pretence has the Art to claim kindred with
Poetry but by its power over the imagination? To this
power the Painter of genius directs him; in this sense
he studies Nature, and often arrives at his end, even by
being unnatural in the confined sense of the word.

"The grand style of Painting requires this minute
attention to be carefully avoided, and must be kept as

separate from it as the style of Poetry from that of History. (Poetical ornaments destroy that air of truth and plainness which ought to characterize History; but the very being of Poetry consists in departing from this plain narrative, and adopting every ornament that will warm the imagination.*) To desire to see the excellences of each style united—to mingle the Dutch with the Italian school, is to join contrarieties which cannot subsist together, and which destroy the efficacy of each other."

We find, first, from this interesting passage, that the writer considers the Dutch and Italian masters as severally representative of the low and high schools; next, that he considers the Dutch painters as excelling in a mechanical imitation, "in which the slowest intellect is always sure to succeed best"; and, thirdly, that he considers the Italian painters as excelling in a style which corresponds to that of imaginative poetry in literature, and which has an exclusive right to be called the grand style.

I wish that it were in my power entirely to concur with the writer, and to enforce this opinion thus distinctly stated. I have never been a zealous partisan of the Dutch School, and should rejoice in claiming Reynolds's authority for the assertion, that their manner was one "in which the slowest intellect is always sure to succeed best." But before his authority can be so claimed, we must observe exactly the meaning of the assertion itself, and separate it from the company of some others not perhaps so admissible. First, I say, we must observe Reynolds's exact meaning, for (though the assertion may at first appear singular) a man who uses accurate language is always more liable to misinterpretation than one who is careless in his expressions. We may assume that the latter means very nearly what we at first suppose him to mean, for words which have been uttered without thought may be received without examination.

---

* I have put this sentence in a parenthesis, because it is inconsistent with the rest of the statement, and with the general teaching of the paper; since that which "attends only to the invariable" cannot certainly adopt "every ornament that will warm the imagination." [Ruskin's note.]

But when a writer or speaker may be fairly supposed
to have considered his expressions carefully, and, after
having revolved a number of terms in his mind, to have
chosen the one which *exactly* means the thing he intends
to say, we may be assured that what costs him time to
select, will require from us time to understand; and that
we shall do him wrong, unless we pause to reflect how the
word which he has actually employed differs from other
words which it seems he *might* have employed. It thus
constantly happens that persons themselves unaccustomed
to think clearly, or speak correctly, misunderstand a logical and careful writer, and are actually in more danger
of being misled by language which is measured and precise, than by that which is loose and inaccurate.

Now, in the instance before us, a person not accustomed to good writing might very rashly conclude that
when Reynolds spoke of the Dutch School as one "in
which the slowest intellect was sure to succeed best," he
meant to say that every successful Dutch painter was
a fool. We have no right to take his assertion in that
sense. He says, the *slowest* intellect. We have no right
to assume that he meant the *weakest*. For it is true,
that in order to succeed in the Dutch style, a man has
need of qualities of mind eminently deliberate and sustained. He must be possessed of patience rather than
of power; and must feel no weariness in contemplating
the expression of a single thought for several months
together. As opposed to the changeful energies of the
imagination, these mental characters may be properly
spoken of as under the general term—slowness of intellect. But it by no means follows that they are necessarily those of weak or foolish men.

We observe, however, farther, that the imitation which
Reynolds supposes to be characteristic of the Dutch
School is that which gives to objects such relief that they
seem real, and that he then speaks of this art of realistic
imitation as corresponding to *history* in literature.

Reynolds, therefore, seems to class these dull works of
the Dutch School under a general head, to which they
are not commonly referred—that of *historical* painting;
while he speaks of the works of the Italian School not as

historical, but as *poetical* painting. His next sentence will farther manifest his meaning.

"The Italian attends only to the invariable, the great and general ideas which are fixed and inherent in universal Nature; the Dutch, on the contrary, to literal truth, and a minute exactness in the detail, as I may say, of Nature modified by accident. The attention to these petty peculiarities is the very cause of this naturalness so much admired in the Dutch pictures, which, if we suppose it to be a beauty, is certainly of a lower order, which ought to give place to a beauty of a superior kind, since one cannot be obtained but by departing from the other.

"If my opinion was asked concerning the works of Michael Angelo, whether they would receive any advantage from possessing this mechanical merit, I should not scruple to say, they would not only receive no advantage, but would lose, in a great measure, the effect which they now have on every mind susceptible of great and noble ideas. His works may be said to be all genius and soul; and why should they be loaded with heavy matter, which can only counteract his purpose by retarding the progress of the imagination?"

Examining carefully this and the preceding passage, we find the author's unmistakable meaning to be, that Dutch painting is *history;* attending to literal truth and "minute exactness in the details of nature modified by accident." That Italian painting is *poetry,* attending only to the invariable; and that works which attend only to the invariable are full of genius and soul; but that literal truth and exact detail are "heavy matter which retards the progress of the imagination."

This being then indisputably what Reynolds means to tell us, let us think a little whether he is in all respects right. And first, as he compares his two kinds of painting to history and poetry, let us see how poetry and history themselves differ, in their use of *variable* and *invariable* details. I am writing at a window which commands a view of the head of the Lake of Geneva; and as I look up from my paper, to consider this point, I see, beyond it, a blue breadth of softly moving water, and the outline of the mountains above Chillon, bathed in morning mist. The first verses which naturally come into my mind are—

> A thousand feet in depth below
> The massy waters meet and flow;
> So far the fathom line was sent
> From Chillon's snow-white battlement.

Let us see in what manner this poetical statement is distinguished from a historical one.

It is distinguished from a truly historical statement, first, in being simply false. The water under the Castle of Chillon is not a thousand feet deep, nor anything like it. Herein, certainly, these lines fulfil Reynolds's first requirement in poetry, "that it should be inattentive to literal truth and minute exactness in detail." In order, however, to make our comparison more closely in other points, let us assume that what is stated is indeed a fact, and that it was to be recorded, first historically, and then poetically.

Historically stating it, then, we should say: "The lake was sounded from the walls of the Castle of Chillon, and found to be a thousand feet deep."

Now, if Reynolds be right in his idea of the difference between history and poetry, we shall find that Byron leaves out of this statement certain *un*necessary details, and retains only the invariable,—that is to say, the points which the Lake of Geneva and Castle of Chillon have in common with all other lakes and castles.

Let us hear, therefore.

> A thousand feet in depth below.

"Below?" Here is, at all events, a word added (instead of anything being taken away); invariable, certainly in the case of lakes, but not absolutely necessary

> The massy waters meet and flow.

"Massy!" why massy? Because deep water is heavy The word is a good word, but it is assuredly an added

detail, and expresses a character, not which the Lake of
Geneva has in common with all other lakes, but which it
has in distinction from those which are narrow, or shallow.

"Meet and flow." Why meet and flow? Partly to
make up a rhyme; partly to tell us that the waters are
forceful as well as massy, and changeful as well as deep.
Observe, a farther addition of details, and of details more
or less peculiar to the spot, or, according to Reynolds's
definition, of "heavy matter, retarding the progress of the
imagination."

> So far the fathom line was sent.

Why fathom line? All lines for sounding are not
fathom lines. If the lake was ever sounded from Chillon,
it was probably sounded in metres, not fathoms. This is
an addition of another particular detail, in which the
only compliance with Reynolds's requirement is, that
there is some chance of its being an inaccurate one.

> From Chillon's snow-white battlement.

Why snow-white? Because castle battlements are not
usually snow-white. This is another added detail, and
a detail quite peculiar to Chillon, and therefore exactly
the most striking word in the whole passage.

"Battlement!" Why battlement? Because all walls
have not battlements, and the addition of the term marks
the castle to be not merely a prison, but a fortress.

This is a curious result. Instead of finding, as we
expected, the poetry distinguished from the history by
the omission of details, we find it consist entirely in the
addition of details; and instead of being characterized
by regard only of the invariable, we find its whole power
to consist in the clear expression of what is singular and
particular!

The reader may pursue the investigation for himself
in other instances. He will find in every case that a
poetical is distinguished from a merely historical statement, not by being more vague, but more specific; and

it might, therefore, at first appear that our author's comparison should be simply reversed, and that the Dutch School should be called poetical, and the Italian historical. But the term poetical does not appear very applicable to the generality of Dutch painting; and a little reflection will show us, that if the Italians represent only the invariable, they cannot be properly compared even to historians. For that which is incapable of change has no history, and records which state only the invariable need not be written, and could not be read.

It is evident, therefore, that our author has entangled himself in some grave fallacy, by introducing this idea of invariableness as forming a distinction between poetical and historical art. What the fallacy is, we shall discover as we proceed; but as an invading army should not leave an untaken fortress in its rear, we must not go on with our inquiry into the views of Reynolds until we have settled satisfactorily the question already suggested to us, in what the essence of poetical treatment really consists. For though, as we have seen, it certainly involves the addition of specific details, it cannot be simply that addition which turns the history into poetry. For it is perfectly possible to add any number of details to a historical statement, and to make it more prosaic with every added word. As, for instance, "The lake was sounded out of a flat-bottomed boat, near the crab-tree at the corner of the kitchen-garden, and was found to be a thousand feet nine inches deep, with a muddy bottom." It thus appears that it is not the multiplication of details which constitutes poetry; nor their subtraction which constitutes history, but that there must be something either in the nature of the details themselves, or the method of using them, which invests them with poetical power or historical propriety.

It seems to me, and may seem to the reader, strange that we should need to ask the question, "What is poetry?" Here is a word we have been using all our lives, and, I suppose, with a very distinct idea attached to it; and when I am now called upon to give a definition of this idea, I find myself at a pause. What is more singular, I do not at present recollect hearing the question often

asked, though surely it is a very natural one; and I
never recollect hearing it answered, or even attempted to
be answered. In general, people shelter themselves under
metaphors, and while we hear poetry described as an
utterance of the soul, an effusion of Divinity, or voice
of nature, or in other terms equally elevated and obscure,
we never attain anything like a definite explanation of
the character which actually distinguishes it from prose.

I come, after some embarrassment, to the conclusion,
that poetry is "the suggestion, by the imagination, of
noble grounds for the noble emotions." * I mean, by the
noble emotions, those four principal sacred passions—
Love, Veneration, Admiration, and Joy (this latter especially, if unselfish); and their opposites—Hatred, indignation (or Scorn), Horror, and Grief,—this last, when
unselfish, becoming Compassion. These passions in their
various combinations constitute what is called "poetical
feeling," when they are felt on noble grounds, that is, on
great and true grounds. Indignation, for instance, is a poetical feeling, if excited by serious injury; but it is not
a poetical feeling if entertained on being cheated out of
a small sum of money. It is very possible the manner
of the cheat may have been such as to justify considerable indignation; but the feeling is nevertheless not poetical unless the grounds of it be large as well as just. In
like manner, energetic admiration may be excited in certain minds by a display of fireworks, or a street of handsome shops; but the feeling is not poetical, because the
grounds of it are false, and therefore ignoble. There is
in reality nothing to deserve admiration either in the
firing of packets of gunpowder, or in the display of the
stocks of warehouses. But admiration excited by the
budding of a flower is a poetical feeling, because it is
impossible that this manifestation of spiritual power and
vital beauty can ever be enough admired.

Farther, it is necessary to the existence of poetry that
the grounds of these feelings should be *furnished by the
imagination*. Poetical feeling, that is to say, mere noble
emotion, is not poetry. It is happily inherent in all

---

* Ruskin added later: "It leaves out rhythm, which I now consider
a defect in said definition; otherwise good."

human nature deserving the name, and is found often to be purest in the least sophisticated. But the power of assembling, by *the help of the imagination,* such images as will excite these feelings, is the power of the poet or literally of the "Maker." *

Now this power of exciting the emotions depends of course on the richness of the imagination, and on its choice of those images which, in combination, will be most effective, or, for the particular work to be done, most fit. And it is altogether impossible for a writer not endowed with invention to conceive what tools a true poet will make use of, or in what way he will apply them, or what unexpected results he will bring out by them; so that it is vain to say that the details of poetry ought to possess, or ever do possess, any *definite* charac-

---

* Take, for instance, the beautiful stanza in the *Affliction of Margaret:*

> I look for ghosts, but none will force
>   Their way to me. 'T is falsely said
> That ever there was intercourse
>   Between the living and the dead;
> For, surely, then, I should have sight
> Of him I wait for, day and night,
> With love and longing infinite.

This we call Poetry, because it is invented or *made* by the writer, entering into the mind of a supposed person. Next, take an instance of the actual feeling truly experienced and simply expressed by a real person.

"Nothing surprised me more than a woman of Argentière, whose cottage I went into to ask for milk, as I came down from the glacier of Argentière, in the month of March, 1764. An epidemic dysentery had prevailed in the village, and, a few months before, had taken away from her, her father, her husband, and her brothers, so that she was left alone, with three children in the cradle. Her face had something noble in it, and its expression bore the seal of a calm and profound sorrow. After having given me milk, she asked me whence I came, and what I came there to do, so early in the year. When she knew that I was of Geneva, she said to me, 'she could not believe that all Protestants were lost souls; that there were many honest people among us, and that God was too good and too great to condemn all without distinction.' Then, after a moment of reflection, she added, in shaking her head, 'But that which is very strange is that of so many who have gone away, none have ever returned. I, she added, with an expression of grief, 'who have so mourned my husband and my brothers, who have never ceased to think of them, who every night conjure them with beseechings to tell me where they are, and in what state they are! Ah, surely, if they lived anywhere, they would not leave me thus! But, perhaps,' she added, 'I am not worthy of this kindness, perhaps the pure and innocent spirits of these children,' and she looked at the cradle, 'may have their presence, and the joy which is denied to *me.*'"—SAUSSURE, *Voyages dans les Alpes,* chap. xxiv.

This we do not call Poetry, merely because it is not invented, but the true utterance of a real person. [Ruskin's note.]

ter. Generally speaking, poetry runs into finer and more delicate details than prose; but the details are not poetical because they are more delicate, but because they are employed so as to bring out an affecting result. For instance, no one but a true poet would have thought of exciting our pity for a bereaved father by describing his way of locking the door of his house:

> Perhaps to himself at that moment he said,
> 'The key I must take, for my Ellen is dead.'
> But of this in my ears not a word did he speak;
> And he went to the chase with a tear on his cheek.

In like manner, in painting, it is altogether impossible to say beforehand what details a great painter may make poetical by his use of them to excite noble emotions: and we shall, therefore, find presently that a painting is to be classed in the great or inferior schools, not according to the kind of details which it represents, but according to the uses for which it employs them.

It is only farther to be noticed, that infinite confusion has been introduced into this subject by the careless and illogical custom of opposing painting to poetry, instead of regarding poetry as consisting in a noble use, whether of colors or words. Painting is properly to be opposed to *speaking* or *writing,* but not to *poetry.* Both painting and speaking are methods of expression. Poetry is the employment of either for the noblest purposes.

This question being thus far determined, we may proceed with our paper in the *Idler.*

"It is very difficult to determine the exact degree of enthusiasm that the arts of Painting and Poetry may admit. There may, perhaps, be too great indulgence as well as too great a restraint of imagination; if the one produces incoherent monsters, the other produces what is full as bad, lifeless insipidity. An intimate knowledge of the passions, and good sense, but not common sense, must at last determine its limits. It has been thought, and I believe with reason, that Michael Angelo sometimes transgressed those limits; and, I think, I have seen figures of him of which it was very difficult to determine whether they were in the highest degree sublime or extremely ridiculous. Such faults may be said to be the ebullitions of genius; but at least he had this merit, that he never was insipid; and whatever passion his works may excite, they will always escape contempt.

"What I have had under consideration is the sublimest style, particularly that of Michael Angelo, the Homer of painting. Other kinds may admit of this naturalness, which of the lowest kind is the chief merit; but in painting, as in poetry, the highest style has the least of common nature."

From this passage we gather three important indications of the supposed nature of the Great Style. That it is the work of men in a state of enthusiasm. That it is like the writing of Homer; and that it has as little as possible of "common nature" in it.

First, it is produced by men in a state of enthusiasm. That is, by men who feel *strongly* and *nobly;* for we do not call a strong feeling of envy, jealousy, or ambition, enthusiasm. That is, therefore, by men who feel poetically. This much we may admit, I think, with perfect safety. Great art is produced by men who feel acutely and nobly; and it is in some sort an expression of this personal feeling. We can easily conceive that there may be a sufficiently marked distinction between such art, and that which is produced by men who do not feel at all, but who reproduce, though ever so accurately, yet coldly, like human mirrors, the scenes which pass before their eyes.

Secondly, Great Art is like the writing of Homer, and this chiefly because it has little of "common nature" in it. We are not clearly informed what is meant by common nature in this passage. Homer seems to describe a great deal of what is common:—cookery, for instance, very carefully in all its processes. I suppose the passage in the *Iliad* which, on the whole, has excited most admiration, is that which describes a wife's sorrow at parting from her husband, and a child's fright at its father's helmet; and I hope, at least, the former feeling may be considered "common nature." But the true greatness of Homer's style is, doubtless, held by our author to consist in his imaginations of things not only uncommon but impossible (such as spirits in brazen armor, or monsters with heads of men and bodies of beasts), and in his occasional delineations of the human character and form in their utmost, or heroic, strength and beauty. We gather then on the whole, that a painter in the Great Style must be enthusiastic, or full of emotion, and must paint the human form in its utmost strength and beauty, and perhaps certain impossible forms besides, liable by persons not in an equally enthusiastic state of mind to be looked upon as in some degree absurd. This I presume to be Reynolds's meaning, and to be all that he intends us to gather from his comparison of the Great Style with the writings of Homer. But if that comparison be a just one in all respects, surely two other corollaries ought to be drawn from it, namely,—first, that these Heroic or Impossible images are to be mingled with others very unheroic and very possible; and, secondly, that in the representation of the Heroic or Impossible forms, the greatest care must be taken in *finishing the details,* so that a painter must not be satisfied with painting well the countenance and the body of his hero, but ought to spend the greatest part of his time (as Homer the greatest number of verses) in elaborating the sculptured pattern on his shield.

Let us, however, proceed with our paper.

"One may very safely recommend a little more enthusiasm to the modern Painters; too much is certainly not the vice of the present age. The Italians seem to have been continually declining in this respect, from the time of Michael Angelo to that of Carlo Maratti, and from thence to the very bathos of insipidity to which they are now sunk; so that there is no need of remarking, that where I mentioned the Italian painters in opposition to the Dutch, I mean not the moderns, but the heads of the old Roman and Bolognian Schools; nor did I mean to include, in my idea of an Italian painter, the Venetian school, *which may be said to be the Dutch part of the Italian genius.* I have only to add a word of advice to the Painters,—that, however excellent they may be in painting naturally, they would not flatter themselves very much upon it; and to the Connoisseurs, that when they see a cat or a fiddle painted so finely, that, as the phrase is, it looks as if you could take it up, they would not for that reason immediately compare the Painter to Raffaelle and Michael Angelo."

In this passage there are four points chiefly to be remarked. The first, that in the year 1759 the Italian painters were, in our author's opinion, sunk in the very bathos of insipidity. The second, that the Venetian painters, *i.e.,* Titian, Tintoret, and Veronese, are, in our author's opinion, to be classed with the Dutch; that is to say, are painters in a style "in which the slowest intellect is always sure to succeed best." Thirdly, that painting naturally is not a difficult thing, nor one on which a painter should pride himself. And, finally, that connoisseurs, seeing a cat or a fiddle successfully painted, ought not therefore immediately to compare the painter to Raphael or Michael Angelo.

Yet Raphael painted fiddles very carefully in the foreground of his St. Cecilia,—so carefully, that they quite look as if they might be taken up. So carefully, that I never yet looked at the picture without wishing that somebody *would* take them up, and out of the way. And I am under a very strong persuasion that Raphael did not think painting "naturally" an easy thing. It will be well to examine into this point a little; and for the present, with the reader's permission, we will pass over the first two statements in this passage (touching the character of Italian art in 1759, and of Venetian art in general), and immediately examine some of the evidence existing as to the real dignity of "natural" painting—that is to say, of painting carried to the point at which it reaches a deceptive appearance of reality.

THE NOVELTY OF LANDSCAPE

[*Modern Painters,* Vol. III, Ch. 11.]

HAVING now obtained, I trust, clear ideas, up to a certain point, of what is generally right and wrong in all art, both in conception and in workmanship, we have to apply these laws of right to the particular branch of art which is the subject of our present inquiry, namely, landscape-painting. Respecting which, after the various meditations into which we have been led on the high duties and ideals of art, it may not improbably occur to us first to ask,—whether it be worth inquiring about at all.

That question, perhaps the reader thinks, should have been asked and answered before I had written, or he read, two volumes and a half about it. So I *had* answered it, in my own mind; but it seems time now to give the grounds for this answer. If, indeed, the reader has never suspected that landscape-painting was anything but good, right, and healthy work, I should be sorry to put any doubt of its being so into his mind; but if, as seems to me more likely, he, living in this busy and perhaps somewhat calamitous age, has some suspicion that landscape-painting is but an idle and empty business, not worth all our long talk about it, then, perhaps, he will be pleased to have such suspicion done away, before troubling himself farther with these disquisitions.

I should rather be glad, than otherwise, that he *had* formed some suspicion on this matter. If he has at all admitted the truth of anything hitherto said respecting great art, and its choices of subject, it seems to me he ought, by this time, to be questioning with himself whether road-side weeds, old cottages, broken stones, and such other materials, be worthy matters for grave men to busy themselves in the imitation of. And I should like him to probe this doubt to the deep of it, and bring all his misgivings out to the broad light, that we may see how we are to deal with them, or ascertain if indeed they are too well founded to be dealt with.

And to this end I would ask him now to imagine himself entering, for the first time in his life, the room of the Old Water-Color Society: and to suppose that he has entered it, not for the sake of a quiet examination of the paintings one by one, but in order to seize such ideas as it may generally suggest respecting the state and meaning of modern, as compared with elder, art. I suppose him, of course, that he may be capable of such a comparison, to be in some degree familiar with the different forms in which art has developed itself within the periods historically known to us; but never, till that moment, to have seen any completely modern work. So prepared, and so unprepared, he would, as his ideas began to arrange themselves, be first struck by the number of paintings representing blue mountains, clear lakes, and ruined castles or cathedrals, and he would say to himself: "There is something strange in the mind of these modern people! Nobody ever cared about blue mountains before, or tried to paint the broken stones of old walls." And the more he considered the subject, the more he would feel the peculiarity; and, as he thought over the art of Greeks and Romans, he would still repeat, with increasing certainty of conviction: "Mountains! I remember none. The Greeks did not seem, as artists, to know that such things were in the world. They carved, or variously represented, men, and horses, and beasts, and birds, and all kinds of living creatures,—yes, even down to cuttle-fish; and trees, in a sort of way; but not so much as the outline of a mountain; and as for lakes, they merely showed they knew the difference between salt and fresh water by the fish they put into each." Then he would pass on to mediæval art; and still he would be obliged to repeat: "Mountains! I remember none. Some careless and jagged arrangements of blue spires or spikes on the horizon, and, here and there, an attempt at representing an overhanging rock with a hole through it; but merely in order to divide the light behind some human figure. Lakes! No, nothing of the kind,—only blue bays of sea put in to fill up the background when the painter could not think of anything else. Broken-down buildings! No; for the most part very complete and well-appointed buildings, if any; and never buildings at all, but to give place or explanation to some circumstance of human conduct." And then he would look up again to the modern pictures, observing, with an increasing astonishment, that here the human interest had, in many cases, altogether disappeared. That mountains, instead of being used only as a blue ground for the relief of the heads of saints, were themselves the exclusive subjects of reverent contemplation; that their ravines, and peaks, and forests, were all painted with an appearance of as much enthusiasm as had formerly been devoted to the dimples of beauty, or the frowns of asceticism; and that all the living interest which was still supposed necessary to the scene, might be supplied by a traveller in a slouched hat, a beggar in a scarlet cloak, or, in default of these, even by a heron or a wild duck.

And if he could entirely divest himself of his own modern habits of thought, and regard the subjects in question with the feelings of a knight or monk of the Middle Ages, it might be a question whether those feelings would not rapidly verge toward contempt. "What!" he might perhaps mutter to himself, "here are human beings spending the whole of their lives in making pictures of bits of stone and runlets of water, withered sticks and flying fogs, and actually not a picture of the gods or the heroes! none of the saints or the martyrs! none of the angels and demons! none of councils or battles, or any other single thing worth the thought of a man! Trees and clouds indeed! as if I should not see as many trees as I cared to see, and more, in the first half of my day's journey to-morrow, or as if it mattered to any man whether the sky were clear or cloudy, so long as his armor did not get too hot in the sun!"

There can be no question that this would have been somewhat the tone of thought with which either a Lacedæmonian, a soldier of Rome in her strength, or a knight of the thirteenth century, would have been apt to regard these particular forms of our present art. Nor can there be any question that, in many respects, their judgment would have been just. It is true that the indignation of the Spartan or Roman would have been equally excited against any appearance of luxurious industry; but the mediæval knight would, to the full, have admitted the nobleness of art; only he would have had it employed in decorating his church or his prayer-book, not in imitating moors and clouds. And the feelings of all the three would have agreed in this,—that their main ground of offence must have been the want of *seriousness* and *purpose* in what they saw. They would all have admitted the nobleness of whatever conduced to the honor of the gods, or the power of the nation; but they would not have understood how the skill of human life could be wisely spent in that which did no honor either to Jupiter or to the Virgin; and which in no wise tended, apparently, either to the accumulation of wealth, the excitement of patriotism, or the advancement of morality.

And exactly so far forth their judgment would be just, as the landscape-painting could indeed be shown, for others as well as for them, to be art of this nugatory kind; and so far forth unjust, as that painting could be shown to depend upon, or cultivate, certain sensibilities which neither the Greek nor mediæval knight possessed, and which have resulted from some extraordinary change in human nature since their time. We have no right to assume, without very accurate examination of it, that this change has been an ennobling one. The simple fact, that we are, in some strange way, different from all the great races that have existed before us, cannot at once be received as the proof of our own greatness; nor can it be granted, without any question, that we have a legitimate subject of complacency in being under the influence of feelings, with which neither Miltiades nor the Black Prince, neither Homer nor Dante, neither Socrates nor St. Francis, could for an instant have sympathized.

Whether, however, this fact be one to excite our pride or not, it is assuredly one to excite our deepest interest. The fact itself is certain. For nearly six thousand years the energies of man have pursued certain beaten paths, manifesting some constancy of feeling throughout all that period, and involving some fellowship at heart, among the various nations who by turns succeeded or surpassed each other in the several aims of art or policy. So that, for these thousands of years, the whole human race might be to some extent described in general terms. Man was a creature separated from all others by his instinctive sense of an Existence superior to his own, invariably manifesting this sense of the being of a God more strongly in proportion to his own perfectness of mind and body; and making enormous and self-denying efforts, in order to obtain some persuasion of the immediate presence or approval of the Divinity. So that, on the whole, the best things he did were done as in the presence, or for the honor, of his gods; and, whether in statues, to help him to imagine them, or temples raised to their honor, or acts of self-sacrifice done in the hope of their love, he brought whatever was best and skilfullest in him into their service, and lived in a perpetual subjection to their unseen power. Also, he was always anxious to know something definite about them; and his chief books, songs, and pictures were filled with legends about them, or especially devoted to illustration of their lives and nature.

Next to these gods, he was always anxious to know something about his human ancestors; fond of exalting the memory, and telling or painting the history of old rulers and benefactors; yet full of an enthusiastic confidence in himself, as having in many ways advanced beyond the best efforts of past time; and eager to record his own doings for future fame. He was a creature eminently warlike, placing his principal pride in dominion; eminently beautiful, and having great delight in his own beauty; setting forth this beauty by every species of invention in dress, and rendering his arms and accoutrements superbly decorative of his form. He took, however, very little interest in anything but what belonged to humanity; caring in no wise for the external world, except as it influenced his own destiny; honoring the lightning because it could strike him, the sea because it could drown him, the fountains because they gave him drink, and the grass because it yielded him seed; but utterly incapable of feeling any special happiness in the love of such things, or any earnest emotion about them, considered as separate from man; therefore giving no time to the study of them;—knowing little of herbs, except only which were hurtful and which healing; of stones, only which would glitter brightest in a crown, or last the longest in a wall; of the wild beasts, which were best for food, and which the stoutest quarry for the hunter;—thus spending only on the lower creatures and inanimate things his waste energy, his dullest thoughts, his most languid emotions, and reserving all his acuter intellect for researches into his own nature and that of the gods; all his strength of will for the acquirement of political or moral power; all his sense of beauty for things immediately connected with his own person and life; and all his deep affections for domestic or divine companionship.

Such, in broad light and brief terms, was man for five thousand years. Such he is no longer. Let us consider what he is now, comparing the descriptions clause by clause.

1. He *was* invariably sensible of the existence of gods, and went about all his speculations or works holding this as an acknowledged fact, making his best efforts in their service. *Now* he is capable of going through life with hardly any positive idea on this subject,—doubting, fearing, suspecting, analyzing,—doing everything, in fact, *but* believing; hardly ever getting quite up to that point which hitherto was wont to be the starting-point for all generations. And human work has accordingly hardly any reference to spiritual beings, but is done either from a patriotic or personal interest,—either to benefit mankind, or reach some selfish end, not (I speak of human work in the broad sense) to please the gods.

II. He *was* a beautiful creature, setting forth this beauty by all means in his power, and depending upon it for much of his authority over his fellows. So that the ruddy cheek of David, and the ivory skin of Atrides, and the towering presence of Saul, and the blue eyes of Cœur de Lion, were among chief reasons why they should be kings; and it was one of the aims of all education, and of all dress, to make the presence of the human form stately and lovely. *Now* it has become the task of grave philosophy partly to depreciate or conceal this bodily beauty; and even by those who esteem it in their hearts, it is not made one of the great ends of education; man has become, upon the whole, an ugly animal, and is not ashamed of his ugliness.

III. He *was* eminently warlike. He is *now* gradually becoming more and more ashamed of all the arts and aims of battle. So that the desire of dominion, which was once frankly confessed or boasted of as a heroic passion, is now sternly reprobated or cunningly disclaimed.

IV. He *used* to take no interest in anything but what immediately concerned himself. *Now,* he has deep interest in the abstract nature of things, inquires as eagerly into the laws which regulate the economy of the material world, as into those of his own being, and manifests a passionate admiration of inanimate objects, closely resembling, in its elevation and tenderness, the affection which he bears to those living souls with which he is brought into the nearest fellowship.

It is this last change only which is to be the subject of our present inquiry; but it cannot be doubted that it is closely connected with all the others, and that we can only thoroughly understand its nature by considering it in this connection. For, regarded by itself, we might, perhaps, too rashly assume it to be a natural consequence of the progress of the race. There appears to be a diminution of selfishness in it, and a more extended and heartfelt desire of understanding the manner of God's working; and this the more, because one of the permanent characters of this change is a greater accuracy in the statement of external facts. When the eyes of men were fixed first upon themselves, and upon nature solely and secondarily as bearing upon their interests, it was of less consequence to them what the ultimate laws of nature were, than what their immediate effects were upon human beings. Hence they could rest satisfied with phenomena instead of principles, and accepted without scrutiny every fable which seemed sufficiently or gracefully to account for those phenomena. But so far as the eyes of men are now withdrawn from themselves, and turned upon the inanimate things about them, the results cease to be of importance, and the laws become essential.

In these respects, it might easily appear to us that this change was assuredly one of steady and natural advance. But when we contemplate the others above noted, of which it is clearly one of the branches or consequences, we may suspect ourselves of over-rashness in our self-congratulation, and admit the necessity of a scrupulous analysis both of the feeling itself and of its tendencies.

Of course a complete analysis, or anything like it, would involve a treatise on the whole history of the world. I shall merely endeavor to note some of the leading and more interesting circumstances bearing on the subject, and to show sufficient practical ground for the conclusion, that landscape-painting is indeed a noble and useful art, though one not long known by man. I shall therefore examine, as best I can, the effect of landscape, 1st, on the Classical mind; 2ndly, on the Mediæval mind; and lastly, on the Modern mind. But there is one point of some interest respecting the effect of it on *any* mind, which must be settled first; and this I will endeavor to do in the next chapter.

THE PATHETIC FALLACY

[*Modern Painters,* Vol. III, Ch. 12.]

GERMAN dulness, and English affectation, have of late much multiplied among us the use of two of the most objectionable words that were ever coined by the troublesomeness of metaphysicians,—namely, "Objective" and "Subjective."

No words can be more exquisitely, and in all points, useless; and I merely speak of them that I may, at once and forever, get them out of my way, and out of my reader's. But to get that done, they must be explained.

The word "Blue," say certain philosophers, means the sensation of color which the human eye receives in looking at the open sky, or at a bell-gentian.

Now, say they farther, as this sensation can only be felt when the eye is turned to the object, and as, therefore, no such sensation is produced by the object when nobody looks at it, therefore the thing, when it is not looked at, is not blue; and thus (say they) there are many qualities of things which depend as much on something else as on themselves. To be sweet, a thing must have a taster; it is only sweet while it is being tasted, and if the tongue had not the capacity of taste, then the sugar would not have the quality of sweetness.

And then they agree that the qualities of things which thus depend upon our perception of them, and upon our human nature as affected by them, shall be called Subjective; and the qualities of things which they always have, irrespective of any other nature, as roundness or squareness, shall be called Objective.

From these ingenious views the step is very easy to a farther opinion, that it does not much matter what things are in themselves, but only what they are to us; and that the only real truth of them is their appearance to, or effect upon, us. From which position, with a hearty desire for mystification, and much egotism, selfishness, shallowness, and impertinence, a philosopher may easily go so far as to believe, and say, that everything in the world depends upon his seeing or thinking of it, and that nothing, therefore, exists but what he sees or thinks of.

Now, to get rid of all these ambiguities and troublesome words at once, be it observed that the word "Blue" does *not* mean the *sensation* caused by a gentian on the human eye; but it means the *power* of producing that sensation: and this power is always there, in the thing, whether we are there to experience it or not, and would remain there though there were not left a man on the face of the earth. Precisely in the same way gunpowder has a power of exploding. It will not explode if you put no match to it. But it has always the power of so exploding, and is therefore called an explosive compound, which it very positively and assuredly is, whatever philosophy may say to the contrary.

In like manner, a gentian does not produce the sensation of blueness, if you don't look at it. But it has always the power of doing so; its particles being everlastingly so arranged by its Maker. And, therefore, the gentian and the sky are always verily blue, whatever philosophy may say to the contrary; and if you do not see them blue when you look at them, it is not their fault, but yours.

Hence I would say to these philosophers: If, instead of

using the sonorous phrase, "It is objectively so," you will use the plain old phrase, "It *is* so," and if instead of the sonorous phrase, "It is subjectively so," you will say, in plain old English, "It does so," or "It seems so to me," you will, on the whole, be more intelligent to your fellow-creatures; and besides, if you find that a thing which generally "does so" to other people (as a gentian looks blue to most men), does *not* so to you, on any particular occasion, you will not fall into the impertinence of saying, that the thing is not so, or did not so, but you will say simply (what you will be all the better for speedily finding out), that something is the matter with you. If you find that you cannot explode the gunpowder, you will not declare that all gunpowder is subjective, and all explosion imaginary, but you will simply suspect and declare yourself to be an ill-made match. Which, on the whole, though there may be a distant chance of a mistake about it, is, nevertheless, the wisest conclusion you can come to until further experiment.

Now, therefore, putting these tiresome and absurd words quite out of our way, we may go on at our ease to examine the point in question,—namely, the difference between the ordinary, proper, and true appearances of things to us; and the extraordinary, or false appearances, when we are under the influence of emotion, or contemplative fancy; false appearances, I say, as being entirely unconnected with any real power or character in the object, and only imputed to it by us.

For instance—

> The spendthrift crocus, bursting through the mould
> Naked and shivering, with his cup of gold.

This is very beautiful, and yet very untrue. The crocus is not a spendthrift, but a hardy plant; its yellow is not gold, but saffron. How is it that we enjoy so much the having it put into our heads that it is anything else than a plain crocus?

It is an important question. For, throughout our past reasonings about art, we have always found that nothing could be good or useful, or ultimately pleasurable, which was untrue. But here is something pleasurable in written poetry, which is nevertheless *untrue*. And what is more, if we think over our favorite poetry, we shall find it full of this kind of fallacy, and that we like it all the more for being so.

It will appear also, on consideration of the matter, that this fallacy is of two principal kinds. Either, as in this case of the crocus, it is the fallacy of wilful fancy, which involves no real expectation that it will be believed; or else it is a fallacy caused by an excited state of the feelings, making us, for the time, more or less irrational. Of the cheating of the fancy we shall have to speak presently; but, in this chapter, I want to examine the nature of the other error, that which the mind admits when affected strongly by emotion. Thus, for instance, in *Alton Locke,*—

> They rowed her in across the rolling foam—
> The cruel, crawling foam.

The foam is not cruel, neither does it crawl. The state of mind which attributes to it these characters of a living creature is one in which the reason is unhinged by grief. All violent feelings have the same effect. They produce in us a falseness in all our impressions of external things, which I would generally characterize as the "pathetic fallacy."

Now we are in the habit of considering this fallacy as eminently a character of poetical description, and the temper of mind in which we allow it, as one eminently poetical, because passionate. But I believe, if we look well into the matter, that we shall find the greatest poets do not often admit this kind of falseness,—that it is only the second order of poets who much delight in it.*

---

* I admit two orders of poets, but no third; and by these two orders I mean the Creative (Shakspeare, Homer, Dante), and Reflective or Perceptive (Wordsworth, Keats, Tennyson). But both of these must be *first*-rate in their range, though their range is different; and with poetry second-rate in' *quality* no one ought to be allowed to trouble mankind. There is quite enough of the best,—much more than we can ever read or enjoy in the length of a life; and it is a literal wrong or sin in any person to encumber us with inferior work. I have no patience with apologies made by young pseudo-poets, "that they believe there is *some* good in what they have written: that they hope to do better in time," etc. *Some* good! If there is not *all* good, there is no

Thus, when Dante describes the spirits falling from the bank of Acheron "as dead leaves flutter from a bough," he gives the most perfect image possible of their utter lightness, feebleness, passiveness, and scattering agony of despair, without, however, for an instant losing his own clear perception that *these* are souls, and *those* are leaves; he makes no confusion of one with the other. But when Coleridge speaks of

> The one red leaf, the last of its clan,
> That dances as often as dance it can,

he has a morbid, that is to say, a so far false, idea about the leaf; he fancies a life in it, and will, which there are not; confuses its powerlessness with choice, its fading death with merriment, and the wind that shakes it with music. Here, however, there is some beauty, even in the morbid passage; but take an instance in Homer and Pope. Without the knowledge of Ulysses, Elpenor, his youngest follower, has fallen from an upper chamber in the Circean palace, and has been left dead, unmissed by his leader or companions, in the haste of their departure. They cross the sea to the Cimmerian land; and Ulysses summons the shades from Tartarus. The first which appears is that of the lost Elpenor. Ulysses, amazed, and in exactly the spirit of bitter and terrified lightness which is seen in Hamlet, addresses the spirit with the simple, startled words:—

"Elpenor! How camest thou under the shadowy darkness? Hast thou come faster on foot than I in my black ship?"

good. If they ever hope to do better, why do they trouble us now? Let them rather courageously burn all they have done, and wait for the better days. There are few men, ordinarily educated, who in moments of strong feeling could not strike out a poetical thought, and afterward polish it so as to be presentable. But men of sense know better than so to waste their time; and those who sincerely love poetry, know the touch of the master's hand on the chords too well to fumble among them after him. Nay, more than this, all inferior poetry is an injury to the good, inasmuch as it takes away the freshness of rhymes, blunders upon and gives a wretched commonalty to good thoughts; and, in general, adds to the weight of human weariness in a most woful and culpable manner. There are few thoughts likely to come across ordinary men, which have not already been expressed by greater men in the best possible way; and it is a wiser, more generous, more noble thing to remember and point out the perfect words, than to invent poorer ones, wherewith to encumber temporarily the world. [Ruskin's note.]

Which Pope renders thus:—

> O, say, what angry power Elpenor led
> To glide in shades, and wander with the dead?
> How could thy soul, by realms and seas disjoined,
> Outfly the nimble sail, and leave the lagging wind?

I sincerely hope the reader finds no pleasure here, either in the nimbleness of the sail, or the laziness of the wind! And yet how is it that these conceits are so painful now, when they have been pleasant to us in the other instances?

For a very simple reason. They are not a *pathetic* fallacy at all, for they are put into the mouth of the wrong passion—a passion which never could possibly have spoken them—agonized curiosity. Ulysses wants to know the facts of the matter; and the very last thing his mind could do at the moment would be to pause, or suggest in anywise what was *not* a fact. The delay in the first three lines, and conceit in the last, jar upon us instantly like the most frightful discord in music. No poet of true imaginative power could possibly have written the passage.*

Therefore we see that the spirit of truth must guide us in some sort, even in our enjoyment of fallacy. Coleridge's fallacy has no discord in it, but Pope's has set our teeth on edge. Without farther questioning, I will endeavor to state the main bearings of this matter.

The temperament which admits the pathetic fallacy, is, as I said above, that of a mind and body in some sort too weak to deal fully with what is before them or upon them; borne away, or overclouded, or overdazzled by

---

* It is worth while comparing the way a similar question is put by the exquisite sincerity of Keats:—

> He wept, and his bright tears
> Went trickling down the golden bow he held.
> Thus, with half-shut, suffused eyes, he stood;
> While from beneath some cumbrous boughs hard by
> With solemn step an awful goddess came,
> And there was purport in her looks for him,
> Which he with eager guess began to read
> Perplex'd, the while melodiously he said,
> *"How camest thou over the unfooted sea?"*
>   *Hyperion*, 3. 42.—[Ruskin's note.]

emotion; and it is a more or less noble state, according
to the force of the emotion which has induced it. For it
is no credit to a man that he is not morbid or inaccurate
in his perceptions, when he has no strength of feeling to
warp them; and it is in general a sign of higher capacity
and stand in the ranks of being, that the emotions should
be strong enough to vanquish, partly, the intellect, and
make it believe what they choose. But it is still a grander
condition when the intellect also rises, till it is strong
enough to assert its rule against, or together with, the
utmost efforts of the passions; and the whole man stands
in an iron glow, white hot, perhaps, but still strong, and
in no wise evaporating; even if he melts, losing none of
his weight.

So, then, we have the three ranks: the man who perceives rightly, because he does not feel, and to whom
the primrose is very accurately the primrose, because he
does not love it. Then, secondly, the man who perceives
wrongly, because he feels, and to whom the primrose is
anything else than a primrose: a star, or a sun, or a
fairy's shield, or a forsaken maiden. And then, lastly,
there is the man who perceives rightly in spite of his
feelings, and to whom the primrose is forever nothing
else than itself—a little flower apprehended in the very
plain and leafy fact of it, whatever and how many soever
the associations and passions may be that crowd around
it. And, in general, these three classes may be rated in
comparative order, as the men who are not poets at all,
and the poets of the second order, and the poets of the
first; only however great a man may be, there are always
some subjects which *ought* to throw him off his balance;
some, by which his poor human capacity of thought should
be conquered, and brought into the inaccurate and vague
state of perception, so that the language of the highest
inspiration becomes broken, obscure, and wild in meta-
phor, resembling that of the weaker man, overborne by
weaker things.

And thus, in full, there are four classes: the men who
feel nothing, and therefore see truly; the men who feel
strongly, think weakly, and see untruly (second order of
poets); the men who feel strongly, think strongly, and

see truly (first order of poets); and the men who, strong
as human creatures can be, are yet submitted to influences stronger than they, and see in a sort untruly, because what they see is inconceivably above them. This
last is the usual condition of prophetic inspiration.

I separate these classes, in order that their character
may be clearly understood; but of course they are united
each to the other by imperceptible transitions, and the
same mind, according to the influences to which it is
subjected, passes at different times into the various states.
Still, the difference between the great and less man is, on
the whole, chiefly in this point of *alterability*. That is to
say, the one knows too much, and perceives and feels too
much of the past and future, and of all things beside
and around that which immediately affects him, to be in
any wise shaken by it. His mind is made up; his thoughts
have an accustomed current; his ways are steadfast; it
is not this or that new sight which will at once un-
balance him. He is tender to impression at the surface,
like a rock with deep moss upon it; but there is too
much mass of him to be moved. The smaller man, with
the same degree of sensibility, is at once carried off his
feet; he wants to do something he did not want to do
before; he views all the universe in a new light through
his tears; he is gay or enthusiastic, melancholy or passionate, as things come and go to him. Therefore the
high creative poet might even be thought, to a great
extent, impassive (as shallow people think Dante stern),
receiving indeed all feelings to the full, but having a
great centre of reflection and knowledge in which he
stands serene, and watches the feeling, as it were, from
far off.

Dante, in his most intense moods, has entire command of himself, and can look around calmly, at all
moments, for the image or the word that will best tell
what he sees to the upper or lower world. But Keats
and Tennyson, and the poets of the second order, are
generally themselves subdued by the feelings under which
they write, or, at least, write as choosing to be so; and
therefore admit certain expressions and modes of thought
which are in some sort diseased or false.

Now so long as we see that the *feeling* is true, we pardon, or are even pleased by, the confessed fallacy of sight which it induces: we are pleased, for instance, with those lines of Kingsley's above quoted, not because they fallaciously describe foam, but because they faithfully describe sorrow. But the moment the mind of the speaker becomes cold, that moment every such expression becomes untrue, as being forever untrue in the external facts. And there is no greater baseness in literature than the habit of using these metaphorical expressions in cool blood. An inspired writer, in full impetuosity of passion, may speak wisely and truly of "raging waves of the sea foaming out their own shame"; but it is only the basest writer who cannot speak of the sea without talking of "raging waves," "remorseless floods," "ravenous billows," etc.; and it is one of the signs of the highest power in a writer to check all such habits of thought, and to keep his eyes fixed firmly on the *pure fact,* out of which if any feeling comes to him or his reader, he knows it must be a true one.

To keep to the waves, I forget who it is who represents a man in despair desiring that his body may be cast into the sea,

> *Whose changing mound, and foam that passed away,*
> Might mock the eye that questioned where I lay.

Observe, there is not here a single false, or even overcharged, expression. "Mound" of the sea wave is perfectly simple and true; "changing" is as familiar as may be; "foam that passed away," strictly literal; and the whole line descriptive of the reality with a degree of accuracy which I know not any other verse, in the range of poetry, that altogether equals. For most people have not a distinct idea of the clumsiness and massiveness of a large wave. The word "wave" is used too generally of ripples and breakers, and bendings in light drapery or grass: it does not by itself convey a perfect image. But the word "mound" is heavy, large, dark, definite; there is no mistaking the kind of wave meant, nor missing the sight of it. Then the term "changing" has a peculiar force also. Most people think of waves as rising and falling. But if they look at the sea carefully, they will perceive that the waves do not rise and fall. They change. Change both place and form, but they do not fall; one wave goes on, and on, and still on; now lower, now higher, now tossing its mane like a horse, now building itself together like a wall, now shaking, now steady, but still the same wave, till at last it seems struck by something, and changes, one knows not how,—becomes another wave.

The close of the line insists on this image, and paints it still more perfectly,—"foam that passed away." Not merely melting, disappearing, but passing on, out of sight, on the career of the wave. Then, having put the absolute ocean fact as far as he may before our eyes, the poet leaves us to feel about it as we may, and to trace for ourselves the opposite fact,—the image of the green mounds that do not change, and the white and written stones that do not pass away; and thence to follow out also the associated images of the calm life with the quiet grave, and the despairing life with the fading foam—

> Let no man move his bones.
> As for Samaria, her king is cut off like the foam upon the water.

But nothing of this is actually told or pointed out, and the expressions, as they stand, are perfectly severe and accurate, utterly uninfluenced by the firmly governed emotion of the writer. Even the word "mock" is hardly an exception, as it may stand merely for "deceive" or "defeat," without implying any impersonation of the waves.

It may be well, perhaps, to give one or two more instances to show the peculiar dignity possessed by all passages, which thus limit their expression to the pure fact, and leave the hearer to gather what he can from it. Here is a notable one from the *Iliad*. Helen, looking from the Scæan gate of Troy over the Grecian host, and telling Priam the names of its captains, says at last:—

"I see all the other dark-eyed Greeks; but two I cannot see,—Castor and Pollux,—whom one mother bore with me. Have they not followed from fair Lacedæmon, or have they indeed come in their sea-wandering ships, but now will not enter into the battle of men, fearing the shame and the scorn that is in Me?"

Then Homer:—

"So she spoke. But them, already, the life-giving earth possessed, there in Lacedæmon, in the dear fatherland." *

Note, here, the high poetical truth carried to the extreme. The poet has to speak of the earth in sadness, but he will not let that sadness affect or change his thoughts of it. No; though Castor and Pollux be dead, yet the earth is our mother still, fruitful, life-giving. These are the facts of the thing. I see nothing else than these. Make what you will of them.

Take another very notable instance from Casimir de la Vigne's terrible ballad, "La Toilette de Constance." I must quote a few lines out of it here and there, to enable the reader who has not the book by him, to understand its close.

> Vite, Anna! vite; au miroir!
> Plus vite, Anna. L'heure s'avance,
> Et je vais au bal ce soir
> Chez l'ambassadeur de France.

> Y pensez-vous? ils sont fanés, ces nœuds;
> Ils sont d'hier; mon Dieu, comme tout passe!
> Que du réseau qui retient mes cheveux
> Les glands d'azur retombent avec grâce.
> Plus haut! Plus bas! Vous ne comprenez rien!
> Que sur mon front ce saphir étincelle:
> Vous me piquez, maladroite. Ah, c'est bien,
> Bien,—chère Anna! Je t'aime, je suis belle.

---

* *Iliad*, 3. 243. In the MS. Ruskin notes, "The insurpassably tender irony in the epithet—'life-giving earth'—of the grave"; and then adds another illustration:—"Compare the hammer-stroke at the close of the [32nd] chapter of *Vanity Fair*—'The darkness came down on the field and city, and Amelia was praying for George, who was lying on his face, dead, with a bullet through his heart.' A great deal might have been said about it. The writer is very sorry for Amelia, neither does he want faith in prayer. He knows as well as any of us that prayer must be answered in some sort; but those are the facts. The man and woman sixteen miles apart—one on her knees on the floor, the other on his face in the clay. So much love in her heart, so much lead in his. Make what you can of it." [Cook and Wedderburn.]

Vite, j'en crois mon miroir,
　　Et mon cœur bat d'espérance.
Vite, Anna, je vais ce soir
　　Chez l'ambassadeur de France.

Celui qu'en vain je voudrais oublier . . .
　　(Anna, ma robe) il y sera, j'espère.
(Ah, fi! profane, est-ce là mon collier?
　　Quoi! ces grains d'or bénits par le Saint-Père!)
Il y sera; Dieu, s'il pressait ma main,
　　En y pensant à peine je respire:
Frère Anselmo doit m'entendre demain,
　　Comment ferai-je, Anna, pour tout lui dire? . . .

　　　Vite! un coup d'œil au miroir,
　　　　Le dernier. ——J'ai l'assurance
　　　Qu'on va m'adorer ce soir
　　　　Chez l'ambassadeur de France.

Près du foyer, Constance s'admirait.
　　Dieu! sur sa robe il vole une étincelle!
Au feu! Courez! Quand l'espoir l'énivrait,
　　Tout perdre ainsi! Quoi! Mourir,—et si belle!
L'horrible feu ronge avec volupté
　　Ses bras, son sein, et l'entoure, et s'élève,
Et sans pitié dévore sa beauté,
　　Ses dix-huit ans, hélas, et son doux rêve!

　　　Adieu, bal, plaisir, amour!
　　　　On disait, Pauvre Constance.
　　　Et l'on dansa, jusqu'au jour,
　　　　Chez l'ambassadeur de France.

Yes, that is the fact of it. Right or wrong, the poet does not say. What you may think about it, he does not know. He has nothing to do with that. There lie the ashes of the dead girl in her chamber. There they danced, till the morning, at the Ambassador's of France. Make what you will of it.

If the reader will look through the ballad, of which I have quoted only about the third part, he will find that there is not, from beginning to end of it, a single poetical (so called) expression, except in one stanza. The girl speaks as simple prose as may be; there is not a word

she would not have actually used as she was dressing.
The poet stands by, impassive as a statue, recording her
words just as they come. At last the doom seizes her,
and in the very presence of death, for an instant, his
own emotions conquer him. He records no longer the
facts only, but the facts as they seem to him. The fire
gnaws *with voluptuousness—without pity*. It is soon past.
The fate is fixed forever; and he retires into his pale
and crystalline atmosphere of truth. He closes all with
the calm veracity,

They said, "Poor Constance!"

Now in this there is the exact type of the consummate
poetical temperament. For, be it clearly and constantly
remembered, that the greatness of a poet depends upon
the two faculties, acuteness of feeling, and command of
it. A poet is great, first in proportion to the strength
of his passion, and then, that strength being granted, in
proportion to his government of it; there being, however,
always a point beyond which it would be inhuman and
monstrous if he pushed this government, and, therefore,
a point at which all feverish and wild fancy becomes just
and true. Thus the destruction of the kingdom of As-
syria cannot be contemplated firmly by a prophet of
Israel. The fact is too great, too wonderful. It overthrows him, dashes him into a confused element of dreams.
All the world is, to his stunned thought, full of strange
voices. "Yea, the fir-trees rejoice at thee, and the cedars
of Lebanon, saying, 'Since thou art gone down to the
grave, no feller is come up against us.'" So, still more,
the thought of the presence of Deity cannot be borne
without this great astonishment. "The mountains and
the hills shall break forth before you into singing, and
all the trees of the field shall clap their hands."
But by how much this feeling is noble when it is justified by the strength of its cause, by so much it is ignoble
when there is not cause enough for it; and beyond all
other ignobleness is the mere affectation of it, in hardness of heart. Simply bad writing may almost always,
as above noticed, be known by its adoption of these

fanciful metaphorical expressions as a sort of current coin; yet there is even a worse, at least a more harmful condition of writing than this, in which such expressions are not ignorantly and feelinglessly caught up, but, by some master, skilful in handling, yet insincere, deliberately wrought out with chill and studied fancy; as if we should try to make an old lava-stream look red-hot again, by covering it with dead leaves, or white-hot, with hoar-frost.

When Young is lost in veneration, as he dwells on the character of a truly good and holy man, he permits himself for a moment to be overborne by the feeling so far as to exclaim—

> Where shall I find him? angels, tell me where.
> You know him; he is near you; point him out.
> Shall I see glories beaming from his brow,
> Or trace his footsteps by the rising flowers?

This emotion has a worthy cause, and is thus true and right. But now hear the cold-hearted Pope say to a shepherd girl—

> Where'er you walk, cool gales shall fan the glade;
> Trees, where you sit, shall crowd into a shade;
> Your praise the birds shall chant in every grove,
> And winds shall waft it to the powers above.
> But would you sing, and rival Orpheus' strain,
> The wondering forests soon should dance again;
> The moving mountains hear the powerful call,
> And headlong streams hang, listening, in their fall.

This is not, nor could it for a moment be mistaken for, the language of passion. It is simple falsehood, uttered by hypocrisy; definite absurdity, rooted in affectation, and coldly asserted in the teeth of nature and fact. Passion will indeed go far in deceiving itself; but it must be a strong passion, not the simple wish of a lover to tempt his mistress to sing. Compare a very closely parallel passage in Wordsworth, in which the lover has lost his mistress:

Three years had Barbara in her grave been laid,
    When thus his moan he made:—

"Oh, move, thou cottage, from behind yon oak,
    Or let the ancient tree uprooted lie,
That in some other way yon smoke
    May mount into the sky.
If still behind yon pine-tree's ragged bough,
    Headlong, the waterfall must come,
    Oh, let it, then, be dumb—
Be anything, sweet stream, but that which thou art now."

Here is a cottage to be moved, if not a mountain, and
a waterfall to be silent, if it is not to hang listening: but
with what different relation to the mind that contem-
plates them! Here, in the extremity of its agony, the
soul cries out wildly for relief, which at the same moment it partly knows to be impossible, but partly believes possible, in a vague impression that a miracle
might be wrought to give relief even to a less sore
distress,—that nature is kind, and God is kind, and that
grief is strong: it knows not well what *is* possible to such
grief. To silence a stream, to move a cottage wall,—
one might think it could do as much as that!

I believe these instances are enough to illustrate the
main point I insist upon respecting the pathetic fallacy,
—that so far as it *is* a fallacy, it is always the sign of a
morbid state of mind, and comparatively of a weak one.
Even in the most inspired prophet it is a sign of the
incapacity of his human sight or thought to bear what
has been revealed to it. In ordinary poetry, if it is found
in the thoughts of the poet himself, it is at once a sign
of his belonging to the inferior school; if in the thoughts
of the characters imagined by him, it is right or wrong
according to the genuineness of the emotion from which
it springs; always, however, implying necessarily *some*
degree of weakness in the character.

Take two most exquisite instances from master hands.
The Jessy of Shenstone, and the Ellen of Wordsworth,
have both been betrayed and deserted. Jessy, in the
course of her most touching complaint, says:

If through the garden's flowery tribes I stray,
  Where bloom the jasmines that could once allure,
"Hope not to find delight in us," they say,
  "For we are spotless, Jessy; we are pure."

Compare with this some of the words of Ellen:

"Ah, why," said Ellen, sighing to herself,
'Why do not words, and kiss, and solemn pledge,
And nature, that is kind in woman's breast,
And reason, that in man is wise and good,
And fear of Him Who is a righteous Judge,—
Why do not these prevail for human life,
To keep two hearts together, that began
Their springtime with one love, and that have need
Of mutual pity and forgiveness sweet
To grant, or be received; while that poor bird—
O, come and hear him! Thou who hast to me
Been faithless, hear him;—though a lowly creature,
One of God's simple children that yet know not
The Universal Parent, *how* he sings!
As if he wished the firmament of heaven
Should listen, and give back to him the voice
Of his triumphant constancy and love;
The proclamation that he makes, how far
His darkness doth transcend our fickle light."

The perfection of both these passages, as far as regards truth and tenderness of imagination in the two poets, is quite insuperable. But of the two characters imagined, Jessy is weaker than Ellen, exactly in so far as something appears to her to be in nature which is not. The flowers do not really reproach her. God meant them to comfort her, not to taunt her; they would do so if she saw them rightly.

Ellen, on the other hand, is quite above the slightest erring emotion. There is not the barest film of fallacy in all her thoughts. She reasons as calmly as if she did not feel. And, although the singing of the bird suggests to her the idea of its desiring to be heard in heaven, she does not for an instant admit any veracity in the thought. "As if," she says,—"I know he means nothing of the kind; but it does verily seem as if." The reader will find, by examining the rest of the poem, that Ellen's character is throughout consistent in this clear though passionate strength.*

It then being, I hope, now made clear to the reader in all respects that the pathetic fallacy is powerful only so far as it is pathetic, feeble so far as it is fallacious, and, therefore, that the dominion of Truth is entire, over this, as over every other natural and just state of the human mind, we may go on to the subject for the dealing with which this prefatory inquiry became necessary; and why necessary, we shall see forthwith.

Modern Landscape

[*Modern Painters,* Vol. III, Ch. 16.]

We turn our eyes, therefore, as boldly and as quickly as may be, from these serene fields and skies of mediæval art, to the most characteristic examples of modern landscape. And, I believe, the first thing that will strike us, or that ought to strike us, is their *cloudiness.*

Out of perfect light and motionless air, we find ourselves on a sudden brought under sombre skies, and into drifting wind; and, with fickle sunbeams flashing in our face, or utterly drenched with sweep of rain, we are reduced to track the changes of the shadows on the grass, or watch the rents of twilight through angry cloud. And we find that whereas all the pleasure of the mediæval was in *stability, definiteness,* and *luminousness,* we are expected to rejoice in darkness, and triumph in mutability; to lay the foundation of happiness in things which momentarily change or fade; and to expect

---

* I cannot quit this subject without giving two more instances, both exquisite, of the pathetic fallacy, which I have just come upon in *Maud:*—

For a great speculation had fail'd;
And ever he mutter'd and madden'd, and ever wann'd with despair;
And out he walk'd, when the wind like a broken worldling wail'd,
And the *flying gold of the ruin'd woodlands drove thro' the air.*

There has fallen a splendid tear
From the passion-flower at the gate.
The red rose cries, "She is near, she is near!"
And the white rose weeps, "She is late."
The larkspur listens, "I hear, I hear!"
And the lily whispers, "I wait."

[Ruskin's note.]

the utmost satisfaction and instruction from what it is impossible to arrest, and difficult to comprehend.

We find, however, together with this general delight in breeze and darkness, much attention to the real form of clouds, and careful drawing of effects of mist; so that the appearance of objects, as seen through it, becomes a subject of science with us; and the faithful representation of that appearance is made of primal importance, under the name of aërial perspective. The aspects of sunset and sunrise, with all their attendant phenomena of cloud and mist, are watchfully delineated; and in ordinary daylight landscape, the sky is considered of so much importance, that a principal mass of foliage, or a whole foreground, is unhesitatingly thrown into shade merely to bring out the form of a white cloud. So that, if a general and characteristic name were needed for modern landscape art, none better could be invented than "the service of clouds."

And this name would, unfortunately, be characteristic of our art in more ways than one. In the last chapter, I said that all the Greeks spoke kindly about the clouds, except Aristophanes; and he, I am sorry to say (since his report is so unfavorable), is the only Greek who had studied them attentively. He tells us, first, that they are "great goddesses to idle men"; then, that they are "mistresses of disputings, and logic, and monstrosities, and noisy chattering"; declares that whoso believes in their divinity must first disbelieve in Jupiter, and place supreme power in the hands of an unknown god "Whirlwind"; and, finally, he displays their influence over the mind of one of their disciples, in his sudden desire "to speak ingeniously concerning smoke."

There is, I fear, an infinite truth in this Aristophanic judgment applied to our modern cloud-worship. Assuredly, much of the love of mystery in our romances, our poetry, our art, and, above all, in our metaphysics, must come under that definition so long ago given by the great Greek, "speaking ingeniously concerning smoke." And much of the instinct, which, partially developed in painting, may be now seen throughout every mode of exertion of mind,—the easily encouraged doubt, easily excited curiosity, habitual agitation, and delight in the changing and the marvellous, as opposed to the old quiet serenity of social custom and religious faith,—is again deeply defined in those few words, the "dethroning of Jupiter," the "coronation of the whirlwind."

Nor of whirlwind merely, but also of darkness or ignorance respecting all stable facts. That darkening of the foreground to bring out the white cloud, is, in one aspect of it, a type of the subjection of all plain and positive fact, to what is uncertain and unintelligible. And, as we examine farther into the matter, we shall be struck by another great difference between the old and modern landscape, namely, that in the old no one ever thought of drawing anything but as well *as he could.* That might not be *well,* as we have seen in the case of rocks; but it was as well as he *could,* and always distinctly. Leaf, or stone, or animal, or man, it was equally drawn with care and clearness, and its essential characters shown. If it was an oak tree, the acorns were drawn; if a flint pebble, its veins were drawn; if an arm of the sea, its fish were drawn; if a group of figures, their faces and dresses were drawn—to the very last subtlety of expression and end of thread that could be got into the space, far off or near. But now our ingenuity is all "concerning smoke." Nothing is truly drawn but that; all else is vague, slight, imperfect; got with as little pains as possible. You examine your closest foreground, and find no leaves; your largest oak, and find no acorns; your human figure, and find a spot of red paint instead of a face; and in all this, again and again, the Aristophanic words come true, and the clouds seem to be "great goddesses to idle men."

The next thing that will strike us, after this love of clouds, is the love of liberty. Whereas the mediæval was always shutting himself into castles, and behind fosses, and drawing brickwork neatly, and beds of flowers primly, our painters delight in getting to the open fields and moors; abhor all hedges and moats; never paint anything but free-growing trees, and rivers gliding "at their own sweet will"; eschew formality down to the smallest detail; break and displace the brickwork which the mediæval would have carefully cemented; leave unpruned the thickets he would have delicately trimmed; and, carrying the love of liberty even to license, and the love of wildness even to ruin, take pleasure at last in every aspect of age and desolation which emancipates the objects of nature from the government of men;—on the castle wall displacing its tapestry with ivy, and spreading, through the garden, the bramble for the rose.

Connected with this love of liberty we find a singular manifestation of love of mountains, and see our painters traversing the wildest places of the globe in order to obtain subjects with craggy foregrounds and purple distances. Some few of them remain content with pollards and flat land; but these are always men of third-rate order; and the leading masters, while they do not reject the beauty of the low grounds, reserve their highest powers to paint Alpine peaks or Italian promontories. And it is eminently noticeable, also, that this pleasure in the mountains is never mingled with fear, or tempered by a spirit of meditation, as with the mediæval; but is always free and fearless, brightly exhilarating, and wholly unreflective; so that the painter feels that his mountain foreground may be more consistently animated by a sportsman than a hermit; and our modern society in general goes to the mountains, not to fast, but to feast, and leaves their glaciers covered with chicken-bones and egg-shells.

Connected with this want of any sense of solemnity in mountain scenery, is a general profanity of temper in regarding all the rest of nature; that is to say, a total absence of faith in the presence of any deity therein. Whereas the mediæval never painted a cloud, but with the purpose of placing an angel in it; and a Greek never entered a wood without expecting to meet a god in it; *we* should think the appearance of an angel in the cloud wholly unnatural, and should be seriously surprised by meeting a god anywhere. Our chief ideas about the wood are connected with poaching. We have no belief that the clouds contain more than so many inches of rain or hail, and from our ponds and ditches expect nothing more divine than ducks and watercresses.

Finally: connected with this profanity of temper is a strong tendency to deny the sacred element of color, and make our boast in blackness. For though occasionally glaring or violent, modern color is on the whole eminently sombre, tending continually to gray or brown, and by many of our best painters consistently falsified, with a confessed pride in what they call chaste or subdued tints; so that, whereas a mediæval paints his sky bright blue and his foreground bright green, gilds the towers of his castles, and clothes his figures with purple and white, we paint our sky gray, our foreground black, and our foliage brown, and think that enough is sacrificed to the sun in admitting the dangerous brightness of a scarlet cloak or a blue jacket.

These, I believe, are the principal points which would strike us instantly, if we were to be brought suddenly into an exhibition of modern landscapes out of a room filled with mediæval work. It is evident that there are both evil and good in this change; but how much evil, or how much good, we can only estimate by considering, as in the former divisions of our inquiry, what are the real roots of the habits of mind which have caused them.

And first, it is evident that the title "Dark Ages," given to the mediæval centuries, is, respecting art, wholly inapplicable. They were, on the contrary, the bright ages; ours are the dark ones. I do not mean metaphysically, but literally. They were the ages of gold; ours are the ages of umber.

This is partly mere mistake in us; we build brown brick walls, and wear brown coats, because we have been blunderingly taught to do so, and go on doing so mechanically. There is, however, also some cause for the change in our own tempers. On the whole, these are much *sadder* ages than the early ones; not sadder in a noble and deep way, but in a dim wearied way,—the way of ennui, and jaded intellect, and uncomfortableness of soul and body. The Middle Ages had their wars and agonies, but also intense delights. Their gold was dashed with blood; but ours is sprinkled with dust. Their life was inwoven with white and purple: ours is one seamless stuff of brown. Not that we are without apparent festivity, but festivity more or less forced, mistaken, embittered, incomplete—not of the heart. How wonderfully, since Shakspeare's time, have we lost the power of laughing at bad jests! The very finish of our wit belies our gayety.

The profoundest reason of this darkness of heart is, I believe, our want of faith. There never yet was a generation of men (savage or civilized) who, taken as a body, so wofully fulfilled the words "having no hope, and without God in the world," as the present civilized European race. A Red Indian or Otaheitan savage has more sense of a divine existence round him, or government over him, than the plurality of refined Londoners and Parisians: and those among us who may in some sense be said to believe, are divided almost without exception into two broad classes, Romanist and Puritan; who, but for the interference of the unbelieving portions of society, would, either of them, reduce the other sect as speedily as possible to ashes; the Romanist having always done so whenever he could, from the beginning of their separation, and the Puritan at this time holding himself in complacent expectation of the destruction of Rome by volcanic fire. Such division as this between persons nominally of one religion, that is to say, believing in the same God, and the same Revelation, cannot but become a stumbling-block of the gravest kind to all thoughtful and far-sighted men,—a stumbling-block which they can only surmount under the most favorable circumstances of early education. Hence, nearly all our powerful men in this age of the world are unbelievers; the best of them in doubt and misery; the worst in reckless defiance; the plurality, in plodding hesitation, doing, as well as they can, what practical work lies ready to their hands. Most of our scientific men are in this last class: our popular authors either set themselves definitely against all religious form, pleading for simple truth and benevolence (Thackeray, Dickens), or give themselves up to bitter and fruitless statement of facts (De Balzac), or surface-painting (Scott), or careless blasphemy, sad or smiling (Byron, Béranger). Our earnest poets and deepest thinkers are doubtful and in-

dignant (Tennyson, Carlyle); one or two, anchored, indeed, but anxious or weeping (Wordsworth, Mrs. Brown-
ing); and of these two, the first is not so sure of his
anchor, but that now and then it drags with him, even
to make him cry out,—

> Great God, I had rather be
> A Pagan suckled in some creed outworn;
> So might I, standing on this pleasant lea,
> Have glimpses that would make me less forlorn.

In politics, religion is now a name; in art, a hypocrisy
or affectation. Over German religious pictures the inscription, "See how Pious I am," can be read at a glance
by any clear-sighted person. Over French and English
religious pictures the inscription, "See how Impious I
am," is equally legible. All sincere and modest art is,
among us, profane.*

This faithlessness operates among us according to our
tempers, producing either sadness or levity, and being
the ultimate root alike of our discontents and of our
wantonnesses. It is marvellous how full of contradiction
it makes us: we are first dull, and seek for wild and
lonely places because we have no heart for the garden;
presently we recover our spirits, and build an assembly-
room among the mountains, because we have no reverence for the desert. I do not know if there be game on
Sinai, but I am always expecting to hear of some one's
shooting over it.

There is, however, another, and a more innocent root
of our delight in wild scenery.

All the Renaissance principles of art tended, as I have
before often explained, to the setting Beauty above Truth,
and seeking for it always at the expense of truth. And
the proper punishment of such pursuit—the punishment
which all the laws of the universe rendered inevitable—
was, that those who thus pursued beauty should wholly
lose sight of beauty. All the thinkers of the age, as we

---

* Pre-Raphaelitism, of course, excepted, which is a new phase of art,
in no wise considered in this chapter. Blake was sincere, but full of
wild creeds, and somewhat diseased in brain. [Ruskin's note.]

saw previously, declared that it did not exist. The age seconded their efforts, and banished beauty, so far as human effort could succeed in doing so, from the face of the earth, and the form of man. To powder the hair, to patch the cheek, to hoop the body, to buckle the foot, were all part and parcel of the same system which reduced streets to brick walls, and pictures to brown stains. One desert of Ugliness was extended before the eyes of mankind; and their pursuit of the beautiful, so recklessly continued, received unexpected consummation in high-heeled shoes and periwigs,—Gower Street, and Gaspar Poussin.

Reaction from this state was inevitable, if any true life was left in the races of mankind; and, accordingly, though still forced, by rule and fashion, to the producing and wearing all that is ugly, men steal out, half-ashamed of themselves for doing so, to the fields and mountains; and, finding among these the color, and liberty, and variety, and power, which are forever grateful to them, delight in these to an extent never before known; rejoice in all the wildest shattering of the mountain side, as an opposition to Gower Street, gaze in a rapt manner at sunsets and sunrises, to see there the blue, and gold, and purple, which glow for them no longer on knight's armor or temple porch; and gather with care out of the fields, into their blotted herbaria, the flowers which the five orders of architecture have banished from their doors and casements.

The absence of care for personal beauty, which is another great characteristic of the age, adds to this feeling in a twofold way: first, by turning all reverent thoughts away from human nature; and making us think of men as ridiculous or ugly creatures, getting through the world as well as they can, and spoiling it in doing so; not ruling it in a kingly way and crowning all its loveliness. In the Middle Ages hardly anything but vice could be caricatured, because virtue was always visibly and personally noble: now virtue itself is apt to inhabit such poor human bodies, that no aspect of it is invulnerable to jest; and for all fairness we have to seek to the flowers; for all sublimity, to the hills.

The same want of care operates, in another way, by lowering the standard of health, increasing the susceptibility to nervous or sentimental impressions, and thus adding to the other powers of nature over us whatever charm may be felt in her fostering the melancholy fancies of brooding idleness.

It is not, however, only to existing inanimate nature that our want of beauty in person and dress has driven us. The imagination of it, as it was seen in our ancestors, haunts us continually; and while we yield to the present fashions, or act in accordance with the dullest modern principles of economy and utility, we look fondly back to the manners of the ages of chivalry, and delight in painting, to the fancy, the fashions we pretend to despise, and the splendors we think it wise to abandon. The furniture and personages of our romance are sought, when the writers desires to please most easily, in the centuries which we profess to have surpassed in everything; the art which takes us into the present times is considered as both daring and degraded; and while the weakest words please us, and are regarded as poetry, which recall the manners of our forefathers, or of strangers, it is only as familiar and vulgar that we accept the description of our own.

In this we are wholly different from all the races that preceded us. All other nations have regarded their ancestors with reverence as saints or heroes; but have nevertheless thought their own deeds and ways of life the fitting subjects for their arts of painting or of verse. We, on the contrary, regard our ancestors as foolish and wicked, but yet find our chief artistic pleasures in descriptions of their ways of life.

The Greeks and mediævals honored, but did not imitate their forefathers; we imitate, but do not honor.

With this romantic love of beauty, forced to seek in history, and in external nature, the satisfaction it cannot find in ordinary life, we mingle a more rational passion, the due and just result of newly awakened powers of attention. Whatever may first lead us to the scrutiny of natural objects, that scrutiny never fails of its reward. Unquestionably they are intended to be regarded by us with both reverence and delight; and every hour we give to them renders their beauty more apparent, and their interest more engrossing. Natural science—which can hardly be considered to have existed before modern times —rendering our knowledge fruitful in accumulation, and exquisite in accuracy, has acted for good or evil, according to the temper of the mind which received it; and though it has hardened the faithlessness of the dull and proud, has shown new grounds for reverence to hearts which were thoughtful and humble. The neglect of the art of war, while it has somewhat weakened and deformed the body,* has given us leisure and opportunity for studies to which, before, time and space were equally wanting; lives which once were early wasted on the battle-field are now passed usefully in the study; nations which exhausted themselves in annual warfare now dispute with each other the discovery of new planets; and the serene philosopher dissects the plants, and analyzes the dust, of lands which were of old only traversed by the knight in hasty march, or by the borderer in heedless rapine.

The elements of progress and decline being thus strangely mingled in the modern mind, we might beforehand anticipate that one of the notable characters of our art would be its inconsistency; that efforts would be made in every direction, and arrested by every conceivable cause and manner of failure; that in all we did, it would become next to impossible to distinguish accurately the grounds for praise or for regret; that all previous canons of practice and methods of thought would be gradually overthrown, and criticism continually defied by successes which no one had expected, and sentiments which no one could define.

Accordingly, while, in our inquiries into Greek and mediæval art, I was able to describe, in general terms, what all men did or felt, I find now many characters in

---

* Of course this is meant only of the modern citizen or country-gentleman, as compared with a citizen of Sparta or old Florence. I leave it to others to say whether the "neglect of the *art* of war" may or may not, in a yet more fatal sense, be predicated of the English nation. War *without* art, we seem, with God's help, able still to wage nobly. [Ruskin's note.]

many men; some, it seems to me, founded on the in
ferior and evanescent principles of modernism, on its
recklessness, impatience, or faithlessness; others founded
on its science, its new affection for nature, its love of
openness and liberty. And among all these characters,
good or evil, I see that some, remaining to us from old
or transitional periods, do not properly belong to us, and
will soon fade away, and others, though not yet distinctly
developed, are yet properly our own, and likely to grow
forward into greater strength.

For instance: our reprobation of bright color is, I think,
for the most part, mere affectation, and must soon be
done away with. Vulgarity, dulness, or impiety, will in
deed always express themselves through art in brown and
gray, as in Rembrandt, Caravaggio, and Salvator; but
we are not wholly vulgar, dull, or impious; nor, as mod
erns, are we necessarily obliged to continue so in any
wise. Our greatest men, whether sad or gay, still delight,
like the great men of all ages, in brilliant hues. The
coloring of Scott and Byron is full and pure; that of
Keats and Tennyson rich even to excess. Our practical
failures in coloring are merely the necessary consequence
of our prolonged want of practice during the periods of
Renaissance affectation and ignorance; and the only dura
ble difference between old and modern coloring, is the
acceptance of certain hues, by the modern, which please
him by expressing that melancholy peculiar to his more
reflective or sentimental character, and the greater va
riety of them necessary to express his greater science.

Again: if we ever become wise enough to dress con
sistently and gracefully, to make health a principal ob
ject in education, and to render our streets beautiful with
art, the external charm of past history will in great meas
ure disappear. There is no essential reason, because we
live after the fatal seventeenth century, that we should
never again be able to confess interest in sculpture, or
see brightness in embroidery; nor, because now we choose
to make the night deadly with our pleasures, and the day
with our labors, prolonging the dance till dawn, and the
toil to twilight, that we should never again learn how
rightly to employ the sacred trusts of strength, beauty

and time. Whatever external charm attaches itself to the past, would then be seen in proper subordination to the brightness of present life; and the elements of romance would exist, in the earlier ages, only in the attraction which must generally belong to whatever is unfamiliar; in the reverence which a noble nation always pays to its ancestors; and in the enchanted light which races, like individuals, must perceive in looking back to the days of their childhood.

Again: the peculiar levity with which natural scenery is regarded by a large number of modern minds cannot be considered as entirely characteristic of the age, inasmuch as it never can belong to its greatest intellects. Men of any high mental power must be serious, whether in ancient or modern days; a certain degree of reverence for fair scenery is found in all our great writers without exception,—even the one who has made us laugh oftenest, taking us to the valley of Chamouni, and to the sea beach, there to give peace after suffering, and change revenge into pity. It is only the dull, the uneducated, or the worldly, whom it is painful to meet on the hillsides; and levity, as a ruling character, cannot be ascribed to the whole nation, but only to its holiday-making apprentices, and its House of Commons.

We need not, therefore, expect to find any single poet or painter representing the entire group of powers, weaknesses, and inconsistent instincts which govern or confuse our modern life. But we may expect that in the man who seems to be given by Providence as the type of the age (as Homer and Dante were given, as the types of classical and mediæval mind), we shall find whatever is fruitful and substantial to be completely present, together with those of our weaknesses, which are indeed nationally characteristic, and compatible with general greatness of mind, just as the weak love of fences, and dislike of mountains, were found compatible with Dante's greatness in other respects.

Farther: as the admiration of mankind is found, in our times, to have in great part passed from men to mountains, and from human emotion to natural phenomena, we may anticipate that the great strength of art will also be warped in this direction; with this notable result for us, that whereas the greatest painters or painter of classical and mediæval periods, being wholly devoted to the representation of humanity, furnished us with but little to examine in landscape, the greatest painters or painter of modern times will in all probability be devoted to landscape principally; and farther, because in representing human emotion words surpass painting, but in representing natural scenery painting surpasses words, we may anticipate also that the painter and poet (for convenience' sake I here use the words in opposition) will somewhat change their relations of rank in illustrating the mind of the age; that the painter will become of more importance, the poet of less; and that the relations between the men who are the types and firstfruits of the age in word and work,—namely, Scott and Turner,—will be, in many curious respects, different from those between Homer and Phidias, or Dante and Giotto.

The Two Boyhoods

[*Modern Painters,* Vol. V, Pt. 9, Ch. 9.]

Born half-way between the mountains and the sea— that young George of Castelfranco—of the Brave Castle: —Stout George they called him, George of Georges, so goodly a boy he was—Giorgione.

Have you ever thought what a world his eyes opened on—fair, searching eyes of youth? What a world of mighty life, from those mountain roots to the shore;— of loveliest life, when he went down, yet so young, to the marble city—and became himself as a fiery heart to it?

A city of marble, did I say? nay, rather a golden city, paved with emerald. For truly, every pinnacle and turret glanced or glowed, overlaid with gold, or bossed with jasper. Beneath, the unsullied sea drew in deep breathing, to and fro, its eddies of green wave. Deep-hearted, majestic, terrible as the sea,—the men of Venice moved in sway of power and war; pure as her pillars of alabaster, stood her mothers and maidens; from foot to brow, all noble, walked her knights; the low bronzed gleaming of sea-rusted armor shot angrily under their blood-red mantle-folds. Fearless, faithful, patient, impenetrable, implacable,—every word a fate—sat her senate. In hope and honor, lulled by flowing of wave around their isles of sacred sand, each with his name written and the cross graved at his side, lay her dead. A wonderful piece of world. Rather, itself a world. It lay along the face of the waters, no larger, as its captains saw it from their masts at evening, than a bar of sunset that could not pass away; but for its power, it must have seemed to them as if they were sailing in the expanse of heaven, and this a great planet, whose orient edge widened through ether. A world from which all ignoble care and petty thoughts were banished, with all the common and poor elements of life. No foulness, nor tumult, in those tremulous streets, that filled, or fell, beneath the moon; but rippled music of majestic change, or thrilling silence. No weak walls could rise above them; no low-roofed cottage, nor straw-built shed. Only the strength as of rock, and the finished setting of stones most precious. And around them, far as the eye could reach, still the soft moving of stainless waters, proudly pure; as not the flower, so neither the thorn nor the thistle, could grow in the glancing fields. Ethereal strength of Alps, dreamlike, vanishing in high procession beyond the Torcellan shore; blue islands of Paduan hills, poised in the golden west. Above, free winds and fiery clouds ranging at their will;—brightness out of the north, and balm from the south, and the stars of the evening and morning clear in the limitless light of arched heaven and circling sea.

Such was Giorgione's school—such Titian's home.

Near the southwest corner of Covent Garden, a square brick pit or well is formed by a close-set block of houses, to the back windows of which it admits a few rays of light. Access to the bottom of it is obtained out of Maiden Lane, through a low archway and an iron gate; and if you stand long enough under the archway to accustom your eyes to the darkness you may see on the left hand a narrow door, which formerly gave quiet access to a respectable barber's shop, of which the front window, looking into Maiden Lane, is still extant, filled, in this year (1860), with a row of bottles, connected, in some defunct manner, with a brewer's business. A more fashionable neighborhood, it is said, eighty years ago than now—never certainly a cheerful one—wherein a boy being born on St. George's day, 1775, began soon after to take interest in the world of Covent Garden, and put to service such spectacles of life as it afforded.

No knights to be seen there, nor, I imagine, many beautiful ladies; their costume at least disadvantageous, depending much on incumbency of hat and feather, and short waists; the majesty of men founded similarly on shoebuckles and wigs;—impressive enough when Reynolds will do his best for it; but not suggestive of much ideal delight to a boy.

"Bello ovile dov' io dormii agnello";* of things beautiful, besides men and women, dusty sunbeams up or down the street on summer mornings; deep furrowed cabbage-leaves at the greengrocer's; magnificence of oranges in wheelbarrows round the corner; and Thames' shore within three minutes' race.

None of these things very glorious; the best, however, that England, it seems, was then able to provide for a boy of gift: who, such as they are, loves them—never, indeed, forgets them. The short waists modify to the last his visions of Greek ideal. His foregrounds had always a succulent cluster or two of greengrocery at the corners. Enchanted oranges gleam in Covent Gardens of the Hesperides; and great ships go to pieces in order to scatter chests of them on the waves. That mist of early sunbeams in the London dawn crosses, many and many a time, the clearness of Italian air; and by Thames' shore, with its stranded barges and glidings of red sail, dearer to us than Lucerne lake or Venetian lagoon,—by Thames' shore we will die.

With such circumstance round him in youth, let us note what necessary effects followed upon the boy. I assume him to have had Giorgione's sensibility (and more than Giorgione's, if that be possible) to color and form. I tell you farther, and this fact you may receive trust-

---

* Dante's allusion to Florence, *Paradiso*, xxv, 5: "Out of the fair Sheepfold, where a lamb I slept." (Norton's tr.).

fully, that his sensibility to human affection and distress was no less keen than even his sense for natural beauty —heart-sight deep as eyesight.

Consequently, he attaches himself with the faithfullest child-love to everything that bears an image of the place he was born in. No matter how ugly it is,—has it anything about it like Maiden Lane, or like Thames' shore? If so, it shall be painted for their sake. Hence, to the very close of life, Turner could endure ugliness which no one else, of the same sensibility, would have borne with for an instant. Dead brick walls, blank square windows, old clothes, market-womanly types of humanity—anything fishy and muddy, like Billingsgate or Hungerford Market, had great attraction for him; black barges, patched sails, and every possible condition of fog.

You will find these tolerations and affections guiding or sustaining him to the last hour of his life; the notablest of all such endurances being that of dirt. No Venetian ever draws anything foul; but Turner devoted picture after picture to the illustration of effects of dinginess, smoke, soot, dust, and dusty texture; old sides of boats, weedy roadside vegetation, dung-hills, straw-yards, and all the soilings and stains of every common labor.

And more than this, he not only could endure, but enjoyed and looked for *litter,* like Covent Garden wreck after the market. His pictures are often full of it, from side to side; their foregrounds differ from all others in the natural way that things have of lying about in them. Even his richest vegetation, in ideal work, is confused; and he delights in shingle, débris, and heaps of fallen stones. The last words he ever spoke to me about a picture were in gentle exultation about his St. Gothard: "that *litter* of stones which I endeavored to represent."

The second great result of this Covent Garden training was, understanding of and regard for the poor, whom the Venetians, we saw, despised; whom, contrarily, Turner loved, and more than loved — understood. He got no romantic sight of them, but an infallible one, as he prowled about the end of his lane, watching night effects in the wintry streets; nor sight of the poor alone, but of the poor in direct relations with the rich. He knew, in good and evil, what both classes thought of, and how they dwelt with, each other.

Reynolds and Gainsborough, bred in country villages, learned there the country boy's reverential theory of "the squire," and kept it. They painted the squire and the squire's lady as centres of the movements of the universe, to the end of their lives. But Turner perceived the younger squire in other aspects about his lane, occurring prominently in its night scenery, as a dark figure, or one of two, against the moonlight. He saw also the working of city commerce, from endless warehouse, towering over Thames, to the back shop in the lane, with its stale herrings—highly interesting these last; one of his father's best friends, whom he often afterward visited affectionately at Bristol, being a fishmonger and glue-boiler; which gives us a friendly turn of mind toward herring-fishing, whaling, Calais poissardes, and many other of our choicest subjects in after-life; all this being connected with that mysterious forest below London Bridge on one side; and, on the other, with these masses of human power and national wealth which weigh upon us, at Covent Garden here, with strange compression, and crush us into narrow Hand Court.

"That mysterious forest below London Bridge"—better for the boy than wood of pine, grove of myrtle. How he must have tormented the watermen, beseeching them to let him crouch anywhere in the bows, quiet as a log, so only that he might get floated down there among the ships, and round and round the ships, and with the ships, and by the ships, and under the ships, staring, and clambering;—these the only quite beautiful things he can see in all the world, except the sky; but these, when the sun is on their sails, filling or falling, endlessly disordered by sway of tide and stress of anchorage, beautiful unspeakably; which ships also are inhabited by glorious creatures—red-faced sailors, with pipes, appearing over the gunwales, true knights, over their castle parapets—the most angelic beings in the whole compass of London world. And Trafalgar happening long before we can draw ships, we, nevertheless, coax all current stories out of the wounded sailors, do our best at present to show Nelson's funeral streaming up the Thames; and vow that

Trafalgar shall have its tribute of memory some day.
Which, accordingly, is accomplished—once, with all our
might, for its death; twice, with all our might, for its
victory; thrice, in pensive farewell to the old *Téméraire,*
and with it, to that order of things.

Now this fond companying with sailors must have divided his time, it appears to me, pretty equally between
Covent Garden and Wapping (allowing for incidental excursions to Chelsea on one side, and Greenwich on the
other), which time he would spend pleasantly, but not
magnificently, being limited in pocket-money, and leading a kind of "Poor Jack" life on the river.

In some respects, no life could be better for a lad.
But it was not calculated to make his ear fine to the nice-
ties of language, nor form his moralities on an entirely
regular standard. Picking up his first scraps of vigorous
English chiefly at Deptford and in the markets, and his
first ideas of female tenderness and beauty among nymphs
of the barge and the barrow,—another boy might, perhaps, have become what people usually term "vulgar."
But the original make and frame of Turner's mind being
not vulgar, but as nearly as possible a combination of the
minds of Keats and Dante, joining capricious wayward-
ness, and intense openness to every fine pleasure of sense,
and hot defiance of formal precedent, with a quite infinite
tenderness, generosity, and desire of justice and truth—
this kind of mind did not become vulgar, but very toler-
ant of vulgarity, even fond of it in some forms; and on
the outside, visibly infected by it, deeply enough; the
curious result, in its combination of elements, being to
most people wholly incomprehensible. It was as if a
cable had been woven of blood-crimson silk, and then
tarred on the outside. People handled it, and the tar
came off on their hands; red gleams were seen through
the black underneath, at the places where it had been
strained. Was it ochre?—said the world—or red lead?

Schooled thus in manners, literature, and general
moral principles at Chelsea and Wapping, we have finally
to inquire concerning the most important point of all.
We have seen the principal differences between this boy
and Giorgione, as respects sight of the beautiful, understanding of poverty, of commerce, and of order of battle;

then follows another cause of difference in our training
—not slight,—the aspect of religion, namely, in the neighborhood of Covent Garden. I say the aspect; for that
was all the lad could judge by. Disposed, for the most
part, to learn chiefly by his eyes, in this special matter
he finds there is really no other way of learning. His
father had taught him "to lay one penny upon another."
Of mother's teaching, we hear of none; of parish pastoral
teaching, the reader may guess how much.

I chose Giorgione rather than Veronese to help me in
carrying out this parallel; because I do not find in
Giorgione's work any of the early Venetian monarchist
element. He seems to me to have belonged more to an
abstract contemplative school. I may be wrong in this;
it is no matter;—suppose it were so, and that he came
down to Venice somewhat recusant, or insentient, concerning the usual priestly doctrines of his day, how would
the Venetian religion, from an outer intellectual standing-point, have *looked* to him?

He would have seen it to be a religion indisputably
powerful in human affairs; often very harmfully so;
sometimes devouring widows' houses, and consuming the
strongest and fairest from among the young: freezing
into merciless bigotry the policy of the old: also, on the
other hand, animating national courage, and raising
souls, otherwise sordid, into heroism: on the whole, always a real and great power; served with daily sacrifice
of gold, time, and thought; putting forth its claims, if
hypocritically, at least in bold hypocrisy, not waiving
any atom of them in doubt or fear; and, assuredly, in
large measure, sincere, believing in itself, and believed:
a goodly system, moreover, in aspect; gorgeous, harmonious, mysterious;—a thing which had either to be obeyed
or combated, but could not be scorned. A religion towering over all the city—many-buttressed—luminous in marble stateliness, as the dome of our Lady of Safety shines
over the sea; many-voiced, also, giving, over all the eastern seas, to the sentinel his watch-word, to the soldier his
war-cry; and, on the lips of all who died for Venice, shaping the whisper of death.

I suppose the boy Turner to have regarded the religion

of his city also from an external intellectual standing-point.

What did he see in Maiden Lane?

Let not the reader be offended with me: I am willing to let him describe, at his own pleasure, what Turner saw there; but to me, it seems to have been this. A religion maintained occasionally, even the whole length of the lane, at point of constable's staff; but, at other times, placed under the custody of the beadle, within certain black and unstately iron railings of St. Paul's, Covent Garden. Among the wheelbarrows and over the vegetables, no perceptible dominance of religion; in the narrow, disquieted streets, none; in the tongues, deeds, daily ways of Maiden Lane, little. Some honesty, indeed, and English industry, and kindness of heart, and general idea of justice; but faith, of any national kind, shut up from one Sunday to the next, not artistically beautiful even in those Sabbatical exhibitions; its paraphernalia being chiefly of high pews, heavy elocution, and cold grimness of behavior.

What chiaroscuro belongs to it—(dependent mostly on candlelight),—we will, however, draw, considerately; no goodliness of escutcheon, nor other respectability being omitted, and the best of their results confessed, a meek old woman and a child being let into a pew, for whom the reading by candlelight will be beneficial.

For the rest, this religion seems to him discreditable —discredited—not believing in itself: putting forth its authority in a cowardly way, watching how far it might be tolerated, continually shrinking, disclaiming, fencing, finessing; divided against itself, not by stormy rents, but by thin fissures, and splittings of plaster from the walls. Not to be either obeyed, or combated, by an ignorant, yet clear-sighted youth! only to be scorned. And scorned not one whit the less, though also the dome dedicated to *it* looms high over distant winding of the Thames; as St. Mark's campanile rose, for goodly landmark, over mirage of lagoon. For St. Mark ruled over life; the Saint of London over death; St. Mark over St. Mark's Place, but St. Paul over St. Paul's Churchyard.

Under these influences pass away the first reflective hours of life, with such conclusion as they can reach. In consequence of a fit of illness, he was taken—I cannot ascertain in what year—to live with an aunt, at Brentford; and here, I believe, received some schooling, which he seems to have snatched vigorously; getting knowledge, at least by translation, of the more picturesque classical authors, which he turned presently to use, as we shall see. Hence also, walks about Putney and Twickenham in the summer time acquainted him with the look of English meadow-ground in its restricted states of paddock and park; and with some round-headed appearances of trees, and stately entrances to houses of mark: the avenue at Bushy, and the iron gates and carved pillars of Hampton, impressing him apparently with great awe and admiration; so that in after-life his little country house is, —of all places in the world,—at Twickenham! Of swans and reedy shores he now learns the soft motion and the green mystery, in a way not to be forgotten.

And at last fortune wills that the lad's true life shall begin; and one summer's evening, after various wonderful stage-coach experiences on the north road, which gave him a love of stage-coaches ever after, he finds himself sitting alone among the Yorkshire hills. For the first time, the silence of Nature round him, her freedom sealed to him, her glory opened to him. Peace at last; no roll of cart-wheel, nor mutter of sullen voices in the back shop; but curlew-cry in space of heaven, and welling of bell-toned streamlet by its shadowy rock. Freedom at last. Dead-wall, dark railing, fenced field, gated garden, all passed away like the dream of a prisoner; and behold, far as foot or eye can race or range, the moor, and cloud. Loveliness at last. It is here then, among these deserted vales! Not among men. Those pale, poverty-struck, or cruel faces;—that multitudinous, marred humanity;—are not the only things that God has made. Here is something He has made which no one has marred. Pride of purple rocks, and river pools of blue, and tender wilderness of glittering trees, and misty lights of evening on immeasurable hills.

Beauty, and freedom, and peace; and yet another teacher, graver than these. Sound preaching at last here, in Kirkstall crypt, concerning fate and life. Here, where the dark pool reflects the chancel pillars, and the cattle lie in unhindered rest, the soft sunshine on their dappled bodies, instead of priests' vestments; their white furry hair ruffled a little, fitfully, by the evening wind deep-scented from the meadow thyme.

Consider deeply the import to him of this, his first sight of ruin, and compare it with the effect of the architecture that was around Giorgione. There were indeed aged buildings, at Venice, in his time, but none in decay. All ruin was removed, and its place filled as quickly as in our London; but filled always by architecture loftier and more wonderful than that whose place it took, the boy himself happy to work upon the walls of it; so that the idea of the passing away of the strength of men and beauty of their works never could occur to him sternly. Brighter and brighter the cities of Italy had been rising and broadening on hill and plain, for three hundred years. He saw only strength and immortality, could not but paint both; conceived the form of man as deathless, calm with power, and fiery with life.

Turner saw the exact reverse of this. In the present work of men, meanness, aimlessness, unsightliness: thin-walled, lath-divided, narrow-garreted houses of clay; booths of a darksome Vanity Fair, busily base.

But on Whitby Hill, and by Bolton Brook, remained traces of other handiwork. Men who could build had been there; and who also had wrought, not merely for their own days. But to what purpose? Strong faith, and steady hands, and patient souls—can this, then, be all you have left? this the sum of your doing on the earth;—a nest whence the night-owl may whimper to the brook, and a ribbed skeleton of consumed arches, looming above the bleak banks of mist, from its cliff to the sea?

As the strength of men to Giorgione, to Turner their weakness and vileness, were alone visible. They themselves, unworthy or ephemeral; their work, despicable, or decayed. In the Venetian's eyes, all beauty depended on man's presence and pride; in Turner's, on the solitude he had left, and the humiliation he had suffered.

And thus the fate and issue of all his work were determined at once. He must be a painter of the strength of nature, there was no beauty elsewhere than in that; he must paint also the labor and sorrow and passing

away of men: this was the great human truth visible to
him.

Their labor, their sorrow, and their death. Mark the
three. Labor; by sea and land, in field and city, at forge
and furnace, helm and plough. No pastoral indolence nor
classic pride shall stand between him and the troubling of
the world; still less between him and the toil of his country,—blind, tormented, unwearied, marvellous England.

Also their Sorrow; Ruin of all their glorious work,
passing away of their thoughts and their honor, mirage
of pleasure, FALLACY OF HOPE; gathering of weed on
temple step; gaining of wave on deserted strand; weeping
of the mother for the children, desolate by her breathless
first-born in the streets of the city, desolate by her last
sons slain, among the beasts of the field.

And their Death. That old Greek question again;—
yet unanswered. The unconquerable spectre still flitting
among the forest trees at twilight; rising ribbed out of
the sea-sand;—white, a strange Aphrodite,—out of the
sea-foam; stretching its gray, cloven wings among the
clouds; turning the light of their sunsets into blood.
This has to be looked upon, and in a more terrible shape
than ever Salvator or Dürer saw it. The wreck of one
guilty country does not infer the ruin of all countries,
and need not cause general terror respecting the laws of
the universe. Neither did the orderly and narrow succession of domestic joy and sorrow in a small German
community bring the question in its breadth, or in any
unresolvable shape, before the mind of Dürer. But the
English death—the European death of the nineteenth
century—was of another range and power; more terrible
a thousand-fold in its merely physical grasp and grief;
more terrible, incalculably, in its mystery and shame.
What were the robber's casual pang, or the range of the
flying skirmish, compared to the work of the axe, and the
sword, and the famine, which was done during this man's
youth on all the hills and plains of the Christian earth,
from Moscow to Gibraltar? He was eighteen years old
when Napoleon came down on Arcola. Look on the map
of Europe and count the blood-stains on it, between Arcola and Waterloo.

Not alone those blood-stains on the Alpine snow, and

the blue of the Lombard plain. The English death was before his eyes also. No decent, calculable, consoled dying; no passing to rest like that of the aged burghers of Nuremberg town. No gentle processions to churchyards among the fields, the bronze crests bossed deep on the memorial tablets, and the skylark singing above them from among the corn. But the life trampled out in the slime of the street, crushed to dust amidst the roaring of the wheel, tossed countlessly away into howling winter wind along five hundred leagues of rock-fanged shore. Or, worst of all, rotted down to forgotten graves through years of ignorant patience, and vain seeking for help from man, for hope in God—infirm, imperfect yearning, as of motherless infants starving at the dawn; oppressed royalties of captive thought, vague ague-fits of bleak, amazed despair.

A goodly landscape this, for the lad to paint, and under a goodly light. Wide enough the light was, and clear; no more Salvator's lurid chasm on jagged horizon, nor Dürer's spotted rest of sunny gleam on hedgerow and field; but light over all the world. Full shone now its awful globe, one pallid charnel-house,—a ball strewn bright with human ashes, glaring in poised sway beneath the sun, all blinding-white with death from pole to pole, —death, not of myriads of poor bodies only, but of will, and mercy, and conscience; death, not once inflicted on the flesh, but daily fastening on the spirit; death, not silent or patient, waiting his appointed hour, but voiceful, venomous; death with the taunting word, and burning grasp, and infixed sting.

"Put ye in the sickle, for the harvest is ripe." The word is spoken in our ears continually to other reapers than the angels,—to the busy skeletons that never tire for stooping. When the measure of iniquity is full, and it seems that another day might bring repentance and redemption,—"Put ye in the sickle." When the young life has been wasted all away, and the eyes are just opening upon the tracks of ruin, and faint resolution rising in the heart for nobler things,—"Put ye in the sickle." When the roughest blows of fortune have been borne long and bravely, and the hand is just stretched to grasp its goal,—"Put ye in the sickle." And when there are but a few in the midst of a nation, to save it, or to teach, or to cherish; and all its life is bound up in those few golden ears,—"Put ye in the sickle, pale reapers, and pour hemlock for your feast of harvest home."

This was the sight which opened on the young eyes, this the watchword sounding within the heart of Turner in his youth.

So taught, and prepared for his life's labor, sat the boy at last alone among his fair English hills; and began to paint, with cautious toil, the rocks, and fields, and trickling brooks, and soft white clouds of heaven.

THE THRONE

[*Stones of Venice,* Vol. II, Ch. 1.]

IN the olden days of travelling, now to return no more, in which distance could not be vanquished without toil, but in which that toil was rewarded, partly by the power of deliberate survey of the countries through which the journey lay, and partly by the happiness of the evening hours, when from the top of the last hill he had surmounted, the traveller beheld the quiet village where he was to rest, scattered among the meadows beside its valley stream; or, from the long hoped for turn in the dusty perspective of the causeway, saw, for the first time, the towers of some famed city, faint in the rays of sunset—hours of peaceful and thoughtful pleasure, for which the rush of the arrival in the railway station is perhaps not always, or to all men, an equivalent,—in those days, I say, when there was something more to be anticipated and remembered in the first aspect of each successive halting-place, than a new arrangement of glass roofing and iron girder, there were few moments of which the recollection was more fondly cherished by the traveller, than that which, as I endeavored to describe in the close of the last chapter, brought him within sight of Venice, as his gondola shot into the open lagoon from the canal of Mestre. Not but that the aspect of the city itself was generally the source of some slight disappointment, for, seen in this direction, its buildings are far less characteristic than those of the other great towns of Italy; but this inferiority was partly disguised by distance, and more than atoned for by the strange rising of its walls and towers out of the midst, as it seemed, of the deep sea, for it was impossible that the mind or the eye could at once comprehend the shallowness of the vast sheet of water which stretched away in leagues of rippling lustre to the north and south, or trace the narrow line of islets bounding it to the east. The salt breeze, the white moaning sea-birds, the masses of black weed separating and disappearing gradually, in knots of heaving shoal, under the advance of the steady tide, all proclaimed it to be indeed the ocean on whose bosom the great city rested so calmly; not such blue, soft, lake-like ocean as bathes the Neapolitan promontories, or sleeps beneath the marble rocks of Genoa, but a sea with the bleak power of our own northern waves, yet subdued into a strange spacious rest, and changed from its angry pallor into a field of burnished gold, as the sun declined behind the belfry tower of the lonely island church, fitly named "St. George of the Seaweed." As the boat drew nearer to the city, the coast which the traveller had just left sank behind him into one long, low, sad-colored line, tufted irregularly with brushwood and willows: but, at what seemed its northern extremity, the hills of Arqua rose in a dark cluster of purple pyramids, balanced on the bright mirage of the lagoon; two or three smooth surges of inferior hill extended themselves about their roots, and beyond these, beginning with the craggy peaks above Vicenza, the chain of the Alps girded the whole horizon to the north—a wall of jagged blue, here and there showing through its clefts a wilderness of misty precipices, fading far back into the recesses of Cadore, and itself rising and breaking away eastward, where the sun struck opposite upon its snow, into mighty fragments of peaked light, standing up behind the barred clouds of evening, one after another, countless, the crown of the Adrian Sea, until the eye turned back from pursuing them, to rest upon the nearer burning of the campaniles of Murano, and on the great city, where it magnified itself along the waves, as the quick silent pacing of the gondola drew nearer and nearer. And at last, when its walls were reached, and the outmost of its untrodden streets was entered, not through towered

gate or guarded rampart, but as a deep inlet between two
rocks of coral in the Indian Sea; when first upon the
traveller's sight opened the long ranges of columned palaces,—each with its black boat moored at the portal,—
each with its image cast down, beneath its feet, upon that
green pavement which every breeze broke into new fan-
tasies of rich tessellation; when first, at the extremity of
the bright vista, the shadowy Rialto threw its colossal
curve slowly forth from behind the palace of the Camer-
lenghi; that strange curve, so delicate, so adamantine,
strong as a mountain cavern, graceful as a bow just bent;
when first, before its moonlike circumference was all
risen, the gondolier's cry, "Ah! Stalì," struck sharp upon
the ear, and the prow turned aside under the mighty
cornices that half met over the narrow canal, where the
plash of the water followed close and loud, ringing along
the marble by the boat's side; and when at last that boat
darted forth upon the breadth of silver sea, across which
the front of the Ducal Palace, flushed with its sanguine
veins, looks to the snowy dome of Our Lady of Salvation,
it was no marvel that the mind should be so deeply entranced by the visionary charm of a scene so beautiful
and so strange, as to forget the darker truths of its history and its being. Well might it seem that such a city
had owed her existence rather to the rod of the enchanter,
than the fear of the fugitive; that the waters which en-
circled her had been chosen for the mirror of her state,
rather than the shelter of her nakedness; and that all
which in nature was wild or merciless,—Time and Decay,
as well as the waves and tempests,—had been won to adorn
her instead of to destroy, and might still spare, for ages
to come, that beauty which seemed to have fixed for its
throne the sands of the hour-glass as well as of the sea.

And although the last few eventful years, fraught with
change to the face of the whole earth, have been more
fatal in their influence on Venice than the five hundred
that preceded them; though the noble landscape of approach to her can now be seen no more, or seen only by
a glance, as the engine slackens its rushing on the iron
line; and though many of her palaces are forever de-
faced, and many in desecrated ruins, there is still so
much of magic in her aspect, that the hurried traveller,

who must leave her before the wonder of that first aspect has been worn away, may still be led to forget the humility of her origin, and to shut his eyes to the depth of her desolation. They, at least, are little to be envied, in whose hearts the great charities of the imagination lie dead, and for whom the fancy has no power to repress the importunity of painful impressions, or to raise what is ignoble, and disguise what is discordant, in a scene so rich in its remembrances, so surpassing in its beauty. But for this work of the imagination there must be no permission during the task which is before us. The impotent feelings of romance, so singularly characteristic of this century, may indeed gild, but never save, the remains of those mightier ages to which they are attached like climbing flowers; and they must be torn away from the magnificent fragments, if we would see them as they stood in their own strength. Those feelings, always as fruitless as they are fond, are in Venice not only incapable of protecting, but even of discerning, the objects to which they ought to have been attached. The Venice of modern fiction and drama is a thing of yesterday, a mere efflorescence of decay, a stage dream which the first ray of daylight must dissipate into dust. No prisoner, whose name is worth remembering, or whose sorrow deserved sympathy, ever crossed that "Bridge of Sighs," which is the centre of the Byronic ideal of Venice; no great merchant of Venice ever saw that Rialto under which the traveller now passes with breathless interest: the statue which Byron makes Faliero address as of one of his great ancestors was erected to a soldier of fortune a hundred and fifty years after Faliero's death; and the most conspicuous parts of the city have been so entirely altered in the course of the last three centuries, that if Henry Dandolo or Francis Foscari could be summoned from their tombs, and stood each on the deck of his galley at the entrance of the Grand Canal, that renowned entrance, the painter's favorite subject, the novelist's favorite scene, where the water first narrows by the steps of the Church of La Salute,—the mighty Doges would not know in what part of the world they stood, would literally not recognize one stone of the great city, for whose sake, and by whose ingratitude, their gray hairs had been brought down with bitterness to the grave.

The remains of *their* Venice lie hidden behind the cumbrous masses which were the delight of the nation in its dotage; hidden in many a grass-grown court, and silent pathway, and lightless canal, where the slow waves have sapped their foundations for five hundred years, and must soon prevail over them forever. It must be our task to glean and gather them forth, and restore out of them some faint image of the lost city; more gorgeous a thousand-fold than that which now exists, yet not created in the day-dream of the prince, nor by the ostentation of the noble, but built by iron hands and patient hearts, contending against the adversity of nature and the fury of man, so that its wonderfulness cannot be grasped by the indolence of imagination, but only after frank inquiry into the true nature of that wild and solitary scene, whose restless tides and trembling sands did indeed shelter the birth of the city, but long denied her dominion.

When the eye falls casually on a map of Europe, there is no feature by which it is more likely to be arrested than the strange sweeping loop formed by the junction of the Alps and Apennines, and enclosing the great basin of Lombardy. This return of the mountain chain upon itself causes a vast difference in the character of the distribution of its débris on its opposite sides. The rock fragments and sediment which the torrents on the other side of the Alps bear into the plains are distributed over a vast extent of country, and, though here and there lodged in beds of enormous thickness, soon permit the firm substrata to appear from underneath them; but all the torrents which descend from the southern side of the High Alps, and from the northern slope of the Apennines, meet concentrically in the recess or mountain bay which the two ridges enclose; every fragment which thunder breaks out of their battlements, and every grain of dust which the summer rain washes from their pastures, is at last laid at rest in the blue sweep of the Lombardic plain; and that plain must have risen within its rocky barriers as a cup fills with wine, but for two contrary influences which continually depress, or disperse from its surface, the accumulation of the ruins of ages.

I will not tax the reader's faith in modern science by insisting on the singular depression of the surface of Lombardy, which appears for many centuries to have taken place steadily and continually; the main fact with which we have to do is the gradual transport, by the Po and its great collateral rivers, of vast masses of the finer sediment to the sea. The character of the Lombardic plains is most strikingly expressed by the ancient walls of its cities, composed for the most part of large rounded Alpine pebbles alternating with narrow courses of brick; and was curiously illustrated in 1848, by the ramparts of these same pebbles thrown up four or five feet high round every field, to check the Austrian cavalry in the battle under the walls of Verona. The finer dust among which these pebbles are dispersed is taken up by the rivers, fed into continual strength by the Alpine snow, so that, however pure their waters may be when they issue from the lakes at the foot of the great chain, they become of the color and opacity of clay before they reach the Adriatic; the sediment which they bear is at once thrown down as they enter the sea, forming a vast belt of low land along the eastern coast of Italy. The powerful stream of the Po of course builds forward the fastest; on each side of it, north and south, there is a tract of marsh, fed by more feeble streams, and less liable to rapid change than the delta of the central river. In one of these tracts is built RAVENNA, and in the other VENICE.

What circumstances directed the peculiar arrangement of this great belt of sediment in the earliest times, it is not here the place to inquire. It is enough for us to know that from the mouths of the Adige to those of the Piave there stretches, at a variable distance of from three to five miles from the actual shore, a bank of sand, divided into long islands by narrow channels of sea. The space between this bank and the true shore consists of the sedimentary deposits from these and other rivers, a great plain of calcareous mud, covered, in the neighborhood of Venice, by the sea at high water, to the depth in most places of a foot or a foot and a half, and nearly everywhere exposed at low tide, but divided by an intricate network of narrow and winding channels, from which the sea never retires. In some places, according to the run of the currents, the land has risen into marshy islets, consolidated, some by art, and some by time, into ground

firm enough to be built upon, or fruitful enough to be
cultivated: in others, on the contrary, it has not reached
the sea level; so that, at the average low water, shallow
lakelets glitter among its irregularly exposed fields of sea-
weed. In the midst of the largest of these, increased in
importance by the confluence of several large river channels toward one of the openings in the sea bank, the city
of Venice itself is built, on a crowded cluster of islands;
the various plots of higher ground which appear to the
north and south of this central cluster, have at different
periods been also thickly inhabited, and now bear, according to their size, the remains of cities, villages, or isolated
convents and churches, scattered among spaces of open
ground, partly waste and encumbered by ruins, partly
under cultivation for the supply of the metropolis.

The average rise and fall of the tide is about three
feet (varying considerably with the seasons); but this
fall, on so flat a shore, is enough to cause continual movement in the waters, and in the main canals to produce a
reflux which frequently runs like a mill stream. At high
water no land is visible for many miles to the north or
south of Venice, except in the form of small islands
crowned with towers or gleaming with villages: there is
a channel, some three miles wide, between the city and
the mainland, and some mile and a half wide between it
and the sandy breakwater called the Lido, which divides
the lagoon from the Adriatic, but which is so low as
hardly to disturb the impression of the city's having been
built in the midst of the ocean, although the secret of its
true position is partly, yet not painfully, betrayed by the
clusters of piles set to mark the deep-water channels,
which undulate far away in spotty chains like the studded
backs of huge sea-snakes, and by the quick glittering of
the crisped and crowded waves that flicker and dance before the strong winds upon the uplifted level of the shallow sea. But the scene is widely different at low tide. A
fall of eighteen or twenty inches is enough to show ground
over the greater part of the lagoon; and at the complete
ebb the city is seen standing in the midst of a dark plain
of sea-weed, of gloomy green, except only where the larger
branches of the Brenta and its associated streams con-
verge toward the port of the Lido. Through this salt and

sombre plain the gondola and the fishing-boat advance by tortuous channels, seldom more than four or five feet deep, and often so choked with slime that the heavier keels furrow the bottom till their crossing tracks are seen through the clear sea water like the ruts upon a wintry road, and the oar leaves blue gashes upon the ground at every stroke, or is entangled among the thick weed that fringes the banks with the weight of its sullen waves, leaning to and fro upon the uncertain sway of the exhausted tide. The scene is often profoundly oppressive, even at this day, when every plot of higher ground bears some fragment of fair building: but, in order to know what it was once, let the traveller follow in his boat at evening the windings of some unfrequented channel far into the midst of the melancholy plain; let him remove, in his imagination, the brightness of the great city that still extends itself in the distance, and the walls and towers from the islands that are near; and so wait, until the bright investiture and sweet warmth of the sunset are withdrawn from the waters, and the black desert of their shore lies in its nakedness beneath the night, pathless, comfortless, infirm, lost in dark languor and fearful silence, except where the salt runlets plash into the tideless pools, or the sea-birds flit from their margins with a questioning cry; and he will be enabled to enter in some sort into the horror of heart with which this solitude was anciently chosen by man for his habitation. They little thought, who first drove the stakes into the sand, and strewed the ocean reeds for their rest, that their children were to be the princes of that ocean, and their palaces its pride; and yet, in the natural laws that rule that sorrowful wilderness, let it be remembered what strange preparation had been made for the things which no human imagination could have foretold, and how the whole existence and fortune of the Venetian nation were anticipated or compelled, by the setting of those bars and doors to the rivers and the sea. Had deeper currents divided their islands, hostile navies would again and again have reduced the rising city into servitude; had stronger surges beaten their shores, all the richness and refinement of the Venetian architecture must have been exchanged for the walls and bulwarks of an ordinary seaport. Had there

been no tide, as in other parts of the Mediterranean, the
narrow canals of the city would have become noisome,
and the marsh in which it was built pestiferous. Had
the tide been only a foot or eighteen inches higher in its
rise, the water-access to the doors of the palaces would
have been impossible: even as it is, there is sometimes a
little difficulty, at the ebb, in landing without setting foot
upon the lower and slippery steps; and the highest tides
sometimes enter the courtyards, and overflow the entrance
halls. Eighteen inches more of difference between the
level of the flood and ebb would have rendered the door-
steps of every palace, at low water, a treacherous mass of
weeds and limpets, and the entire system of water-carriage
for the higher classes, in their easy and daily intercourse,
must have been done away with. The streets of the city
would have been widened, its network of canals filled up,
and all the peculiar character of the place and the people
destroyed.

The reader may perhaps have felt some pain in the
contrast between this faithful view of the site of the
Venetian Throne and the romantic conception of it which
we ordinarily form: but this pain, if he have felt it, ought
to be more than counterbalanced by the value of the instance thus afforded to us at once of the inscrutableness
and the wisdom of the ways of God. If, two thousand
years ago, we had been permitted to watch the slow settling of the slime of those turbid rivers into the polluted
sea, and the gaining upon its deep and fresh waters of
the lifeless, impassable, unvoyageable plain, how little
could we have understood the purpose with which those
islands were shaped out of the void, and the torpid waters
enclosed with their desolate walls of sand! How little
could we have known, any more than of what now seems
to us most distressful, dark, and objectless, the glorious
aim which was then in the mind of Him in whose hand
are all the corners of the earth! how little imagined that
in the laws which were stretching forth the gloomy margins of those fruitless banks, and feeding the bitter grass
among their shallows, there was indeed a preparation, and
the only preparation possible, for the founding of a city
which was to be set like a golden clasp on the girdle of
the earth, to write her history on the white scrolls of the

sea-surges, and to word it in their thunder, and to gather and give forth, in world-wide pulsation, the glory of the West and of the East, from the burning heart of her Fortitude and Splendor.

ST. MARK'S

[Stones of Venice, Vol. II, Ch. 4.]

"AND so Barnabas took Mark, and sailed unto Cyprus." If as the shores of Asia lessened upon his sight, the spirit of prophecy had entered into the heart of the weak disciple who had turned back when his hand was on the plough, and who had been judged, by the chiefest of Christ's captains, unworthy thenceforward to go forth with him to the work, how wonderful would he have thought it, that by the lion symbol in future ages he was to be represented among men! how woful, that the war-cry of his name should so often reanimate the rage of the soldier, on those very plains where he himself had failed in the courage of the Christian, and so often dye with fruitless blood that very Cypriot Sea, over whose waves, in repentance and shame, he was following the Son of Consolation!

That the Venetians possessed themselves of his body in the ninth century, there appears no sufficient reason to doubt, nor that it was principally in consequence of their having done so, that they chose him for their patron saint. There exists, however, a tradition that before he went into Egypt he had founded the church at Aquileia, and was thus in some sort the first bishop of the Venetian isles and people. I believe that this tradition stands on nearly as good grounds as that of St. Peter having been the first bishop of Rome; but, as usual, it is enriched by various later additions and embellishments, much resembling the stories told respecting the church of Murano. Thus we find it recorded by the Santo Padre who compiled the *Vite de' Santi spettanti alle Chiese di Venezia,* that "St. Mark having seen the people of Aquileia well grounded in religion, and being called to Rome by St. Peter, before setting off took with him the holy bishop Hermagoras, and went in a small boat to the marshes of Venice. There were at that period some houses built upon a certain high bank called Rialto, and the boat being driven by the wind was anchored in a marshy place, when St. Mark, snatched into ecstacy, heard the voice of an angel saying to him: 'Peace be to thee, Mark; here shall thy body rest.'" The angel goes on to foretell the building of "una stupenda, ne più veduta Città"; but the fable is hardly ingenious enough to deserve farther relation.

But whether St. Mark was first bishop of Aquileia or not, St. Theodore was the first patron of the city; nor can he yet be considered as having entirely abdicated his early right, as his statue, standing on a crocodile, still companions the winged lion on the opposing pillar of the piazzetta. A church erected to this Saint is said to have occupied, before the ninth century, the site of St. Mark's; and the traveller, dazzled by the brilliancy of the great square, ought not to leave it without endeavoring to imagine its aspect in that early time, when it was a green field, cloister-like and quiet, divided by a small canal, with a line of trees on each side; and extending between the two churches of St. Theodore and St. Gemanium, as the little piazza of Torcello lies between its "palazzo" and cathedral.

But in the year 813, when the seat of government was finally removed to the Rialto, a Ducal Palace, built on the spot where the present one stands, with a Ducal Chapel beside it, gave a very different character to the Square of St. Mark; and fifteen years later, the acquisition of the body of the Saint, and its deposition in the Ducal Chapel, perhaps not yet completed, occasioned the investiture of that Chapel with all possible splendor. St. Theodore was deposed from his patronship, and his church destroyed, to make room for the aggrandizement of the one attached to the Ducal Palace, and thenceforward known as "St. Mark's."

This first church was however destroyed by fire, when the Ducal Palace was burned in the revolt against Candiano, in 976. It was partly rebuilt by his successor, Pietro Orseolo, on a larger scale; and, with the assistance of Byzantine architects, the fabric was carried on under successive Doges for nearly a hundred years; the main building being completed in 1071, but its incrustation with marble not till considerably later. It was consecrated on the 8th of October, 1085, according to Sansovino and the author of the *Chiesa Ducale di S. Marco*, in 1094, according to Lazari, but certainly between 1084 and 1096, those years being the limits of the reign of Vital Falier; I incline to the supposition that it was soon after his accession to the throne in 1085, though Sansovino writes, by mistake, Ordelafo instead of Vital Falier. But, at all events, before the close of the eleventh century the great consecration of the church took place. It was again injured by fire in 1106, but repaired; and from that time to the fall of Venice there was probably no Doge who did not in some slight degree embellish or alter the fabric, so that few parts of it can be pronounced boldly to be of any given date. Two periods of interference are, however, notable above the rest: the first, that in which the Gothic school had superseded the Byzantine toward the close of the fourteenth century, when the pinnacles, upper archivolts, and window traceries were added to the exterior, and the great screen, with various chapels and tabernacle-work, to the interior; the second, when the Renaissance school superseded the Gothic, and the pupils of Titian and Tintoret substituted, over one-half of the church, their own compositions for the Greek mosaics with which it was originally decorated; happily, though with no good-will, having left enough to enable us to imagine and lament what they destroyed. Of this irreparable loss we shall have more to say hereafter; meantime, I wish only to fix in the reader's mind the succession of periods of alterations as firmly and simply as possible.

We have seen that the main body of the church may be broadly stated to be of the eleventh century, the Gothic additions of the fourteenth, and the restored mosaics of the seventeenth. There is no difficulty in distinguishing at a glance the Gothic portions from the Byzantine; but there is considerable difficulty in ascertaining how long, during the course of the twelfth and thirteenth centuries, additions were made to the Byzantine church, which cannot be easily distinguished from the work of the eleventh century, being purposely executed in the same manner. Two of the most important pieces of evidence on this point are, a mosaic in the south transept, and another over the northern door of the façade; the first representing the interior, the second the exterior, of the ancient church.

It has just been stated that the existing building was consecrated by the Doge Vital Falier. A peculiar solemnity was given to that act of consecration, in the minds of the Venetian people, by what appears to have been one of the best arranged and most successful impostures ever attempted by the clergy of the Romish church. The body of St. Mark had, without doubt, perished in the conflagration of 976; but the revenues of the church depended too much upon the devotion excited by these relics to permit the confession of their loss. The following is the account given by Corner, and believed to this day by the Venetians, of the pretended miracle by which it was concealed.

"After the repairs undertaken by the Doge Orseolo, the place in which the body of the holy Evangelist rested had been altogether forgotten; so that the Doge Vital Falier was entirely ignorant of the place of the venerable deposit. This was no light affliction, not only to the pious Doge, but to all the citizens and people; so that at last, moved by confidence in the Divine mercy, they determined to implore, with prayer and fasting, the manifestation of so great a treasure, which did not now depend upon any human effort. A general fast being therefore proclaimed, and a solemn procession appointed for the 25th day of June, while the people assembled in the church interceded with God in fervent prayers for the desired boon, they beheld, with as much amazement as joy, a slight shaking in the marbles of a pillar (near the place where the altar of the Cross is now), which, presently falling to the earth, exposed to the view of the rejoicing people the chest of bronze in which the body of the Evangelist was laid."

Of the main facts of this tale there is no doubt. They were embellished afterward, as usual, by many fanciful traditions; as, for instance, that, when the sarcophagus was discovered, St. Mark extended his hand out of it, with a gold ring on one of the fingers, which he permitted a noble of the Dolfin family to remove; and a quaint and delightful story was further invented of this ring, which I shall not repeat here, as it is now as well known as any tale of the Arabian Nights. But the fast and the discovery of the coffin, by whatever means effected, are facts;

and they are recorded in one of the best-preserved mosaics of the south transept, executed very certainly not long after the event had taken place, closely resembling in its treatment that of the Bayeux tapestry, and showing, in a conventional manner, the interior of the church, as it then was, filled by the people, first in prayer, then in thanksgiving, the pillar standing open before them, and the Doge, in the midst of them, distinguished by his crimson bonnet embroidered with gold, but more unmistakably by the inscription "Dux" over his head, as uniformly is the case in the Bayeux tapestry, and most other pictorial works of the period. The church is, of course, rudely represented, and the two upper stories of it reduced to a small scale in order to form a background to the figures; one of those bold pieces of picture history which we in our pride of perspective, and a thousand things besides, never dare attempt. We should have put in a column or two, of the real or perspective size, and subdued it into a vague background: the old workman crushed the church together that he might get it all in, up to the cupolas; and has, therefore, left us some useful notes of its ancient form, though any one who is familiar with the method of drawing employed at the period will not push the evidence too far. The two pulpits are there, however, as they are at this day, and the fringe of mosaic flowerwork which then encompassed the whole church, but which modern restorers have destroyed, all but one fragment still left in the south aisle. There is no attempt to represent the other mosaics on the roof, the scale being too small to admit of their being represented with any success; but some at least of those mosaics had been executed at that period, and their absence in the representation of the entire church is especially to be observed, in order to show that we must not trust to any negative evidence in such works. M. Lazari has rashly concluded that the central archivolt of St. Mark's *must* be posterior to the year 1205, because it does not appear in the representation of the exterior of the church over the northern door; but he justly observes that this mosaic (which is the other piece of evidence we possess respecting the ancient form of the building) cannot itself be earlier than 1205, since it represents the bronze horses which were brought from Constantinople in that year. And this one fact renders it very difficult to speak with confidence respecting the date of any part of the exterior of St. Mark's; for we have above seen that it was consecrated in the eleventh century, and yet here is one of its most important exterior decorations assuredly retouched, if not entirely added, in the thirteenth, although its style would have led us to suppose it had been an original part of the fabric. However, for all our purposes, it will be enough for the reader to remember that the earliest parts of the building belong to the eleventh, twelfth, and first part of the thirteenth century; the Gothic portions to the fourteenth; some of the altars and embellishments to the fifteenth and sixteenth; and the modern portion of the mosaics to the seventeenth.

This, however, I only wish him to recollect in order that I may speak generally of the Byzantine architecture of St. Mark's, without leading him to suppose the whole church to have been built and decorated by Greek artists. Its later portions, with the single exception of the seventeenth century mosaics, have been so dexterously accommodated to the original fabric that the general effect is still that of a Byzantine building; and I shall not, except when it is absolutely necessary, direct attention to the discordant points, or weary the reader with anatomical criticism. Whatever in St. Mark's arrests the eye, or affects the feelings, is either Byzantine, or has been modified by Byzantine influence; and our inquiry into its architectural merits need not therefore be disturbed by the anxieties of antiquarianism, or arrested by the obscurities of chronology.

And now I wish that the reader, before I bring him into St. Mark's Place, would imagine himself for a little time in a quiet English cathedral town, and walk with me to the west front of its cathedral. Let us go together up the more retired street, at the end of which we can see the pinnacles of one of the towers, and then through the low gray gateway, with its battlemented top and small latticed window in the centre, into the inner private-looking road or close, where nothing goes in but the carts of the tradesmen who supply the bishop and the chapter, and where there are little shaven grass-plots, fenced in by neat rails, before old-fashioned groups of somewhat diminutive and excessively trim houses, with little oriel and bay windows jutting out here and there, and deep wooden cornices and eaves painted cream color and white, and small porches to their doors in the shape of cockle-shells, or little, crooked, thick, indescribable wooden gables warped a little on one side; and so forward till we come to larger houses, also old-fashioned, but of red brick, and with garden behind them, and fruit walls, which show here and there, among the nectarines, the vestiges of an old cloister arch or shaft, and looking in front on the cathedral square itself, laid out in rigid divisions of smooth grass and gravel walk, yet not uncheerful, especially on the sunny side, where the canon's children are walking with their nursery maids. And so, taking care not to tread on the grass, we will go along the straight walk to the west front, and there stand for a time, looking up at its deep-pointed porches and the dark places between their pillars where there were statues once, and where the fragments, here and there, of a stately figure are still left, which has in it the likeness of a king, perhaps indeed a king on earth, perhaps a saintly king long ago in heaven; and so higher and higher up to the great mouldering wall of rugged sculpture and confused arcades, shattered, and gray, and grisly with heads of dragons and mocking fiends, worn by the rain and swirling winds into yet unseemlier shape, and colored on their stony scales by the deep russet-orange lichen, melancholy gold; and so, higher still, to the bleak towers, so far above that the eye loses itself among the bosses of their traceries, though they are rude and strong, and only sees like a drift of eddying black points, now closing, now scattering, and now settling suddenly into invisible places among the bosses and flowers, the crowd of restless birds that fill the whole square with that strange clangor of theirs, so harsh and yet so soothing, like the cries of birds on a solitary coast between the cliffs and sea.

Think for a little while of that scene, and the meaning of all its small formalisms, mixed with its serene sublimity. Estimate its secluded, continuous, drowsy felicities, and its evidence of the sense and steady performance of such kind of duties as can be regulated by the cathedral clock; and weigh the influence of those dark towers on all who have passed through the lonely square at their feet for centuries, and on all who have seen them rising far away over the wooded plain, or catching on their square masses the last rays of the sunset, when the city at their feet was indicated only by the mist at the bend of the river. And then let us quickly recollect that we are in Venice, and land at the extremity of the Calla Lunga San Moisè, which may be considered as there answering to the secluded street that led us to our English cathedral gateway.

We find ourselves in a paved alley, some seven feet wide where it is widest, full of people, and resonant with cries of itinerant salesmen,—a shriek in their beginning, and dying away into a kind of brazen ringing, all the worse for its confinement between the high houses of the passage along which we have to make our way. Over head, an inextricable confusion of rugged shutters, and iron balconies and chimney flues, pushed out on brackets to save room, and arched windows with projecting sills of Istrian stone, and gleams of green leaves here and there where a fig-tree branch escapes over a lower wall from some inner cortile, leading the eye up to the narrow stream of blue sky high over all. On each side, a row of shops, as densely set as may be, occupying, in fact, intervals between the square stone shafts, about eight feet high, which carry the first floors: intervals of which one is narrow and serves as a door; the other is, in the more respectable shops, wainscoted to the height of the counter and glazed above, but in those of the poorer tradesmen left open to the ground, and the wares laid on benches and tables in the open air, the light in all cases entering at the front only, and fading away in a few feet from the threshold into a gloom which the eye from without cannot penetrate, but which is generally broken by a ray or two from a feeble lamp at the back of the shop, suspended before a print of the Virgin. The less pious shopkeeper sometimes leaves his lamp unlighted, and is contented with a penny print; the more religious one has his print colored and set in a little shrine with a gilded or figured fringe, with perhaps a faded flower or two on each side, and his lamp burning brilliantly. Here, at the fruiterer's, where the dark-green watermelons are heaped upon the counter like cannon balls, the Madonna has a tabernacle of fresh laurel leaves; but the pewterer next door has let his lamp out, and there is nothing to be seen in his shop but the dull gleam of the studded patterns on the copper pans, hanging from his roof in the darkness. Next comes a "Vendita Frittole e Liquori," where the Virgin, enthroned in a very humble manner beside a tallow candle on a back shelf, presides over certain ambrosial morsels of a nature too ambiguous to be defined or enumerated. But a few steps farther on, at the regular wine-shop of the calle, where we are offered "Vino Nostrani a Soldi 28.32," the Madonna is in great glory, enthroned above ten or a dozen large red casks of three-year-old vintage, and flanked by goodly ranks of bottles of Maraschino, and two crimson lamps; and for the evening, when the gondoliers will come to drink out, under her auspices, the money they have gained during the day, she will have a whole chandelier.

A yard or two farther, we pass the hostelry of the Black Eagle, and glancing as we pass through the square door of marble, deeply moulded, in the outer wall, we see the shadows of its pergola vines resting on an ancient well, with a pointed shield carved on its side; and so presently emerge on the bridge and Campo San Moisè, whence to the entrance into St. Mark's Place, called the Bocca di Piazza (mouth of the square), the Venetian character is nearly destroyed, first by the frightful façade of San Moisè, which we will pause at another time to examine, and then by the modernizing of the shops as they near the piazza, and the mingling with the lower Venetian populace of lounging groups of English and Austrians. We will push fast through them into the shadow of the pillars at the end of the "Bocca di Piazza," and then we forget them all; for between those pillars there opens a great light, and, in the midst of it, as we advance slowly, the vast tower of St. Mark seems to lift itself visibly forth from the level field of checkered stones; and, on each side, the countless arches prolong themselves into ranged symmetry, as if the rugged and irregular houses that pressed together above us in the dark alley had been struck back into sudden obedience and lovely order, and

all their rude casements and broken walls had been transformed into arches charged with goodly sculpture, and
fluted shafts of delicate stone.

And well may they fall back, for beyond those troops
of ordered arches there rises a vision out of the earth,
and all the great square seems to have opened from it in
a kind of awe, that we may see it far away;—a multitude
of pillars and white domes, clustered into a long low
pyramid of colored light; a treasure-heap, it seems, partly
of gold, and partly of opal and mother-of-pearl, hollowed
beneath into five great vaulted porches, ceiled with fair
mosaic, and beset with sculpture of alabaster, clear as
amber and delicate as ivory,—sculpture fantastic and involved, of palm leaves and lilies, and grapes and pome-
granates, and birds clinging and fluttering among the
branches, all twined together into an endless network of
buds and plumes; and, in the midst of it, the solemn
forms of angels, sceptred, and robed to the feet, and leaning to each other across the gates, their figures indistinct
among the gleaming of the golden ground through the
leaves beside them, interrupted and dim, like the morning light as it faded back among the branches of Eden,
when first its gates were angel-guarded long ago. And
round the walls of the porches there are set pillars of
variegated stones, jasper and porphyry, and deep-green
serpentine spotted with flakes of snow, and marbles, that
half refuse and half yield to the sunshine, Cleopatra-like,
"their bluest veins to kiss"—the shadow, as it steals back
from them, revealing line after line of azure undulation,
as a receding tide leaves the waved sand; their capitals
rich with interwoven tracery, rooted knots of herbage, and
drifting leaves of acanthus and vine, and mystical signs,
all beginning and ending in the Cross; and above them,
in the broad archivolts, a continuous chain of language
and of life—angels, and the signs of heaven, and the
labors of men, each in its appointed season upon the
earth; and above these, another range of glittering pinnacles, mixed with white arches edged with scarlet flowers,
—a confusion of delight, amidst which the breasts of the
Greek horses are seen blazing in their breadth of golden
strength, and the St. Mark's lion, lifted on a blue field
covered with stars, until at last, as if in ecstasy, the crests

of the arches break into a marble foam, and toss themselves far into the blue sky in flashes and wreaths of sculptured spray, as if the breakers on the Lido shore had been frost-bound before they fell, and the sea-nymphs had inlaid them with coral and amethyst.

Between that grim cathedral of England and this, what an interval! There is a type of it in the very birds that haunt them; for, instead of the restless crowd, hoarse-voiced and sable-winged, drifting on the bleak upper air, the St. Mark's porches are full of doves, that nestle among the marble foliage, and mingle the soft iridescence of their living plumes, changing at every motion, with the tints, hardly less lovely, that have stood unchanged for seven hundred years.

And what effect has this splendor on those who pass beneath it? You may walk from sunrise to sunset, to and fro, before the gateway of St. Mark's, and you will not see an eye lifted to it, nor a countenance brightened by it. Priest and layman, soldier and civilian, rich and poor, pass by it alike regardlessly. Up to the very recesses of the porches, the meanest tradesmen of the city push their counters; nay, the foundations of its pillars are themselves the seats—not "of them that sell doves" for sacrifice, but of the venders of toys and caricatures. Round the whole square in front of the church there is almost a continuous line of cafés, where the idle Venetians of the middle classes lounge, and read empty journals; in its center the Austrian bands play during the time of vespers, their martial music jarring with the organ notes,—the march drowning the miserere, and the sullen crowd thickening round them,—a crowd, which, if it had its will, would stiletto every soldier that pipes to it. And in the recesses of the porches, all day long, knots of men of the lowest classes, unemployed and listless, lie basking in the sun like lizards; and unregarded children, —every heavy glance of their young eyes full of desperation and stony depravity, and their throats hoarse with cursing,—gamble, and fight, and snarl, and sleep, hour after hour, clashing their bruised centesimi upon the marble ledges of the church porch. And the images of Christ and His angels look down upon it continually.

That we may not enter the church out of the midst of

the horror of this, let us turn aside under the portico which looks across the sea, and passing round within the two massive pillars brought from St. Jean d'Acre, we shall find the gate of the Baptistery; let us enter there. The heavy door closes behind us instantly, and the light and the turbulence of the Piazzetta are together shut out by it.

We are in a low vaulted room; vaulted, not with arches but with small cupolas starred with gold, and checkered with gloomy figures: in the center is a bronze font charged with rich bas-reliefs, a small figure of the Baptist standing above it in a single ray of light that glances across the narrow room, dying as it falls from a window high in the wall, and the first thing that it strikes, and the only thing that it strikes brightly, is a tomb. We hardly know if it be a tomb indeed; for it is like a narrow couch set beside the window, low-roofed and curtained, so that it might seem, but that it is some height above the pavement, to have been drawn toward the window, that the sleeper might be wakened early;—only there are two angels, who have drawn the curtain back, and are looking down upon him. Let us look also, and thank that gentle light that rests upon his forehead forever, and dies away upon his breast.

The face is of a man in middle life, but there are two deep furrows right across the forehead, dividing it like the foundations of a tower: the height of it above is bound by the fillet of the ducal cap. The rest of the features are singularly small and delicate, the lips sharp, perhaps the sharpness of death being added to that of the natural lines; but there is a sweet smile upon them, and a deep serenity upon the whole countenance. The roof of the canopy above has been blue, filled with stars; beneath, in the centre of the tomb on which the figure rests, is a seated figure of the Virgin, and the border of it all around is of flowers and soft leaves, growing rich and deep, as if in a field in summer.

It is the Doge Andrea Dandolo, a man early great among the great of Venice; and early lost. She chose him for her king in his 36th year; he died ten years later, leaving behind him that history to which we owe half of what we know of her former fortunes.

Look around at the room in which he lies. The floor of it is of rich mosaic, encompassed by a low seat of red marble, and its walls are of alabaster, but worn and shattered, and darkly stained with age, almost a ruin,— in places the slabs of marble have fallen away altogether, and the rugged brickwork is seen through the rents, but all beautiful; the ravaging fissures fretting their way among the islands and channelled zones of the alabaster, and the time-stains on its translucent masses darkened into fields of rich golden brown, like the color of seaweed when the sun strikes on it through deep sea. The light fades away into the recess of the chamber toward the altar, and the eye can hardly trace the lines of the bas-relief behind it of the baptism of Christ: but on the vaulting of the roof the figures are distinct, and there are seen upon it two great circles, one surrounded by the "Principalities and powers in heavenly places," of which Milton has expressed the ancient division in the single massy line,

"Thrones, Dominations, Princedoms, Virtues, Powers,"

and around the other, the Apostles; Christ the centre of both: and upon the walls, again and again repeated, the gaunt figure of the Baptist, in every circumstance of his life and death; and the streams of the Jordan running down between their cloven rocks; the axe laid to the root of a fruitless tree that springs up on their shore. "Every tree that bringeth not forth good fruit shall be hewn down, and cast into the fire." Yes, verily: to be baptized with fire, or to be cast therein; it is the choice set before all men. The march-notes still murmur through the grated window, and mingle with the sounding in our ears of the sentence of judgment, which the Old Greek has writ-ten on that Baptistery wall. Venice has made her choice.

He who lies under that stony canopy would have taught her another choice, in his day, if she would have listened to him; but he and his counsels have long been forgotten by her, and the dust lies upon his lips.

Through the heavy door whose bronze network closes the place of his rest, let us enter the church itself. It is lost in still deeper twilight, to which the eye must be ac-

customed for some moments before the form of the building can be traced; and then there opens before us a vast
cave, hewn out into the form of a Cross, and divided into
shadowy aisles by many pillars. Round the domes of its
roof the light enters only through narrow apertures like
large stars; and here and there a ray or two from some
far-away casement wanders into the darkness, and casts
a narrow phosphoric stream upon the waves of marble
that heave and fall in a thousand colors along the floor.
What else there is of light is from torches, or silver lamps,
burning ceaselessly in the recesses of the chapels; the
roof sheeted with gold, and the polished walls covered
with alabaster, give back at every curve and angle some
feeble gleaming to the flames; and the glories round the
heads of the sculptured saints flash out upon us as we
pass them, and sink again into the gloom. Under foot
and over head, a continual succession of crowded imagery,
one picture passing into another, as in a dream; forms
beautiful and terrible mixed together; dragons and serpents, and ravening beasts of prey, and graceful birds that
in the midst of them drink from running fountains and
feed from vases of crystal; the passions and the pleasures
of human life symbolized together, and the mystery of
its redemption; for the mazes of interwoven lines and
changeful pictures lead always at last to the Cross, lifted
and carved in every place and upon every stone; sometimes with the serpent of eternity wrapped round it,
sometimes with doves beneath its arms, and sweet herbage growing forth from its feet; conspicuous most of all
on the great rood that crosses the church before the altar,
raised in bright blazonry against the shadow of the apse.
And although in the recesses of the aisles and chapels,
when the mist of the incense hangs heavily, we may see
continually a figure traced in faint lines upon their marble, a woman standing with her eyes raised to heaven, and
the inscription above her, "Mother of God," she is not
here the presiding deity. It is the Cross that is first seen,
and always, burning in the centre of the temple; and
every dome and hollow of its roof has the figure of Christ
in the utmost height of it, raised in power, or returning
in judgment.

Nor is this interior without effect on the minds of the

people. At every hour of the day there are groups collected before the various shrines, and solitary worshippers scattered through the darker places of the church, evidently in prayer both deep and reverent, and, for the most part, profoundly sorrowful. The devotees at the greater number of the renowned shrines of Romanism may be seen murmuring their appointed prayers with wandering eyes and unengaged gestures; but the step of the stranger does not disturb those who kneel on the pavement of St. Mark's; and hardly a moment passes, from early morning to sunset, in which we may not see some half-veiled figure enter beneath the Arabian porch, cast itself into long abasement on the floor of the temple, and then rising slowly with more confirmed step, and with a passionate kiss and clasp of the arms given to the feet of the crucifix, by which the lamps burn always in the northern aisle, leave the church, as if comforted.

But we must not hastily conclude from this that the nobler characters of the building have at present any influence in fostering a devotional spirit. There is distress enough in Venice to bring many to their knees, without excitement from external imagery; and whatever there may be in the temper of the worship offered in St. Mark's more than can be accounted for by reference to the unhappy circumstances of the city, is assuredly not owing either to the beauty of its architecture or to the impressiveness of the Scripture histories embodied in its mosaics. That it has a peculiar effect, however slight, on the popular mind, may perhaps be safely conjectured from the number of worshippers which it attracts, while the churches of St. Paul and the Frari, larger in size and more central in position, are left comparatively empty. But this effect is altogether to be ascribed to its richer assemblage of those sources of influence which address themselves to the commonest instincts of the human mind, and which, in all ages and countries, have been more or less employed in the support of superstition. Darkness and mystery; confused recesses of building; artificial light employed in small quantity, but maintained with a constancy which seems to give it a kind of sacredness; preciousness of material easily comprehended by the vulgar eye; close air loaded with a sweet and peculiar odor associated only with religious services, solemn music, and tangible idols or images having popular legends attached to them,—these, the stage properties of superstition, which have been from the beginning of the world, and must be to the end of it, employed by all nations, whether openly savage or nominally civilized, to produce a false awe in minds incapable of apprehending the true nature of the Deity, are assembled in St. Mark's to a degree, as far as I know, unexampled in any other European church. The arts of the Magus and the Brahmin are exhausted in the animation of a paralyzed Christianity; and the popular sentiment which these arts excite is to be regarded by us with no more respect than we should have considered ourselves justified in rendering to the devotion of the worshippers at Eleusis, Ellora, or Edfou.

THE LAMP OF MEMORY

[Seven Lamps, Ch. 6.]

AMONG the hours of his life to which the writer looks back with peculiar gratitude, as having been marked by more than ordinary fulness of joy or clearness of teaching, is one passed, now some years ago, near time of sunset, among the broken masses of pine forest which skirt the course of the Ain, above the village of Champagnole, in the Jura. It is a spot which has all the solemnity, with none of the savageness, of the Alps; where there is a sense of a great power beginning to be manifested in the earth, and of a deep and majestic concord in the rise of the long low lines of piny hills; the first utterance of those mighty mountain symphonies, soon to be more loudly lifted and wildly broken along the battlements of the Alps. But their strength is as yet restrained; and the far-reaching ridges of pastoral mountain succeed each other, like the long and sighing swell which moves over quiet waters from some far off stormy sea. And there is a deep tenderness pervading that vast monotony. The destructive forces and the stern expression of the central ranges are alike withdrawn. No frost-ploughed, dust-encumbered paths of ancient glacier fret the soft Jura pastures; no splintered heaps of ruin break the fair ranks

f her forest; no pale, defiled, or furious rivers send their
ude and changeful ways among her rocks. Patiently,
ddy by eddy, the clear green streams wind along their
vell-known beds; and under the dark quietness of the
undisturbed pines, there spring up, year by year, such
ompany of joyful flowers as I know not the like of among
ll the blessings of the earth. It was spring time, too;
nd all were coming forth in clusters crowded for very
ove; there was room enough for all, but they crushed
heir leaves into all manner of strange shapes only to be
earer each other. There was the wood anemone, star
fter star, closing every now and then into nebulæ; and
here was the oxalis, troop by troop, like virginal proces-
ions of the Mois de Marie, the dark vertical clefts in
he limestone choked up with them as with heavy snow,
nd touched with ivy on the edges—ivy as light and
ovely as the vine; and, ever and anon, a blue gush of
iolets, and cowslip bells in sunny places; and in the
nore open ground, the vetch, and comfrey, and meze-
eon, and the small sapphire buds of the Polygala Al-
ina, and the wild strawberry, just a blossom or two,
ll showered amidst the golden softness of deep, warm,
mber-colored moss. I came out presently on the edge
f the ravine: the solemn murmur of its waters rose
uddenly from beneath, mixed with the singing of the
hrushes among the pine boughs; and, on the opposite
ide of the valley, walled all along as it was by gray
liffs of limestone, there was a hawk sailing slowly off
heir brow, touching them nearly with his wings, and
vith the shadows of the pines flickering upon his plu-
nage from above; but with the fall of a hundred fathoms
inder his breast, and the curling pools of the green river
liding and glittering dizzily beneath him, their foam
globes moving with him as he flew. It would be difficult
o conceive a scene less dependent upon any other in-
erest than that of its own secluded and serious beauty;
ut the writer well remembers the sudden blankness and
hill which were cast upon it when he endeavored, in
rder more strictly to arrive at the sources of its im-
ressiveness, to imagine it, for a moment, a scene in
ome aboriginal forest of the New Continent. The flow-
rs in an instant lost their light, the river its music; the

hills became oppressively desolate; a heaviness in th
boughs of the darkened forest showed how much of thei
former power had been dependent upon a life which wa
not theirs, how much of the glory of the imperishable
or continually renewed, creation is reflected from thing
more precious in their memories than it, in its renew
ing. Those ever springing flowers and ever flowing
streams had been dyed by the deep colors of human en
durance, valor, and virtue; and the crests of the sabl
hills that rose against the evening sky received a deepe
worship, because their far shadows fell eastward over th
iron walls of Joux, and the four-square keep of Granson

It is as the centralization and protectress of this
sacred influence, that Architecture is to be regarded by
us with the most serious thought. We may live withou
her, and worship without her, but we cannot remembe
without her. How cold is all history, how lifeless al
imagery, compared to that which the living nation writes
and the uncorrupted marble bears!—how many pages o
doubtful record might we not often spare, for a few
stones left one upon another! The ambition of the ol
Babel builders was well directed for this world: there
are but two strong conquerors of the forgetfulness o
men, Poetry and Architecture; and the latter in some
sort includes the former, and is mightier in its reality
it is well to have, not only what men have thought and
felt, but what their hands have handled, and thei
strength wrought, and their eyes beheld, all the days o
their life. The age of Homer is surrounded with darkness, his very personality with doubt. Not so that of
Pericles: and the day is coming when we shall confess,
that we have learned more of Greece out of the crum-
bled fragments of her sculpture than even from her
sweet singers or soldier historians. And if indeed there
be any profit in our knowledge of the past, or any joy in
the thought of being remembered hereafter, which can
give strength to present exertion, or patience to present
endurance, there are two duties respecting national architecture whose importance it is impossible to overrate:
the first, to render the architecture of the day, historical;
and, the second, to preserve, as the most precious of in-
heritances, that of past ages.

It is in the first of these two directions that Memory may truly be said to be the Sixth Lamp of Architecture; for it is in becoming memorial or monumental that a true perfection is attained by civil and domestic buildings; and this partly as they are, with such a view, built in a more stable manner, and partly as their decorations are consequently animated by a metaphorical or historical meaning.

As regards domestic buildings, there must always be a certain limitation to views of this kind in the power, as well as in the hearts, of men; still I cannot but think it an evil sign of a people when their houses are built to last for one generation only. There is a sanctity in a good man's house which cannot be renewed in every tenement that rises on its ruins: and I believe that good men would generally feel this; and that having spent their lives happily and honorably, they would be grieved, at the close of them, to think that the place of their earthly abode, which had seen, and seemed almost to sympathize in, all their honor, their gladness, or their suffering,—that this, with all the record it bare of them, and of all material things that they had loved and ruled over, and set the stamp of themselves upon—was to be swept away, as soon as there was room made for them in the grave; that no respect was to be shown to it, no affection felt for it, no good to be drawn from it by their children; that though there was a monument in the church, there was no warm monuments in the hearth and house to them; that all that they ever treasured was despised, and the places that had sheltered and comforted them were dragged down to the dust. I say that a good man would fear this; and that, far more, a good son, a noble descendant, would fear doing it to his father's house. I say that if men lived like men indeed, their houses would be temples—temples which we should hardly dare to injure, and in which it would make us holy to be permitted to live; and there must be a strange dissolution of natural affection, a strange unthankfulness for all that homes have given and parents taught, a strange consciousness that we have been unfaithful to our fathers' honor, or that our own lives are not such as would make our dwellings sacred to our children, when each man would fain build to himself, and build for the little revolution of his own life only. And I look upon those pitiful concretions of lime and clay which spring up, in mildewed forwardness, out of the kneaded fields about our capital—upon those thin, tottering, foundationless shells of splintered wood and imitated stone—upon those gloomy rows of formalized minuteness, alike without difference and without fellowship, as solitary as similar—not merely with the careless disgust of an offended eye, not merely with sorrow for a desecrated landscape, but with a painful foreboding that the roots of our national greatness must be deeply cankered when they are thus loosely struck in their native ground; that those comfortless and unhonored dwellings are the signs of a great and spreading spirit of popular discontent; that they mark the time when every man's aim is to be in some more elevated sphere than his natural one, and every man's past life is his habitual scorn; when men build in the hope of leaving the places they have built, and live in the hope of forgetting the years that they have lived; when the comfort, the peace, the religion of home have ceased to be felt; and the crowded tenements of a struggling and restless population differ only from the tents of the Arab or the Gypsy by their less healthy openness to the air of heaven, and less happy choice of their spot of earth; by their sacrifice of liberty without the gain of rest, and of stability without the luxury of change.

This is no slight, no consequenceless evil; it is ominous, infectious, and fecund of other fault and misfortune. When men do not love their hearths, nor reverence their thresholds, it is a sign that they have dishonored both, and that they have never acknowledged the true universality of that Christian worship which was indeed to supersede the idolatry, but not the piety, of the pagan. Our God is a household God, as well as a heavenly one; He has an altar in every man's dwelling; let men look to it when they rend it lightly and pour out its ashes. It is not a question of mere ocular delight, it is no question of intellectual pride, or of cultivated and critical fancy, how, and with what aspect of durability and of completeness, the domestic buildings of a nation shall be raised. It is one of those moral duties, not with more impunity to be neglected because the perception of them depends on a finely toned and balanced conscientiousness, to build our dwellings with care, and patience, and fondness, and diligent completion, and with a view to their duration at least for such a period as, in the ordinary course of national revolutions, might be supposed likely to extend to the entire alteration of the direction of local interests. This at the least; but it would be better if, in every possible instance, men built their own houses on a scale commensurate rather with their condition at the commencement, than their attainments at the termination, of their worldly career; and built them to stand as long as human work at its strongest can be hoped to stand; recording to their children what they had been, and from what, if so it had been permitted them, they had risen. And when houses are thus built, we may have that true domestic architecture, the beginning of all other, which does not disdain to treat with respect and thoughtfulness the small habitation as well as the large, and which invests with the dignity of contented manhood the narrowness of worldly circumstance.

I look to this spirit of honorable, proud, peaceful self-possession, this abiding wisdom of contented life, as probably one of the chief sources of great intellectual power in all ages, and beyond dispute as the very primal source of the great architecture of old Italy and France. To this day, the interest of their fairest cities depends, not on the isolated richness of palaces, but on the cherished and exquisite decoration of even the smallest tenements of their proud periods. The most elaborate piece of architecture in Venice is a small house at the head of the Grand Canal, consisting of a ground floor with two stories above, three windows in the first, and two in the second. Many of the most exquisite buildings are on the narrower canals, and of no larger dimensions. One of the most interesting pieces of fifteenth century architecture in north Italy, is a small house in a back street, behind the market-place of Vicenza; it bears date 1481, and the motto, *Il. n'est. rose. sans. épine.*; it has also only a ground floor and two stories, with three windows in each, separated by rich flower-work, and with balconies, supported, the central one by an eagle with open wings, the lateral ones by winged griffins standing on cornucopiæ. The idea that a house must be large in order to be well built, is altogether of modern growth, and is parallel with the idea, that no picture can be historical, except of a size admitting figures larger than life.

I would have, then, our ordinary dwelling-houses built to last, and built to be lovely; as rich and full of pleasantness as may be, within and without; with what degree of likeness to each other in style and manner, I will say presently, under another head; but, at all events, with such differences as might suit and express each man's character and occupation, and partly his history. This right over the house, I conceive, belongs to its first builder, and is to be respected by his children; and it would be well that blank stones should be left in places, to be inscribed with a summary of his life and of its experience, raising thus the habitation into a kind of monument, and developing, into more systematic instructiveness, that good custom which was of old universal, and which still remains among some of the Swiss and Germans, of acknowledging the grace of God's permission to build and possess a quiet resting-place, in such sweet words as may well close our speaking of these things. I have taken them from the front of a cottage lately built among the green pastures which descend from the village of Grindelwald to the lower glacier:—

"Mit herzlichem Vertrauen
Hat Johannes Mooter und Maria Rubi
Dieses Haus bauen lassen.
Der liebe Gott woll uns bewahren
Vor allem Unglück and Gefahren
Und es in Segen lassen stehn
Auf der Reise durch diese Jammerzeit
Nach dem himmlischen Paradiese,
Wo alle Frommen wohnen,
Da wird Gott sie belohnen
Mit der Friedenskrone
Zu alle Ewigkeit." *

* "With heartfelt trust Have Johannes Mooter and Maria Rubi Had this house built. The dear God will shield us From all misfortune and danger, And let it stand in blessedness On the journey, through this

In public buildings the historical purpose should be still more definite. It is one of the advantages of Gothic architecture,—I use the word Gothic in the most extended sense as broadly opposed to classical,—that it admits of a richness of record altogether unlimited. Its minute and multitudinous sculptural decorations afford means of expressing, either symbolically or literally, all that need be known of national feeling or achievement. More decoration will, indeed, be usually required than can take so elevated a character; and much, even in the most thoughtful periods, has been left to the freedom of fancy, or suffered to consist of mere repetitions of some national bearing or symbol. It is, however, generally unwise, even in mere surface ornament, to surrender the power and privilege of variety which the spirit of Gothic architecture admits; much more in important features—capitals of columns or bosses, and string-courses, as of course in all confessed bas-reliefs. Better the rudest work that tells a story or records a fact, than the richest without meaning. There should not be a single ornament put upon great civic buildings, without some intellectual intention. Actual representation of history has in modern times been checked by a difficulty, mean indeed, but steadfast; that of unmanageable costume: nevertheless, by a sufficiently bold imaginative treatment, and frank use of symbols, all such obstacles may be vanquished; not perhaps in the degree necessary to produce sculpture in itself satisfactory, but at all events so as to enable it to become a grand and expressive element of architectural composition. Take, for example, the management of the capitals of the ducal palace at Venice. History, as such, was indeed entrusted to the painters of its interior, but every capital of its arcades was filled with meaning. The large one, the corner stone of the whole, next the entrance, was devoted to the symbolization of Abstract Justice; above it is a sculpture of the Judgment of Solomon, remarkable for a beautiful subjection in its treatment to its decorative purpose. The figures, if the subject had been entirely composed of them, would

---

time of sorrow. To the heavenly Paradise, Where all good people dwell, There will God reward them With the Crown of Peace To all Eternity." [Translation of Cook and Wedderburn.]

have awkwardly interrupted the line of the angle, and
diminished its apparent strength; and therefore in the
midst of them, entirely without relation to them, and indeed actually between the executioner and interceding
mother, there rises the ribbed trunk of a massy tree, which
supports and continues the shaft of the angle, and whose
leaves above overshadow and enrich the whole. The capital below bears among its leafage a throned figure of Justice, Trajan doing justice to the widow, Aristotle "che
die legge," and one or two other subjects now unintelligible from decay. The capitals next in order represent the
virtues and vices in succession, as preservative or destructive of national peace and power, concluding with Faith,
with the inscription "Fides optima in Deo est." A figure
is seen on the opposite side of the capital, worshipping
the sun. After these, one or two capitals are fancifully
decorated with birds, and then come a series representing, first the various fruits, then the national costumes,
and then the animals of the various countries subject to
Venetian rule.

Now, not to speak of any more important public building, let us imagine our own India House adorned in this
way, by historical or symbolical sculpture: massively
built in the first place; then chased with bas-reliefs of
our Indian battles, and fretted with carvings of Oriental
foliage, or inlaid with Oriental stones; and the more important members of its decoration composed of groups of
Indian life and landscape, and prominently expressing the
phantasms of Hindoo worship in their subjection to the
Cross. Would not one such work be better than a thousand histories? If, however, we have not the invention
necessary for such efforts, or if, which is probably one of
the most noble excuses we can offer for our deficiency in
such matters, we have less pleasure in talking about ourselves, even in marble, than the Continental nations, at
least we have no excuse for any want of care in the points
which insure the building's endurance. And as this question is one of great interest in its relations to the choice
of various modes of decoration, it will be necessary to
enter into it at some length.

The benevolent regards and purposes of men in masses
seldom can be supposed to extend beyond their own gener-

ation. They may look to posterity as an audience, may hope for its attention, and labor for its praise: they may trust to its recognition of unacknowledged merit, and demand its justice for contemporary wrong. But all this is mere selfishness, and does not involve the slightest regard to, or consideration of, the interest of those by whose numbers we would fain swell the circle of our flatterers, and by whose authority we would gladly support our presently disputed claims. The idea of self-denial for the sake of posterity, of practising present economy for the sake of debtors yet unborn, of planting forests that our descendants may live under their shade, or of raising cities for future nations to inhabit, never, I suppose, efficiently takes place among publicly recognized motives of exertion. Yet these are not the less our duties; nor is our part fitly sustained upon the earth, unless the range of our intended and deliberate usefulness include, not only the companions, but the successors of our pilgrimage. God has lent us the earth for our life; it is a great entail. It belongs as much to those who are to come after us, and whose names are already written in the book of creation, as to us; and we have no right, by anything that we do or neglect, to involve them in unnecessary penalties, or deprive them of benefits which it was in our power to bequeath. And this the more, because it is one of the appointed conditions of the labor of men that, in proportion to the time between the seed-sowing and the harvest, is the fulness of the fruit; and that generally, therefore, the farther off we place our aim, and the less we desire to be ourselves the witnesses of what we have labored for, the more wide and rich will be the measure of our success. Men cannot benefit those that are with them as they can benefit those who come after them; and of all the pulpits from which human voice is ever sent forth, there is none from which it reaches so far as from the grave.

Nor is there, indeed, any present loss, in such respect, for futurity. Every human action gains in honor, in grace, in all true magnificence, by its regard to things that are to come. It is the far sight, the quiet and confident patience, that, above all other attributes, separate man from man, and near him to his Maker; and there is no action nor art, whose majesty we may not measure by this test. Therefore, when we build, let us think that we build forever. Let it not be for present delight, nor for present use alone; let it be such work as our descendants will thank us for, and let us think, as we lay stone on stone, that a time is to come when those stones will be held sacred because our hands have touched them, and that men will say as they look upon the labor and wrought substance of them, "See! this our fathers did for us." For, indeed, the greatest glory of a building is not in its stones, nor in its gold. Its glory is in its Age, and in that deep sense of voicefulness, of stern watching, of mysterious sympathy, nay, even of approval or condemnation, which we feel in walls that have long been washed by the passing waves of humanity. It is in their lasting witness against men, in their quiet contrast with the transitional character of all things, in the strength which, through the lapse of seasons and times, and the decline and birth of dynasties, and the changing of the face of the earth, and of the limits of the sea, maintains its sculptured shapeliness for a time insuperable, connects forgotten and following ages with each other, and half constitutes the identity, as it concentrates the sympathy, of nations: it is in that golden stain of time, that we are to look for the real light, and color, and preciousness of architecture; and it is not until a building has assumed this character, till it has been entrusted with the fame, and hallowed by the deeds of men, till its walls have been witnesses of suffering, and its pillars rise out of the shadows of death, that its existence, more lasting as it is than that of the natural objects of the world around it, can be gifted with even so much as these possess, of language and of life.

For that period, then, we must build; not, indeed, refusing to ourselves the delight of present completion, nor hesitating to follow such portions of character as may depend upon delicacy of execution to the highest perfection of which they are capable, even although we may know that in the course of years such details must perish; but taking care that for work of this kind we sacrifice no enduring quality, and that the building shall not depend for its impressiveness upon anything that is perishable. This would, indeed, be the law of good composition under any circumstances, the arrangement of the larger masses being always a matter of greater importance than the treatment of the smaller; but in architecture there is much in that very treatment which is skilful or otherwise in proportion to its just regard to the probable effects of time: and (which is still more to be considered) there is a beauty in those effects themselves, which nothing else can replace, and which it is our wisdom to consult and to desire. For though, hitherto, we have been speaking of the sentiment of age only, there is an actual beauty in the marks of it, such and so great as to have become not unfrequently the subject of especial choice among certain schools of art, and to have impressed upon those schools the character usually and loosely expressed by the term "picturesque." It is of some importance to our present purpose to determine the true meaning of this expression, as it is now generally used; for there is a principle to be developed from that use which, while it has occultly been the ground of much that is true and just in our judgment of art, has never been so far understood as to become definitely serviceable. Probably no word in the language, (exclusive of theological expressions) has been the subject of so frequent or so prolonged dispute; yet none remain more vague in their acceptance, and it seems to me to be a matter of no small interest to investigate the essence of that idea which all feel, and (to appearance) with respect to similar things, and yet which every attempt to define has, as I believe, ended either in mere enumeration of the effects and objects to which the term has been attached, or else in attempts at abstraction more palpably nugatory than any which have disgraced metaphysical investigation on other subjects. A recent critic on Art, for instance, has gravely advanced the theory that the essence of the picturesque consists in the expression of "universal decay." It would be curious to see the result of an attempt to illustrate this idea of the picturesque, in a painting of dead flowers and decayed fruit; and equally curious to trace the steps of any reasoning which, on such a theory, should account for the picturesqueness of an ass colt as opposed to a horse foal. But there is much excuse for even the most utter failure in reasonings of this kind, since the subject is, indeed, one of the most obscure of all that may legitimately be submitted to human reason; and the idea is itself so varied in the minds of different men, according to their subjects of study, that no definition can be expected to embrace more than a certain number of its infinitely multiplied forms.

That peculiar character, however, which separates the picturesque from the characters of subject belonging to the higher walks of art (and this is all that it is necessary for our present purpose to define), may be shortly and decisively expressed. Picturesqueness, in this sense, is *Parasitical Sublimity.* Of course all sublimity, as well as all beauty, is, in the simple etymological sense, picturesque, that is to say, fit to become the subject of a picture; and all sublimity is, even in the peculiar sense which I am endeavoring to develop, picturesque, as opposed to beauty; that is to say, there is more picturesqueness in the subject of Michael Angelo than of Perugino, in proportion to the prevalence of the sublime element over the beautiful. But that character, of which the extreme pursuit is generally admitted to be degrading to art, is *parasitical* sublimity; *i.e.,* a sublimity dependent on the accidents, or on the least essential characters, of the objects to which it belongs; and the picturesque is *developed distinctively exactly in proportion to the distance from the centre of thought of those points of character in which the sublimity is found.* Two ideas, therefore, are essential to picturesqueness,—the first, that of sublimity (for pure beauty is not picturesque at all, and becomes so only as the sublime element mixes with it), and the second, the subordinate or parasitical position of that sublimity. Of course, therefore, whatever characters of line or shade or expression are productive of sublimity, will become productive of picturesqueness; what these characters are I shall endeavor hereafter to show at length; but, among those which are generally acknowledged, I may name angular and broken lines, vigorous oppositions of light and shadow, and grave, deep, or boldly contrasted color; and all these are in a still higher degree effective, when, by resemblance or association, they remind us of objects on which a true and essential sublimity exists, as of rocks or mountains, or stormy clouds or waves. Now if these characters, or any others of a higher and more abstract sublimity, be found in the very heart and substance of what we contemplate, as the sublimity of Michael Angelo depends on the expression of mental character in his figures far more than even on the noble lines of their arrangement, the art which represents such characters cannot be properly called picturesque: but, if they be found in the accidental or external qualities, the distinctive picturesque will be the result.

Thus, in the treatment of the features of the human face by Francia or Angelico, the shadows are employed only to make the contours of the features thoroughly felt; and to those features themselves the mind of the observer is exclusively directed (that is to say, to the essential characters of the thing represented). All power and all sublimity rest on these; the shadows are used only for the sake of the features. On the contrary, by Rembrandt, Salvator, or Caravaggio, the features are used *for the sake of the shadows;* and the attention is directed, and the power of the painter addressed, to characters of accidental light and shade across or around those features. In the case of Rembrandt there is often an essential sublimity in invention and expression besides, and always a high degree of it in the light and shade itself; but it is, for the most part, parasitical or engrafted sublimity as regards the subject of the painting, and, just so far, picturesque.

Again, in the management of the sculptures of the Parthenon, shadow is frequently employed as a dark field on which the forms are drawn. This is visibly the case in the metopes, and must have been nearly as much so in the pediment. But the use of that shadow is entirely to show the confines of the figures; and it is to *their lines,* and not to the shapes of the shadows behind them, that the art and the eye are addressed. The figures themselves are conceived, as much as possible, in full light, aided by bright reflections; they are drawn exactly as, on vases, white figures on a dark ground; and the sculptors have dispensed with, or even struggled to avoid, all shadows which were not absolutely necessary to the explaining of the form. On the contrary, in Gothic sculpture, the shadow becomes itself a subject of thought. It is considered as a dark color, to be arranged in certain agree-

able masses; the figures are very frequently made even
subordinate to the placing of its divisions: and their
costume is enriched at the expense of the forms underneath, in order to increase the complexity and variety of
the points of shade.   There are thus, both in sculpture
and painting, two, in some sort, opposite schools, of which
the one follows for its subject the essential forms of
things, and the other the accidental lights and shades
upon them.   There are various degrees of their contrari-
ety: middle steps, as in the works of Correggio, and
all degrees of nobility and of degradation in the several
manners: but the one is always recognized as the pure
and the other as the picturesque school.   Portions of picturesque treatment will be found in Greek work, and of
pure and unpicturesque in Gothic; and in both there are
countless instances, as preeminently in the works of
Michael Angelo, in which shadows become valuable as
media of expression, and therefore take rank among essential characteristics.   Into these multitudinous distinctions and exceptions I cannot now enter, desiring only
to prove the broad applicability of the general definition.

Again, the distinction will be found to exist, not only
between forms and shades as subjects of choice, but between essential and inessential forms.   One of the chief
distinctions between the dramatic and picturesque schools
of sculpture is found in the treatment of the hair.   By
the artists of the time of Pericles it was considered as
an excrescence, indicated by few and rude lines, and
subordinated, in every particular, to the principality of
the features and person.   How completely this was an
artistical, not a national idea, it is unnecessary to prove.
We need but remember the employment of the Lacedæ-
monians, reported by the Persian spy on the evening before the battle of Thermopylæ, or glance at any Homeric
description of ideal form, to see how purely *sculpturesque*
was the law which reduced the markings of the hair, lest,
under the necessary disadvantages of material, they
should interfere with the distinctness of the personal
forms.   On the contrary, in later sculpture, the hair receives almost the principal care of the workman; and,
while the features and limbs are clumsily and bluntly
executed, the hair is curled and twisted, cut into bold and

shadowy projections, and arranged in masses elaborately ornamental: there is true sublimity in the lines and the chiaroscuro of these masses, but it is, as regards the creature represented, parasitical and therefore picturesque. In the same sense we may understand the application of the term to modern animal painting, distinguished as it has been by peculiar attention to the colors, lustre, and texture of skin; nor is it in art alone that the definition will hold. In animals themselves, when their sublimity depends upon their muscular forms or motions, or necessary and principal attributes, as perhaps more than all others in the horse, we do not call them picturesque, but consider them as peculiarly fit to be associated with pure historical subject. Exactly in proportion as their character of sublimity passes into excrescences;—into mane and beard as in the lion, into horns as in the stag, into shaggy hide as in the instance above given of the ass colt, into variegation as in the zebra, or into plumage,— they become picturesque, and are so in art exactly in proportion to the prominence of these excrescential characters. It may be often most expedient that they should be prominent; often there is in them the highest degree of majesty, as in those of the leopard and boar; and in the hands of men like Tintoret and Rubens, such attributes become means of deepening the very highest and most ideal impressions. But the picturesque direction of their thoughts is always distinctly recognizable, as clinging to the surface, to the less essential character, and as developing out of this a sublimity different from that of the creature itself; a sublimity which is, in a sort, common to all the objects of creation, and the same in its constituent elements, whether it be sought in the clefts and folds of shaggy hair, or in the chasms and rents of rocks, or in the hanging of thickets or hill sides, or in the alternations of gayety and gloom in the variegation of the shell, the plume, or the cloud.

Now, to return to our immediate subject, it so happens that, in architecture, the superinduced and accidental beauty is most commonly inconsistent with the preservation of original character, and the picturesque is therefore sought in ruin, and supposed to consist in decay. Whereas, even when so sought, it consists in the mere sublimity of the rents, or fractures, or stains, or vegetation, which assimilate the architecture with the work of Nature, and bestow upon it those circumstances of color and form which are universally beloved by the eye of man. So far as this is done, to the extinction of the true characters of the architecture, it is picturesque, and the artist who looks to the stem of the ivy instead of the shaft of the pillar, is carrying out in more daring freedom the debased sculptor's choice of the hair instead of the countenance. But so far as it can be rendered consistent with the inherent character, the picturesque or extraneous sublimity of architecture has just this of nobler function in it than that of any other object whatsoever, that it is an exponent of age, of that in which, as has been said, the greatest glory of the building consists; and, therefore, the external signs of this glory, having power and purpose greater than any belonging to their mere sensible beauty, may be considered as taking rank among pure and essential characters; so essential to my mind, that I think a building cannot be considered as in its prime until four or five centuries have passed over it; and that the entire choice and arrangement of its details should have reference to their appearance after that period, so that none should be admitted which would suffer material injury either by the weather-staining, or the mechanical degradation which the lapse of such a period would necessitate.

It is not my purpose to enter into any of the questions which the application of this principle involves. They are of too great interest and complexity to be even touched upon within my present limits, but this is broadly to be noticed, that those styles of architecture which are picturesque in the sense above explained with respect to sculpture, that is to say, whose decoration depends on the arrangement of points of shade rather than on purity of outline, do not suffer, but commonly gain in richness of effect when their details are partly worn away; hence such styles, preeminently that of French Gothic, should always be adopted when the materials to be employed are liable to degradation, as brick, sandstone, or soft limestone; and styles in any degree dependent on purity of line, as the Italian Gothic, must be practised altogether in hard and undecomposing materials, granite, serpentine, or crystalline marbles. There can be no doubt that the nature of the accessible materials influenced the formation of both styles; and it should still more authoritatively determine our choice of either.

It does not belong to my present plan to consider at length the second head of duty of which I have above spoken; the preservation of the architecture we possess: but a few words may be forgiven, as especially necessary in modern times. Neither by the public, nor by those who have the care of public monuments, is the true meaning of the word *restoration* understood. It means the most total destruction which a building can suffer: a destruction out of which no remnants can be gathered: a destruction accompanied with false description of the thing destroyed. Do not let us deceive ourselves in this important matter; it is *impossible,* as impossible as to raise the dead, to restore anything that has ever been great or beautiful in architecture. That which I have above insisted upon as the life of the whole, that spirit which is given only by the hand and eye of the workman, never can be recalled. Another spirit may be given by another time, and it is then a new building; but the spirit of the dead workman cannot be summoned up, and commanded to direct other hands, and other thoughts. And as for direct and simple copying, it is palpably impossible. What copying can there be of surfaces that have been worn half an inch down? The whole finish of the work was in the half inch that is gone; if you attempt to restore that finish, you do it conjecturally; if you copy what is left, granting fidelity to be possible, (and what care, or watchfulness, or cost can secure it,) how is the new work better than the old? There was yet in the old *some* life, some mysterious suggestion of what it had been, and of what it had lost; some sweetness in the gentle lines which rain and sun had wrought. There can be none in the brute hardness of the new carving. Look at the animals which I have given in Plate XIV., as an instance of living work, and suppose the markings of the scales and hair once worn away, or the wrinkles of the brows, and who shall ever restore them? The first step to restoration, (I have seen it, and that again and again—seen it on the Baptistery of Pisa, seen it on the Casa d' Oro at Venice, seen it on the Cathedral of Lisieux,) is to dash the old work to pieces; the second is usually to put up the cheapest and basest imitation which can escape detection, but in all cases, however careful, and however labored, an imitation still, a cold model of such parts as *can* be modelled, with conjectural supplements; and my experience has as yet furnished me with only one instance, that of the Palais de Justice at Rouen, in which even this, the utmost degree of fidelity which is possible, has been attained, or even attempted.

Do not let us talk then of restoration. The thing is a Lie from beginning to end. You may make a model of a building as you may of a corpse, and your model may have the shell of the old walls within it as your cast might have the skeleton, with what advantage I neither see nor care: but the old building is destroyed, and that more totally and mercilessly than if it had sunk into a heap of dust, or melted into a mass of clay: more has been gleaned out of desolated Nineveh than ever will be out of re-built Milan. But, it is said, there may come a necessity for restoration! Granted. Look the necessity full in the face, and understand it on its own terms. It is a necessity for destruction. Accept it as such, pull the building down, throw its stones into neglected corners, make ballast of them, or mortar, if you will; but do it honestly, and do not set up a Lie in their place. And look that necessity in the face before it comes, and you may prevent it. The principle of modern times, (a principle which, I believe, at least in France, to be *systematically acted on by the masons,* in order to find themselves work, as the abbey of St. Ouen was pulled down by the magistrates of the town by way of giving work to some vagrants,) is to neglect buildings first, and restore them afterward. Take proper care of your monuments, and you will not need to restore them. A few sheets of lead put in time upon a roof, a few dead leaves and sticks swept in time out of a water-course, will save both roof and walls from ruin. Watch an old building with an anxious care; guard it as best you may, and at *any* cost, from every influence of dilapidation. Count its stones as you would jewels of a crown; set watches about it as

if at the gates of a besieged city; bind it together with
iron where it loosens; stay it with timber where it de-
clines; do not care about the unsightliness of the aid:
better a crutch than a lost limb; and do this tenderly,
and reverently, and continually, and many a generation
will still be born and pass away beneath its shadow. Its
evil day must come at last; but let it come declaredly and
openly, and let no dishonoring and false substitute deprive it of the funeral offices of memory.

Of more wanton or ignorant ravage it is vain to speak;
my words will not reach those who commit them, and yet,
be it heard or not, I must not leave the truth unstated,
that it is again no question of expediency or feeling
whether we shall preserve the buildings of past times or
not. *We have no right whatever to touch them.* They are
not ours. They belong partly to those who built them, and
partly to all the generations of mankind who are to follow us. The dead have still their right in them: that
which they labored for, the praise of achievement or the
expression of religious feeling, or whatsoever else it might
be which in those buildings they intended to be permanent, we have no right to obliterate. What we have ourselves built, we are at liberty to throw down; but what
other men gave their strength and wealth and life to accomplish, their right over does not pass away with their
death; still less is the right to the use of what they have
left vested in us only. It belongs to all their successors.
It may hereafter be a subject of sorrow, or a cause of injury, to millions, that we have consulted our present convenience by casting down such buildings as we choose to
dispense with. That sorrow, that loss, we have no right
to inflict. Did the cathedral of Avranches belong to the
mob who destroyed it, any more than it did to us, who
walk in sorrow to and fro over its foundation? Neither
does any building whatever belong to those mobs who do
violence to it. For a mob it is, and must be always; it
matters not whether enraged, or in deliberate folly;
whether countless, or sitting in committees; the people
who destroy anything causelessly are a mob, and Architecture is always destroyed causelessly. A fair building
is necessarily worth the ground it stands upon, and will
be so until Central Africa and America shall have be-

come as populous as Middlesex: nor is any cause whatever valid as a ground for its destruction. If ever valid, certainly not now, when the place both of the past and future is too much usurped in our minds by the restless and discontented present. The very quietness of nature is gradually withdrawn from us; thousands who once in their necessarily prolonged travel were subjected to an influence, from the silent sky and slumbering fields, more effectual than known or confessed, now bear with them even there the ceaseless fever of their life; and along the iron veins that traverse the frame of our country, beat and flow the fiery pulses of its exertion, hotter and faster every hour. All vitality is concentrated through those throbbing arteries into the central cities; the country is passed over like a green sea by narrow bridges, and we are thrown back in continually closer crowds upon the city gates. The only influence which can in any wise *there* take the place of that of the woods and fields, is the power of ancient Architecture. Do not part with it for the sake of the formal square, or of the fenced and planted walk, nor of the goodly street nor opened quay. The pride of a city is not in these. Leave them to the crowd; but remember that there will surely be some within the circuit of the disquieted walls who would ask for some other spots than these wherein to walk; for some other forms to meet their sight familiarly: like him who sat so often where the sun struck from the west, to watch the lines of the dome of Florence drawn on the deep sky, or like those, his Hosts, who could bear daily to behold, from their palace chambers, the places where their fathers lay at rest, at the meeting of the dark streets of Verona.

THE LAMP OF OBEDIENCE

[Seven Lamps, Ch. 7.]

IT has been my endeavor to show in the preceding pages how every form of noble architecture is in some sort the embodiment of the Polity, Life, History, and Religious Faith of nations. Once or twice in doing this, I have named a principle to which I would now assign a definite place among those which direct that embodiment; the last place, not only as that to which its own humility would incline, but rather as belonging to it in the aspect of the crowning grace of all the rest; that principle, I mean, to which Polity owes its stability, Life its happiness, Faith its acceptance, Creation its continuance,— Obedience.

Nor is it the least among the sources of more serious satisfaction which I have found in the pursuit of a subject that at first appeared to bear but slightly on the grave interests of mankind, that the conditions of material perfection which it leads me in conclusion to consider, furnish a strange proof how false is the conception, how frantic the pursuit, of that treacherous phantom which men call Liberty: most treacherous, indeed, of all phantoms; for the feeblest ray of reason might surely show us, that not only its attainment, but its being, was impossible. There is no such thing in the universe. There can never be. The stars have it not; the earth has it not; the sea has it not; and we men have the mockery and semblance of it only for our heaviest punishment.

In one of the noblest poems for its imagery and its music belonging to the recent school of our literature, the writer has sought in the aspect of inanimate nature the expression of that Liberty which, having once loved, he had seen among men in its true dyes of darkness. But with what strange fallacy of interpretation! since in one noble line of his invocation he has contradicted the assumptions of the rest, and acknowledged the presence of a subjection, surely not less severe because eternal. How could he otherwise? since if there be any one principle more widely than another confessed by every utterance, or more sternly than another imprinted on every atom, of the visible creation, that principle is not Liberty, but Law.

The enthusiast would reply that by Liberty he meant the Law of Liberty. Then why use the single and misunderstood word? If by liberty you mean chastisement of the passions, discipline of the intellect, subjection of the will; if you mean the fear of inflicting the shame of committing a wrong; if you mean respect for all who are in authority, and consideration for all who are in dependence; veneration for the good, mercy to the evil, sympathy with the weak; if you mean watchfulness over all thoughts, temperance in all pleasures, and perseverance in all toils; if you mean, in a word, that Service which is defined in the liturgy of the English Church to be perfect Freedom, why do you name this by the same word by which the luxurious mean license, and the reckless mean change; by which the rogue means rapine, and the fool, equality; by which the proud mean anarchy, and the malignant mean violence? Call it by any name rather than this, but its best and truest is Obedience. Obedience is, indeed, founded on a kind of freedom, else it would become mere subjugation, but that freedom is only granted that obedience may be more perfect; and thus, while a measure of license is necessary to exhibit the individual energies of things, the fairness and pleasantness and perfection of them all consist in their Restraint. Compare a river that has burst its banks with one that is bound by them, and the clouds that are scattered over the face of the whole heaven with those that are marshalled into ranks and orders by its winds. So that though restraint, utter and unrelaxing, can never be comely, this is not because it is in itself an evil, but only because, when too great, it overpowers the nature of the thing restrained, and so counteracts the other laws of which that nature is itself composed. And the balance wherein consists the fairness of creation is between the laws of life and being in the things governed, and the laws of general sway to which they are subjected; and the suspension or infringement of either kind of law, or, literally, disorder, is equivalent to, and synonymous with, disease; while the increase of both honor and beauty is habitually on the side of restraint (or the action of superior law) rather than of character (or the action of inherent law). The noblest word in the catalogue of social virtue is "Loyalty," and the sweetest which men have learned in the pastures of the wilderness is "Fold."

Nor is this all; but we may observe, that exactly in proportion to the majesty of things in the scale of being, is the completeness of their obedience to the laws that are set over them. Gravitation is less quietly, less instantly obeyed by a grain of dust than it is by the sun and moon; and the ocean falls and flows under influences which the lake and river do not recognize. So also in estimating the dignity of any action or occupation of men, there is perhaps no better test than the question "are its laws strait?" For their severity will probably be commensurate with the greatness of the numbers whose labor it concentrates or whose interest it concerns.

This severity must be singular, therefore, in the case of that art, above all others, whose productions are the most vast and the most common; which requires for its practice the cooperation of bodies of men, and for its perfection the perseverance of successive generations. And, taking into account also what we have before so often observed of Architecture, her continual influence over the emotions of daily life, and her realism, as opposed to the two sister arts which are in comparison but the picturing of stories and of dreams, we might beforehand expect that we should find her healthy state and action dependent on far more severe laws than theirs: that the license which they extend to the workings of individual mind would be withdrawn by her; and that, in assertion of the relations which she holds with all that is universally important to man, she would set forth, by her own majestic subjection, some likeness of that on which man's social happiness and power depend. We might, therefore, without the light of experience, conclude, that Architecture never could flourish except when it was subjected to a national law as strict and as minutely authoritative as the laws which regulate religion, policy, and social relations; nay, even more authoritative than these, because both capable of more enforcement, as over more passive matter; and needing more enforcement, as the purest type not of one law nor of another, but of the common authority of all. But in this matter experience speaks more loudly than reason. If there be any one condition which, in watching the progress of architecture, we see distinct and general; if, amidst the counter-evidence of success attending opposite accidents of character and circumstance, any one conclusion may be constantly and indisputably drawn, it is this; that the architecture of a nation is great only when it is as universal and as established as its language; and when provincial differ-

ences of style are nothing more than so many dialects.
Other necessities are matters of doubt: nations have been
alike successful in their architecture in times of poverty
and of wealth; in times of war and of peace; in times of
barbarism and of refinement; under governments the
most liberal or the most arbitrary; but this one condition
has been constant, this one requirement clear in all places
and at all times, that the work shall be that of a *school,*
that no individual caprice shall dispense with, or materially vary, accepted types and customary decorations;
and that from the cottage to the palace, and from the
chapel to the basilica, and from the garden fence to the
fortress wall, every member and feature of the architecture of the nation shall be as commonly current, as frankly
accepted, as its language or its coin.

A day never passes without our hearing our English
architects called upon to be original, and to invent a new
style: about as sensible and necessary an exhortation as
to ask of a man who has never had rags enough on his
back to keep out cold, to invent a new mode of cutting a
coat. Give him a whole coat first, and let him concern
himself about the fashion of it afterward. We want no
new style of architecture. Who wants a new style of
painting or sculpture? But we want *some* style. It is of
marvellously little importance, if we have a code of laws
and they be good laws, whether they be new or old, foreign or native, Roman or Saxon, or Norman, or English
laws. But it is of considerable importance that we should
have a code of laws of one kind or another, and that code
accepted and enforced from one side of the island to
another, and not one law made ground of judgment at
York and another in Exeter. And in like manner it does
not matter one marble splinter whether we have an old
or new architecture, but it matters everything whether
we have an architecture truly so called or not; that is,
whether an architecture whose laws might be taught at
our schools from Cornwall to Northumberland, as we
teach English spelling and English grammar, or an architecture which is to be invented fresh every time we
build a workhouse or a parish school. There seems to me
to be a wonderful misunderstanding among the majority
of architects at the present day as to the very nature and

meaning of Originality, and of all wherein it consists.
Originality in expression does not depend on invention
of new words; nor originality in poetry on invention of
new measures; nor, in painting, on invention of new colors, or new modes of using them. The chords of music,
the harmonies of color, the general principles of the arrangement of sculptural masses, have been determined
long ago, and, in all probability, cannot be added to any
more than they can be altered. Granting that they may
be, such additions or alterations are much more the work
of time and of multitudes than of individual inventors.
We may have one Van Eyck, who will be known as the
introducer of a new style once in ten centuries, but he
himself will trace his invention to some accidental by-
play or pursuit; and the use of that invention will depend
altogether on the popular necessities or instincts of the
period. Originality depends on nothing of the kind. A
man who has the gift, will take up any style that is going, the style of his day, and will work in that, and be
great in that, and make everything that he does in it look
as fresh as if every thought of it had just come down
from heaven. I do not say that he will not take liberties
with his materials, or with his rules: I do not say that
strange changes will not sometimes be wrought by his
efforts, or his fancies, in both. But those changes will
be instructive, natural, facile, though sometimes marvel-
ous; they will never be sought after as things necessary
to his dignity or to his independence; and those liberties
will be like the liberties that a great speaker takes with
the language, not a defiance of its rules for the sake of
singularity; but inevitable, uncalculated, and brilliant
consequences of an effort to express what the language,
without such infraction, could not. There may be times
when, as I have above described, the life of an art is
manifested in its changes, and in its refusal of ancient
imitations: so there are in the life of an insect; and
there is great interest in the state of both the art and
the insect at those periods when, by their natural progress
and constitutional power, such changes are about to be
wrought. But as that would be both an uncomfortable
and foolish caterpillar which, instead of being contented
with a caterpillar's life and feeding on caterpillar's food,

was always striving to turn itself into a chrysalis; and
as that would be an unhappy chrysalis which should lie
awake at night and roll restlessly in its cocoon, in effort
to turn itself prematurely into a moth; so will that art
be unhappy and unprosperous which, instead of support-
ing itself on the food, and contenting itself with the customs, which have been enough for the support and guidance of other arts before it and like it, is struggling and
fretting under the natural limitations of its existence,
and striving to become something other than it is. And
though it is the nobility of the highest creatures to look
forward to, and partly to understand the changes which
are appointed for them, preparing for them beforehand;
and if, as is usual with *appointed* changes, they be into
a higher state, even desiring them, and rejoicing in the
hope of them, yet it is the strength of every creature, be
it changeful or not, to rest, for the time being, contented
with the conditions of its existence, and striving only to
bring about the changes which it desires, by fulfilling to
the uttermost the duties for which its present state is
appointed and continued.

Neither originality, therefore, nor change, good though
both may be, and this is commonly a most merciful and
enthusiastic supposition with respect to either, is ever
to be sought in itself, or can ever be healthily obtained
by any struggle or rebellion against common laws. We
want neither the one nor the other. The forms of architecture already known are good enough for us, and far
far better than any of us: and it will be time enough to
think of changing them for better when we can use them
as they are. But there are some things which we not
only want, but cannot do without; and which all the
struggling and raving in the world, nay more, which all
the real talent and resolution in England, will never
enable us to do without: and these are Obedience, Unity,
Fellowship, and Order. And all our schools of design
and committees of taste; all our academies and lectures
and journalisms, and essays; all the sacrifices which we
are beginning to make, all the truth which there is in our
English nature, all the power of our English will, and
the life of our English intellect, will in this matter be as
useless as efforts and emotions in a dream, unless we are

ontented to submit architecture and all art, like other
hings, to English law.

I say architecture and all art; for I believe architec-
ure must be the beginning of arts, and that the others
must follow her in their time and order; and I think the
rosperity of our schools of painting and sculpture, in
which no one will deny the life, though many the health,
epends upon that of our architecture. I think that all
will languish until that takes the lead, and (this I do
ot *think*, but I proclaim, as confidently as I would as-
ert the necessity, for the safety of society, of an under-
tood and strongly administered legal government) our
rchitecture *will* languish, and that in the very dust, un-
il the first principle of common sense be manfully obeyed,
nd a universal system of form and workmanship be
verywhere adopted and enforced. It may be said that
his is impossible. It may be so—I fear it is so: I have
othing to do with the possibility or impossibility of it;
simply know and assert the necessity of it. If it be im-
ossible, English art is impossible. Give it up at once.
ou are wasting time, and money, and energy upon it,
nd though you exhaust centuries and treasures, and
reak hearts for it, you will never raise it above the
erest dilettanteism. Think not of it. It is a dangerous
anity, a mere gulf in which genius after genius will
e swallowed up, and it will not close. And so it will
ontinue to be, unless the one bold and broad step be
aken at the beginning. We shall not manufacture art
ut of pottery and printed stuffs: we shall not reason out
rt by our philosophy; we shall not stumble upon art by
ur experiments, nor create it by our fancies: I do not
ay that we can even build it out of brick and stone; but
here is a chance for us in these, and there is none else;
nd that chance rests on the bare possibility of obtain-
ng the consent, both of architects and of the public, to
hoose a style, and to use it universally.

How surely its principles ought at first to be limited,
e may easily determine by the consideration of the
ecessary modes of teaching any other branch of gen-
ral knowledge. When we begin to teach children writ-
ng, we force them to absolute copyism, and require abso-
ate accuracy in the formation of the letters; as they

obtain command of the received modes of literal expre
sion, we cannot prevent their falling into such variation
as are consistent with their feeling, their circumstance
or their characters. So, when a boy is first taught t
write Latin, an authority is required of him for ever
expression he uses; as he becomes master of the languag
he may take a license, and feel his right to do so withou
any authority, and yet write better Latin than when h
borrowed every separate expression. In the same wa
our architects would have to be taught to write the ac
cepted style. We must first determine what building
are to be considered Augustan in their authority; the
modes of construction and laws of proportion are to b
studied with the most penetrating care; then the diffe
ent forms and uses of their decorations are to be classe
and catalogued, as a German grammarian classes th
powers of prepositions; and under this absolute, irrefraga
ble authority, we are to begin to work; admitting not s
much as an alteration in the depth of a cavetto, or th
breadth of a fillet. Then, when our sight is once accu
tomed to the grammatical forms and arrangements, an
our thoughts familiar with the expression of them al
when we can speak this dead language naturally, an
apply it to whatever ideas we have to render, that is t
say, to every practical purpose of life; then, and not ti
then, a license might be permitted, and individual au
thority allowed to change or to add to the received form
always within certain limits; the decorations, especiall
might be made subjects of variable fancy, and enriche
with ideas either original or taken from other school
And thus, in process of time, and by a great nation
movement, it might come to pass that a new style shoul
arise, as language itself changes; we might perhaps con
to speak Italian instead of Latin, or to speak modern i
stead of old English; but this would be a matter of enti
indifference, and a matter, besides, which no determin
tion or desire could either hasten or prevent. That alon
which it is in our power to obtain, and which it is ou
duty to desire, is a unanimous style of some kind, an
such comprehension and practice of it as would enab
us to adapt its features to the peculiar character of ever
several building, large or small, domestic, civil, or eccles

astical. I have said that it was immaterial what style was adopted, so far as regards the room for originality which its development would admit: it is not so, however, when we take into consideration the far more important questions of the facility of adaptation to general purposes, and of the sympathy with which this or that style would be popularly regarded. The choice of Classical or Gothic, again using the latter term in its broadest sense, may be questionable when it regards some single and considerable public building; but I cannot conceive it questionable, for an instant, when it regards modern uses in general: I cannot conceive any architect insane enough to project the vulgarization of Greek architecture. Neither can it be rationally questionable whether we should adopt early or late, original or derivative Gothic; if the latter were chosen, it must be either some impotent and ugly degradation, like our own Tudor, or else a style whose grammatical laws it would be nearly impossible to limit or arrange, like the French Flamboyant. We are equally precluded from adopting styles essentially infantine or barbarous, however Herculean their infancy, or majestic their outlawry, such as our own Norman, or the Lombard Romanesque. The choice would lie I think between four styles:—1. The Pisan Romanesque; 2. The early Gothic of the Western Italian Republics, advanced as far and as fast as our art would enable us to the Gothic of Giotto; 3. The Venetian Gothic in its purest development; 4. The English earliest decorated. The most natural, perhaps the safest choice, would be of the last, well fenced from chance of again stiffening into the perpendicular; and perhaps enriched by some mingling of decorative elements from the exquisite decorated Gothic of France, of which, in such cases, it would be needful to accept some well-known examples, as the north door of Rouen and the church of St. Urbain at Troyes, for final and limiting authorities on the side of decoration.

It is almost impossible for us to conceive, in our present state of doubt and ignorance, the sudden dawn of intelligence and fancy, the rapidly increasing sense of power and facility, and, in its *proper sense,* of Freedom, which such wholesome restraint would instantly cause throughout the whole circle of the arts. Freed from the

agitation and embarrassment of that liberty of choice
which is the cause of half the discomforts of the world;
freed from the accompanying necessity of studying all
past, present, or even possible styles; and enabled, by con-
centration of individual, and cooperation of multitudinous energy, to penetrate into the uttermost secrets of
the adopted style, the architect would find his whole understanding enlarged, his practical knowledge certain and
ready to hand, and his imagination playful and vigorous,
as a child's would be within a walled garden, who would
sit down and shudder if he were left free in a fenceless
plain. How many and how bright would be the results
in every direction of interest, not to the arts merely, but
to national happiness and virtue, it would be as difficult
to preconceive as it would seem extravagant to state: but
the first, perhaps the least, of them would be an increased
sense of fellowship among ourselves, a cementing of every
patriotic bond of union, a proud and happy recognition
of our affection for and sympathy with each other, and
our willingness in all things to submit ourselves to every
law that could advance the interest of the community; a
barrier, also, the best conceivable, to the unhappy rivalry
of the upper and middle classes, in houses, furniture, and
establishments; and even a check to much of what is as
vain as it is painful in the oppositions of religious parties
respecting matters of ritual. These, I say, would be the
first consequences. Economy increased tenfold, as it
would be by the simplicity of practice; domestic comforts uninterfered with by the caprice and mistakes of
architects ignorant of the capacities of the styles they
use, and all the symmetry and sightliness of our harmonized streets and public buildings, are things of slighter
account in the catalogue of benefits. But it would be
mere enthusiasm to endeavor to trace them farther. I
have suffered myself too long to indulge in the specu-
lative statement of requirements which perhaps we have
more immediate and more serious work than to supply,
and of feelings which it may be only contingently in our
power to recover. I should be unjustly thought unaware
of the difficulty of what I have proposed, or of the un-
importance of the whole subject as compared with many
which are brought home to our interests and fixed upon

our consideration by the wild course of the present century. But of difficulty and of importance it is for others to judge. I have limited myself to the simple statement of what, if we desire to have architecture, we MUST primarily endeavor to feel and do: but then it may not be desirable for us to have architecture at all. There are many who feel it to be so; many who sacrifice much to that end; and I am sorry to see their energies wasted and their lives disquieted in vain. I have stated, therefore, the only ways in which that end is attainable, without venturing even to express an opinion as to its real desirableness. I have an opinion, and the zeal with which I have spoken may sometimes have betrayed it, but I hold to it with no confidence. I know too well the undue importance which the study that every man follows must assume in his own eyes, to trust my own impressions of the dignity of that of Architecture; and yet I think I cannot be utterly mistaken in regarding it as at least useful in the sense of a National employment. I am confirmed in this impression by what I see passing among the states of Europe at this instant. All the horror, distress, and tumult which oppress the foreign nations, are traceable, among the other secondary causes through which God is working out His will upon them, to the simple one of their not having enough to do. I am not blind to the distress among their operatives; nor do I deny the nearer and visibly active causes of the movement: the recklessness of villainy in the leaders of revolt, the absence of common moral principle in the upper classes, and of common courage and honesty in the heads of governments. But these causes themselves are ultimately traceable to a deeper and simpler one: the recklessness of the demagogue, the immorality of the middle class, and the effeminacy and treachery of the noble, are traceable in all these nations to the commonest and most fruitful cause of calamity in households—idleness. We think too much in our benevolent efforts, more multiplied and more vain day by day, of bettering men by giving them advice and instruction. There are few who will take either: the chief thing they need is occupation. I do not mean work in the sense of bread,—I mean work in the sense of mental interest; for those who either are

placed above the necessity of labor for their bread, or
who will not work although they should. There is a vast
quantity of idle energy among European nations at this
time, which ought to go into handicrafts; there are multitudes of idle semi-gentlemen who ought to be shoemakers
and carpenters; but since they will not be these so long
as they can help it, the business of the philanthropist is
to find them some other employment than disturbing
governments. It is of no use to tell them they are fools,
and that they will only make themselves miserable in the
end as well as others: if they have nothing else to do,
they will do mischief; and the man who will not work,
and who has no means of intellectual pleasure, is as sure
to become an instrument of evil as if he had sold himself
bodily to Satan. I have myself seen enough of the daily
life of the young educated men of France and Italy, to
account for, as it deserves, the deepest national suffering
and degradation; and though, for the most part, our commerce and our national habits of industry preserve us
from a similar paralysis, yet it would be wise to consider
whether the forms of employment which we chiefly adopt
or promote, are as well calculated as they might be to
improve and elevate us.

We have just spent, for instance, a hundred and fifty
millions, with which we have paid men for digging ground
from one place and depositing it in another. We have
formed a large class of men, the railway navvies, especially reckless, unmanageable, and dangerous. We have
maintained besides (let us state the benefits as fairly as
possible) a number of ironfounders in an unhealthy and
painful employment; we have developed (this is at least
good) a very large amount of mechanical ingenuity; and
we have, in fine, attained the power of going fast from
one place to another. Meantime we have no mental interest or concern ourselves in the operations we have set
on foot, but have been left to the usual vanities and
cares of our existence. Suppose, on the other hand, that
we had employed the same sums in building beautiful
houses and churches. We should have maintained the
same number of men, not in driving wheelbarrows, but
in a distinctly technical, if not intellectual, employment;
and those who were more intelligent among them would

have been especially happy in that employment, as having room in it for the development of their fancy, and being directed by it to that observation of beauty which, associated with the pursuit of natural science, at present forms the enjoyment of many of the more intelligent manufacturing operatives. Of mechanical ingenuity, there is, I imagine, at least as much required to build a cathedral as to cut a tunnel or contrive a locomotive: we should, therefore, have developed as much science, while the artistical element of intellect would have been added to the gain. Meantime we should ourselves have been made happier and wiser by the interest we should have taken in the work with which we were personally concerned; and when all was done, instead of the very doubtful advantage of the power of going fast from place to place, we should have had the certain advantage of increased pleasure in stopping at home.

There are many other less capacious, but more constant, channels of expenditure, quite as disputable in their beneficial tendency; and we are, perhaps, hardly enough in the habit of inquiring, with respect to any particular form of luxury or any customary appliance of life, whether the kind of employment it gives to the operative or the dependent be as healthy and fitting an employment as we might otherwise provide for him. It is not enough to find men absolute subsistence; we should think of the manner of life which our demands necessitate; and endeavor, as far as may be, to make all our needs such as may, in the supply of them, raise, as well as feed, the poor. It is far better to give work which is above the men, than to educate the men to be above their work. It may be doubted, for instance, whether the habits of luxury, which necessitate a large train of men servants, be a wholesome form of expenditure; and more, whether the pursuits which have a tendency to enlarge the class of the jockey and the groom be a philanthropic form of mental occupation. So again, consider the large number of men whose lives are employed by civilized nations in cutting facets upon jewels. There is much dexterity of hand, patience and ingenuity thus bestowed, which are simply burned out in the blaze of the tiara, without, so far as I see, bestowing any pleasure upon those who wear

or who behold, at all compensatory for the loss of life
and mental power which are involved in the employment
of the workman. He would be far more healthily and
happily sustained by being set to carve stone; certain
qualities of his mind, for which there is no room in his
present occupation, would develop themselves in the no
bler; and I believe that most women would, in the end,
prefer the pleasure of having built a church, or con
tributed to the adornment of a cathedral, to the pride
of bearing a certain quantity of adamant on their fore
heads.

I could pursue this subject willingly, but I have some
strange notions about it which it is perhaps wiser not
loosely to set down. I content myself with finally reas-
serting, what had been throughout the burden of the pre
ceding pages, that whatever rank, or whatever impor
tance, may be attributed or attached to their immediate
subject, there is at least some value in the analogies with
which its pursuit has presented us, and some instruction
in the frequent reference of its commonest necessities to
the mighty laws, in the sense and scope of which all men
are Builders, whom every hour sees laying the stubble or
the stone.

I have paused, not once nor twice, as I wrote, and
often have checked the course of what might otherwise
have been importunate persuasion, as the thought has
crossed me, how soon all Architecture may be vain, except that which is not made with hands. There is something ominous in the light which has enabled us to look
back with disdain upon the ages among whose lovely
vestiges we have been wandering. I could smile when I
hear the hopeful exultation of many, at the new reach
of worldly science, and vigor of worldly effort; as if we
were again at the beginning of days. There is thunder
on the horizon as well as dawn. The sun was risen upon
the earth when Lot entered into Zoar.

IV. ART AND SOCIETY

The Nature of Gothic

[Stones of Venice, Vol. II, Ch. 6.]

If the reader will look back to the division of our subject which was made in the first chapter of the first volume, he will find that we are now about to enter upon the examination of that school of Venetian architecture which forms an intermediate step between the Byzantine and Gothic forms; but which I find may be conveniently considered in its connection with the latter style. In order that we may discern the tendency of each step of this change, it will be wise in the outset to endeavor to form some general idea of its final result. We know already what the Byzantine architecture is from which the transition was made, but we ought to know something of the Gothic architecture into which it led. I shall endeavor therefore to give the reader in this chapter an idea, at once broad and definite, of the true nature of *Gothic* architecture, properly so called; not of that of Venice only, but of universal Gothic: for it will be one of the most interesting parts of our subsequent inquiry to find out how far Venetian architecture reached the universal or perfect type of Gothic, and how far it either fell short of it, or assumed foreign and independent forms.

The principal difficulty in doing this arises from the fact that every building of the Gothic period differs in some important respect from every other; and many include features which, if they occurred in other buildings, would not be considered Gothic at all; so that all we have to reason upon is merely, if I may be allowed so to express it, a greater or less degree of *Gothicness* in each building we examine. And it is this Gothicness,—the character which, according as it is found more or less in a building, makes it more or less Gothic,—of which I want to define the nature; and I feel the same kind of difficulty in doing so which would be encountered by any one who undertook to explain, for instance, the nature of Redness, without any actually red thing to point to, but only orange and purple things. Suppose he had only a piece of heather and a dead oak-leaf to do it with. He might

213

say, the color which is mixed with the yellow in this oak
leaf, and with the blue in this heather, would be red, if
you had it separate; but it would be difficult, neverthe
less, to make the abstraction perfectly intelligible: and
it is so in a far greater degree to make the abstraction of
the Gothic character intelligible, because that character
itself is made up of many mingled ideas, and can consist
only in their union.   That is to say, pointed arches do
not constitute Gothic, nor vaulted roofs, nor flying but
tresses, nor grotesque sculptures; but all or some of these
things, and many other things with them, when they
come together so as to have life.

Observe also, that, in the definition proposed, I shall
only endeavor to analyze the idea which I suppose already
to exist in the reader's mind.   We all have some notion
most of us a very determined one, of the meaning of the
term Gothic, but I know that many persons have this
idea in their minds without being able to define it: that
is to say, understanding generally that Westminster Ab
bey is Gothic, and St. Paul's is not, that Strasburg Ca
thedral is Gothic, and St. Peter's is not, they have, never
theless, no clear notion of what it is that they recognize
in the one or miss in the other, such as would enable
them to say how far the work at Westminster or Stras
burg is good and pure of its kind; still less to say of any
nondescript building, like St. James's Palace or Windsor
Castle, how much right Gothic element there is in it, and
how much wanting.   And I believe this inquiry to be a
pleasant and profitable one; and that there will be found
something more than usually interesting in tracing out
this gray, shadowy, many-pinnacled image of the Gothic
spirit within us; and discerning what fellowship there is
between it and our northern hearts.   And if, at any point
of the inquiry, I should interfere with any of the reader's
previously formed conceptions, and use the term Gothic
in any sense which he would not willingly attach to it,
I do not ask him to accept, but only to examine and un
derstand, my interpretation, as necessary to the intelligi
bility of what follows in the rest of the work.

We have, then, the Gothic character submitted to our
analysis, just as the rough mineral is submitted to that
of the chemist, entangled with many other foreign sub

stances, itself perhaps in no place pure, or ever to be obtained or seen in purity for more than an instant; but nevertheless a thing of definite and separate nature, however inextricable or confused in appearance. Now observe: the chemist defines his mineral by two separate kinds of character; one external, its crystalline form, hardness, lustre, etc.; the other internal, the proportions and nature of its constituent atoms. Exactly in the same manner, we shall find that Gothic architecture has external forms and internal elements. Its elements are certain mental tendencies of the builders, legibly expressed in it; as fancifulness, love of variety, love of richness, and such others. Its external forms are pointed arches, vaulted roofs, etc. And unless both the elements and the forms are there, we have no right to call the style Gothic. It is not enough that it has the Form, if it have not also the power and life. It is not enough that it has the Power, if it have not the form. We must therefore inquire into each of these characters successively; and determine first, what is the Mental Expression, and secondly, what the Material Form of Gothic architecture, properly so called.

Mental Power or Expression. What characters, we have to discover, did the Gothic builders love, or instinctively express in their work, as distinguished from all other builders?

Let us go back for a moment to our chemistry, and note that, in defining a mineral by its constituent parts, it is not one nor another of them, that can make up the mineral, but the union of all: for instance, it is neither in charcoal, nor in oxygen, nor in lime, that there is the making of chalk, but in the combination of all three in certain measures; they are all found in very different things from chalk, and there is nothing like chalk either in charcoal or in oxygen, but they are nevertheless necessary to its existence.

So in the various mental characters which make up the soul of Gothic. It is not one nor another that produces it; but their union in certain measures. Each one of them is found in many other architectures besides Gothic; but Gothic cannot exist where they are not found, or, at least, where their place is not in some way supplied. Only there is this great difference between the composition of the mineral and of the architectural style, that if we withdraw one of its elements from the stone, its form is utterly changed, and its existence as such and such a mineral is destroyed; but if we withdraw one of its mental elements from the Gothic style, it is only a little less Gothic than it was before, and the union of two or three of its elements is enough already to bestow a certain Gothicness of character, which gains in intensity as we add the others, and loses as we again withdraw them.

I believe, then, that the characteristic or moral elements of Gothic are the following, placed in the order of their importance:

1. Savageness.
2. Changefulness.
3. Naturalism.
4. Grotesqueness.
5. Rigidity.
6. Redundance.

These characters are here expressed as belonging to the building; as belonging to the builder, they would be expressed thus:—1. Savageness or Rudeness. 2. Love of Change. 3. Love of Nature. 4. Disturbed Imagination. 5. Obstinacy. 6. Generosity. And I repeat, that the withdrawal of any one, or any two, will not at once destroy the Gothic character of a building, but the removal of a majority of them will. I shall proceed to examine them in their order.

1. SAVAGENESS.—I am not sure when the word "Gothic" was first generally applied to the architecture of the North; but I presume that, whatever the date of its original usage, it was intended to imply reproach, and express the barbaric character of the nations among whom that architecture arose. It never implied that they were literally of Gothic lineage, far less that their architecture had been originally invented by the Goths themselves but it did imply that they and their buildings together exhibited a degree of sternness and rudeness, which, in contradistinction to the character of southern and eastern nations, appeared like a perpetual reflection of the

contrast between the Goth and the Roman in their first encounter. And when that fallen Roman, in the utmost impotence of his luxury, and insolence of his guilt, became the model for the imitation of civilized Europe, at the close of the so-called Dark Ages, the word Gothic became a term of unmitigated contempt, not unmixed with aversion. From that contempt, by the exertion of the antiquaries and architects of this century, Gothic architecture has been sufficiently vindicated; and perhaps some among us, in our admiration of the magnificent science of its structure, and sacredness of its expression, might desire that the term of ancient reproach should be withdrawn, and some other, of more apparent honorableness, adopted in its place. There is no chance, as there is no need, of such a substitution. As far as the epithet was used scornfully, it was used falsely; but there is no reproach in the word, rightly understood; on the contrary, there is a profound truth, which the instinct of mankind almost unconsciously recognizes. It is true, greatly and deeply true, that the architecture of the North is rude and wild; but it is not true, that, for this reason, we are to condemn it, or despise. Far otherwise: I believe it is in this very character that it deserves our profoundest reverence.

The charts of the world which have been drawn up by modern science have thrown into a narrow space the expression of a vast amount of knowledge, but I have never yet seen any one pictorial enough to enable the spectator to imagine the kind of contrast in physical character which exists between Northern and Southern countries. We know the differences in detail, but we have not that broad glance and grasp which would enable us to feel them in their fulness. We know that gentians grow on the Alps, and olives on the Apennines; but we do not enough conceive for ourselves that variegated mosaic of the world's surface which a bird sees in its migration, that difference between the district of the gentian and of the olive which the stork and the swallow see far off, as they lean upon the sirocco wind. Let us, for a moment, try to raise ourselves even above the level of their flight, and imagine the Mediterranean lying beneath us like an irregular lake, and all its ancient promontories sleeping in the sun: here and there an angry spot of thunder, a gray stain of storm, moving upon the burning field; and here and there a fixed wreath of white volcano smoke, surrounded by its circle of ashes; but for the most part a great peacefulness of light, Syria and Greece, Italy and Spain, laid like pieces of a golden pavement into the sea-blue, chased, as we stoop nearer to them, with bossy beaten work of mountain chains, and glowing softly with terraced gardens, and flowers heavy with frankincense, mixed among masses of laurel, and orange, and plumy palm, that abate with their gray-green shadows the burning of the marble rocks, and of the ledges of porphyry sloping under lucent sand. Then let us pass farther toward the north, until we see the orient colors change gradually into a vast belt of rainy green, where the pastures of Switzerland, and poplar valleys of France, and dark forests of the Danube and Carpathians stretch from the mouths of the Loire to those of the Volga, seen through clefts in gray swirls of rain-cloud and flaky veils of the mist of the brooks, spreading low along the pasture lands: and then, farther north still, to see the earth heave into mighty masses of leaden rock and heathy moor, bordering with a broad waste of gloomy purple that belt of field and wood, and splintering into irregular and grisly islands amidst the northern seas, beaten by storm, and chilled by ice-drift, and tormented by furious pulses of contending tide, until the roots of the last forests fail from among the hill ravines, and the hunger of the north wind bites their peaks into barrenness; and, at last, the wall of ice, durable like iron, sets, deathlike, its white teeth against us out of the polar twilight. And, having once traversed in thought this gradation of the zoned iris of the earth in all its material vastness, let us go down nearer to it, and watch the parallel change in the belt of animal life; the multitudes of swift and brilliant creatures that glance in the air and sea, or tread the sands of the southern zone; striped zebras and spotted leopards, glistening serpents, and birds arrayed in purple and scarlet. Let us contrast their delicacy and brilliancy of color, and swiftness of motion, with the frost-cramped strength, and shaggy covering, and dusky plumage of the northern tribes; contrast the Arabian horse with the Shetland, the tiger and leopard with the wolf and bear, the antelope with the elk, the bird of paradise with the osprey; and then, submissively acknowleging the great laws by which the earth and all that it bears are ruled throughout their being, let us not condemn but rejoice in the expression by man of his own rest in the statutes of the lands that gave him birth. Let us watch him with reverence as he sets side by side the burning gems, and smooths with soft sculpture the jasper pillars, that are to reflect a ceaseless sunshine, and rise into a cloudless sky: but not with less reverence let us stand by him, when, with rough strength and hurried stroke, he smites an uncouth animation out of the rocks which he has torn from among the moss of the moorland, and heaves into the darkened air the pile of iron buttress and rugged wall, instinct with work of an imagination as wild and wayward as the northern sea; creatures of ungainly shape and rigid limb, but full of wolfish life; fierce as the winds that beat, and changeful as the clouds that shade them.

There is, I repeat, no degradation, no reproach in this, but all dignity and honorableness: and we should err grievously in refusing either to recognize as an essential character of the existing architecture of the North, or to admit as a desirable character in that which it yet may be, this wildness of thought, and roughness of work; this look of mountain brotherhood between the cathedral and the Alp; this magnificence of sturdy power, put forth only the more energetically because the fine finger-touch was chilled away by the frosty wind, and the eye dimmed by the moor-mist, or blinded by the hail; this outspeaking of the strong spirit of men who may not gather redundant fruitage from the earth, nor bask in dreamy benignity of sunshine, but must break the rock for bread, and cleave the forest for fire, and show, even in what they did for their delight, some of the hard habits of the arm and heart that grew on them as they swung the ax or pressed the plough.

If, however, the savageness of Gothic architecture, merely as an expression of its origin among Northern nations, may be considered, in some sort, a noble character, it possesses a higher nobility still, when considered as an index, not of climate, but of religious principle.

In the 13th and 14th paragraphs of Chapter XXI of the first volume of this work, it was noticed that the systems of architectural ornament, properly so called, might be divided into three:—1. Servile ornament, in which the execution or power of the inferior workman is entirely subjected to the intellect of the higher;—2. Constitutional ornament, in which the executive inferior power is, to a certain point, emancipated and independent, having a will of its own, yet confessing its inferiority and rendering obedience to higher powers;—and 3. Revolutionary ornament, in which no executive inferiority is admitted at all. I must here explain the nature of these divisions at somewhat greater length.

Of Servile ornament, the principal schools are the Greek, Ninevite, and Egyptian; but their servility is of different kinds. The Greek master-workman was far advanced in knowledge and power above the Assyrian or Egyptian. Neither he nor those for whom he worked could endure the appearance of imperfection in anything; and, therefore, what ornament he appointed to be done by those beneath him was composed of mere geometrical forms,—balls, ridges, and perfectly symmetrical foliage, —which could be executed with absolute precision by line and rule, and were as perfect in their way, when completed, as his own figure sculpture. The Assyrian and Egyptian, on the contrary, less cognizant of accurate form in anything, were content to allow their figure sculpture to be executed by inferior workmen, but lowered the method of its treatment to a standard which every workman could reach, and then trained him by discipline so rigid, that there was no chance of his falling beneath the standard appointed. The Greek gave to the lower workman no subject which he could not perfectly execute. The Assyrian gave him subjects which he could only execute imperfectly, but fixed a legal standard for his imperfection. The workman was, in both systems, a slave.*

---

* The third kind of ornament, the Renaissance, is that in which the inferior detail becomes principal, the executor of every minor portion being required to exhibit skill and possess knowledge as great as that which is possessed by the master of the design; and in the endeavor to endow him with this skill and knowledge, his own original power is overwhelmed, and the whole building becomes a wearisome exhibition of well-educated imbecility. We must fully inquire into the nature of this form of error, when we arrive at the examination of the Renaissance schools. [Ruskin's note.]

But in the mediæval, or especially Christian, system of ornament, this slavery is done away with altogether; Christianity having recognized, in small things as well as great, the individual value of every soul. But it not only recognizes its value; it confesses its imperfection, in only bestowing dignity upon the acknowledgment of unworthiness. That admission of lost power and fallen nature, which the Greek or Ninevite felt to be intensely painful, and, as far as might be, altogether refused, the Christian makes daily and hourly, contemplating the fact of it without fear, as tending, in the end, to God's greater glory. Therefore, to every spirit which Christianity summons to her service, her exhortation is: Do what you can, and confess frankly what you are unable to do; neither let your effort be shortened for fear of failure, nor your confession silenced for fear of shame. And it is, perhaps, the principal admirableness of the Gothic schools of architecture, that they thus receive the results of the labor of inferior minds; and out of fragments full of imperfection, and betraying that imperfection in every touch, indulgently raise up a stately and unaccusable whole.

But the modern English mind has this much in common with that of the Greek, that it intensely desires, in all things, the utmost completion or perfection compatible with their nature. This is a noble character in the abstract, but becomes ignoble when it causes us to forget the relative dignities of that nature itself, and to prefer the perfectness of the lower nature to the imperfection of the higher; not considering that as, judged by such a rule, all the brute animals would be preferable to man, because more perfect in their functions and kind, and yet are always held inferior to him, so also in the works of man, those which are more perfect in their kind are always inferior to those which are, in their nature, liable to more faults and shortcomings. For the finer the nature, the more flaws it will show through the clearness of it; and it is a law of this universe, that the best things shall be seldomest seen in their best form. The wild grass grows well and strongly, one year with another; but the wheat is, according to the greater nobleness of its nature, liable to the bitterer blight. And therefore, while in all things that we see or do, we are to desire perfection, and

strive for it, we are nevertheless not to set the meaner
thing, in its narrow accomplishment, above the nobler
thing, in its mighty progress; not to esteem smooth minuteness above shattered majesty; not to prefer mean
victory to honorable defeat; not to lower the level of our
aim, that we may the more surely enjoy the complacency
of success. But, above all, in our dealings with the souls
of other men, we are to take care how we check, by severe
requirement or narrow caution, efforts which might otherwise lead to a noble issue; and, still more, how we with-
hold our admiration from great excellencies, because they
are mingled with rough faults. Now, in the make and
nature of every man, however rude or simple, whom we
employ in manual labor, there are some powers for better
things; some tardy imagination, torpid capacity of emotion, tottering steps of thought, there are, even at the
worst; and in most cases it is all our own fault that they
are tardy or torpid. But they cannot be strengthened,
unless we are content to take them in their feebleness,
and unless we prize and honor them in their imperfection
above the best and most perfect manual skill. And this
is what we have to do with all our laborers; to look for
the *thoughtful* part of them, and get that out of them,
whatever we lose for it, whatever faults and errors we are
obliged to take with it. For the best that is in them cannot manifest itself, but in company with much error. Understand this clearly: You can teach a man to draw a
straight line, and to cut one; to strike a curved line, and
to carve it; and to copy and carve any number of given
lines or forms, with admirable speed and perfect precision;
and you find his work perfect of its kind: but if you ask
him to think about any of those forms, to consider if he
cannot find any better in his own head, he stops; his execution becomes hesitating; he thinks, and ten to one he
thinks wrong; ten to one he makes a mistake in the first
touch he gives to his work as a thinking being. But you
have made a man of him for all that. He was only a machine before, an animated tool.

And observe, you are put to stern choice in this matter.
You must either make a tool of the creature, or a man of
him. You cannot make both. Men were not intended to
work with the accuracy of tools, to be precise and perfect

in all their actions. If you will have that precision out of them, and make their fingers measure degrees like cog-wheels, and their arms strike curves like compasses, you must unhumanize them. All the energy of their spirits must be given to make cogs and compasses of themselves. All their attention and strength must go to the accomplishment of the mean act. The eye of the soul must be bent upon the finger-point, and the soul's force must fill all the invisible nerves that guide it, ten hours a day, that it may not err from its steely precision, and so soul and sight be worn away, and the whole human being be lost at last—a heap of sawdust, so far as its intellectual work in this world is concerned: saved only by its Heart, which cannot go into the form of cogs and compasses, but expands, after the ten hours are over, into fireside humanity. On the other hand, if you will make a man of the working creature, you cannot make a tool. Let him but begin to imagine, to think, to try to do anything worth doing; and the engine-turned precision is lost at once. Out come all his roughness, all his dulness, all his incapability; shame upon shame, failure upon failure, pause after pause: but out comes the whole majesty of him also; and we know the height of it only when we see the clouds settling upon him. And, whether the clouds be bright or dark, there will be transfiguration behind and within them.

And now, reader, look round this English room of yours, about which you have been proud so often, because the work of it was so good and strong, and the ornaments of it so finished. Examine again all those accurate mouldings, and perfect polishings, and unerring adjustments of the seasoned wood and tempered steel. Many a time you have exulted over them, and thought how great England was, because her slightest work was done so thoroughly. Alas! if read rightly, these perfectnesses are signs of a slavery in our England a thousand times more bitter and more degrading than that of the scourged African, or helot Greek. Men may be beaten, chained, tormented, yoked like cattle, slaughtered like summer flies, and yet remain in one sense, and the best sense, free. But to smother their souls within them, to blight and hew into rotting pollards the suckling branches of their human intelligence, to make the flesh and skin which, after the worm's work on it, is to see God, into leathern thongs to yoke machinery with,—this it is to be slave-masters indeed; and there might be more freedom in England, though her feudal lords' lightest words were worth men's lives, and though the blood of the vexed husbandman dropped in the furrows of her fields, than there is while the animation of her multitudes is sent like fuel to feed the factory smoke, and the strength of them is given daily to be wasted into the fineness of a web, or racked into the exactness of a line.

And, on the other hand, go forth again to gaze upon the old cathedral front, where you have smiled so often at the fantastic ignorance of the old sculptors: examine once more those ugly goblins, and formless monsters, and stern statues, anatomiless and rigid; but do not mock at them, for they are signs of the life and liberty of every workman who struck the stone; a freedom of thought, and rank in scale of being, such as no laws, no charters, no charities can secure; but which it must be the first aim of all Europe at this day to regain for her children.

Let me not be thought to speak wildly or extravagantly. It is verily this degradation of the operative into a machine, which, more than any other evil of the times, is leading the mass of the nations everywhere into vain, incoherent, destructive struggling for a freedom of which they cannot explain the nature to themselves. Their universal outcry against wealth, and against nobility, is not forced from them either by the pressure of famine, or the sting of mortified pride. These do much, and have done much in all ages; but the foundations of society were never yet shaken as they are at this day. It is not that men are ill fed, but that they have no pleasure in the work by which they make their bread, and therefore look to wealth as the only means of pleasure. It is not that men are pained by the scorn of the upper classes, but they cannot endure their own; for they feel that the kind of labor to which they are condemned is verily a degrading one, and makes them less than men. Never had the upper classes so much sympathy with the lower, or charity for them, as they have at this day, and yet never were they so much hated by them: for, of old, the separation between the noble and the poor was merely a wall built by law; now it is a veritable difference in level of standing, a precipice between upper and lower grounds in the field of humanity, and there is pestilential air at the bottom of it. I know not if a day is ever to come when the nature of right freedom will be understood, and when men will see that to obey another man, to labor for him, yield reverence to him or to his place, is not slavery. It is often the best kind of liberty,—liberty from care. The man who says to one, Go, and he goeth, and to another, Come, and he cometh, has, in most cases, more sense of restraint and difficulty than the man who obeys him. The movements of the one are hindered by the burden on his shoulder; of the other, by the bridle on his lips: there is no way by which the burden may be lightened; but we need not suffer from the bridle if we do not champ at it. To yield reverence to another, to hold ourselves and our lives at his disposal, is not slavery; often it is the noblest state in which a man can live in this world. There is, indeed, a reverence which is servile, that is to say, irrational or selfish: but there is also noble reverence, that is to say, reasonable and loving; and a man is never so noble as when he is reverent in this kind; nay, even if the feeling pass the bounds of mere reason, so that it be loving, a man is raised by it. Which had, in reality, most of the serf nature in him,—the Irish peasant who was lying in wait yesterday for his landlord, with his musket muzzle thrust through the ragged hedge; or that old mountain servant, who 200 years ago, at Inverkeithing, gave up his own life and the lives of his seven sons for his chief?— as each fell, calling forth his brother to the death, "Another for Hector!" And therefore, in all ages and all countries, reverence has been paid and sacrifice made by men to each other, not only without complaint, but rejoicingly; and famine, and peril, and sword, and all evil, and all shame, have been borne willingly in the causes of masters and kings; for all these gifts of the heart ennobled the men who gave, not less than the men who received them, and nature prompted, and God rewarded the sacrifice. But to feel their souls withering within them, unthanked, to find their whole being sunk into an unrecognized abyss, to be counted off into a heap of mechanism,

numbered with its wheels, and weighed with its hammer
strokes,—this, nature bade not,—this, God blesses not,—
this, humanity for no long time is able to endure.

We have much studied and much perfected, of late, the
great civilized invention of the division of labor; only
we give it a false name. It is not, truly speaking, the
labor that is divided; but the men:—Divided into mere
segments of men—broken into small fragments and
crumbs of life; so that all the little piece of intelligence
that is left in a man is not enough to make a pin, or a
nail, but exhausts itself in making the point of a pin or
the head of a nail. Now it is a good and desirable thing,
truly, to make many pins in a day; but if we could only
see with what crystal sand their points were polished,—
sand of human soul, much to be magnified before it can
be discerned for what it is,—we should think there might
be some loss in it also. And the great cry that rises from
all our manufacturing cities, louder than their furnace
blast, is all in very deed for this,—that we manufacture
everything there except men; we blanch cotton, and
strengthen steel, and refine sugar, and shape pottery; but
to brighten, to strengthen, to refine, or to form a single
living spirit, never enters into our estimate of advantages.
And all the evil to which that cry is urging our myriads
can be met only in one way: not by teaching nor preaching, for to teach them is but to show them their misery,
and to preach to them, if we do nothing more than preach,
is to mock at it. It can be met only by a right understanding, on the part of all classes, of what kinds of labor
are good for men, raising them, and making them happy;
by a determined sacrifice of such convenience, or beauty,
or cheapness as is to be got only by the degradation of
the workman; and by equally determined demand for the
products and results of healthy and ennobling labor.

And how, it will be asked, are these products to be
recognized, and this demand to be regulated? Easily: by
the observance of three broad and simple rules:

1. Never encourage the manufacture of any article not
absolutely necessary, in the production of which *Invention* has no share.

2. Never demand an exact finish for its own sake, but
only for some practical or noble end.

) 3. Never encourage imitation or copying of any kind, except for the sake of preserving record of great works.

The second of these principles is the only one which directly rises out of the consideration of our immediate subject; but I shall briefly explain the meaning and extent of the first also, reserving the enforcement of the third for another place.

1. Never encourage the manufacture of anything not necessary, in the production of which invention has no share.

For instance. Glass beads are utterly unnecessary, and there is no design or thought employed in their manufacture. They are formed by first drawing out the glass into rods; these rods are chopped up into fragments of the size of beads by the human hand, and the fragments are then rounded in the furnace. The men who chop up the rods sit at their work all day, their hands vibrating with a perpetual and exquisitely timed palsy, and the beads dropping beneath their vibration like hail. Neither they, nor the men who draw out the rods or fuse the fragments, have the smallest occasion for the use of any single human faculty; and every young lady, therefore, who buys glass beads is engaged in the slave-trade, and in a much more cruel one than that which we have so long been endeavoring to put down.

But glass cups and vessels may become the subjects of exquisite invention; and if in buying these we pay for the invention, that is to say, for the beautiful form, or color, or engraving, and not for mere finish of execution, we are doing good to humanity.

So, again, the cutting of precious stones, in all ordinary cases, requires little exertion of any mental faculty; some tact and judgment in avoiding flaws, and so on, but nothing to bring out the whole mind. Every person who wears cut jewels merely for the sake of their value is, therefore, a slave-driver.

But the working of the goldsmith, and the various designing of grouped jewellery and enamel-work, may become the subject of the most noble human intelligence. Therefore, money spent in the purchase of well-designed plate, of precious engraved vases, cameos, or enamels, does good to humanity; and, in work of this kind, jewels may be employed to heighten its splendor; and their cutting is then a price paid for the attainment of a noble end, and thus perfectly allowable.

I shall perhaps press this law farther elsewhere, but our immediate concern is chiefly with the second, namely, never to demand an exact finish, when it does not lead to a noble end. For observe, I have only dwelt upon the rudeness of Gothic, or any other kind of imperfectness, as admirable, where it was impossible to get design or thought without it. If you are to have the thought of a rough and untaught man, you must have it in a rough and untaught way; but from an educated man, who can without effort express his thoughts in an educated way, take the graceful expression, and be thankful. Only *get* the thought, and do not silence the peasant because he cannot speak good grammar, or until you have taught him his grammar. Grammar and refinement are good things, both, only be sure of the better thing first. And thus in art, delicate finish is desirable from the greatest masters, and is always given by them. In some places Michael Angelo, Leonardo, Phidias, Perugino, Turner, all finished with the most exquisite care; and the finish they give always leads to the fuller accomplishment of their noble purposes. But lower men than these cannot finish, for it requires consummate knowledge to finish consummately, and then we must take their thoughts as they are able to give them. So the rule is simple: Always look for invention first, and after that, for such execution as will help the invention, and as the inventor is capable of without painful effort, and *no more*. Above all, demand no refinement of execution where there is no thought, for that is slaves' work, unredeemed. Rather choose rough work than smooth work, so only that the practical purpose be answered, and never imagine there is reason to be proud of anything that may be accomplished by patience and sand-paper.

I shall only give one example, which however will show the reader what I mean, from the manufacture already alluded to, that of glass. Our modern glass is exquisitely clear in its substance, true in its form, accurate in its cutting. We are proud of this. We ought to be ashamed of it. The old Venice glass was muddy, inaccurate in all its forms, and clumsily cut, if at all. And the old Venetian was justly proud of it. For there is this difference between the English and Venetian workman, that the former thinks only of accurately matching his patterns, and getting his curves perfectly true and his edges perfectly sharp, and becomes a mere machine for rounding curves and sharpening edges; while the old Venetian cared not a whit whether his edges were sharp or not, but he invented a new design for every glass that he made, and never moulded a handle or a lip without a new fancy in it. And therefore, though some Venetian glass is ugly and clumsy enough when made by clumsy and unintive workmen, other Venetian glass is so lovely in its forms that no price is too great for it; and we never see the same form in it twice. Now you cannot have the finish and the varied form too. If the workman is thinking about his edges, he cannot be thinking of his design; if of his design, he cannot think of his edges. Choose whether you will pay for the lovely form or the perfect finish, and choose at the same moment whether you will make the worker a man or a grindstone.

Nay, but the reader interrupts me,—"If the workman can design beautifully, I would not have him kept at the furnace. Let him be taken away and made a gentleman, and have a studio, and design his glass there, and I will have it blown and cut for him by common workmen, and so I will have my design and my finish too."

All ideas of this kind are founded upon two mistaken suppositions: the first, that one man's thoughts can be, or ought to be, executed by another man's hands; the second, that manual labor is a degradation, when it is governed by intellect.

On a large scale, and in work determinable by line and rule, it is indeed both possible and necessary that the thoughts of one man should be carried out by the labor of others; in this sense I have already defined the best architecture to be the expression of the mind of manhood by the hands of childhood. But on a smaller scale, and in a design which cannot be mathematically defined, one man's thoughts can never be expressed by another: and the difference between the spirit of touch of the man who is inventing, and of the man who is obeying directions, is often all the difference between a great and a common work of art. How wide the separation is between original and second-hand execution, I shall endeavor to show elsewhere; it is not so much to our purpose here as to mark the other and more fatal error of despising manual labor when governed by intellect; for it is no less fatal an error to despise it when thus regulated by intellect, than to value it for its own sake. We are always in these days endeavoring to separate the two; we want one man to be always thinking, and another to be always working, and we call one a gentleman, and the other an operative; whereas the workman ought often to be thinking, and the thinker often to be working, and both should be gentlemen, in the best sense. As it is, we make both ungentle, the one envying, the other despising, his brother; and the mass of society is made up of morbid thinkers, and miserable workers. Now it is only by labor that thought can be made healthy, and only by thought that labor can be made happy, and the two cannot be separated with impunity. It would be well if all of us were good handicraftsmen in some kind, and the dishonor of manual labor done away with altogether; so that though there should still be a trenchant distinction of race between nobles and commoners, there should not, among the latter, be a trenchant distinction of employment, as between idle and working men, or between men of liberal and illiberal professions. All professions should be liberal, and there should be less pride felt in peculiarity of employment, and more in excellence of achievement. And yet more, in each several profession, no master should be too proud to do its hardest work. The painter should grind his own colors; the architect work in the mason's yard with his men; the master-manufacturer be himself a more skilful operative than any man in his mills; and the distinction between one man and another be only in experience and skill, and the authority and wealth which these must naturally and justly obtain.

I should be led far from the matter in hand, if I were to pursue this interesting subject. Enough, I trust, has been said to show the reader that the rudeness or imperfection which at first rendered the term "Gothic" one of reproach is indeed, when rightly understood, one of the most noble characters of Christian architecture, and not only a noble but an *essential* one. It seems a fantastic paradox, but it is nevertheless a most important truth, that no architecture can be truly noble which is *not* imperfect. And this is easily demonstrable. For since the architect, whom we will suppose capable of doing all in perfection, cannot execute the whole with his own hands, he must either make slaves of his workmen in the old Greek, and present English fashion, and level his work to a slave's capacities, which is to degrade it; or else he must take his workmen as he finds them, and let them show their weaknesses together with their strength, which will involve the Gothic imperfection, but render the whole work as noble as the intellect of the age can make it.

But the principle may be stated more broadly still. I have confined the illustration of it to architecture, but I must not leave it as if true of architecture only. Hitherto I have used the words imperfect and perfect merely to distinguish between work grossly unskilful, and work executed with average precision and science; and I have been pleading that any degree of unskilfulness should be admitted, so only that the laborer's mind had room for expression. But, accurately speaking, no good work whatever can be perfect, and *the demand for perfection is always a sign of a misunderstanding of the ends of art.*

This for two reasons, both based on everlasting laws. The first, that no great man ever stops working till he has reached his point of failure: that is to say, his mind is always far in advance of his powers of execution, and the latter will now and then give way in trying to follow it; besides that he will always give to the inferior portions of his work only such inferior attention as they require; and according to his greatness he becomes so accustomed to the feeling of dissatisfaction with the best he can do, that in moments of lassitude or anger with himself he will not care though the beholder be dissatisfied also. I believe there has only been one man who would not acknowledge this necessity, and strove always to reach perfection, Leonardo; the end of his vain effort being merely that he would take ten years to a picture and leave it unfinished. And therefore, if we are to have great men working at all, or less men doing their best, the work will be imperfect, however beautiful. Of human work none but what is bad can be perfect, in its own bad way.*

The second reason is, that imperfection is in some sort essential to all that we know of life. It is the sign of life in a mortal body, that is to say, of a state of progress and change. Nothing that lives is, or can be, rigidly perfect; part of it is decaying, part nascent. The fox-glove blossom,—a third part bud, a third part past, a third part in full bloom,—is a type of the life of this world. And in all things that live there are certain ir-regularities and deficiencies which are not only signs of life, but sources of beauty. No human face is exactly the same in its lines on each side, no leaf perfect in its lobes, no branch in its symmetry. All admit irregularity as they imply change; and to banish imperfection is to de-stroy expression, to check exertion, to paralyze vitality. All things are literally better, lovelier, and more beloved for the imperfections which have been divinely appointed, that the law of human life may be Effort, and the law of human judgment, Mercy.

Accept this then for a universal law, that neither ar-chitecture nor any other noble work of man can be good unless it be imperfect; and let us be prepared for the otherwise strange fact, which we shall discern clearly as we approach the period of the Renaissance, that the first cause of the fall of the arts of Europe was a relentless requirement of perfection, incapable alike either of being silenced by veneration for greatness, or softened into for-giveness of simplicity.

Thus far then of the Rudeness or Savageness, which is the first mental element of Gothic architecture. It is an element in many other healthy architectures also, as in Byzantine and Romanesque; but true Gothic cannot exist without it.

The second mental element above named was CHANGE-FULNESS, or Variety.

I have already enforced the allowing independent oper-

---

* The Elgin marbles are supposed by many persons to be "perfect." In the most important portions they indeed approach perfection, but only there. The draperies are unfinished, the hair and wool of the animals are unfinished, and the entire bas-reliefs of the frieze are roughly cut. [Ruskin's note.]

ation to the inferior workman, simply as a duty *to him,* and as ennobling the architecture by rendering it more Christian. We have now to consider what reward we obtain for the performance of this duty, namely, the perpetual variety of every feature of the building.

Wherever the workman is utterly enslaved, the parts of the building must of course be absolutely like each other; for the perfection of his execution can only be reached by exercising him in doing one thing, and giving him nothing else to do. The degree in which the workman is degraded may be thus known at a glance, by observing whether the several parts of the building are similar or not; and if, as in Greek work, all the capitals are alike, and all the mouldings unvaried, then the degradation is complete; if, as in Egyptian or Ninevite work, though the manner of executing certain figures is always the same, the order of design is perpetually varied, the degradation is less total; if, as in Gothic work, there is perpetual change both in design and execution, the workman must have been altogether set free.

How much the beholder gains from the liberty of the laborer may perhaps be questioned in England, where one of the strongest instincts in nearly every mind is that Love of Order which makes us desire that our house windows should pair like our carriage horses, and allows us to yield our faith unhesitatingly to architectural theories which fix a form for everything, and forbid variation from it. I would not impeach love of order: it is one of the most useful elements of the English mind; it helps us in our commerce and in all purely practical matters; and it is in many cases one of the foundation-stones of morality. Only do not let us suppose that love of order is love of art. It is true that order, in its highest sense, is one of the necessities of art, just as time is a necessity of music; but love of order has no more to do with our right enjoyment of architecture or painting, than love of punctuality with the appreciation of an opera. Experience, I fear, teaches us that accurate and methodical habits in daily life are seldom characteristic of those who either quickly perceive, or richly possess, the creative powers of art; there is, however, nothing inconsistent between the two instincts, and nothing to hinder us from retaining our business habits, and yet fully allowing and enjoying the noblest gifts of Invention. We already do so, in every other branch of art except architecture, and we only do *not* so there because we have been taught that it would be wrong. Our architects gravely inform us that, as there are four rules of arithmetic, there are five orders of architecture; we, in our simplicity, think that this sounds consistent, and believe them. They inform us also that there is one proper form for Corinthian capitals, another for Doric, and another for Ionic. We, considering that there is also a proper form for the letters A, B, and C, think that this also sounds consistent, and accept the proposition. Understanding, therefore, that one form of the said capitals is proper, and no other, and having a conscientious horror of all impropriety, we allow the architect to provide us with the said capitals, of the proper form, in such and such a quantity, and in all other points to take care that the legal forms are observed; which having done, we rest in forced confidence that we are well housed.

But our higher instincts are not deceived. We take no pleasure in the building provided for us, resembling that which we take in a new book or a new picture. We may be proud of its size, complacent in its correctness, and happy in its convenience. We may take the same pleasure in its symmetry and workmanship as in a well-ordered room, or a skilful piece of manufacture. And this we suppose to be all the pleasure that architecture was ever intended to give us. The idea of reading a building as we would read Milton or Dante, and getting the same kind of delight out of the stones as out of the stanzas, never enters our minds for a moment. And for good reason:—There is indeed rhythm in the verses, quite as strict as the symmetries or rhythm of the architecture, and a thousand times more beautiful, but there is something else than rhythm. The verses were neither made to order, nor to match, as the capitals were; and we have therefore a kind of pleasure in them other than a sense of propriety. But it requires a strong effort of common sense to shake ourselves quit of all that we have been taught for the last two centuries, and wake to the perception of a truth just as simple and certain as it is new: that great art, whether expressing itself in words, colors,

or stones, does *not* say the same thing over and over
again; that the merit of architectural, as of every other
art, consists in its saying new and different things; that
to repeat itself is no more a characteristic of genius in
marble than it is of genius in print; and that we may,
without offending any laws of good taste, require of an
architect, as we do of a novelist, that he should be not
only correct, but entertaining.

Yet all this is true, and self-evident; only hidden from
us, as many other self-evident things are, by false teaching. Nothing is a great work of art, for the production
of which either rules or models can be given. Exactly so
far as architecture works on known rules, and from given
models, it is not an art, but a manufacture; and it is, of
the two procedures, rather less rational (because more
easy) to copy capitals or mouldings from Phidias, and
call ourselves architects, than to copy heads and hands
from Titian, and call ourselves painters.

Let us then understand at once that change or variety
is as much a necessity to the human heart and brain in
buildings as in books; that there is no merit, though
there is some occasional use, in monotony; and that we
must no more expect to derive either pleasure or profit
from an architecture whose ornaments are of one pattern,
and whose pillars are of one proportion, than we should
out of a universe in which the clouds were all of one
shape, and the trees all of one size.

And this we confess in deeds, though not in words. All
the pleasure which the people of the nineteenth century
take in art, is in pictures, sculpture, minor objects of
virtù, or mediæval architecture, which we enjoy under
the term picturesque: no pleasure is taken anywhere in
modern buildings, and we find all men of true feeling
delighting to escape out of modern cities into natural
scenery: hence, as I shall hereafter show, that peculiar
love of landscape, which is characteristic of the age. It
would be well, if, in all other matters, we were as ready
to put up with what we dislike, for the sake of compliance with established law, as we are in architecture.

How so debased a law ever came to be established, we
shall see when we come to describe the Renaissance
schools: here we have only to note, as the second most

essential element of the Gothic spirit, that it broke through that law wherever it found it in existence; it not only dared, but delighted in, the infringement of every servile principle; and invented a series of forms of which the merit was, not merely that they were new, but that they were *capable of perpetual novelty*. The pointed arch was not merely a bold variation from the round, but it admitted of millions of variations in itself; for the proportions of a pointed arch are changeable to infinity, while a circular arch is always the same. The grouped shaft was not merely a bold variation from the single one, but it admitted of millions of variations in its grouping, and in the proportions resultant from its grouping. The introduction of tracery was not only a startling change in the treatment of window lights, but admitted endless changes in the interlacement of the tracery bars themselves. So that, while in all living Christian architecture the love of variety exists, the Gothic schools exhibited that love in culminating energy; and their influence, wherever it extended itself, may be sooner and farther traced by this character than by any other; the tendency to the adoption of Gothic types being always first shown by greater irregularity, and richer variation in the forms of the architecture it is about to supersede, long before the appearance of the pointed arch or of any other recognizable *outward* sign of the Gothic mind.

We must, however, herein note carefully what distinction there is between a healthy and a diseased love of change; for as it was in healthy love of change that the Gothic architecture rose, it was partly in consequence of diseased love of change that it was destroyed. In order to understand this clearly, it will be necessary to consider the different ways in which change and monotony are presented to us in nature; both having their use, like darkness and light, and the one incapable of being enjoyed without the other: change being most delightful after some prolongation of monotony, as light appears most brilliant after the eyes have been for some time closed.

I believe that the true relations of monotony and change may be most simply understood by observing them in music. We may therein notice first, that there is a sublimity and majesty in monotony, which there is not in rapid or frequent variation. This is true throughout all nature. The greater part of the sublimity of the sea depends on its monotony; so also that of desolate moor and mountain scenery; and especially the sublimity of motion, as in the quiet, unchanged fall and rise of an engine beam. So also there is sublimity in darkness which there is not in light.

Again, monotony after a certain time, or beyond a certain degree, becomes either uninteresting or intolerable, and the musician is obliged to break it in one or two ways: either while the air or passage is perpetually repeated, its notes are variously enriched and harmonized; or else, after a certain number of repeated passages, an entirely new passage is introduced, which is more or less delightful according to the length of the previous monotony. Nature, of course, uses both these kinds of variation perpetually. The sea-waves, resembling each other in general mass, but none like its brother in minor divisions and curves, are a monotony of the first kind; the great plain, broken by an emergent rock or clump of trees, is a monotony of the second.

Farther: in order to the enjoyment of the change in either case, a certain degree of patience is required from the hearer or observer. In the first case, he must be satisfied to endure with patience the recurrence of the great masses of sound or form, and to seek for entertainment in a careful watchfulness of the minor details. In the second case, he must bear patiently the infliction of the monotony for some moments, in order to feel the full refreshment of the change. This is true even of the shortest musical passage in which the element of monotony is employed. In cases of more majestic monotony, the patience required is so considerable that it becomes a kind of pain,—a price paid for the future pleasure.

Again: the talent of the composer is not in the monotony, but in the changes: he may show feeling and taste by his use of monotony in certain places or degrees; that is to say, by his *various* employment of it; but it is always in the new arrangement or invention that his intellect is shown, and not in the monotony which relieves it.

Lastly: if the pleasure of change be too often repeated,

it ceases to be delightful, for then change itself becomes monotonous, and we are driven to seek delight in extreme and fantastic degrees of it. This is the diseased love of change of which we have above spoken.

From these facts we may gather generally that monotony is, and ought to be, in itself painful to us, just as darkness is; that an architecture which is altogether monotonous is a dark or dead architecture; and of those who love it, it may be truly said, "they love darkness rather than light." But monotony in certain measure, used in order to give value to change, and above all, that *transparent* monotony, which, like the shadows of a great painter, suffers all manner of dimly suggested form to be seen through the body of it, is an essential in architectural as in all other composition; and the endurance of monotony has about the same place in a healthy mind that the endurance of darkness has: that is to say, as a strong intellect will have pleasure in the solemnities of storm and twilight, and in the broken and mysterious lights that gleam among them, rather than in mere brilliancy and glare, while a frivolous mind will dread the shadow and the storm; and as a great man will be ready to endure much darkness of fortune in order to reach greater eminence of power or felicity, while an inferior man will not pay the price; exactly in like manner a great mind will accept, or even delight in, monotony which would be wearisome to an inferior intellect, because it has more patience and power of expectation, and is ready to pay the full price for the great future pleasure of change. But in all cases it is not that the noble nature loves monotony, any more than it loves darkness or pain. But it can bear with it, and receive a high pleasure in the endurance or patience, a pleasure necessary to the well-being of this world; while those who will not submit to the temporary sameness, but rush from one change to another, gradually dull the edge of change itself, and bring a shadow and weariness over the whole world from which there is no more escape.

From these general uses of variety in the economy of the world, we may at once understand its use and abuse in architecture. The variety of the Gothic schools is the more healthy and beautiful, because in many cases it is entirely unstudied, and results, not from mere love of change, but from practical necessities. For in one point of view Gothic is not only the best, but the *only rational* architecture, as being that which can fit itself most easily to all services, vulgar or noble. Undefined in its slope of roof, height of shaft, breadth of arch, or disposition of ground plan, it can shrink into a turret, expand into a hall, coil into a staircase, or spring into a spire, with undegraded grace and unexhausted energy; and whenever it finds occasion for change in its form or purpose, it submits to it without the slightest sense of loss either to its unity or majesty,—subtle and flexible like a fiery serpent, but ever attentive to the voice of the charmer. And it is one of the chief virtues of the Gothic builders, that they never suffered ideas of outside symmetries and consistencies to interfere with the real use and value of what they did. If they wanted a window, they opened one; a room, they added one; a buttress, they built one; utterly regardless of any established conventionalities of external appearance, knowing (as indeed it always happened) that such daring interruptions of the formal plan would rather give additional interest to its symmetry than injure it. So that, in the best times of Gothic, a useless window would rather have been opened in an unexpected place for the sake of the surprise, than a useful one forbidden for the sake of symmetry. Every successive architect, employed upon a great work, built the pieces he added in his own way, utterly regardless of the style adopted by his predecessors; and if two towers were raised in nominal correspondence at the sides of a cathedral front, one was nearly sure to be different from the other, and in each the style at the top to be different from the style at the bottom.

These marked variations were, however, only permitted as part of the great system of perpetual change which ran through every member of Gothic design, and rendered it as endless a field for the beholder's inquiry as for the builder's imagination: change, which in the best schools is subtle and delicate, and rendered more delightful by intermingling of a noble monotony; in the more barbaric schools is somewhat fantastic and redundant; but, in all, a necessary and constant condition of the life of the school. Sometimes the variety is in one feature, sometimes in another; it may be in the capitals or crockets, in the niches or the traceries, or in all together, but in some one or other of the features it will be found always. If the mouldings are constant, the surface sculpture will change; if the capitals are of a fixed design, the traceries will change; if the traceries are monotonous, the capitals will change; and if even, as in some fine schools, the early English for example, there is the slightest approximation to an unvarying type of mouldings, capitals, and floral decoration, the variety is found in the disposition of the masses, and in the figure sculpture.

I must now refer for a moment, before we quit the consideration of this, the second mental element of Gothic, to the opening of the third chapter of the *Seven Lamps of Architecture,* in which the distinction was drawn (§ 2) between man gathering and man governing; between his acceptance of the sources of delight from nature, and his development of authoritative or imaginative power in their arrangement: for the two mental elements, not only of Gothic, but of all good architecture, which we have just been examining, belong to it, and are admirable in it, chiefly as it is, more than any other subject of art, the work of man, and the expression of the average power of man. A picture or poem is often little more than a feeble utterance of man's admiration of something out of himself; but architecture approaches more to a creation of his own, born of his necessities, and expressive of his nature. It is also, in some sort, the work of the whole race, while the picture or statue is the work of one only, in most cases more highly gifted than his fellows. And therefore we may expect that the first two elements of good architecture should be expressive of some great truths commonly belonging to the whole race, and necessary to be understood or felt by them in all their work that they do under the sun. And observe what they are: the confession of Imperfection, and the confession of Desire of Change. The building of the bird and the bee needs not express anything like this. It is perfect and unchanging. But just because we are something better than birds or bees, our building must confess that we have not reached the perfection we can imagine, and cannot rest in the condition we have attained. If we pretend to have reached either perfection or satisfaction, we have degraded ourselves and our work. God's work only may express that; but ours may never have that sentence written upon it,—"And behold, it was very good." And, observe again, it is not merely as it renders the edifice a book of various knowledge, or a mine of precious thought, that variety is essential to its nobleness. The vital principle is not the love of *Knowledge,* but the love of *Change.* It is that strange *disquietude* of the Gothic spirit that is its greatness; that restlessness of the dreaming mind, that wanders hither and thither among the niches, and flickers feverishly around the pinnacles, and frets and fades in labyrinthine knots and shadows along wall and roof, and yet is not satisfied, nor shall be satisfied. The Greek could stay in his triglyph furrow, and be at peace; but the work of the Gothic heart is fretwork still, and it can neither rest in, nor from, its labor, but must pass on, sleeplessly, until its love of change shall be pacified forever in the change that must come alike on them that wake and them that sleep. . . . . . .

Last, because the least essential, of the constituent elements of this noble school, was placed that of RE-DUNDANCE,—the uncalculating bestowal of the wealth of its labor. There is, indeed, much Gothic, and that of the best period, in which this element is hardly traceable, and which depends for its effect almost exclusively on loveliness of simple design and grace of uninvolved proportion; still, in the most characteristic buildings, a certain portion of their effect depends upon accumulation of ornament; and many of those which have most influence on the minds of men, have attained it by means of this attribute alone. And although, by careful study of the school, it is possible to arrive at a condition of taste which shall be better contented by a few perfect lines than by a whole façade covered with fretwork, the building which only satisfies such a taste is not to be considered the best. For the very first requirement of Gothic architecture being, as we saw above, that it shall both admit the aid, and appeal to the admiration, of the rudest as well as the most refined minds, the richness of the work is, paradoxical as the statement may appear, a part of its humility. No architecture is so haughty as that which is simple; which refuses to address the eye, except in a few clear and forceful lines; which implies, in offering so little to our regards, that all it has offered is perfect; and disdains, either by the complexity or the attractiveness of its features, to embarrass our investigation, or betray us into delight. That humility, which is the very life of the Gothic school, is shown not only in the imperfection, but in the accumulation, of ornament. The inferior rank of the workman is often shown as much in the richness, as the roughness, of his work; and if the cooperation of every hand, and the sympathy of every heart, are to be received, we must be content to allow the redundance which disguises the failure of the feeble, and wins the regard of the inattentive. There are, however, far nobler interests mingling, in the Gothic heart, with the rude love of decorative accumulation: a magnificent enthusiasm, which feels as if it never could do enough to reach the fulness of its ideal; an unselfishness of sacrifice, which would rather cast fruitless labor before the altar than stand idle in the market; and, finally, a profound sympathy with the fulness and wealth of the material universe, rising out of that Naturalism whose operation we have already endeavored to define. The sculptor who sought for his models among the forest leaves, could not but quickly and deeply feel that complexity need not involve the loss of grace, nor richness that of repose; and every hour which he spent in the study of the minute and various work of Nature, made him feel more forcibly the barrenness of what was best in that of man: nor is it to be wondered at, that, seeing her perfect and exquisite creations poured forth in a profusion which conception could not grasp nor calculation sum, he should think that it ill became him to be niggardly of his own rude craftsmanship; and where he saw throughout the universe a faultless beauty lavished on measureless spaces of broidered field and blooming mountain, to grudge his poor and imperfect labor to the few stones that he had raised one upon another, for habitation or memorial. The years of his life passed away before his task was accomplished; but generation succeeded generation with unwearied enthusiasm, and the cathedral front was at last lost in the tapestry of its traceries, like a rock among the thickets and herbage of spring.

Modern Manufacture and Design

[*The Two Paths,* Lecture III.]

BEAUTIFUL art can only be produced by people who have beautiful things about them, and leisure to look at them; and unless you provide some elements of beauty for your workmen to be surrounded by, you will find that no elements of beauty can be invented by them.

I was struck forcibly by the bearing of this great fact upon our modern efforts at ornamentation in an afternoon walk, last week, in the suburbs of one of our large manufacturing towns. I was thinking of the difference in the effect upon the designer's mind, between the scene which I then came upon, and the scene which would have presented itself to the eyes of any designer of the Middle Ages, when he left his workshop. Just outside the town I came upon an old English cottage, or mansion, I hardly know which to call it, set close under the hill, and beside the river, perhaps built somewhere in the Charleses' times, with mullioned windows and a low arched porch; round which, in the little triangular garden, one can imagine the family as they used to sit in old summer times, the ripple of the river heard faintly through the sweetbriar hedge, and the sheep on the far-off wolds shining in the evening sunlight. There, uninhabited for many and many a year, it had been left in unregarded havoc of ruin; the garden-gate still swung loose to its latch; the garden, blighted utterly into a field of ashes, not even a weed taking root there; the roof torn into shapeless rents; the shutters hanging about the windows in rags of rotten wood; before its gate, the stream which had gladdened it now soaking slowly by, black as ebony and thick with curdling scum; the bank above it trodden into unctuous, sooty slime: far in front of it, between it and the old hills, the furnaces of the city foaming forth perpetual plague of sulphurous darkness; the volumes of their storm clouds coiling low over a waste of grassless fields, fenced from each other, not by hedges, but by slabs of square stone, like gravestones, riveted together with iron.

That was your scene for the designer's contemplation in his afternoon walk at Rochdale. Now fancy what was the scene which presented itself, in his afternoon walk, to a designer of the Gothic school of Pisa—Nino Pisano, or any of his men.

On each side of a bright river he saw rise a line of brighter palaces, arched and pillared, and inlaid with deep red porphyry, and with serpentine; along the quays before their gates were riding troops of knights, noble in face and form, dazzling in crest and shield; horse and man one labyrinth of quaint color and gleaming light— the purple, and silver, and scarlet fringes flowing over the strong limbs and clashing mail, like sea-waves over rocks at sunset. Opening on each side from the river were gardens, courts, and cloisters; long successions of white pillars among wreaths of vine; leaping of fountains through buds of pomegranate and orange: and still along the garden paths, and under and through the crimson of the pomegranate shadows, moving slowly, groups of the fairest women that Italy ever saw—fairest, because purest and thoughtfullest; trained in all high knowledge, as in all courteous art—in dance, in song, in sweet wit, in lofty learning, in loftier courage, in loftiest love—able alike to cheer, to enchant, or save the souls of men. Above all this scenery of perfect human life rose dome and bell-tower, burning with white alabaster and gold; beyond dome and bell-tower the slopes of mighty hills, hoary with olive; far in the north above a purple sea of peaks of solemn Apennine, the clear, sharp-cloven Carrara mountains sent up their steadfast flames of marble summit into amber sky; the great sea itself, scorching with expanse of light, stretching from their feet to the Gorgonian isles; and over all these, ever present, near or far—seen through the leaves of vine, or imaged with all its march of clouds in the Arno's stream, or set with its depth of blue close against the golden hair and burning cheek of lady and knight,—that untroubled and sacred sky, which was to all men, in those days of innocent faith, indeed the unquestioned abode of spirits, as the earth was of men; and which opened straight through its gates of cloud and veils of dew into the awfulness of the eternal world;—a heaven in which every cloud that passed was literally the chariot of an angel, and every ray of its Evening and Morning streamed from the throne of God.

What think you of that for a school of design?

I do not bring this contrast before you as a ground of hopelessness in our task; neither do I look for any possible renovation of the Republic of Pisa, at Bradford, in the nineteenth century; but I put it before you in order that you may be aware precisely of the kind of difficulty you have to meet, and may then consider with yourselves how far you can meet it. To men surrounded by the depressing and monotonous circumstances of English manufacturing life, depend upon it, design is simply impossible. This is the most distinct of all the experiences I have had in dealing with the modern workman. He is intelligent and ingenious in the highest degree—subtle in touch and keen in sight: but he is, generally speaking, wholly destitute of designing power. And if you want to give him the power, you must give him the materials, and put him in the circumstances for it. Design is not the offspring of idle fancy: it is the studied result of accumulative observation and delightful habit. Without observation and experience, no design—without peace and pleasurableness in occupation, no design—and all the lecturings, and teachings, and prizes, and principles of art, in the world, are of no use, so long as you don't surround your men with happy influences and beautiful things. It is impossible for them to have right ideas about color, unless they see the lovely colors of nature unspoiled; impossible for them to supply beautiful incident and action in their ornament, unless they see beautiful incident and action in the world about them. Inform their minds, refine their habits, and you form and refine their designs; but keep them illiterate, uncomfortable, and in the midst of unbeautiful things, and whatever they do will still be spurious, vulgar, and valueless.

I repeat, that I do not ask you nor wish you to build a new Pisa for them. We don't want either the life or the decorations of the thirteenth century back again; and the circumstances with which you must surround your workmen are those simply of happy modern English life, because the designs you have now to ask for from your workmen are such as will make modern English life beautiful. All that gorgeousness of the Middle Ages, beautiful as it sounds in description, noble as in many respects it was in reality, had, nevertheless, for foundation and for end, nothing but the pride of life—the pride of the so-called superior classes; a pride which supported itself by violence and robbery, and led in the end to the destruction both of the arts themselves and the States in which they flourished.

The great lesson of history is, that all the fine arts hitherto—having been supported by the selfish power of the noblesse, and never having extended their range to the comfort or the relief of the mass of the people—the arts, I say, thus practised, and thus matured, have only accelerated the ruin of the States they adorned; and at the moment which, in any kingdom, you point to the triumphs of its greatest artists, you point also to the determined hour of the kingdom's decline. The names of great painters are like passing bells: in the name of Velasquez, you hear sounded the fall of Spain; in the name of Titian, that of Venice; in the name of Leonardo, that of Milan; in the name of Raphael, that of Rome. And there is profound justice in this; for in proportion to the nobleness of the power is the guilt of its use for purposes vain or vile; and hitherto the greater the art, the more surely has it been used, and used solely, for the decoration of pride, or the provoking of sensuality. Another course lies open to us. We may abandon the hope—or if you like the words better, we may disdain the temptation—of the pomp and grace of Italy in her youth. For us there can be no more the throne of marble—for us no more the vault of gold—but for us there is the loftier and lovelier privilege of bringing the power and charm of art within the reach of the humble and the poor; and as the magnificence of past ages failed by its narrowness and its pride, ours may prevail and continue by its universality and its lowliness.

And thus, between the picture of too laborious England, which we imagined as future, and the picture of too luxurious Italy, which we remember in the past, there may exist—there will exist, if we do our duty—an intermediate condition, neither oppressed by labor nor wasted in vanity—the condition of a peaceful and thoughtful temperance in aims, and acts, and arts.

We are about to enter upon a period of our world's history in which domestic life, aided by the arts of peace, will slowly, but at last entirely, supersede public life and the arts of war. For our own England, she will not, I believe, be blasted throughout with furnaces; nor will she be encumbered with palaces. I trust she will keep her green fields, her cottages, and her homes of middle life; but these ought to be, and I trust will be, enriched with a useful, truthful, substantial form of art. We want now no more feasts of the gods, nor martyrdoms of saints; we have no need of sensuality, no place for superstition, or for costly insolence. Let us have learned and faithful historical painting—touching and thoughtful representations of human nature, in dramatic painting; poetical and familiar renderings of natural objects and of landscape; and rational, deeply felt realizations of the events which are the subjects of our religious faith. And let these things we want, as far as possible, be scattered abroad and made accessible to all men.

So, also, in manufacture: we require work substantial rather than rich in make; and refined, rather than splendid in design. Your stuffs need not be such as would catch the eye of a duchess; but they should be such as may at once serve the need, and refine the taste, of a cottager. The prevailing error in English dress, especially among the lower orders, is a tendency to flimsiness and gaudiness, arising mainly from the awkward imitation of their superiors.* It should be one of the first

---

* If their superiors would give them simplicity and economy to imitate, it would, in the issue, be well for themselves, as well as for those whom they guide. The typhoid fever of passion for dress, and all other display, which has struck the upper classes of Europe at this time, is one of the most dangerous political elements we have to deal with. Its wickedness I have shown elsewhere; but its wickedness is, in the minds of most persons, a matter of no importance. I wish I had time also to show them its danger. I cannot enter here into political investigation; but this is a certain fact, that the wasteful and vain expenses at present indulged in by the upper classes are hastening

objects of all manufacturers to produce stuffs not only beautiful and quaint in design, but also adapted for every-day service, and decorous in humble and secluded life. And you must remember always that your business, as manufacturers, is to form the market, as much as to supply it. If, in short-sighted and reckless eagerness for wealth, you catch at every humor of the populace as it shapes itself into momentary demand—if, in jealous rivalry with neighboring States, or with other producers, you try to attract attention by singularities, novelties, and gaudinesses—to make every design an advertisement, and pilfer every idea of a successful neighbor's, that you may insidiously imitate it, or pompously eclipse—no good design will ever be possible to you, or perceived by you. You may, by accident, snatch the market; or, by energy, command it; you may obtain the confidence of the public, and cause the ruin of opponent houses; or you may, with equal justice of fortune, be ruined by them. But whatever happens to you, this, at least, is certain, that the whole of your life will have been spent in corrupting public taste and encouraging public extravagance. Every preference you have won by gaudiness must have been based on the purchaser's vanity; every demand you have created by novelty has fostered in the consumer a habit of discontent; and when you retire into inactive life, you may, as a subject of consolation for your declining years, reflect that precisely according to the extent of your past operations, your life has been successful in retarding the arts, tarnishing the virtues, and confusing the manners of your country.

But, on the other hand, if you resolve from the first that, so far as you can ascertain or discern what is best, you will produce what is best, on an intelligent consideration of the probable tendencies and possible tastes of the people whom you supply, you may literally become more influential for all kinds of good than many lecturers on art, or many treatise-writers on morality. Con-

---

the advance of republicanism more than any other element of modern change. No agitators, no clubs, no epidemical errors, ever were, or will be, fatal to social order in any nation. Nothing but the guilt of the upper classes, wanton, accumulated, reckless, and merciless, ever overthrows them. Of such guilt they have now much to answer for—let them look to it in time.

sidering the materials dealt with, and the crude state of art knowledge at the time, I do not know that any more wide or effective influence in public taste was ever exercised than that of the Staffordshire manufacture of pottery under William Wedgwood; and it only rests with the manufacturer in every other business to determine whether he will, in like manner, make his wares educational instruments, or mere drugs of the market. You all should be, in a certain sense, authors: you must, indeed, first catch the public eye, as an author must the public ear; but once gain your audience, or observance, and as it is in the writer's power thenceforward to publish what will educate as it amuses—so it is in yours to publish what will educate as it adorns. Nor is this surely a subject of poor ambition. I hear it said continually that men are too ambitious: alas! to me, it seems, they are never enough ambitious. How many are content to be merely the thriving merchants of a state, when they might be its guides, counsellors, and rulers—wielding powers of subtle but gigantic beneficence, in restraining its follies while they supplied its wants. Let such duty, such ambition, be once accepted in their fulness, and the best glory of European art and of European manufacture may yet be to come. The paintings of Raphael and of Buonarroti gave force to the falsehoods of superstition, and majesty to the imaginations of sin; but the arts of England may have, for their task, to inform the soul with truth, and touch the heart with compassion. The steel of Toledo and the silk of Genoa did but give strength to oppression and lustre to pride: let it be for the furnace and for the loom of England, as they have already richly earned, still more abundantly to bestow, comfort on the indigent, civilization on the rude, and to dispense, through the peaceful homes of nations, the grace and the preciousness of simple adornment, and useful possession.

The Division of Arts

[*Aratra Pentelici,* Lecture I.]

If, as is commonly believed, the subject of study which it is my special function to bring before you had no relation to the great interests of mankind, I should have less courage in asking for your attention to-day than when I first addressed you; though, even then, I did not do so without painful diffidence. For at this moment, even supposing that in other places it were possible for men to pursue their ordinary avocations undisturbed by indignation or pity,—here, at least, in the midst of the deliberative and religious influences of England, only one subject, I am well assured, can seriously occupy your thoughts—the necessity, namely, of determining how it has come to pass that, in these recent days, iniquity the most reckless and monstrous can be committed unanimously, by men more generous than ever yet in the world's history were deceived into deeds of cruelty; and that prolonged agony of body and spirit, such as we should shrink from inflicting wilfully on a single criminal, has become the appointed and accepted portion of unnumbered multitudes of innocent persons, inhabiting the districts of the world which, of all others, as it seemed, were best instructed in the laws of civilization, and most richly invested with the honor, and indulged in the felicity, of peace.

Believe me, however, the subject of Art—instead of being foreign to these deep questions of social duty and peril—is so vitally connected with them, that it would be impossible for me now to pursue the line of thought in which I began these lectures, because so ghastly an emphasis would be given to every sentence by the force of passing events. It is well, then, that in the plan I have laid down for your study, we shall now be led into the examination of technical details, or abstract conditions of sentiment; so that the hours you spend with me may be times of repose from heavier thoughts. But it chances strangely that, in this course of minutely detailed study, I have first to set before you the most essential piece of human workmanship, the plough, at the very moment when (you may see the announcement in the journals either of yesterday or the day before) the swords of your soldiers have been sent for *to be sharpened,* and not at all to be beaten into ploughshares. I permit myself, therefore, to remind you of the watchword of all my earnest writings—"Soldiers of the Ploughshare, instead of Soldiers of the Sword,"—and I know it my duty to assert to you that the work we enter upon to-day is no trivial one, but full of solemn hope; the hope, namely, that among you there may be found men wise enough to lead the national passions toward the arts of peace, instead of the arts of war.

I say, the work "we enter upon," because the first four lectures I gave in the spring were wholly prefatory; and the following three only defined for you methods of practice. To-day we begin the systematic analysis and progressive study of our subject.

In general, the three great, or fine, Arts of Painting, Sculpture, and Architecture, are thought of as distinct from the lower and more mechanical formative arts, such as carpentry or pottery. But we cannot, either verbally, or with any practical advantage, admit such classification. How are we to distinguish painting on canvas from painting on china?—or painting on china from painting on glass?—or painting on glass from infusion of color into any vitreous substance, such as enamel?—or the infusion of color into glass and enamel from the infusion of color into wool or silk, and weaving of pictures in tapestry, or patterns in dress? You will find that although, in ultimately accurate use of the word, painting must be held to mean only the laying of a pigment on a surface with a soft instrument; yet, in broad comparison of the functions of Art, we must conceive of one and the same great artistic faculty, as governing *every mode of disposing colors in a permanent relation on, or in, a solid substance;* whether it be by tinting canvas, or dyeing stuffs; inlaying metals with fused flint, or coating walls with colored stone.

Similarly, the word "Sculpture,"—though in ultimate accuracy it is to be limited to the development of form in hard substances by cutting away portions of their mass —in broad definition, must be held to signify *the reduc-*

tion of any shapeless mass of solid matter into an intended shape, whatever the consistence of the substance, or nature of the instrument employed; whether we carve a granite mountain, or a piece of box-wood, and whether we use, for our forming instrument, axe, or hammer, or chisel, or our own hands, or water to soften, or fire to fuse;—whenever and however we bring a shapeless thing into shape, we do so under the laws of the one great art of Sculpture.

Having thus broadly defined painting and sculpture, we shall see that there is, in the third place, a class of work separated from both, in a specific manner, and including a great group of arts which neither, of necessity, *tint,* nor for the sake of form merely, *shape* the substances they deal with; but construct or arrange them with a view to the resistance of some external force. We construct, for instance, a table with a flat top, and some support of prop, or leg, proportioned in strength to such weights as the table is intended to carry. We construct a ship out of planks, or plates of iron, with reference to certain forces of impact to be sustained, and of inertia to be overcome; or we construct a wall or roof with distinct reference to forces of pressure and oscillation, to be sustained or guarded against; and, therefore, in every case, with especial consideration of the strength of our materials, and the nature of that strength, elastic, tenacious, brittle, and the like.

Now, although this group of arts nearly always involves the putting of two or more separate pieces together, we must not define it by that accident. The blade of an oar is not less formed with reference to external force than if it were made of many pieces; and the frame of a boat, whether hollowed out of a tree-trunk, or constructed of planks nailed together, is essentially the same piece of art, to be judged by its buoyancy and capacity of progression. Still, from the most wonderful piece of all architecture, the human skeleton, to this simple one,* the ploughshare, on which it depends for its

---

* I had a real ploughshare on my lecture-table; but it would interrupt the drift of the statements in the text too long if I attempted here to illustrate by figures the relation of the coulter to the share, and of the hard to the soft pieces of metal in the share itself. [Ruskin's note.]

subsistence, *the putting of two or more pieces together*
is curiously necessary to the perfectness of every fine
instrument; and the peculiar mechanical work of Dæda-
lus,—inlaying,—becomes all the more delightful to us in
external aspect, because, as in the jawbone of a Saurian,
or the wood of a bow, it is essential to the finest capacities
of tension and resistance.

And observe how unbroken the ascent from this, the
simplest architecture, to the loftiest. The placing of the
timbers in a ship's stem, and the laying of the stones in
a bridge buttress, are similar in art to the construction
of the ploughshare, differing in no essential point, either
in that they deal with other materials, or because, of the
three things produced, one has to divide earth by advancing through it, another to divide water by advancing
through it, and the third to divide water which advances
against it. And again, the buttress of a bridge differs
only from that of a cathedral in having less weight to
sustain, and more to resist. We can find no term in
the gradation, from the ploughshare to the cathedral buttress, at which we can set a logical distinction.

Thus then we have simply three divisions of Art—one,
that of giving colors to substance; another, that of giving
form to it without question of resistance to force; and
the third, that of giving form or position which will make
it capable of such resistance. All the fine arts are em-
braced under these three divisions. Do not think that it
is only a logical or scientific affectation to mass them together in this manner; it is, on the contrary, of the first
practical importance to understand that the painter's
faculty, or masterhood over color, being as subtle as a
musician's over sound, must be looked to for the government of every operation in which color is employed; and
that, in the same manner, the appliance of any art whatsoever to minor objects cannot be right, unless under the
direction of a true master of that art. Under the present
system, you keep your Academician occupied only in producing tinted pieces of canvas to be shown in frames,
and smooth pieces of marble to be placed in niches; while
you expect your builder or constructor to design colored
patterns in stone and brick, and your chinaware merchant to keep a separate body of workwomen who can

paint china, but nothing else. By this division of labor, you ruin all the arts at once. The work of the Academician becomes mean and effeminate, because he is not used to treat color on a grand scale and in rough materials; and your manufacturers become base, because no well-educated person sets hand to them. And therefore it is necessary to understand, not merely as a logical statement, but as a practical necessity, that wherever beautiful color is to be arranged, you need a Master of Painting; and wherever noble form is to be given, a Master of Sculpture; and wherever complex mechanical force is to be resisted, a Master of Architecture.

But over this triple division there must rule another yet more important. Any of these three arts may be either imitative of natural objects or limited to useful appliance. You may either paint a picture that represents a scene, or your street door, to keep it from rotting; you may mould a statue, or a plate; build the resemblance of a cluster of lotus stalks, or only a square pier. Generally speaking, Painting and Sculpture will be imitative, and Architecture merely useful; but there is a great deal of Sculpture—as this crystal ball, for instance, which is not imitative, and a great deal of architecture which, to some extent, is so, as the so-called foils of Gothic apertures; and for many other reasons you will find it necessary to keep distinction clear in your minds between the arts—of whatever kind—which are imitative, and produce a resemblance or image of something which is not present; and those which are limited to the production of some useful reality, as the blade of a knife, or the wall of a house. You will perceive also, as we advance, that sculpture and painting are indeed in this respect only one art; and that we shall have constantly to speak and think of them as simply *graphic,* whether with chisel or color, their principal function being to make us, in the words of Aristotle, «Θεωρητικοὶ τοῦ περὶ τὰ σώματα κάλλους» (Polit. 8, 3), "having capacity and habit of contemplation of the beauty that is in material things"; while architecture, and its correlative arts, are to be practised under quite other conditions of sentiment.

Now it is obvious that so far as the fine arts consist either in imitation or mechanical construction, the right judgment of them must depend on our knowledge of the things they imitate, and forces they resist: and my function of teaching here would (for instance) so far resolve itself, either into demonstration that this painting of a peach does resemble a peach, or explanation of the way in which this ploughshare (for instance) is shaped so as to throw the earth aside with least force of thrust. And in both of these methods of study, though of course your own diligence must be your chief master, to a certain extent your Professor of Art can always guide you securely, and can show you, either that the image does truly resemble what it attempts to resemble, or that the structure is rightly prepared for the service it has to perform. But there is yet another virtue of fine art which is, perhaps, exactly that about which you will expect your Professor to teach you most, and which, on the contrary, is exactly that about which you must teach yourselves all that it is essential to learn.

I have here in my hand one of the simplest possible examples of the union of the graphic and constructive powers,—one of my breakfast plates. Since all the finely architectural arts, we said, began in the shaping of the cup and the platter, we will begin, ourselves, with the platter.

Why has it been made round? For two structural reasons: first, the greatest holding surface may be gathered into the smallest space; and secondly, that in being pushed past other things on the table, it may come into least contact with them.

Next, why has it a rim? For two other structural reasons: first, that it is convenient to put salt or mustard upon; but secondly, and chiefly, that the plate may be easily laid hold of. The rim is the simplest form of continuous handle.

Farther, to keep it from soiling the cloth, it will be wise to put this ridge beneath, round the bottom; for as the rim is the simplest possible form of continuous handle, so this is the simplest form of continuous leg. And we get the section given beneath the figure for the essential one of a rightly made platter.

Thus far our art has been strictly utilitarian, having respect to conditions of collision, of carriage, and of support. But now, on the surface of our piece of pottery, here are various bands and spots of color which are presumably set there to make it pleasanter to the eye. Six of the spots, seen closely, you discover are intended to represent flowers. These then have as distinctly a graphic purpose as the other properties of the plate have an architectural one, and the first critical question we have to ask about them is, whether they are like roses or not. I will anticipate what I have to say in subsequent lectures so far as to assure you that, if they are to be like roses at all, the liker they can be, the better. Do not suppose, as many people will tell you, that because this is a common manufactured article, your roses on it are the better for being ill-painted, or half-painted. If they had been painted by the same hand that did this peach, the plate would have been all the better for it; but, as it chanced, there was no hand such as William Hunt's to paint them, and their graphic power is not distinguished. In any case, however, that graphic power must have been subordinate to their effect as pink spots, while the band of green-blue round the plate's edge, and the spots of gold, pretend to no graphic power at all, but are meaningless spaces of color or metal. Still less have they any mechanical office: they add nowise to the serviceableness of the plate; and their agreeableness, if they possess any, depends, therefore, neither on any imitative, nor any structural, character; but on some inherent pleasantness in themselves, either of mere colors to the eye (as of taste to the tongue), or in the placing of those colors in relations which obey some mental principle of order, or physical principle of harmony.

These abstract relations and inherent pleasantnesses, whether in space, number, or time, and whether of colors or sounds, form what we may properly term the musical or harmonic element in every art; and the study of them is an entirely separate science. It is the branch of art-philosophy to which the word "æsthetics" should be strictly limited, being the inquiry into the nature of things that in themselves are pleasant to the human senses or instincts, though they represent nothing, and serve for nothing, their only service *being* their pleasantness. Thus it is the province of æsthetics to tell you (if you did not know it before), that the taste and color of a peach are

pleasant, and to ascertain, if it be ascertainable (and you
have any curiosity to know), why they are so.

The information would, I presume, to most of you, be
gratuitous. If it were not, and you chanced to be in a
sick state of body in which you disliked peaches, it would
be, for the time, to you false information, and, so far as
it was true of other people, to you useless. Nearly the
whole study of æsthetics is in like manner either gratuitous or useless. Either you like the right things without
being recommended to do so, or, if you dislike them, your
mind cannot be changed by lectures on the laws of taste.
You recollect the story of Thackeray, provoked, as he was
helping himself to strawberries, by a young coxcomb's
telling him that "he never took fruit or sweets." "That,"
replied, or is said to have replied, Thackeray, "is because
you are a sot, and a glutton." And the whole science of
æsthetics is, in the depth of it, expressed by one passage
of Goethe's in the end of the second part of *Faust;*—the
notable one that follows the song of the Lemures, when
the angels enter to dispute with the fiends for the soul of
Faust. They enter singing—"Pardon to sinners and life
to the dust." Mephistopheles hears them first, and ex-
claims to his troop, "Discord I hear, and filthy jingling"
—"Mis-töne höre ich: garstiges Geklimper." This, you
see, is the extreme of bad taste in music. Presently the
angelic host begin strewing roses, which discomfits the
diabolic crowd altogether. Mephistopheles in vain calls
to them—"What do you duck and shrink for—is that
proper hellish behavior? Stand fast, and let them strew"
—"Whas duckt und zucht ihr; ist das Höllenbrauch? So
haltet stand, und lasst sie streuen." There you have, also,
the extreme of bad taste in sight and smell. And in the
whole passage is a brief embodiment for you of the ultimate fact that all æsthetics depend on the health of soul
and body, and the proper exercise of both, not only
through years, but generations. Only by harmony of both
collateral and successive lives can the great doctrine of
the Muses be received which enables men «Χαίρειν ὀρθῶς,»
—"to have pleasure rightly"; and there is no other
definition of the beautiful, nor of any subject of delight to the æsthetic faculty, than that it is what one
noble spirit has created, seen and felt by another of simi-

lar or equal nobility. So much as there is in you of ox, or of swine, perceives no beauty, and creates none; what is human in you, in exact proportion to the perfectness of its humanity, can create it, and receive.

ATHENA ERGANE *

[*Queen of the Air,* Lecture III.]

IN different places of my writings, and through many years of endeavor to define the laws of art, I have insisted on this rightness in work, and on its connection with virtue of character, in so many partial ways, that the impression left on the reader's mind—if, indeed, it was ever impressed at all—has been confused and uncertain. In beginning the series of my corrected works, I wish this principle (in my own mind the foundation of every other) to be made plain, if nothing else is: and will try, therefore, to make it so, as far as, by any effort, I can put it into unmistakable words. And, first, here is a very simple statement of it, given lately in a lecture on the Architecture of the Valley of the Somme, which will be better read in this place than in its incidental connection with my account of the porches of Abbeville.

I had used, in a preceding part of the lecture, the expression, "by what faults" this Gothic architecture fell. We continually speak thus of works of art. We talk of their faults and merits, as of virtues and vices. What do we mean by talking of the faults of a picture, or the merits of a piece of stone?

The faults of a work of art are the faults of its workman, and its virtues his virtues.

Great art is the expression of the mind of a great man, and mean art, that of the want of mind of a weak man. A foolish person builds foolishly, and a wise one, sensibly; a virtuous one, beautifully; and a vicious one, basely. If stone work is well put together, it means that a thoughtful man planned it, and a careful man cut it, and an honest man cemented it. If it has too much ornament, it means that its carver was too greedy of pleasure; if

---

* "Athena the worker, or having rule over work." The name was first given to her by the Athenians. [Ruskin's note.]

too little, that he was rude, or insensitive, or stupid, and the like. So that when once you have learned how to spell these most precious of all legends,—pictures and buildings,—you may read the characters of men, and of nations, in their art, as in a mirror;—nay, as in a micro-scope, and magnified a hundredfold; for the character be-comes passionate in the art, and intensifies itself in all its noblest or meanest delights. Nay, not only as in a micro-scope, but as under a scalpel, and in dissection; for a man may hide himself from you, or misrepresent himself to you, every other way; but he cannot in his work: there, be sure, you have him to the inmost. All that he likes, all that he sees,—all that he can do,—his imagina-tion, his affections, his perseverance, his impatience, his clumsiness, cleverness, everything is there. If the work is a cobweb, you know it was made by a spider; if a honeycomb, by a bee; a worm-cast is thrown up by a worm, and a nest wreathed by a bird; and a house built by a man, worthily, if he is worthy, and ignobly, if he is ignoble.

And always, from the least to the greatest, as the made thing is good or bad, so is the maker of it.

You all use this faculty of judgment more or less, whether you theoretically admit the principle or not. Take that floral gable;* you don't suppose the man who built Stonehenge could have built that, or that the man who built that, *would* have built Stonehenge? Do you think an old Roman would have liked such a piece of filigree work? or that Michael Angelo would have spent his time in twisting these stems of roses in and out? Or, of modern handicraftsmen, do you think a burglar, or a brute, or a pickpocket could have carved it? Could Bill Sykes have done it? or the Dodger, dexterous with finger and tool? You will find in the end, that *no man could have done it but exactly the man who did it;* and by look-ing close at it, you may, if you know your letters, read precisely the manner of man he was.

Now I must insist on this matter, for a grave reason. Of all facts concerning art, this is the one most neces-

---

* The elaborate pediment above the central porch at the west end of Rouen Cathedral, pierced into a transparent web of tracery, and enriched with a border of "twisted eglantine." [Ruskin's note.]

sary to be known, that, while manufacture is the work
of hands only, art is the work of the whole spirit of man;
and as that spirit is, so is the deed of it: and by whatever power of vice or virtue any art is produced, the same
vice or virtue it reproduces and teaches. That which is
born of evil begets evil; and that which is born of valor
and honor, teaches valor and honor. All art is either in-
fection or education. It *must* be one or other of these.

This, I repeat, of all truths respecting art, is the one
of which understanding is the most precious, and denial
the most deadly. And I assert it the more, because it
has of late been repeatedly, expressly, and with contumely
denied; and that by high authority: and I hold it one of
the most sorrowful facts connected with the decline of
the arts among us, that English gentlemen, of high standing as scholars and artists, should have been blinded into
the acceptance, and betrayed into the assertion of a fallacy which only authority such as theirs could have rendered for an instant credible. For the contrary of it is
written in the history of all great nations; it is the one
sentence always inscribed on the steps of their thrones;
the one concordant voice in which they speak to us out
of their dust.

All such nations first manifest themselves as a pure
and beautiful animal race, with intense energy and imagination. They live lives of hardship by choice, and by
grand instinct of manly discipline: they become fierce
and irresistible soldiers; the nation is always its own
army, and their king, or chief head of government, is
always their first soldier. Pharaoh, or David, or Leonidas,
or Valerius, or Barbarossa, or Cœur de Lion, or St. Louis,
or Dandolo, or Frederick the Great:—Egyptian, Jew,
Greek, Roman, German, English, French, Venetian,—
that is inviolable law for them all; their king must be
their first soldier, or they cannot be in progressive power.
Then, after their great military period, comes the domestic period; in which, without betraying the discipline of
war, they add to their great soldiership the delights and
possessions of a delicate and tender home-life: and then,
for all nations, is the time of their perfect art, which is
the fruit, the evidence, the reward of their national ideal
of character, developed by the finished care of the occu-

pations of peace. That is the history of all true art that ever was, or can be: palpably the history of it,—unmistakably,—written on the forehead of it in letters of light, —in tongues of fire, by which the seal of virtue is branded as deep as ever iron burned into a convict's flesh the seal of crime. But always, hitherto, after the great period, has followed the day of luxury, and pursuit of the arts for pleasure only. And all has so ended.

Thus far of Abbeville building. Now I have here asserted two things,—first, the foundation of art in moral character; next, the foundation of moral character in war. I must make both these assertions clearer, and prove them.

First, of the foundation of art in moral character. Of course art-gift and amiability of disposition are two different things; a good man is not necessarily a painter, nor does an eye for color necessarily imply an honest mind. But great art implies the union of both powers: it is the expression, by an art-gift, of a pure soul. If the gift is not there, we can have no art at all; and if the soul—and a right soul too—is not there, the art is bad, however dexterous.

But also, remember, that the art-gift itself is only the result of the moral character of generations. A bad woman may have a sweet voice; but that sweetness of voice comes of the past morality of her race. That she can sing with it at all, she owes to the determination of laws of music by the morality of the past. Every act, every impulse, of virtue and vice, affects in any creature, face, voice, nervous power, and vigor and harmony of invention, at once. Perseverance in rightness of human conduct, renders, after a certain number of generations, human art possible; every sin clouds it, be it ever so little a one; and persistent vicious living and following of pleasure render, after a certain number of generations, all art impossible. Men are deceived by the long-suffering of the laws of nature; and mistake, in a nation, the reward of the virtue of its sires for the issue of its own sins. The time of their visitation will come, and that inevitably; for, it is always true, that if the fathers have eaten sour grapes, the children's teeth are set on edge. And for the individual, as soon as you have learned to read, you may, as I have said, know him to the heart's core, through his art. Let his art-gift be never so great, and cultivated to the height by the schools of a great race of men; and it is still but a tapestry thrown over his own being and inner soul; and the bearing of it will show, infallibly, whether it hangs on a man, or on a skeleton. If you are dim-eyed, you may not see the difference in the fall of the folds at first, but learn how to look, and the folds themselves will become transparent, and you shall see through them the death's shape, or the divine one, making the tissue above it as a cloud of light, or as a winding-sheet.

Then farther, observe, I have said (and you will find it true, and that to the uttermost) that, as all lovely art is rooted in virtue, so it bears fruit of virtue, and is didactic in its own nature. It is often didactic also in actually expressed thought, as Giotto's, Michael Angelo's, Dürer's, and hundreds more; but that is not its special function,—it is didactic chiefly by being beautiful; but beautiful with haunting thought, no less than with form, and full of myths that can be read only with the heart.

For instance, at this moment there is open beside me as I write, a page of Persian manuscript, wrought with wreathed azure and gold, and soft green, and violet, and ruby and scarlet, into one field of pure resplendence. It is wrought to delight the eyes only; and does delight them; and the man who did it assuredly had eyes in his head; but not much more. It is not didactic art, but its author was happy: and it will do the good, and the harm, that mere pleasure can do. But, opposite me, is an early Turner drawing of the lake of Geneva, taken about two miles from Geneva, on the Lausanne road, with Mont Blanc in the distance. The old city is seen lying beyond the waveless waters, veiled with a sweet misty veil of Athena's weaving: a faint light of morning, peaceful exceedingly, and almost colorless, shed from behind the Voirons, increases into soft amber along the slope of the Salève, and is just seen, and no more, on the fair warm fields of its summit, between the folds of a white cloud that rests upon the grass, but rises, high and towerlike, into the zenith of dawn above.

There is not as much color in that low amber light upon the hill-side as there is in the palest dead leaf. The lake is not blue, but gray in mist, passing into deep shadows beneath the Voirons' pines; a few dark clusters of leaves, a single white flower—scarcely seen—are all the gladness given to the rocks of the shore. One of the ruby spots of the eastern manuscript would give color enough for all the red that is in Turner's entire drawing. For the mere pleasure of the eye, there is not so much in all those lines of his, throughout the entire landscape, as in half an inch square of the Persian's page. What made him take pleasure in the low color that is only like the brown of a dead leaf? in the cold gray of dawn—in the one white flower among the rocks—in these—and no more than these?

He took pleasure in them because he had been bred among English fields and hills; because the gentleness of a great race was in his heart, and its power of thought in his brain; because he knew the stories of the Alps, and of the cities at their feet; because he had read the Homeric legends of the clouds, and beheld the gods of dawn, and the givers of dew to the fields; because he knew the faces of the crags, and the imagery of the passionate mountains, as a man knows the face of his friend; because he had in him the wonder and sorrow concerning life and death, which are the inheritance of the Gothic soul from the days of its first sea kings; and also the compassion and the joy that are woven into the innermost fabric of every great imaginative spirit, born now in countries that have lived by the Christian faith with any courage or truth. And the picture contains also, for us, just this which its maker had in him to give; and can convey it to us, just so far as we are of the temper in which it must be received. It is didactic, if we are worthy to be taught, no otherwise. The pure heart, it will make more pure; the thoughtful, more thoughtful. It has in it no words for the reckless or the base.

[*Lectures on Art,* Lecture I.]

THE duty which is to-day laid on me, of introducing, among the elements of education appointed in this great University, one not only new, but such as to involve in its possible results some modification of the rest, is, as you well feel, so grave, that no man could undertake it without laying himself open to the imputation of a kind of insolence; and no man could undertake it rightly, without being in danger of having his hands shortened by dread of his task, and mistrust of himself.

And it has chanced to me, of late, to be so little acquainted either with pride or hope, that I can scarcely recover so much as I now need, of the one for strength, and of the other for foresight, except by remembering that noble persons, and friends of the high temper that judges most clearly where it loves best, have desired that this trust should be given me; and by resting also in the conviction that the goodly tree whose roots, by God's help, we set in earth to-day, will not fail of its height because the planting of it is under poor auspices, or the first shoots of it enfeebled by ill gardening.

The munificence of the English gentleman to whom we owe the founding of this Professorship at once in our three great Universities, has accomplished the first great group of a series of changes now taking gradual effect in our system of public education; which, as you well know, are the sign of a vital change in the national mind, respecting both the principles on which that education should be conducted, and the ranks of society to which it should extend. For, whereas it was formerly thought that the discipline necessary to form the character of youth was best given in the study of abstract branches of literature and philosophy, it is now thought that the same, or a better, discipline may be given by informing men in early years of the things it will be of chief practical advantage to them afterward to know; and by permitting to them the choice of any field of study which they may feel to be best adapted to their personal dispositions. I have always used what poor influence I possessed in advancing this change; nor can anyone rejoice more than I in its practical results. But the completion—I will not venture to say correction—of a system established by the highest wisdom of noble ancestors, cannot be too reverently undertaken: and it is necessary for the English people, who are sometimes violent in change in proportion to the reluctance with which they admit its necessity, to be now, oftener than at other times, reminded that the object of instruction here is not primarily attainment, but discipline; and that a youth is sent to our Universities, not (hitherto at least) to be apprenticed to a trade, nor even always to be advanced in a profession; but, always, to be made a gentleman and a scholar.

To be made these,—if there is in him the making of either. The populaces of civilized countries have lately been under a feverish impression that it is possible for all men to be both; and that having once become, by passing through certain mechanical processes of instruction, gentle and learned, they are sure to attain in the sequel the consummate beatitude of being rich.

Rich, in the way and measure in which it is well for them to be so, they may, without doubt, *all* become. There is indeed a land of Havilah open to them, of which the wonderful sentence is literally true—"The gold of *that* land is good." But they must first understand, that education, in its deepest sense, is not the equalizer, but the discerner, of men; and that, so far from being instruments for the collection of riches, the first lesson of wisdom is to disdain them, and of gentleness, to diffuse.

It is not therefore, as far as we can judge, yet possible for all men to be gentlemen and scholars. Even under the best training some will remain too selfish to refuse wealth, and some too dull to desire leisure. But many more might be so than are now; nay, perhaps all men in England might one day be so, if England truly desired her supremacy among the nations to be in kindness and in learning. To which good end, it will indeed contribute that we add some practice of the lower arts to our scheme of University education; but the thing which is vitally necessary is, that we should extend the spirit of University education to the practice of the lower arts.

And, above all, it is needful that we do this by redeeming them from their present pain of self-contempt, and by giving them *rest*. It has been too long boasted as the pride of England, that out of a vast multitude of men, confessed to be in evil case, it was possible for individuals, by strenuous effort, and rare good fortune, occasionally to emerge into the light, and look back with self-gratulatory scorn upon the occupations of their parents, and the circumstances of their infancy. Ought we not rather to aim at an ideal of national life, when, of the employments of Englishmen, though each shall be distinct, none shall be unhappy or ignoble; when mechanical operations, acknowledged to be debasing in their tendency, shall be deputed to less fortunate and more covetous races; when advance from rank to rank, though possible to all men, may be rather shunned than desired by the best; and the chief object in the mind of every citizen may not be extrication from a condition admitted to be disgraceful, but fulfilment of a duty which shall be also a birthright?*

And then, the training of all these distinct classes will not be by Universities of general knowledge, but by distinct schools of such knowledge as shall be most useful for every class: in which, first the principles of their special business may be perfectly taught, and whatever higher learning, and cultivation of the faculties for receiving and giving pleasure, may be properly joined with that labor, taught in connection with it. Thus, I do not despair of seeing a School of Agriculture, with its fully endowed institutes of zoology, botany, and chemistry; and a School of Mercantile Seamanship, with its institutes of astronomy, meteorology, and natural history of the sea: and, to name only one of the finer, I do not say higher, arts, we shall, I hope, in a little time, have a perfect school of Metal-work, at the head of which will be, not the iron-masters, but the goldsmiths; and therein, I believe, that artists, being taught how to deal wisely with the most precious of metals, will take into due government the uses of all others.

But I must not permit myself to fail in the estimate

---

* Ruskin called [1887] this paragraph "the most pregnant summary of my political and social principles I have ever been able to give."

of my immediate duty, while I debate what that duty may hereafter become in the hands of others; and I will therefore now, so far as I am able, lay before you a brief general view of the existing state of the arts in England, and of the influence which her Universities, through these newly founded lectureships, may, I hope, bring to bear upon it for good.

We have first to consider the impulse which has been given to the practice of all the arts by the extension of our commerce, and enlarged means of intercourse with foreign nations, by which we now become more familiarly acquainted with their works in past and in present times. The immediate result of these new opportunities, I regret to say, has been to make us more jealous of the genius of others, than conscious of the limitations of our own; and to make us rather desire to enlarge our wealth by the sale of art, than to elevate our enjoyments by its acquisition.

Now, whatever efforts we make, with a true desire to produce, and possess, things that are intrinsically beautiful, have in them at least one of the essential elements of success. But efforts having origin only in the hope of enriching ourselves by the sale of our productions, are *assuredly* condemned to dishonorable failure; not because, ultimately, a well-trained nation is forbidden to profit by the exercise of its peculiar art-skill; but because that peculiar art-skill can never be developed *with a view* to profit. The right fulfilment of national power in art depends always on the direction of its aim by the experience of ages. Self-knowledge is not less difficult, nor less necessary for the direction of its genius, to a people than to an individual; and it is neither to be acquired by the eagerness of unpractised pride, nor during the anxieties of improvident distress. No nation ever had, or will have, the power of suddenly developing, under the pressure of necessity, faculties it had neglected when it was at ease; nor of teaching itself, in poverty, the skill to produce what it has never, in opulence, had the sense to admire.

Connected also with some of the worst parts of our social system, but capable of being directed to better result than this commercial endeavor, we see lately a most powerful impulse given to the production of costly works of art, by the various causes which promote the sudden accumulation of wealth in the hands of private persons. We have thus a vast and new patronage, which, in its present agency, is injurious to our schools; but which is nevertheless in a great degree earnest and conscientious, and far from being influenced chiefly by motives of ostentation. Most of our rich men would be glad to promote the true interests of art in this country: and even those who buy for vanity, found their vanity on the possession of what they suppose to be best.

It is therefore in a great measure the fault of artists themselves if they suffer from this partly unintelligent, but thoroughly well-intended, patronage. If they seek to attract it by eccentricity, to deceive it by superficial qualities, or take advantage of it by thoughtless and facile production, they necessarily degrade themselves and it together, and have no right to complain afterward that it will not acknowledge better-grounded claims. But if every painter of real power would do only what he knew to be worthy of himself, and refuse to be involved in the contention for undeserved or accidental success, there is indeed, whatever may have been thought or said to the contrary, true instinct enough in the public mind to follow such firm guidance. It is one of the facts which the experience of thirty years enables me to assert without qualification, that a really good picture is ultimately always approved and bought, unless it is wilfully rendered offensive to the public by faults which the artist has been either too proud to abandon or too weak to correct.

The development of whatever is healthful and serviceable in the two modes of impulse which we have been considering, depends however, ultimately, on the direction taken by the true interest in art which has lately been aroused by the great and active genius of many of our living, or but lately lost, painters, sculptors, and architects. It may perhaps surprise, but I think it will please you to hear me, or (if you will forgive me, in my own Oxford, the presumption of fancying that some may recognize me by an old name) to hear the author of *Modern Painters* say, that his chief error in earlier days was not in overestimating, but in too slightly acknowledging the merit of living men. The great painter whose power, while he was yet among us, I was able to perceive, was the first to reprove me for my disregard of the skill of his fellow-artists; and, with this inauguration of the study of the art of all time,—a study which can only by true modesty end in wise admiration,—it is surely well that I connect the record of these words of his, spoken then too truly to myself, and true always more or less for all who are untrained in that toil,—"You don't know how difficult it is."

You will not expect me, within the compass of this lecture, to give you any analysis of the many kinds of excellent art (in all the three great divisions) which the complex demands of modern life, and yet more varied instincts of modern genius, have developed for pleasure or service. It must be my endeavor, in conjunction with my colleagues in other Universities, hereafter to enable you to appreciate these worthily; in the hope that also the members of the Royal Academy, and those of the Institute of British Architects, may be induced to assist, and guide, the efforts of the Universities, by organizing such a system of art-education for their own students, as shall in future prevent the waste of genius in any mistaken endeavors; especially removing doubt as to the proper substance and use of materials; and requiring compliance with certain elementary principles of right, in every picture and design exhibited with their sanction. It is not indeed possible for talent so varied as that of English artists to be compelled into the formalities of a determined school; but it must certainly be the function of every academical body to see that their younger students are guarded from what must in every school be error; and that they are practised in the best methods of work hitherto known, before their ingenuity is directed to the invention of others.

I need scarcely refer, except for the sake of completeness in my statement, to one form of demand for art which is wholly unenlightened, and powerful only for evil;—namely, the demand of the classes occupied solely in the pursuit of pleasure, for objects and modes of art that can amuse indolence or excite passion. There is no need for any discussion of these requirements, or of their forms of influence, though they are very deadly at present in their operation on sculpture, and on jewellers' work. They cannot be checked by blame, nor guided by instruction; they are merely the necessary result of whatever defects exist in the temper and principles of a luxurious society; and it is only by moral changes, not by art-criticism, that their action can be modified.

Lastly, there is a continually increasing demand for popular art, multipliable by the printing-press, illustrative of daily events, of general literature, and of natural science. Admirable skill, and some of the best talent of modern times, are occupied in supplying this want; and there is no limit to the good which may be effected by rightly taking advantage of the powers we now possess of placing good and lovely art within the reach of the poorest classes. Much has been already accomplished; but great harm has been done also,—first, by forms of art definitely addressed to depraved tastes; and, secondly, in a more subtle way, by really beautiful and useful engravings which are yet not good enough to retain their influence on the public mind;—which weary it by redundant quantity of monotonous average excellence, and diminish or destroy its power of accurate attention to work of a higher order.

Especially this is to be regretted in the effect produced on the schools of line engraving, which had reached in England an executive skill of a kind before unexampled, and which of late have lost much of their more sterling and legitimate methods. Still, I have seen plates produced quite recently, more beautiful, I think, in some qualities than anything ever before attained by the burin: and I have not the slightest fear that photography, or any other adverse or competitive operation, will in the least ultimately diminish,—I believe they will, on the contrary, stimulate and exalt—the grand old powers of the wood and the steel.

Such are, I think, briefly the present conditions of art with which we have to deal; and I conceive it to be the function of this Professorship, with respect to them, to establish both a practical and critical school of fine art for English gentlemen: practical, so that, if they draw at all, they may draw rightly; and critical, so that, being first directed to such works of existing art as will best reward their study, they may afterward make their patronage of living artists delightful to themselves in their consciousness of its justice, and, to the utmost, beneficial to their country, by being given to the men who deserve it; in the early period of their lives, when they both need it most and can be influenced by it to the best advantage.

And especially with reference to this function of patronage, I believe myself justified in taking into account future probabilities as to the character and range of art in England: and I shall endeavor at once to organize with you a system of study calculated to develop chiefly the knowledge of those branches in which the English schools have shown, and are likely to show, peculiar excellence.

Now, in asking your sanction both for the nature of the general plans I wish to adopt, and for what I conceive to be necessary limitations of them, I wish you to be fully aware of my reasons for both: and I will therefore risk the burdening of your patience while I state the directions of effort in which I think English artists are liable to failure, and those also in which past experience has shown they are secure of success.

I referred, but now, to the effort we are making to improve the designs of our manufactures. Within certain limits I believe this improvement may indeed take effect: so that we may no more humor momentary fashions by ugly results of chance instead of design; and may produce both good tissues, of harmonious colors, and good forms and substance of pottery and glass. But we shall never excel in decorative design. Such design is usually produced by people of great natural powers of mind, who have no variety of subjects to employ themselves on, no oppressive anxieties, and are in circumstances either of natural scenery or of daily life, which cause pleasurable excitement. *We* cannot design, because we have too much to think of, and we think of it too anxiously. It has long been observed how little real anxiety exists in the minds of the partly savage races which excel in decorative art; and we must not suppose that the temper of the Middle Ages was a troubled one, because every day brought its danger or its change. The very eventfulness of the life rendered it careless, as generally is still the case with soldiers and sailors. Now, when there are great powers of thought, and little to think of, all the waste energy and fancy are thrown into the manual work, and you have so much intellect as would direct the affairs of a large mercantile concern for a day, spent all at once, quite unconsciously, in drawing an ingenious spiral.

Also, powers of doing fine ornamental work are only to be reached by a perpetual discipline of the hand as well as of the fancy; discipline as attentive and painful as that which a juggler has to put himself through, to overcome the more palpable difficulties of his profession. The execution of the best artists is always a splendid tour-de-force; and much that in painting is supposed to be dependent on material is indeed only a lovely and quite inimitable legerdemain. Now, when powers of fancy, stimulated by this triumphant precision of manual dexterity, descend uninterrupted from generation to generation, you have at last, what is not so much a trained artist, as a new species of animal, with whose instinctive gifts you have no chance of contending. And thus all our imitations of other people's work are futile. We must learn first to make honest English wares, and afterward to decorate them as may please the then approving Graces.

Secondly—and this is an incapacity of a graver kind, yet having its own good in it also—we shall never be successful in the highest fields of ideal or theological art.

For there is one strange, but quite essential, character in us—ever since the Conquest, if not earlier—a delight in the forms of burlesque which are connected in some degree with the foulness in evil. I think the most perfect type of a true English mind in its best possible temper, is that of Chaucer; and you will find that, while it is for the most part full of thoughts of beauty, pure and wild like that of an April morning, there are, even in the midst of this, sometimes momentarily jesting passages which stoop to play with evil—while the power of listening to and enjoying the jesting of entirely gross persons, whatever the feeling may be which permits it, afterward degenerates into forms of humor which render some of quite the greatest, wisest, and most moral of English writers now almost useless for our youth. And yet you will find that whenever Englishmen are wholly without this instinct, their genius is comparatively weak and restricted.

Now, the first necessity for the doing of any great work in ideal art, is the looking upon all foulness with horror, as a contemptible though dreadful enemy. You may easily understand what I mean, by comparing the feelings with which Dante regards any form of obscenity or of base jest, with the temper in which the same things are regarded by Shakespeare. And this strange earthly instinct of ours, coupled as it is, in our good men, with great simplicity and common sense, renders them shrewd and perfect observers and delineators of actual nature, low or high; but precludes them from that specialty of art which is properly called sublime. If ever we try anything in the manner of Michael Angelo or of Dante, we catch a fall, even in literature, as Milton in the battle of the angels, spoiled from Hesiod; while in art, every attempt in this style has hitherto been the sign either of the presumptuous egotism of persons who had never really learned to be workmen, or it has been connected with very tragic forms of the contemplation of death,— it has always been partly insane, and never once wholly successful.

But we need not feel any discomfort in these limitations of our capacity. We can do much that others cannot, and more than we have ever yet ourselves completely done. Our first great gift is in the portraiture of living people—a power already so accomplished in both Reynolds and Gainsborough that nothing is left for future masters but to add the calm of perfect workmanship to their vigor and felicity of perception. And of what value a true school of portraiture may become in the future, when worthy men will desire only to be known, and others will not fear to know them, for what they truly were, we cannot from any past records of art influence yet conceive. But in my next address it will be partly my endeavor to show you how much more useful, because more humble, the labor of great masters

might have been, had they been content to bear record
of the souls that were dwelling with them on earth, instead of striving to give a deceptive glory to those they
dreamed of in heaven.

Secondly, we have an intense power of invention and
expression in domestic drama (King Lear and Hamlet
being essentially domestic in their strongest motives of
interest). There is a tendency at this moment toward
a noble development of our art in this direction, checked
by many adverse conditions, which may be summed in
one,—the insufficiency of generous civic or patriotic passion in the heart of the English people; a fault which
makes its domestic affections selfish, contracted, and,
therefore, frivolous.

Thirdly, in connection with our simplicity and good-
humor, and partly with that very love of the grotesque
which debases our ideal, we have a sympathy with the
lower animals which is peculiarly our own; and which,
though it has already found some exquisite expression
in the works of Bewick and Landseer, is yet quite undeveloped. This sympathy, with the aid of our now
authoritative science of physiology, and in association
with our British love of adventure, will, I hope, enable
us to give to the future inhabitants of the globe an almost perfect record of the present forms of animal life
upon it, of which many are on the point of being ex-
tinguished. . . .

While I myself hold this professorship, I shall direct
you in these exercises very definitely to natural history,
and to landscape; not only because in these two branches
I am probably able to show you truths which might be
despised by my successors; but because I think the vital
and joyful study of natural history quite the principal
element requiring introduction, not only into University,
but into national, education, from highest to lowest; and
I even will risk incurring your ridicule by confessing
one of my fondest dreams, that I may succeed in making
some of you English youths like better to look at a bird
than to shoot it; and even desire to make wild creatures
tame, instead of tame creatures wild. And for the study
of landscape, it is, I think, now calculated to be of use
in deeper, if not more important modes, than that of

natural science, for reasons which I will ask you to let me state at some length.

Observe first;—no race of men which is entirely bred in wild country, far from cities, ever enjoys landscape. They may enjoy the beauty of animals, but scarcely even that: a true peasant cannot see the beauty of cattle; but only qualities expressive of their serviceableness. I waive discussion of this to-day; permit my assertion of it, under my confident guarantee of future proof. Landscape can only be enjoyed by cultivated persons; and it is only by music, literature, and painting, that cultivation can be given. Also, the faculties which are thus received are hereditary; so that the child of an educated race has an innate instinct for beauty, derived from arts practised hundreds of years before its birth. Now farther note this, one of the loveliest things in human nature. In the children of noble races, trained by surrounding art, and at the same time in the practice of great deeds, there is an intense delight in the landscape of their country as *memorial;* a sense not taught to them, nor teachable to any others; but, in them, innate; and the seal and reward of persistence in great national life;—the obedience and the peace of ages having extended gradually the glory of the revered ancestors also to the ancestral land; until the Motherhood of the dust, the mystery of the Demeter from whose bosom we came, and to whose bosom we return, surrounds and inspires, everywhere, the local awe of field and fountain; the sacredness of landmark that none may remove, and of wave that none may pollute; while records of proud days, and of dear persons, make every rock monumental with ghostly inscription, and every path lovely with noble desolateness.

Now, however checked by lightness of temperament, the instinctive love of landscape in us has this deep root, which, in your minds, I will pray you to disencumber from whatever may oppress or mortify it, and to strive to feel with all the strength of your youth that a nation is only worthy of the soil and the scenes that it has inherited, when, by all its acts and arts, it is making them more lovely for its children. . . .

But if either our work, or our enquiries, are to be indeed successful in their own field, they must be connected with others of a sterner character. Now listen to me, if I have in these past details lost or burdened your attention; for this is what I have chiefly to say to you. The art of any country *is the exponent of its social and political virtues.* I will show you that it is so in some detail, in the second of my subsequent course of lectures; meantime accept this as one of the things, and the most important of all things, I can positively declare to you. The art, or general productive and formative energy, of any country, is an exact exponent of its ethical life. You can have noble art only from noble persons, associated under laws fitted to their time and circumstances. And the best skill that any teacher of art could spend here in your help, would not end in enabling you even so much as rightly to draw the water-lilies in the Cherwell (and though it did, the work when done would not be worth the lilies themselves) unless both he and you were seeking, as I trust we shall together seek, in the laws which regulate the finest industries, the clue to the laws which regulate *all* industries, and in better obedience to which we shall actually have henceforward to live: not merely in compliance with our own sense of what is right, but under the weight of quite literal necessity. For the trades by which the British people has believed it to be the highest of destinies to maintain itself, cannot now long remain undisputed in its hands; its unemployed poor are daily becoming more violently criminal; and a certain distress in the middle classes, arising, *partly from their vanity in living always up to their incomes, and partly from their folly in imagining that they can subsist in idleness upon usury,* will at last compel the sons and daughters of English families to acquaint themselves with the principles of providential economy; and to learn that food can only be got out of the ground, and competence only secured by frugality; and that although it is not possible for all to be occupied in the highest arts, nor for any, guiltlessly, to pass their days in a succession of pleasures, the most perfect mental culture possible to men is founded on their useful energies, and their best arts and brightest happiness are consistent, and consistent only, with their virtue.

This, I repeat, gentlemen, will soon become manifest

to those among us, and there are yet many, who are honest-hearted. And the future fate of England depends upon the position they then take, and on their courage in maintaining it.

There is a destiny now possible to us—the highest ever set before a nation to be accepted or refused. We are still undegenerate in race; a race mingled of the best northern blood. We are not yet dissolute in temper, but still have the firmness to govern, and the grace to obey. We have been taught a religion of pure mercy, which we must either now betray, or learn to defend by fulfilling. And we are rich in an inheritance of honor, bequeathed to us through a thousand years of noble history, which it should be our daily thirst to increase with splendid avarice, so that Englishmen, if it be a sin to covet honor, should be the most offending souls alive. Within the last few years we have had the laws of natural science opened to us with a rapidity which has been blinding by its brightness; and means of transit and communication given to us, which have made but one kingdom of the habitable globe. One kingdom;—but who is to be its king? Is there to be no king in it, think you, and every man to do that which is right in his own eyes? Or only kings of terror, and the obscene empires of Mammon and Belial? Or will you, youths of England, make your country again a royal throne of kings; a sceptred isle, for all the world a source of light, a centre of peace; mistress of Learning and of the Arts;—faithful guardian of great memories in the midst of irreverent and ephemeral visions;—faithful servant of time-tried principles, under temptation from fond experiments and licentious desires; and amidst the cruel and clamorous jealousies of the nations, worshipped in her strange valor of good-will toward men?

"Vexilla regis prodeunt." * Yes, but of which king? There are the two oriflammes; which shall we plant on the farthest islands,—the one that floats in heavenly fire, or that hangs heavy with foul tissue of terrestrial gold? There is indeed a course of beneficent glory open to us, such as never was yet offered to any poor group

---

* "The royal banners forward go." One of the great Latin hymns of the Church.

of mortal souls. But it must be—it *is* with us, now, "Reign or Die." And if it shall be said of this country, "Fece per viltate, il gran rifiuto," * that refusal of the crown will be, of all yet recorded in history, the shamefullest and most untimely.

And this is what she must either do, or perish: she must found colonies as fast and as far as she is able, formed of her most energetic and worthiest men;—seizing every piece of fruitful waste ground she can set her foot on, and there teaching these her colonists that their chief virtue is to be fidelity to their country, and that their first aim is to be to advance the power of England by land and sea: and that, though they live on a distant plot of ground, they are no more to consider themselves therefore disfranchised from their native land, than the sailors of her fleets do, because they float on distant waves. So that literally, these colonies must be fastened fleets; and every man of them must be under authority of captains and officers, whose better command is to be over fields and streets instead of ships of the line; and England, in these her motionless navies (or, in the true and mightiest sense, motionless *churches,* ruled by pilots on the Galilean lake of all the world), is to "expect every man to do his duty"; recognizing that duty is indeed possible no less in peace than war; and that if we can get men, for little pay, to cast themselves against cannonmouths for love of England, we may find men also who will plough and sow for her, who will behave kindly and righteously for her, who will bring up their children to love her, and who will gladden themselves in the brightness of her glory, more than in all the light of tropic skies.

But that they may be able to do this, she must make her own majesty stainless; she must give them thoughts of their home of which they can be proud. The England who is to be mistress of half the earth, cannot remain herself a heap of cinders, trampled by contending and miserable crowds; she must yet again become the England she was once, and in all beautiful ways,—more: so happy, so secluded, and so pure, that in her sky—polluted

---

* Dante, *Inferno* III, 60: "Who made, through cowardice, the great refusal." (Norton's translation.)

by no unholy clouds—she may be able to spell rightly of every star that heaven doth show; and in her fields, ordered and wide and fair, of every herb that sips the dew; and under the green avenues of her enchanted garden, a sacred Circe, true Daughter of the Sun, she must guide the human arts, and gather the divine knowledge, of distant nations, transformed from savageness to manhood, and redeemed from despairing into peace.

You think that an impossible ideal. Be it so; refuse to accept it if you will; but see that you form your own in its stead. All that I ask of you is to have a fixed purpose of some kind for your country and yourselves; no matter how restricted, so that it be fixed and unselfish. I know what stout hearts are in you, to answer acknowledged need: but it is the fatallest form of error in English youths to hide their hardihood till it fades for lack of sunshine, and to act in disdain of purpose, till all purpose is vain. It is not by deliberate, but by careless selfishness; not by compromise with evil, but by dull following of good, that the weight of national evil increases upon us daily. Break through at least this pretence of existence; determine what you will be, and what you would win. You will not decide wrongly if you will resolve to decide at all. Were even the choice between lawless pleasure and loyal suffering, you would not, I believe, choose basely. But your trial is not so sharp. It is between drifting in confused wreck among the castaways of Fortune, who condemns to assured ruin those who know not either how to resist her, or obey; between this, I say, and the taking of your appointed part in the heroism of Rest; the resolving to share in the victory which is to the weak rather than the strong; and the binding yourselves by that law, which, thought on through lingering night and laboring day, makes a man's life to be as a tree planted by the water-side, that bringeth forth his fruit in his season;—

"ET FOLIUM EJUS NON DEFLUET,
    ET OMNIA, QUÆCUNQUE FACIET, PROSPERABUNTUR."

The Relation of Art to Use

[Lectures on Art, Lecture IV.]

OUR subject of enquiry to-day, you will remember, is the mode in which fine art is founded upon, or may contribute to, the practical requirements of human life.

Its offices in this respect are mainly twofold: it gives Form to knowledge, and Grace to utility; that is to say, it makes permanently visible to us things which otherwise could neither be described by our science, nor retained by our memory; and it gives delightfulness and worth to the implements of daily use, and materials of dress, furniture and lodging. In the first of these offices it gives precision and charm to truth; in the second it gives precision and charm to service. For, the moment we make anything useful thoroughly, it is a law of nature that we shall be pleased with ourselves, and with the thing we have made; and become desirous therefore to adorn or complete it, in some dainty way, with finer art expressive of our pleasure.

And the point I wish chiefly to bring before you to-day is this close and healthy connection of the fine arts with material use; but I must first try briefly to put in clear light the function of art in giving Form to truth.

Much that I have hitherto tried to teach has been disputed on the ground that I have attached too much importance to art as representing natural facts, and too little to it as a source of pleasure. And I wish, in the close of these four prefatory lectures, strongly to assert to you, and, so far as I can in the time, convince you, that the entire vitality of art depends upon its being either full of truth, or full of use; and that, however pleasant, wonderful or impressive it may be in itself, it must yet be of inferior kind, and tend to deeper inferiority, unless it has clearly one of these main objects,—either *to state a true thing,* or to *adorn a serviceable one.* It must never exist alone—never for itself; it exists rightly only when it is the means of knowledge, or the grace of agency for life.

Now, I pray you to observe—for though I have said this often before, I have never yet said it clearly enough

—every good piece of art, to whichever of these ends it may be directed, involves first essentially the evidence of human skill, and the formation of an actually beautiful thing by it.

Skill, and beauty, always then; and, beyond these, the formative arts have always one or other of the two objects which I have just defined to you—truth, or serviceableness; and without these aims neither the skill nor their beauty will avail; only by these can either legitimately reign. All the graphic arts begin in keeping the outline of shadow that we have loved, and they end in giving to it the aspect of life; and all the architectural arts begin in the shaping of the cup and the platter, and they end in a glorified roof.

Therefore, you see, in the graphic arts you have Skill, Beauty, and Likeness; and in the architectural arts, Skill, Beauty, and Use: and you *must* have the three in each group, balanced and coordinate; and all the chief errors of art consist in losing or exaggerating one of these elements.

For instance, almost the whole system and hope of modern life are founded on the notion that you may substitute mechanism for skill, photograph for picture, cast-iron for sculpture. That is your main nineteenth-century faith, or infidelity. You think you can get everything by grinding—music, literature, and painting. You will find it grievously not so; you can get nothing but dust by mere grinding. Even to have the barley-meal out of it, you must have the barley first; and that comes by growth, not grinding. But essentially, we have lost our delight in Skill; in that majesty of it which I was trying to make clear to you in my last address, and which long ago I tried to express, under the head of ideas of power. The entire sense of that, we have lost, because we ourselves do not take pains enough to do right, and have no conception of what the right costs; so that all the joy and reverence we ought to feel in looking at a strong man's work have ceased in us. We keep them yet a little in looking at a honeycomb or a bird's-nest; we understand that these differ, by divinity of skill, from a lump of wax or a cluster of sticks. But a picture, which is a much more wonderful thing than a honeycomb or a bird's-nest,—have we not known people, and sensible people too, who expected to be taught to produce that, in six lessons?

Well, you must have the skill, you must have the beauty, which is the highest moral element; and then lastly, you must have the verity or utility, which is not the moral, but the vital element; and this desire for verity and use is the one aim of the three that always leads in great schools, and in the minds of great masters, without any exception. They will permit themselves in awkwardness, they will permit themselves in ugliness; but they will never permit themselves in uselessness or in unveracity.

And farther, as their skill increases, and as their grace so much more, their desire for truth. It is impossible to find the three motives in fairer balance and harmony than in our own Reynolds. He rejoices in showing you his skill; and those of you who succeed in learning what painter's work really is, will one day rejoice also, even to laughter—that highest laughter which springs of pure delight, in watching the fortitude and the fire of a hand which strikes forth its will upon the canvas as easily as the wind strikes it on the sea. He rejoices in all abstract beauty and rhythm and melody of design; he will never give you a color that is not lovely, nor a shade that is unnecessary, nor a line that is ungraceful. But all his power and all his invention are held by him subordinate —and the more obediently because of their nobleness,— to his true leading purpose of setting before you such likeness of the living presence of an English gentleman or an English lady, as shall be worthy of being looked upon forever.

But farther, you remember, I hope—for I said it in a way that I thought would shock you a little, that you might remember it—my statement, that art had never done more than this, never more than given the likeness of a noble human being. Not only so, but it very seldom does so much as this; and the best pictures that exist of the great schools are all portraits, or groups of portraits, often of very simple and nowise noble persons. You may have much more brilliant and impressive qualities in imaginative pictures; you may have figures scattered like clouds, or garlanded like flowers; you may have light and shade, as of a tempest, and color, as of the rainbow; but all that is child's play to the great men, though it is astonishment to us. Their real strength is tried to the utmost, and as far as I know, it is never elsewhere brought out so thoroughly, as in painting one man or woman, and the soul that was in them; nor that always the highest soul, but often only a thwarted one that was capable of height; or perhaps not even that, but faultful and poor, yet seen through, to the poor best of it, by the masterful sight. So that in order to put before you in your Standard Series, the best art possible, I am obliged, even from the very strongest men, to take the portraits, before I take the idealism. Nay, whatever is best in the great compositions themselves has depended on portraiture; and the study necessary to enable you to understand invention will also convince you that the mind of man never invented a greater thing than the form of man, animated by faithful life. Every attempt to refine or exalt such healthy humanity has weakened or caricatured it; or else consists only in giving it, to please our fancy, the wings of birds, or the eyes of antelopes. Whatever is truly great in either Greek or Christian art, is also restrictedly human; and even the raptures of the redeemed souls who enter, "celestemente ballando," the gate of Angelico's Paradise, were seen first in the terrestrial, yet most pure, mirth of Florentine maidens.

I am aware that this cannot but at present appear gravely questionable to those of my audience who are strictly cognizant of the phases of Greek art; for they know that the moment of its decline is accurately marked, by its turning from abstract form to portraiture. But the reason of this is simple. The progressive course of Greek art was in subduing monstrous conceptions to natural ones; it did this by general laws; it reached absolute truth of generic human form, and if this ethical force had remained, would have advanced into healthy portraiture. But at the moment of change the national life ended in Greece; and portraiture, there, meant insult to her religion, and flattery to her tyrants. And her skill perished, not because she became true in sight, but because she became vile at heart. . . .

But I have told you enough, it seems to me, at least to-day, of this function of art in recording fact; let me now finally, and with all distinctness possible to me, state to you its main business of all;—its service in the actual uses of daily life.

You are surprised, perhaps, to hear me call this its main business. That is indeed so, however. The giving brightness to picture is much, but the giving brightness to life more. And remember, were it as patterns only, you cannot, without the realities, have the pictures. *You cannot have a landscape by Turner, without a country for him to paint; you cannot have a portrait by Titian, without a man to be portrayed.* I need not prove that to you, I suppose, in these short terms; but in the outcome I can get no soul to believe that the beginning of art *is in getting our country clean, and our people beautiful.* I have been ten years trying to get this very plain certainty—I do not say believed—but even thought of, as anything but a monstrous proposition. To get your country clean, and your people lovely;—I assure you that is a necessary work of art to begin with! There has indeed been art in countries where people lived in dirt to serve God, but never in countries where they lived in dirt to serve the devil. There has indeed been art where the people were not all lovely—where even their lips were thick—and their skins black, because the sun had looked upon them; but never in a country where the people were pale with miserable toil and deadly shade, and where the lips of youth, instead of being full with blood, were pinched by famine, or warped with poison. And now, therefore, note this well, the gist of all these long prefatory talks. I said that the two great moral instincts were those of Order and Kindness. Now, all the arts are founded on agriculture by the hand, and on the graces and kindness of feeding, and dressing, and lodging your people. Greek art begins in the gardens of Alcinous—perfect order, leeks in beds, and fountains in pipes. And Christian art, as it arose out of chivalry, was only possible so far as chivalry compelled both kings and knights to care for the right personal training of their people; it perished utterly when those kings and knights became δημοβόροι, devourers of the people. And it will become

possible again only, when, literally, the sword is beaten
into the ploughshare, when your St. George of England
shall justify his name, and Christian art shall be known
as its Master was, in breaking of bread.

Now look at the working out of this broad principle
in minor detail; observe how, from highest to lowest,
health of art has first depended on reference to industrial
use. There is first the need of cup and platter, especially
of cup; for you can put your meat on the Harpies', or
on any other, tables; but you must have your cup to drink
from. And to hold it conveniently, you must put a handle to it; and to fill it when it is empty you must have
a large pitcher of some sort; and to carry the pitcher
you may most advisably have two handles. Modify the
forms of these needful possessions according to the various requirements of drinking largely and drinking delicately; of pouring easily out, or of keeping for years
the perfume in; of storing in cellars, or bearing from
fountains; of sacrificial libation, of Panathenaic treasure
of oil, and sepulchral treasure of ashes,—and you have
a resultant series of beautiful form and decoration, from
the rude amphora of red earth up to Cellini's vases of
gems and crystal, in which series, but especially in the
more simple conditions of it, are developed the most beautiful lines and most perfect types of severe composition
which have yet been attained by art.

But again, that you may fill your cup with pure water,
you must go to the well or spring; you need a fence
round the well; you need some tube or trough, or other
means of confining the stream at the spring. For the
conveyance of the current to any distance you must
build either enclosed or open aqueduct; and in the hot
square of the city where you set it free, you find it good
for health and pleasantness to let it leap into a fountain.
On these several needs you have a school of sculpture
founded; in the decoration of the walls of wells in level
countries, and of the sources of springs in mountainous
ones, and chiefly of all, where the women of household or
market meet at the city fountain.

There is, however, a farther reason for the use of art
here than in any other material service, so far as we may,
by art, express our reverence or thankfulness. Whenever

a nation is in its right mind, it always has a deep sense of divinity in the gift of rain from heaven, filling its heart with food and gladness; and all the more when that gift becomes gentle and perennial in the flowing of springs. It literally is not possible that any fruitful power of the Muses should be put forth upon a people which disdains their Helicon; still less is it possible that any Christian nation should grow up "tanquam lignum quod plantatum est secus decursus aquarum," which cannot recognize the lesson meant in their being told of the places where Rebekah was met;—where Rachel,—where Zipporah,—and she who was asked for water under Mount Gerizim by a Stranger, weary, who had nothing to draw with.

And truly, when our mountain springs are set apart in vale or craggy glen, or glade of wood green through the drought of summer, far from cities, then it is best let them stay in their own happy peace; but if near towns, and liable therefore to be defiled by common usage, we could not use the loveliest art more worthily than by sheltering the spring and its first pools with precious marbles: nor ought anything to be esteemed more important, as a means of healthy education, than the care to keep the streams of it afterward, to as great a distance as possible, pure, full of fish, and easily accessible to children. There used to be, thirty years ago, a little rivulet of the Wandel, about an inch deep, which ran over the carriage-road and under a foot-bridge just under the last chalk hill near Croydon. Alas! men came and went; and it—did *not* go on forever. It has long since been bricked over by the parish authorities; but there was more education in that stream with its minnows than you could get out of a thousand pounds spent yearly in the parish schools, even though you were to spend every farthing of it in teaching the nature of oxygen and hydrogen, and the names, and rate per minute, of all the rivers in Asia and America.

Well, the gist of this matter lies here then. Suppose we want a school of pottery again in England, all we poor artists are ready to do the best we can, to show you how pretty a line may be that is twisted first to one side, and then to the other; and how a plain household blue will make a pattern on white; and how ideal art may be got out of the spaniel's colors of black and tan. But I tell you beforehand, all that we can do will be utterly useless, unless you teach your peasant to say grace, not only before meat, but before drink; and having provided him with Greek cups and platters, provide him also with something that is not poisoned to put into them.

There cannot be any need that I should trace for you the conditions of art that are directly founded on serviceableness of dress, and of armor; but it is my duty to affirm to you, in the most positive manner, that after recovering, for the poor, wholesomeness of food, your next step toward founding schools of art in England must be in recovering, for the poor, decency and wholesomeness of dress; thoroughly good in substance, fitted for their daily work, becoming to their rank in life, and worn with order and dignity. And this order and dignity must be taught them by the women of the upper and middle classes, whose minds can be in nothing right, as long as they are so wrong in this matter as to endure the squalor of the poor, while they themselves dress gayly. And on the proper pride and comfort of both poor and rich in dress, must be founded the true arts of dress; carried on by masters of manufacture no less careful of the perfectness and beauty of their tissues, and of all that in substance and in design can be bestowed upon them, than ever the armorers of Milan and Damascus were careful of their steel.

Then, in the third place, having recovered some wholesome habits of life as to food and dress, we must recover them as to lodging. I said just now that the best architecture was but a glorified roof. Think of it. The dome of the Vatican, the porches of Rheims or Chartres, the vaults and arches of their aisles, the canopy of the tomb, and the spire of the belfry, are all forms resulting from the mere requirement that a certain space shall be strongly covered from heat and rain. More than that— as I have tried all through *The Stones of Venice* to show, —the lovely forms of these were every one of them developed in civil and domestic building, and only after their invention, employed ecclesiastically on the grandest scale. I think you cannot but have noticed here in Oxford, as elsewhere, that our modern architects never seem to know what to do with their roofs. Be assured, until the roofs are right, nothing else will be; and there are just two ways of keeping them right. Never build them of iron, but only of wood or stone; and secondly, take care that in every town the little roofs are built before the large ones, and that everybody who wants one has got one. And we must try also to make everybody want one. That is to say, at some not very advanced period of life, men should desire to have a home, which they do not wish to quit any more, suited to their habits of life, and likely to be more and more suitable to them until their death. And men must desire to have these their dwelling-places built as strongly as possible, and furnished and decorated daintily, and set in pleasant places, in bright light, and good air, being able to choose for themselves that at least as well as swallows. And when the houses are grouped together in cities, men must have so much civic fellowship as to subject their architecture to a common law, and so much civic pride as to desire that the whole gathered group of human dwellings should be a lovely thing, not a frightful one, on the face of the earth. Not many weeks ago an English clergyman, a master of this University, a man not given to sentiment, but of middle age, and great practical sense, told me, by accident, and wholly without reference to the subject now before us, that he never could enter London from his country parsonage but with closed eyes, lest the sight of the blocks of houses which the railroad intersected in the suburbs should unfit him, by the horror of it, for his day's work.

Now, it is not possible—and I repeat to you, only in more deliberate assertion, what I wrote just twenty-two years ago in the last chapter of the *Seven Lamps of Architecture*—it is not possible to have any right morality, happiness, or art, in any country where the cities are thus built, or thus, let me rather say, clotted and coagulated; spots of a dreadful mildew, spreading by patches and blotches over the country they consume. You must have lovely cities, crystallized, not coagulated, into form; limited in size, and not casting out the scum and scurf

of them into an encircling eruption of shame, but girded
each with its sacred pomœrium, and with garlands of
gardens full of blossoming trees and softly guided streams.

That is impossible, you say! it may be so. I have
nothing to do with its possibility, but only with its in-
dispensability. More than that must be possible, however, before you can have a school of art; namely, that
you find places elsewhere than in England, or at least
in otherwise unserviceable parts of England, for the establishment of manufactories needing the help of fire,
that is to say, of all the τέχναι βαναυσικαὶ and ἐπίρρητοι, of
which it was long ago known to be the constant nature that
«ἀσχολίας μάλιστα ἔχουσι καὶ φίλων καὶ πόλεως συνεπιμελεῖσθαι»,*
and to reduce such manufacturers to their lowest limit,
so that nothing may ever be made of iron that can
as effectually be made of wood or stone; and nothing
moved by steam than can be as effectually moved by
natural forces. And observe, that for all mechanical
effort required in social life and in cities, water power
is infinitely more than enough; for anchored mills on
the large rivers, and mills moved by sluices from reser-
voirs filled by the tide, will give you command of any
quantity of constant motive power you need.

Agriculture by the hand, then, and absolute refusal or
banishment of unnecessary igneous force, are the first
conditions of a school of art in any country. And until
you do this, be it soon or late, things will continue in
that triumphant state to which, for want of finer art,
your mechanism has brought them;—that, though England is deafened with spinning wheels, her people have
not clothes—though she is black with digging of fuel,
they die of cold—and though she has sold her soul for
gain, they die of hunger. Stay in that triumph, if you
choose; but be assured of this, it is not one which the
fine arts will ever share with you.

---

* Xenophon, *Economist,* IV. 2, 3: "the arts which are mechanical
and infamous peculiarly involve want of leisure for caring for friends
or city." [Cook and Wedderburn's note.]

TRAFFIC

[The Crown of Wild Olive, Lecture II.]

MY good Yorkshire friends, you asked me down here among your hills that I might talk to you about this Exchange you are going to build; but, earnestly and seriously asking you to pardon me, I am going to do nothing of the kind. I cannot talk, or at least can say very little, about this same Exchange. I must talk of quite other things, though not willingly;—I could not deserve your pardon, if, when you invited me to speak on one subject, I *wilfully* spoke on another. But I cannot speak, to purpose, of anything about which I do not care; and most simply and sorrowfully I have to tell you, in the outset, that I do *not* care about this Exchange of yours.

If, however, when you sent me your invitation, I had answered, "I won't come, I don't care about the Exchange of Bradford," you would have been justly offended with me, not knowing the reasons of so blunt a carelessness. So I have come down, hoping that you will patiently let me tell you why, on this, and many other occasions, I now remain silent, when formerly I should have caught at the opportunity of speaking to a gracious audience.

In a word, then, I do not care about this Exchange—because *you* don't; and because you know perfectly well I cannot make you. Look at the essential conditions of the case, which you, as business men, know perfectly well, though perhaps you think I forget them. You are going to spend £30,000, which to you, collectively, is nothing; the buying a new coat is, as to the cost of it, a much more important matter of consideration to me, than building a new Exchange is to you. But you think you may as well have the right thing for your money. You know there are a great many odd styles of architecture about; you don't want to do anything ridiculous; you hear of me, among others, as a respectable architectural man-milliner; and you send for me, that I may tell you the leading fashion; and what is, in our shops, for the moment, the newest and sweetest thing in pinnacles.

Now, pardon me for telling you frankly, you cannot have good architecture merely by asking people's advice on occasion. All good architecture is the expression of national life and character, and it is produced by a prevalent and eager national taste, or desire for beauty. And I want you to think a little of the deep significance of this word "taste"; for no statement of mine has been more earnestly or oftener controverted than that good taste is essentially a moral quality. "No," say many of my antagonists, "taste is one thing, morality is another. Tell us what is pretty: we shall be glad to know that; but we need no sermons—even were you able to preach them, which may be doubted."

Permit me, therefore, to fortify this old dogma of mine somewhat. Taste is not only a part and an index of morality;—it is the ONLY morality. The first, and last, and closest trial question to any living creature is, "What do you like?" Tell me what you like, and I'll tell you what you are. Go out into the street, and ask the first man or woman you meet, what their "taste" is; and if they answer candidly, you know them, body and soul. "You, my friend in the rags, with the unsteady gait, what do *you* like?" "A pipe and a quartern of gin." I know you. "You, good woman, with the quick step and tidy bonnet, what do you like?" "A swept hearth, and a clean tea-table; and my husband opposite me, and a baby at my breast." Good, I know you also. "You, little girl with the golden hair and the soft eyes, what do you like?" "My canary, and a run among the wood hyacinths." "You, little boy with the dirty hands, and the low forehead, what do you like?" "A shy at the sparrows, and a game at pitch farthing." Good; we know them all now. What more need we ask?

"Nay," perhaps you answer; "we need rather to ask what these people and children do, than what they like. If they *do* right, it is no matter that they like what is wrong; and if they *do* wrong, it is no matter that they like what is right. Doing is the great thing; and it does not matter that the man likes drinking, so that he does not drink; nor that the little girl likes to be kind to her canary, if she will not learn her lessons; nor that the little boy likes throwing stones at the sparrows, if he goes to the Sunday school." Indeed, for a short time, and in a provisional sense, this is true. For if, resolutely people do what is right, in time to come they like doing it. But they only are in a right moral state when they *have* come to like doing it; and as long as they don't like it, they are still in a vicious state. The man is not in health of body who is always thinking of the bottle in the cupboard, though he bravely bears his thirst; but the man who heartily enjoys water in the morning, and wine in the evening, each in its proper quantity and time. And the entire object of true education is to make people not merely *do* the right things, but *enjoy* the right things:—not merely industrious, but to love industry — not merely learned, but to love knowledge — not merely pure, but to love purity—not merely just, but to hunger and thirst after justice.

But you may answer or think, "Is the liking for outside ornaments,—for pictures, or statues, or furniture or architecture, a moral quality?" Yes, most surely, if a rightly set liking. Taste for *any* pictures or statues is not a moral quality, but taste for good ones is. Only here again we have to define the word "good." I don't mean by "good," clever—or learned—or difficult in the doing. Take a picture by Teniers, of sots quarrelling over their dice; it is an entirely clever picture; so clever that nothing in its kind has ever been done equal to it; but it is also an entirely base and evil picture. It is an expression of delight in the prolonged contemplation of a vile thing, and delight in that is an "unmannered," or "immoral" quality. It is "bad taste" in the profoundest sense—it is the taste of the devils. On the other hand, a picture of Titian's, or a Greek statue, or a Greek coin, or a Turner landscape, expresses delight in the perpetual contemplation of a good and perfect thing. That is an entirely moral quality—it is the taste of the angels. And all delight in art, and all love of it, resolve themselves into simple love of that which deserves love. That deserving is the quality which we call "loveliness"—(we ought to have an opposite word, hateliness, to be said of the things which deserve to be hated); and it is not an indifferent nor optional thing whether we love this or that; but it is just the vital function of all our being. What we *like* determines what we *are,* and is the sign of what we are; and to teach taste is inevitably to form character.

As I was thinking over this, in walking up Fleet Street the other day, my eye caught the title of a book standing open in a bookseller's window. It was—"On the necessity of the diffusion of taste among all classes." "Ah," I thought to myself, "my classifying friend, when you have diffused your taste, where will your classes be? The man who likes what you like, belongs to the same class with you, I think. Inevitably so. You may put him to other work if you choose; but, by the condition you have brought him into, he will dislike the work as much as you would yourself. You get hold of a scavenger or a costermonger, who enjoyed the Newgate Calendar for literature, and 'Pop goes the Weasel' for music. You think you can make him like Dante and Beethoven? I wish you joy of your lessons; but if you do, you have made a gentleman of him:—he won't like to go back to his costermongering."

And so completely and unexceptionally is this so, that, if I had time to-night, I could show you that a nation cannot be affected by any vice, or weakness, without expressing it, legibly, and forever, either in bad art, or by want of art; and that there is no national virtue, small or great, which is not manifestly expressed in all the art which circumstances enable the people possessing that virtue to produce. Take, for instance, your great English virtue of enduring and patient courage. You have at present in England only one art of any consequence— that is, iron-working. You know thoroughly well how to cast and hammer iron. Now, do you think, in those masses of lava which you build volcanic cones to melt, and which you forge at the mouths of the Infernos you have created; do you think, on those iron plates, your courage and endurance are not written forever,—not merely with an iron pen, but on iron parchment? And take also your great English vice—European vice—vice of all the world—vice of all other worlds that roll or shine in heaven, bearing with them yet the atmosphere of hell—the vice of jealousy, which brings competition

into your commerce, treachery into your councils, and
dishonor into your wars—that vice which has rendered
for you, and for your next neighboring nation, the daily
occupations of existence no longer possible, but with the
mail upon your breasts and the sword loose in its sheath
so that at last, you have realized for all the multitudes
of the two great peoples who lead the so-called civilization of the earth,—you have realized for them all, I say
in person and in policy, what was once true only of the
rough Border riders of your Cheviot hills—

> "They carved at the meal
> With gloves of steel,
> And they drank the red wine through the helmet barr'd;"—

do you think that this national shame and dastardliness
of heart are not written as legibly on every rivet of your
iron armor as the strength of the right hands that forged
it?

Friends, I know not whether this thing be the more
ludicrous or the more melancholy. It is quite unspeakably both. Suppose, instead of being now sent for by
you, I had been sent for by some private gentleman,
living in a suburban house, with his garden separated
only by a fruit wall from his next door neighbor's; and
he had called me to consult with him on the furnishing
of his drawing-room. I begin looking about me, and
find the walls rather bare; I think such and such a paper
might be desirable—perhaps a little fresco here and there
on the ceiling—a damask curtain or so at the windows.
"Ah," says my employer, "damask curtains, indeed!
That's all very fine, but you know I can't afford that
kind of thing just now!" "Yet the world credits you
with a splendid income!" "Ah, yes," says my friend,
"but do you know, at present I am obliged to spend it
nearly all in steel-traps?" "Steel-traps! for whom?"
"Why, for that fellow on the other side the wall, you
know: we're very good friends, capital friends; but we
are obliged to keep our traps set on both sides of the
wall; we could not possibly keep on friendly terms without them, and our spring guns. The worst of it is, we

are both clever fellows enough; and there's never a day
passes that we don't find out a new trap, or a new gun-
barrel, or something; we spend about fifteen millions a
year each in our traps, take it altogether; and I don't
see how we're to do with less." A highly comic state of
life for two private gentlemen! but for two nations, it
seems to me, not wholly comic. Bedlam would be comic,
perhaps, if there were only one madman in it; and your
Christmas pantomime is comic, when there is only one
clown in it; but when the whole world turns clown, and
paints itself red with its own heart's blood instead of
vermilion, it is something else than comic, I think.

Mind, I know a great deal of this is play, and willingly allow for that. You don't know what to do with
yourselves for a sensation; fox-hunting and cricketing
will not carry you through the whole of this unendurably
long mortal life: you liked pop-guns when you were
schoolboys, and rifles and Armstrongs are only the same
things better made: but then the worst of it is, that
what was play to you when boys, was not play to the
sparrows; and what is play to you now, is not play to
the small birds of State neither; and for the black eagles,
you are somewhat shy of taking shots at them, if I mistake not.

I must get back to the matter in hand, however. Believe me, without further instance, I could show you, in
all time, that every nation's vice, or virtue, was written
in its art: the soldiership of early Greece; the sensuality
of late Italy; the visionary religion of Tuscany; the
splendid human energy of Venice. I have no time to do
this to-night (I have done it elsewhere before now); but
I proceed to apply the principle to ourselves in a more
searching manner.

I notice that among all the new buildings which cover
your once wild hills, churches and schools are mixed in
due, that is to say, in large proportion, with your mills
and mansions; and I notice also that the churches and
schools are almost always Gothic, and the mansions and
mills are never Gothic. May I ask the meaning of this?
for, remember, it is peculiarly a modern phenomenon.
When Gothic was invented, houses were Gothic as well
as churches; and when the Italian style superseded the

Gothic, churches were Italian as well as houses. If there is a Gothic spire to the cathedral of Antwerp, there is a Gothic belfry to the Hôtel de Ville at Brussels; if Inigo Jones builds an Italian Whitehall, Sir Christopher Wren builds an Italian St. Paul's. But now you live under one school of architecture, and worship under another. What do you mean by doing this? Am I to understand that you are thinking of changing your architecture back to Gothic; and that you treat your churches experimentally, because it does not matter what mistakes you make in a church? Or am I to understand that you consider Gothic a preeminently sacred and beautiful mode of building, which you think, like the fine frank-incense, should be mixed for the tabernacle only, and reserved for your religious services? For if this be the feeling, though it may seem at first as if it were graceful and reverent, at the root of the matter, it signifies neither more nor less than that you have separated your religion from your life.

For consider what a wide significance this fact has: and remember that it is not you only, but all the people of England, who are behaving thus, just now.

You have all got into the habit of calling the church "the house of God." I have seen, over the doors of many churches, the legend actually carved, *"This* is the house of God and this is the gate of heaven." Now, note where that legend comes from, and of what place it was first spoken. A boy leaves his father's house to go on a long journey on foot, to visit his uncle: he has to cross a wild hill-desert; just as if one of your own boys had to cross the wolds to visit an uncle at Carlisle. The second or third day your boy finds himself somewhere between Hawes and Brough, in the midst of the moors, at sunset. It is stony ground, and boggy; he cannot go one foot farther that night. Down he lies, to sleep, on Wharnside, where best he may, gathering a few of the stones together to put under his head;—so wild the place is, he cannot get anything but stones. And there, lying under the broad night, he has a dream; and he sees a ladder set up on the earth, and the top of it reaches to heaven, and the angels of God are seen ascending and descending upon it. And when he wakes out of his sleep, he says, "How dreadful is this place; surely this is none other than the house of God, and this is the gate of heaven." This PLACE, observe; not this church; not this city; not this stone, even, which he puts up for a memorial—the piece of flint on which his head has lain. But this *place;* this windy slope of Wharnside; this moorland hollow, torrent-bitten, snow-blighted; this *any* place where God lets down the ladder. And how are you to know where that will be? or how are you to determine where it may be, but by being ready for it always? Do you know where the lightning is to fall next? You *do* know that, partly; you can guide the lightning; but you cannot guide the going forth of the Spirit, which is as that lightning when it shines from the east to the west.

But the perpetual and insolent warping of that strong verse to serve a merely ecclesiastical purpose, is only one of the thousand instances in which we sink back into gross Judaism. We call our churches "temples." Now, you know perfectly well they are *not* temples. They have never had, never can have, anything whatever to do with temples. They are "synagogues"—"gathering places"— where you gather yourselves together as an assembly; and by not calling them so, you again miss the force of another mighty text—"Thou, when thou prayest, shalt not be as the hypocrites are; for they love to pray standing in the *churches"* [we should translate it], "that they may be seen of men. But thou, when thou prayest, enter into thy closet, and when thou hast shut thy door, pray to thy Father,"—which is, not in chancel nor in aisle, but "in secret."

Now, you feel, as I say this to you—I know you feel— as if I were trying to take away the honor of your churches. Not so; I am trying to prove to you the honor of your houses and your hills; not that the Church is not sacred—but that the whole Earth is. I would have you feel what careless, what constant, what infectious sin there is in all modes of thought, whereby, in calling your churches only "holy," you call your hearths and homes "profane"; and have separated yourselves from the heathen by casting all your household gods to the ground, instead of recognizing, in the places of their many and feeble Lares, the presence of your One and Mighty Lord and Lar.

"But what has all this to do with our Exchange?" you ask me, impatiently. My dear friends, it has just everything to do with it; on these inner and great questions depend all the outer and little ones; and if you have asked me down here to speak to you, because you had before been interested in anything I have written, you must know that all I have yet said about architecture was to show this. The book I called *The Seven Lamps* was to show that certain right states of temper and moral feeling were the magic powers by which all good architecture, without exception, had been produced. *The Stones of Venice* had, from beginning to end, no other aim than to show that the Gothic architecture of Venice had arisen out of, and indicated in all its features, a state of pure national faith, and of domestic virtue; and that its Renaissance architecture had arisen out of, and in all its features indicated, a state of concealed national infidelity, and of domestic corruption. And now, you ask me what style is best to build in, and how can I answer, knowing the meaning of the two styles, but by another question—do you mean to build as Christians or as Infidels? And still more—do you mean to build as honest Christians or as honest Infidels? as thoroughly and confessedly either one or the other? You don't like to be asked such rude questions. I cannot help it; they are of much more importance than this Exchange business; and if they can be at once answered, the Exchange business settles itself in a moment. But before I press them farther, I must ask leave to explain one point clearly.

In all my past work, my endeavor has been to show that good architecture is essentially religious—the production of a faithful and virtuous, not of an infidel and corrupted people. But in the course of doing this, I have had also to show that good architecture is not *ecclesiastical*. People are so apt to look upon religion as the business of the clergy, not their own, that the moment they hear of anything depending on "religion," they think it must also have depended on the priesthood; and I have had to take what place was to be occupied between these two errors, and fight both, often with seem-

ing contradiction. Good architecture is the work of good
and believing men; therefore, you say, at least some
people say, "Good architecture must essentially have been
the work of the clergy, not of the laity." No—a thousand
times no; good architecture * has always been the work
of the commonalty, *not* of the clergy. "What," you say,
"those glorious cathedrals — the pride of Europe — did
their builders not form Gothic architecture?" No; they
corrupted Gothic architecture. Gothic was formed in the
baron's castle, and the burgher's street. It was formed
by the thoughts, and hands, and powers of laboring citizens and warrior kings. By the monk it was used as an
instrument for the aid of his superstition: when that
superstition became a beautiful madness, and the best
hearts of Europe vainly dreamed and pined in the cloister, and vainly raged and perished in the crusade,—
through that fury of perverted faith and wasted war, the
Gothic rose also to its loveliest, most fantastic, and,
finally, most foolish dreams; and in those dreams was
lost.

I hope, now, that there is no risk of your misunderstanding me when I come to the gist of what I want to
say to-night;—when I repeat, that every great national
architecture has been the result and exponent of a great
national religion. You can't have bits of it here, bits
there—you must have it everywhere or nowhere. It is
not the monopoly of a clerical company—it is not the
exponent of a theological dogma—it is not the hiero-
glyphic writing of an initiated priesthood; it is the
manly language of a people inspired by resolute and
common purpose, and rendering resolute and common
fidelity to the legible laws of an undoubted God.

Now there have as yet been three distinct schools of
European architecture. I say, European, because Asiatic
and African architectures belong so entirely to other
races and climates, that there is no question of them
here; only, in passing, I will simply assure you that
whatever is good or great in Egypt, and Syria, and India, is just good or great for the same reasons as the
buildings on our side of the Bosphorus. We Europeans,

---

* And all other arts, for the most part; even of incredulous and
seculary-minded commonalties. [Ruskin's note.]

then, have had three great religions: the Greek, which was the worship of the God of Wisdom and Power; the Mediæval, which was the worship of the God of Judgment and Consolation; the Renaissance, which was the worship of the God of Pride and Beauty: these three we have had—they are past,—and now, at last, we English have got a fourth religion, and a God of our own, about which I want to ask you. But I must explain these three old ones first.

I repeat, first, the Greeks essentially worshipped the God of Wisdom; so that whatever contended against their religion,—to the Jews a stumbling-block,—was, to the Greeks—*Foolishness*.

The first Greek idea of deity was that expressed in the word, of which we keep the remnant in our words "*Di*-urnal" and "*Di*-vine"—the god of *Day*, Jupiter the revealer. Athena is his daughter, but especially daughter of the Intellect, springing armed from the head. We are only with the help of recent investigation beginning to penetrate the depth of meaning couched under the Athenaic symbols: but I may note rapidly, that her ægis the mantle with the serpent fringes, in which she often in the best statues, is represented as folding up her left hand, for better guard; and the Gorgon, on her shield, are both representative mainly of the chilling horror and sadness (turning men to stone, as it were) of the outmost and superficial spheres of knowledge—that knowledge which separates, in bitterness, hardness, and sorrow, the heart of the full-grown man from the heart of the child. For out of imperfect knowledge spring terror, dissension, danger, and disdain; but from perfect knowledge, given by the full-revealed Athena, strength and peace, in sign of which she is crowned with the olive spray, and bears the resistless spear.

This, then, was the Greek conception of purest Deity; and every habit of life, and every form of his art developed themselves from the seeking this bright, serene, resistless wisdom; and setting himself, as a man, to do things evermore rightly and strongly;* not with any

---

* It is an error to suppose that the Greek worship, or seeking, was chiefly of Beauty. It was essentially of rightness and strength, founded on Forethought: the principal character of Greek art is not

ardent affection or ultimate hope; but with a resolute and continent energy of will, as knowing that for failure there was no consolation, and for sin there was no remission. And the Greek architecture rose unerring, bright, clearly defined, and self-contained.

Next followed in Europe the great Christian faith, which was essentially the religion of Comfort. Its great doctrine is the remission of sins; for which cause, it happens, too often, in certain phases of Christianity, that sin and sickness themselves are partly glorified, as if, the more you had to be healed of, the more divine was the healing. The practical result of this doctrine, in art, is a continual contemplation of sin and disease, and of imaginary states of purification from them; thus we have an architecture conceived in a mingled sentiment of melancholy and aspiration, partly severe, partly luxuriant, which will bend itself to every one of our needs, and every one of our fancies, and be strong or weak with us, as we are strong or weak ourselves. It is, of all architecture, the basest, when base people build it—of all, the noblest, when built by the noble.

And now note that both these religions—Greek and Mediæval—perished by falsehood in their own main purpose. The Greek religion of Wisdom perished in a false philosophy—"Oppositions of science, falsely so called." The Mediæval religion of Consolation perished in false comfort; in remission of sins given lyingly. It was the selling of absolution that ended the Mediæval faith; and I can tell you more, it is the selling of absolution which, to the end of time, will mark false Christianity. Pure Christianity gives her remission of sins only by *ending* them; but false Christianity gets her remission of sins by *compounding for* them. And there are many ways of compounding for them. We English have beautiful little quiet ways of buying absolution, whether in low Church or high, far more cunning than any of Tetzel's trading.

beauty, but design: and the Dorian Apollo-worship and Athenian Virgin-worship are both expressions of adoration of divine wisdom and purity. Next to these great deities, rank, in power over the national mind, Dionysus and Ceres, the givers of human strength and life; then, for heroic example, Hercules. There is no Venus-worship among the Greeks in the great times: and the Muses are essentially teachers of Truth, and of its harmonies. [Ruskin's note.]

Then, thirdly, there followed the religion of Pleasure, in which all Europe gave itself to luxury, ending in death. First, *bals masqués* in every saloon, and then guillotines in every square. And all these three worships issue in vast temple building. Your Greek worshipped Wisdom, and built you the Parthenon—the Virgin's temple. The Mediæval worshipped· Consolation, and built you Virgin temples also—but to our Lady of Salvation. Then the Revivalist worshipped beauty, of a sort, and built you Versailles and the Vatican. Now, lastly, will you tell me what *we* worship, and what *we* build?

You know we are speaking always of the real, active, continual, national worship; that by which men act, while they live; not that which they talk of, when they die. Now, we have, indeed, a nominal religion, to which we pay tithes of property and sevenths of time; but we have also a practical and earnest religion, to which we devote nine-tenths of our property and sixth-sevenths of our time. And we dispute a great deal about the nominal religion: but we are all unanimous about this practical one; of which I think you will admit that the ruling goddess may be best generally described as the "Goddess of Getting-on," or "Britannia of the Market." The Athenians had an "Athena Agoraia," or Athena of the Market; but she was a subordinate type of their goddess, while our Britannia Agoraia is the principal type of ours. And all your great architectural works are, of course, built to her. It is long since you built a great cathedral; and how you would laugh at me if I proposed building a cathedral on the top of one of these hills of yours, to make it an Acropolis! But your railroad mounds, vaster than the walls of Babylon; your railroad stations, vaster than the temple of Ephesus, and innumerable; your chimneys, how much more mighty and costly than cathedral spires! your harbor-piers; your warehouses; your exchanges!—all these are built to your great Goddess of "Getting-on"; and she has formed, and will continue to form, your architecture, as long as you worship her; and it is quite vain to ask me to tell you how to build to *her;* you know far better than I.

There might, indeed, on some theories, be a conceivably good architecture for Exchanges—that is to say, if

there were any heroism in the fact or deed of exchange
which might be typically carved on the outside of your
building. For, you know, all beautiful architecture must
be adorned with sculpture or painting; and for sculpture
or painting, you must have a subject. And hitherto it
has been a received opinion among the nations of the
world that the only right subjects for either, were *heroisms* of some sort. Even on his pots and his flagons, the
Greek put a Hercules slaying lions, or an Apollo slaying
serpents, or Bacchus slaying melancholy giants, and
earthborn despondencies. On his temples, the Greek put
contests of great warriors in founding states, or of gods
with evil spirits. On his houses and temples alike, the
Christian put carvings of angels conquering devils; or
of hero-martyrs exchanging this world for another; subject inappropriate, I think, to our direction of exchange
here. And the Master of Christians not only left His
followers without any orders as to the sculpture of affairs of exchange on the outside of buildings, but gave
some strong evidence of His dislike of affairs of exchange
within them. And yet there might surely be a heroism
in such affairs; and all commerce become a kind of selling of doves, not impious. The wonder has always been
great to me, that heroism has never been supposed to be
in any wise consistent with the practice of supplying
people with food, or clothes; but rather with that of
quartering one's self upon them for food, and stripping
them of their clothes. Spoiling of armor is a heroic
deed in all ages; but the selling of clothes, old or new,
has never taken any color of magnanimity. Yet one
does not see why feeding the hungry and clothing the
naked should ever become base businesses, even when
engaged in on a large scale. If one could contrive to
attach the notion of conquest to them anyhow! so that,
supposing there were anywhere an obstinate race, who
refused to be comforted, one might take some pride in
giving them compulsory comfort! and, as it were, *"occupying* a country" with one's gifts, instead of one's armies?
If one could only consider it as much a victory to get a
barren field sown, as to get an eared field stripped; and
contend who should build villages, instead of who should
"carry" them! Are not all forms of heroism conceivable

in doing these serviceable deeds? You doubt who i
strongest? It might be ascertained by push of spade, a
well as push of sword. Who is wisest? There are witt
things to be thought of in planning other business tha
campaigns. Who is bravest? There are always the ele
ments to fight with, stronger than men; and nearly a
merciless.

The only absolutely and unapproachable heroic elemen
in the soldier's work seems to be—that he is paid littl
for it—and regularly: while you traffickers, and ex
changers, and others occupied in presumably benevolen
business, like to be paid much for it—and by chance.
never can make out how it is that a *knight*-errant doe
not expect to be paid for his trouble, but a *pedler*-erran
always does;—that people are willing to take hard knock
for nothing, but never to sell ribands cheap; that the
are ready to go on fervent crusades, to recover the tom
of a buried God, but never on any travels to fulfil th
orders of a living one;—that they will go anywhere bar
foot to preach their faith, but must be well bribed t
practise it, and are perfectly ready to give the Gosp
gratis, but never the loaves and fishes.

If you chose to take the matter up on any such so
dierly principle; to do your commerce, and your feedin
of nations, for fixed salaries; and to be as particula
about giving people the best food, and the best clotl
as soldiers are about giving them the best gunpowder,
could carve something for you on your exchange wort
looking at. But I can only at present suggest decoratin
its frieze with pendant purses; and making its pilla
broad at the base, for the sticking of bills. And in th
innermost chambers of it there might be a statue c
Britannia of the Market, who may have, perhaps ac
visably, a partridge for her crest, typical at once of h
courage in fighting for noble ideas, and of her interes
in game; and round its neck, the inscription in golde
letters, "Perdix fovit quæ non peperit." Then, for h
spear, she might have a weaver's beam; and on her shiel
instead of St. George's Cross, the Milanese boar, sem
fleeced, with the town of Gennesaret proper, in the fiel
and the legend, "In the best market," and her corsle
of leather, folded over her heart in the shape of a purs

with thirty slits in it, for a piece of money to go in at,
on each day of the month. And I doubt not but that
people would come to see your exchange, and its goddess,
with applause.

Nevertheless, I want to point out to you certain strange
characters in this goddess of yours. She differs from the
great Greek and Mediæval deities essentially in two
things—first, as to the continuance of her presumed
power; secondly, as to the extent of it.

First, as to the Continuance.

The Greek Goddess of Wisdom gave continual increase
of wisdom, as the Christian Spirit of Comfort (or Com-
forter) continual increase of comfort. There was no
question, with these, of any limit or cessation of function. But with your Agora Goddess, that is just the
most important question. Getting on—but where to?
Gathering together—but how much? Do you mean to
gather always—never to spend? If so, I wish you joy
of your goddess, for I am just as well off as you, without
the trouble of worshipping her at all. But if you do not
spend, somebody else will—somebody else must. And it
is because of this (among many other such errors) that
I have fearlessly declared your so-called science of Political Economy to be no science; because, namely, it
has omitted the study of exactly the most important
branch of the business—the study of *spending*. For
spend you must, and as much as you make, ultimately.
You gather corn:—will you bury England under a heap
of grain; or will you, when you have gathered, finally
eat? You gather gold:—will you make your house-roofs
of it, or pave your streets with it? That is still one way
of spending it. But if you keep it, that you may get
more, I'll give you more; I'll give you all the gold you
want—all you can imagine—if you can tell me what
you'll do with it. You shall have thousands of gold
pieces;—thousands of thousands—millions—mountains,
of gold: where will you keep them? Will you put an
Olympus of silver upon a golden Pelion—make Ossa like
a wart? Do you think the rain and dew would then
come down to you, in the streams from such mountains,
more blessedly than they will down the mountains which
God has made for you, of moss and whinstone? But it

is not gold that you want to gather! What is it? greenbacks? No; not those neither. What is it then—is it ciphers after a capital I? Cannot you practise writing ciphers, and write as many as you want! Write ciphers for an hour every morning, in a big book, and say every evening, I am worth all those naughts more than I was yesterday. Won't that do? Well, what in the name of Plutus is it you want? Not gold, not greenbacks, not ciphers after a capital I? You will have to answer, after all, "No; we want, somehow or other, money's *worth*." Well, what is that? Let your Goddess of Getting-on discover it, and let her learn to stay therein.

Second. But there is yet another question to be asked respecting this Goddess of Getting-on. The first was of the continuance of her power; the second is of its extent.

Pallas and the Madonna were supposed to be all the world's Pallas, and all the world's Madonna. They could teach all men, and they could comfort all men. But, look strictly into the nature of the power of your Goddess of Getting-on; and you will find she is the Goddess—not of everybody's getting on—but only of somebody's getting on. This is a vital, or rather deathful, distinction. Examine it in your own ideal of the state of national life which this Goddess is to evoke and maintain. I asked you what it was, when I was last here;—you have never told me. Now, shall I try to tell you?

Your ideal of human life then is, I think, that it should be passed in a pleasant undulating world, with iron and coal everywhere underneath it. On each pleasant bank of this world is to be a beautiful mansion, with two wings; and stables, and coach-houses; a moderately-sized park; a large garden and hot-houses; and pleasant carriage drives through the shrubberies. In this mansion are to live the favored votaries of the Goddess; the English gentleman, with his gracious wife, and his beautiful family; be always able to have the boudoir and the jewels for the wife, and the beautiful ball dresses, for the daughters, and hunters for the sons, and a shooting in the Highlands for himself. At the bottom of the bank, is to be the mill; not less than a quarter of a mile long, with one steam engine at each end, and two in the middle, and a chimney three hundred feet high. In this mill are to be in constant employment from eight hundred to a thousand workers, who never drink, never strike, always go to church on Sunday, and always express themselves in respectful language.

Is not that, broadly, and in the main features, the kind of thing you propose to yourselves? It is very pretty indeed, seen from above; not at all so pretty, seen from below. For, observe, while to one family this deity is indeed the Goddess of Getting-on, to a thousand families she is the Goddess of *not* Getting-on. "Nay," you say, "they have all their chance." Yes, so has every one in a lottery, but there must always be the same number of blanks. "Ah! but in a lottery it is not skill and intelligence which take the lead, but blind chance." What then! do you think the old practice, that "they should take who have the power, and they should keep who can," is less iniquitous, when the power has become power of brains instead of fist? and that, though we may not take advantage of a child's or a woman's weakness, we may of a man's foolishness? "Nay, but finally, work must be done, and someone must be at the top, someone at the bottom." Granted, my friends. Work must always be, and captains of work must always be; and if you in the least remember the tone of any of my writings, you must know that they are thought unfit for this age, because they are always insisting on need of government, and speaking with scorn of liberty. But I beg you to observe that there is a wide difference between being captains or governors of work, and taking the profits of it. It does not follow, because you are general of an army, that you are to take all the treasure, or land, it wins (if it fight for treasure or land); neither, because you are king of a nation, that you are to consume all the profits of the nation's work. Real kings, on the contrary, are known invariably by their doing quite the reverse of this,—by their taking the least possible quantity of the nation's work for themselves. There is no test of real kinghood so infallible as that. Does the crowned creature live simply, bravely, unostentatiously? probably he *is* a King. Does he cover his body with jewels, and his table with delicates? in all probability he is *not* a King. It is possible he may be, as Solomon was; but that is when the nation shares his splendor with him. Solomon made gold, not only to be in his own palace as stones, but to be in Jerusalem as stones. But, even so, for the most part, these splendid kinghoods expire in ruin, and only the true kinghoods live, which are of royal laborers governing loyal laborers; who, both leading rough lives, establish the true dynasties. Conclusively you will find that because you are king of a nation, it does not follow that you are to gather for yourself all the wealth of that nation; neither, because you are king of a small part of the nation, and lord over the means of its maintenance —over field, or mill, or mine,—are you to take all the produce of that piece of the foundation of national existence for yourself.

You will tell me I need not preach against these things, for I cannot mend them. No, good friends, I cannot; but you can, and you will; or something else can and will. Even good things have no abiding power—and shall these evil things persist in victorious evil? All history shows, on the contrary, that to be the exact thing they never can do. Change *must* come; but it is ours to determine whether change of growth, or change of death. Shall the Parthenon be in ruins on its rock, and Bolton priory in its meadow, but these mills of yours be the consummation of the buildings of the earth, and their wheels be as the wheels of eternity? Think you that "men may come, and men may go," but—mills—go on forever? Not so; out of these, better or worse shall come; and it is for you to choose which.

I know that none of this wrong is done with deliberate purpose. I know, on the contrary, that you wish your workmen well; that you do much for them, and that you desire to do more for them, if you saw your way to such benevolence safely. I know that even all this wrong and misery are brought about by a warped sense of duty, each of you striving to do his best; but, unhappily, not knowing for whom this best should be done. And all our hearts have been betrayed by the plausible impiety of the modern economist, telling us that, "To do the best for ourselves, is finally to do the best for others." Friends, our great Master said not so; and most absolutely we shall find this world is not made so. Indeed, to do the best for others, is finally to do the best for ourselves; but it will not do to have our eyes fixed on that issue. The Pagans had got beyond that. Hear what a Pagan says of this matter; hear what were, perhaps, the last written words of Plato,—if not the last actually written (for this we cannot know), yet assuredly in fact and power his parting words—in which, endeavoring to give full crowning and harmonious close to all his thoughts, and to speak the sum of them by the imagined sentence of the Great Spirit, his strength and his heart fail him, and the words cease, broken off forever. They are at the close of the dialogue called *Critias,* in which he describes, partly from real tradition, partly in ideal dream, the early state of Athens; and the genesis, and order, and religion, of the fabled isle of Atlantis; in which genesis he conceives the same first perfection and final degeneracy of man, which in our own Scriptural tradition is expressed by saying that the Sons of God intermarried with the daughters of men, for he supposes the earliest race to have been indeed the children of God; and to have corrupted themselves, until "their spot was not the spot of his children." And this, he says, was the end; that indeed "through many generations, so long as the God's nature in them yet was full, they were submissive to the sacred laws, and carried themselves lovingly to all that had kindred with them in divineness; for their uttermost spirit was faithful and true, and in every wise great; so that, in *all meekness of wisdom, they dealt with each other,* and took all the chances of life; and despising all things except virtue, they cared little what happened day by day, and *bore lightly the burden* of gold and of possessions; for they saw that, if *only their common love and virtue increased, all these things would be increased together with them;* but to set their esteem and ardent pursuit upon material possession would be to lose that first, and their virtue and affection together with it. And by such reasoning, and what of the divine nature remained in them, they gained all this greatness of which we have already told; but when the God's part of them faded and became extinct, being mixed again and again, and effaced by the prevalent mortality; and the human nature at last ex-

ceeded, they then became unable to endure the courses
of fortune; and fell into shapelessness of life, and baseness in the sight of him who could see, having lost everything that was fairest of their honor; while to the blind
hearts which could not discern the true life, tending to
happiness, it seemed that they were then chiefly noble
and happy, being filled with all iniquity of inordinate
possession and power. Whereupon, the God of Gods,
whose Kinghood is in laws, beholding a once just nation
thus cast into misery, and desiring to lay such punishment upon them as might make them repent into restraining, gathered together all the gods into his dwelling
place, which from heaven's centre overlooks whatever has
part in creation; and having assembled them, he said"—

The rest is silence. Last words of the chief wisdom
of the heathen, spoken of this idol of riches; this idol
of yours; this golden image, high by measureless cubits,
set up where your green fields of England are furnace-
burned into the likeness of the plain of Dura: this idol,
forbidden to us, first of all idols, by our own Master and
faith; forbidden to us also by every human lip that has
ever, in any age or people, been accounted of as able to
speak according to the purposes of God. Continue to
make that forbidden deity your principal one, and soon
no more art, no more science, no more pleasure will be
possible. Catastrophe will come; or, worse than catastrophe, slow mouldering and withering into Hades. But
if you can fix some conception of a true human state of
life to be striven for—life, good for all men, as for yourselves; if you can determine some honest and simple order
of existence; following those trodden ways of wisdom,
which are pleasantness, and seeking her quiet and withdrawn paths, which are peace;—then, and so sanctifying
wealth into "commonwealth," all your art, your literature, your daily labors, your domestic affection, and citizen's duty, will join and increase into one magnificent
harmony. You will know then how to build, well enough;
you will build with stone well, but with flesh better; temples not made with hands, but riveted of hearts; and that
kind of marble, crimson-veined, is indeed eternal.

V. SOCIETY

THE ROOTS OF HONOR

[*Unto This Last,* Essay I.]

AMONG the delusions which at different periods have possessed themselves of the minds of large masses of the human race, perhaps the most curious — certainly the least creditable—is the modern *soi-disant* science of political economy, based on the idea that an advantageous code of social action may be determined irrespectively of the influence of social affection.

Of course, as in the instances of alchemy, astrology, witchcraft, and other such popular creeds, political economy has a plausible idea at the root of it. "The social affections," says the economist, "are accidental and disturbing elements in human nature; but avarice and the desire of progress are constant elements. Let us eliminate the inconstants, and, considering the human being merely as a covetous machine, examine by what laws of labor, purchase, and sale, the greatest accumulative result in wealth is attainable. Those laws once determined, it will be for each individual afterward to introduce as much of the disturbing affectionate element as he chooses, and to determine for himself the result on the new conditions supposed."

This would be a perfectly logical and successful method of analysis, if the accidentals afterward to be introduced were of the same nature as the powers first examined. Supposing a body in motion to be influenced by constant and inconstant forces, it is usually the simplest way of examining its course to trace it first under the persistent conditions, and afterward introduce the causes of variation. But the disturbing elements in the social problem are not of the same nature as the constant ones: they alter the essence of the creature under examination the moment they are added; they operate, not mathematically, but chemically, introducing conditions which render all our previous knowledge unavailable. We made learned experiments upon pure nitrogen, and have convinced ourselves that it is a very manageable gas: but, behold! the thing which we have practically to deal with is its chloride; and this, the moment we touch it on our established principles, sends us and our apparatus through the ceiling.

Observe, I neither impugn nor doubt the conclusion of the science, if its terms are accepted. I am simply uninterested in them, as I should be in those of a science of gymnastics which assumed that men had no skeletons. It might be shown, on that supposition, that it would be advantageous to roll the students up into pellets, flatten them into cakes, or stretch them into cables; and that when these results were effected, the reinsertion of the skeleton would be attended with various inconveniences to their constitution. The reasoning might be admirable, the conclusions true, and the science deficient only in applicability. Modern political economy stands on a precisely similar basis. Assuming, not that the human being has no skeleton, but that it is all skeleton, it founds an ossifiant theory of progress on this negation of a soul; and having shown the utmost that may be made of bones, and constructed a number of interesting geometrical figures with death's-head and humeri, successfully proves the inconvenience of the reappearance of a soul among these corpuscular structures. I do not deny the truth of this theory: I simply deny its applicability to the present phase of the world.

This inapplicability has been curiously manifested during the embarrassment caused by the late strikes of our workmen. Here occurs one of the simplest cases, in a pertinent and positive form, of the first vital problem which political economy has to deal with (the relation between employer and employed); and, at a severe crisis, when lives in multitudes and wealth in masses are at stake, the political economists are helpless—practically mute: no demonstrable solution of the difficulty can be given by them, such as may convince or calm the opposing parties. Obstinately the masters take one view of the matter; obstinately the operatives another; and no political science can set them at one.

It would be strange if it could, it being not by "science" of any kind that men were ever intended to be set at one. Disputant after disputant vainly tries to show that the interests of the masters are, or are not, antagonistic to those of the men: none of the pleaders ever seeming to remember that it does not absolutely or always follow that the persons must be antagonistic because their interests are. If there is only a crust of bread in the house, and mother and children are starving, their interests are not the same. If the mother eats it, the children want it; if the children eat it, the mother must go hungry to her work. Yet it does not necessarily follow that there will be "antagonism" between them, that they will fight for the crust, and that the mother, being strongest, will get it, and eat it. Neither, in any other case, whatever the relations of the persons may be, can it be assumed for certain that, because their interests are diverse, they must necessarily regard each other with hostility, and use violence or cunning to obtain the advantage.

Even if this were so, and it were as just as it is convenient to consider men as actuated by no other moral influences than those which affect rats or swine, the logical conditions of the question are still indeterminable. It can never be shown generally either that the interests of master and laborer are alike, or that they are opposed; for, according to circumstances, they may be either. It is, indeed, always the interest of both that the work should be rightly done, and a just price obtained for it; but, in the division of profits, the gain of the one may or may not be the loss of the other. It is not the master's interest to pay wages so low as to leave the men sickly and depressed, nor the workman's interest to be paid high wages if the smallness of the master's profit hinders him from enlarging his business, or conducting it in a safe and liberal way. A stoker ought not to desire high pay if the company is too poor to keep the engine-wheels in repair.

And the varieties of circumstance which influence these reciprocal interests are so endless, that all endeavor to deduce rules of action from balance of expediency is in vain. And it is meant to be in vain. For no human actions ever were intended by the Maker of men to be guided by balances of expediency, but by balances of justice. He has therefore rendered all endeavors to determine expediency futile forever more. No man ever knew, or can know, what will be the ultimate result to

himself, or to others, of any given line of conduct. But
every man may know, and most of us do know, what is
a just and unjust act. And all of us may know also,
that the consequences of justice will be ultimately the
best possible, both to others and ourselves, though we
can neither say what *is* best, or how it is likely to come
to pass.

I have said balances of justice, meaning, in the term
justice, to include affection,—such affection as one man
owes to another. All right relations between master and
operative, and all their best interests, ultimately depend
on these.

We shall find the best and simplest illustration of the
relations of master and operative in the position of domestic servants.

We will suppose that the master of a household desires only to get as much work out of his servants as he
can, at the rate of wages he gives. He never allows them
to be idle; feeds them as poorly and lodges them as ill
as they will endure, and in all things pushes his requirements to the exact point beyond which he cannot
go without forcing the servant to leave him. In doing
this, there is no violation on his part of what is commonly called "justice." He agrees with the domestic
for his whole time and service, and takes them;—the
limits of hardship in treatment being fixed by the practice of other masters in his neighborhood; that is to say,
by the current rate of wages for domestic labor. If the
servant can get a better place, he is free to take one, and
the master can only tell what is the real market value of
his labor, by requiring as much as he will give.

This is the politico-economical view of the case, according to the doctors of that science; who assert that
by this procedure the greatest average of work will be
obtained from the servant, and therefore the greatest
benefit to the community, and through the community,
by reversion, to the servant himself.

That, however, is not so. It would be so if the servant
were an engine of which the motive power was steam,
magnetism, gravitation, or any other agent of calculable
force. But he being, on the contrary, an engine whose
motive power is a Soul, the force of this very peculiar

agent, as an unknown quantity, enters into all the political economist's equations, without his knowledge, and falsifies every one of their results. The largest quantity of work will not be done by this curious engine for pay, or under pressure, or by help of any kind of fuel which may be applied by the chaldron. It will be done only when the motive force, that is to say, the will or spirit of the creature, is brought to its greatest strength by its own proper fuel: namely, by the affections.

It may indeed happen, and does happen often, that if the master is a man of sense and energy, a large quantity of material work may be done under mechanical pressure, enforced by strong will and guided by wise method; also it may happen, and does happen often, that if the master is indolent and weak (however good-natured), a very small quantity of work, and that bad, may be produced by the servant's undirected strength, and contemptuous gratitude. But the universal law of the matter is that, assuming any given quantity of energy and sense in master and servant, the greatest material result obtainable by them will be, not through antagonism to each other, but through affection for each other; and that, if the master, instead of endeavoring to get as much work as possible from the servant, seeks rather to render his appointed and necessary work beneficial to him, and to forward his interests in all just and wholesome ways, the real amount of work ultimately done, or of good rendered, by the person so cared for, will indeed be the greatest possible.

Observe, I say, "of good rendered," for a servant's work is not necessarily or always the best thing he can give his master. But good of all kinds, whether in material service, in protective watchfulness of his master's interest and credit, or in joyful readiness to seize unexpected and irregular occasions of help.

Nor is this one whit less generally true because indulgence will be frequently abused, and kindness met with ingratitude. For the servant who, gently treated, is ungrateful, treated ungently, will be revengeful; and the man who is dishonest to a liberal master will be injurious to an unjust one.

In any case, and with any person, this unselfish treatment will produce the most effective return. Observe, I am here considering the affections wholly as a motive power; not at all as things in themselves desirable or noble, or in any other way abstractedly good. I look at them simply as an anomalous force, rendering every one of the ordinary political economist's calculations nugatory; while, even if he desired to introduce this new element into his estimates, he has no power of dealing with it; for the affections only become a true motive power when they ignore every other motive and condition of political economy. Treat the servant kindly, with the idea of turning his gratitude to account, and you will get, as you deserve, no gratitude, nor any value for your kindness; but treat him kindly without any economical purpose, and all economical purposes will be answered; in this, as in all other matters, whosoever will save his life shall lose it, whoso loses it shall find it.*

The next clearest and simplest example of relation between master and operative is that which exists between the commander of a regiment and his men.

Supposing the officer only desires to apply the rules of discipline so as, with least trouble to himself, to make the regiment most effective, he will not be able, by any

---

* The difference between the two modes of treatment, and between their effective material results, may be seen very accurately by a comparison of the relations of Esther and Charlie in *Bleak House* with those of Miss Brass and the Marchioness in *Master Humphrey's Clock.*

The essential value and truth of Dickens's writings have been unwisely lost sight of by many thoughtful persons, merely because he presents his truth with some color of caricature. Unwisely, because Dickens's caricature, though often gross, is never mistaken. Allowing for his manner of telling them, the things he tells us are always true. I wish that he could think it right to limit his brilliant exaggeration to works written only for public amusement; and when he takes up a subject of high national importance, such as that which he handled in *Hard Times,* that he would use severer and more accurate analysis. The usefulness of that work (to my mind, in several respects the greatest he has written) is with many persons seriously diminished because Mr. Bounderby is a dramatic monster, instead of a characteristic example of a worldly master; and Stephen Blackpool a dramatic perfection, instead of a characteristic example of an honest workman. But let us not lose the use of Dickens's wit and insight, because he chooses to speak in a circle of stage fire. He is entirely right in his main drift and purpose in every book he has written; and all of them, but especially *Hard Times,* should be studied with close and earnest care by persons interested in social questions. They will find much that is partial, and, because partial, apparently unjust; but if they examine all the evidence on the other side, which Dickens seems to overlook, it will appear, after all their trouble, that his view was the finally right one, grossly and sharply told. [Ruskin's note.]

rules or administration of rules, on this selfish principle, to develop the full strength of his subordinates. If a man of sense and firmness, he may, as in the former instance, produce a better result than would be obtained by the irregular kindness of a weak officer; but let the sense and firmness be the same in both cases, and assuredly the officer who has the most direct personal relations with his men, the most care for their interests, and the most value for their lives, will develop their effective strength, through their affection for his own person, and trust in his character, to a degree wholly unattainable by other means. This law applies still more stringently as the numbers concerned are larger: a charge may often be successful, though the men dislike their officers; a battle has rarely been won, unless they loved their general.

Passing from these simple examples to the more complicated relations existing between a manufacturer and his workmen, we are met first by certain curious difficulties, resulting, apparently, from a harder and colder state of moral elements. It is easy to imagine an enthusiastic affection existing among soldiers for the colonel. Not so easy to imagine an enthusiastic affection among cotton-spinners for the proprietor of the mill. A body of men associated for purposes of robbery (as a Highland clan in ancient times) shall be animated by perfect affection, and every member of it be ready to lay down his life for the life of his chief. But a band of men associated for purposes of legal production and accumulation is usually animated, it appears, by no such emotions, and none of them is in anywise willing to give his life for the life of his chief. Not only are we met by this apparent anomaly, in moral matters, but by others connected with it, in administration of system. For a servant or a soldier is engaged at a definite rate of wages, for a definite period; but a workman at a rate of wages variable according to the demand for labor, and with the risk of being at any time thrown out of his situation by chances of trade. Now, as, under these contingencies, no action of the affections can take place, but only an explosive action of *dis*affections, two points offer themselves for consideration in the matter.

The first—How far the rate of wages may be so regulated as not to vary with the demand for labor.

The second—How far it is possible that bodies of workmen may be engaged and maintained at such fixed rate of wages (whatever the state of trade may be), without enlarging or diminishing their number, so as to give them permanent interest in the establishment with which they are connected, like that of the domestic servants in an old family, or an *esprit de corps,* like that of the soldiers in a crack regiment.

The first question is, I say, how far it may be possible to fix the rate of wages, irrespectively of the demand for labor.

Perhaps one of the most curious facts in the history of human error is the denial by the common political economist of the possibility of thus regulating wages; while, for all the important, and much of the unimportant, labor, on the earth, wages are already so regulated.

We do not sell our prime-ministership by Dutch auction; nor, on the decease of a bishop, whatever may be the general advantages of simony, do we (yet) offer his diocese to the clergyman who will take the episcopacy at the lowest contract. We (with exquisite sagacity of political economy!) do indeed sell commissions; but not openly, generalships: sick, we do not inquire for a physician who takes less than a guinea; litigious, we never think of reducing six-and-eightpence to four-and-sixpence; caught in a shower, we do not canvass the cabmen, to find one who values his driving at less than sixpence a mile.

It is true that in all these cases there is, and in every conceivable case there must be, ultimate reference to the presumed difficulty of the work, or number of candidates for the office. If it were thought that the labor necessary to make a good physician would be gone through by a sufficient number of students with the prospect of only half-guinea fees, public consent would soon withdraw the unnecessary half-guinea. In this ultimate sense, the price of labor is indeed always regulated by the demand for it; but, so far as the practical and immediate administration of the matter is regarded, the best labor always has been, and is, as *all* labor ought to be, paid by an invariable standard.

"What!" the reader perhaps answers amazedly: "pay good and bad workmen alike?"

Certainly. The difference between one prelate's sermons and his successor's — or between one physician's opinion and another's — is far greater, as respects the qualities of mind involved, and far more important in result to you personally, than the difference between good and bad laying of bricks (though that is greater than most people suppose). Yet you pay with equal fee, contentedly, the good and bad workmen upon your soul, and the good and bad workmen upon your body; much more may you pay, contentedly, with equal fees, the good and bad workmen upon your house.

"Nay, but I choose my physician and (?) my clergyman, thus indicating my sense of the quality of their work." By all means, also, choose your bricklayer; that is the proper reward of the good workman, to be "chosen." The natural and right system respecting all labor is, that it should be paid at a fixed rate, but the good workman employed, and the bad workman unemployed. The false, unnatural, and destructive system is when the bad workman is allowed to offer his work at half-price, and either take the place of the good, or force him by his competition to work for an inadequate sum.

This equality of wages, then, being the first object toward which we have to discover the directest available road; the second is, as above stated, that of maintaining constant numbers of workmen in employment, whatever may be the accidental demand for the article they produce.

I believe the sudden and extensive inequalities of demand, which necessarily arise in the mercantile operations of an active nation, constitute the only essential difficulty which has to be overcome in a just organization of labor. The subject opens into too many branches to admit of being investigated in a paper of this kind; but the following general facts bearing on it may be noted.

The wages which enable any workman to live are necessarily higher, if his work is liable to intermission, than if it is assured and continuous; and however severe

the struggle for work may become, the general law will
always hold, that men must get more daily pay if, on the
average, they can only calculate on work three days a
week than they would require if they were sure of work
six days a week. Supposing that a man cannot live on
less than a shilling a day, his seven shillings he must
get, either for three days' violent work, or six days' deliberate work. The tendency of all modern mercantile
operations is to throw both wages and trade into the
form of a lottery, and to make the workman's pay depend on intermittent exertion, and the principal's profit
on dexterously used chance.

In what partial degree, I repeat, this may be necessary
in consequence of the activities of modern trade, I do
not here investigate; contenting myself with the fact,
that in its fatalest aspects it is assuredly unnecessary,
and results merely from love of gambling on the part of
the masters, and from ignorance and sensuality in the
men. The masters cannot bear to let any opportunity
of gain escape them, and frantically rush at every gap
and breach in the walls of Fortune, raging to be rich,
and affronting, with impatient covetousness, every risk
of ruin, while the men prefer three days of violent labor,
and three days of drunkenness, to six days of moderate
work and wise rest. There is no way in which a principal, who really desires to help his workmen, may do it
more effectually than by checking these disorderly habits
both in himself and them; keeping his own business operations on a scale which will enable him to pursue them
securely, not yielding to temptations of precarious gain;
and at the same time, leading his workmen into regular
habits of labor and life, either by inducing them rather
to take low wages, in the form of a fixed salary, than
high wages, subject to the chance of their being thrown
out of work; or, if this be impossible, by discouraging
the system of violent exertion for nominally high day
wages, and leading the men to take lower pay for more
regular labor.

In effecting any radical changes of this kind, doubtless
there would be great inconvenience and loss incurred by
all the originators of movement. That which can be done
with perfect convenience and without loss, is not always

the thing that most needs to be done, or which we are most imperatively required to do.

I have already alluded to the difference hitherto existing between regiments of men associated for purposes of violence, and for purposes of manufacture; in that the former appear capable of self-sacrifice—the latter, not; which singular fact is the real reason of the general lowness of estimate in which the profession of commerce is held, as compared with that of arms. Philosophically, it does not, at first sight, appear reasonable (many writers have endeavored to prove it unreasonable) that a peaceable and rational person, whose trade is buying and selling, should be held in less honor than an unpeaceable and often irrational person, whose trade is slaying. Nevertheless, the consent of mankind has always, in spite of the philosophers, given precedence to the soldier.

And this is right.

For the soldier's trade, verily and essentially, is not slaying, but being slain. This, without well knowing its own meaning, the world honors it for. A bravo's trade is slaying; but the world has never respected bravos more than merchants: the reason it honors the soldier is, because he holds his life at the service of the State. Reckless he may be—fond of pleasure or of adventure—all kinds of bye-motives and mean impulses may have determined the choice of his profession, and may affect (to all appearance exclusively) his daily conduct in it; but our estimate of him is based on this ultimate fact—of which we are well assured—that put him in a fortress breach, with all the pleasures of the world behind him, and only death and his duty in front of him, he will keep his face to the front; and he knows that his choice may be put to him at any moment—and has beforehand taken his part—virtually takes such part continually—does, in reality, die daily.

Not less is the respect we pay to the lawyer and physician, founded ultimately on their self-sacrifice. Whatever the learning or acuteness of a great lawyer, our chief respect for him depends on our belief that, set in a judge's seat, he will strive to judge justly, come of it what may. Could we suppose that he would take bribes, and use his acuteness and legal knowledge to give plausibility to iniquitous decisions, no degree of intellect would win for him our respect. Nothing will win it, short of our tacit conviction, that in all important acts of his life justice is first with him; his own interest, second.

In the case of a physician, the ground of the honor we render him is clearer still. Whatever his science, we would shrink from him in horror if we found him regard his patients merely as subjects to experiment upon; much more, if we found that, receiving bribes from persons interested in their deaths, he was using his best skill to give poison in the mask of medicine.

Finally, the principle holds with utmost clearness as it respects clergymen. No goodness of disposition will excuse want of science in a physician, or of shrewdness in an advocate; but a clergyman, even though his power of intellect be small, is respected on the presumed ground of his unselfishness and serviceableness.

Now, there can be no question but that the tact, foresight, decision, and other mental powers, required for the successful management of a large mercantile concern, if not such as could be compared with those of a great lawyer, general, or divine, would at least match the general conditions of mind required in the subordinate officers of a ship, or of a regiment, or in the curate of a country parish. If, therefore, all the efficient members of the so-called liberal professions are still, somehow, in public estimate of honor, preferred before the head of a commercial firm, the reason must lie deeper than in the measurement of their several powers of mind.

And the essential reason for such preference will be found to lie in the fact that the merchant is presumed to act always selfishly. His work may be very necessary to the community; but the motive of it is understood to be wholly personal. The merchant's first object in all his dealings must be (the public believe) to get as much for himself, and leave as little to his neighbor (or customer) as possible. Enforcing this upon him, by political statute, as the necessary principle of his action; recommending it to him on all occasions, and themselves reciprocally adopting it; proclaiming vociferously, for law of the universe, that a buyer's function is to cheapen, and a seller's to cheat,—the public, nevertheless, involuntarily condemn the man of commerce for his compliance with their own statement, and stamp him forever as belonging to an inferior grade of human personality.

This they will find, eventually, they must give up doing. They must not cease to condemn selfishness; but they will have to discover a kind of commerce which is not exclusively selfish. Or, rather, they will have to discover that there never was, or can be, any other kind of commerce; that this which they have called commerce was not commerce at all, but cozening; and that a true merchant differs as much from a merchant according to laws of modern political economy, as the hero of the *Excursion* from Autolycus. They will find that commerce is an occupation which gentlemen will every day see more need to engage in, rather than in the businesses of talking to men, or slaying them; that, in true commerce, as in true preaching, or true fighting, it is necessary to admit the idea of occasional voluntary loss:— that sixpences have to be lost, as well as lives, under a sense of duty; that the market may have its martyrdoms as well as the pulpit; and trade its heroisms as well as war.

May have—in the final issue, must have—and only has not had yet, because men of heroic temper have always been misguided in their youth into other fields; not recognizing what is in our days, perhaps, the most important of all fields; so that, while many a zealous person loses his life in trying to teach the form of a gospel, very few will lose a hundred pounds in· showing the practice of one.

The fact is, that people never have had clearly explained to them the true functions of a merchant with respect to other people. I should like the reader to be very clear about this.

Five great intellectual professions, relating to daily necessities of life, have hitherto existed — three exist necessarily, in every civilized nation:

The Soldier's profession is to *defend* it.

The Pastor's to *teach* it.

The Physician's to *keep it in health.*

The Lawyer's to *enforce justice* in it.

The Merchant's to *provide* for it.

And the duty of all these men is, on due occasion, to *die* for it.

"On due occasion," namely:—

The Soldier, rather than leave his post in battle.

The Physician, rather than leave his post in plague.

The Pastor, rather than teach Falsehood.

The Lawyer, rather than countenance Injustice.

The Merchant—what is *his* "due occasion" of death?

It is the main question for the merchant, as for all of us. For, truly, the man who does not know when to die, does not know how to live.

Observe, the merchant's function (or manufacturer's, for in the broad sense in which it is here used the word must be understood to include both) is to provide for the nation. It is no more his function to get profit for himself out of that provision than it is a clergyman's function to get his stipend. The stipend is a due and necessary adjunct, but not the object of his life, if he be a true clergyman, any more than his fee (or honorarium) is the object of life to a true physician. Neither is his fee the object of life to a true merchant. All three, if true men, have a work to be done irrespective of fee— to be done even at any cost, or for quite the contrary of fee; the pastor's function being to teach, the physician's to heal, and the merchant's, as I have said, to provide. That is to say, he has to understand to their very root the qualities of the thing he deals in, and the means of obtaining or producing it; and he has to apply all his sagacity and energy to the producing or obtaining it in perfect state, and distributing it at the cheapest possible price where it is most needed.

And because the production or obtaining of any commodity involves necessarily the agency of many lives and hands, the merchant becomes in the course of his business the master and governor of large masses of men in a more direct, though less confessed way, than a military officer or pastor; so that on him falls, in great part, the responsibility for the kind of life they lead: and it becomes his duty, not only to be always considering how to produce what he sells, in the purest and cheapest forms, but how to make the various employments involved in the production, or transference of it, most beneficial to the men employed.

And as into these two functions, requiring for their right exercise the highest intelligence, as well as patience, kindness, and tact, the merchant is bound to put all his energy, so for their just discharge he is bound, as soldier or physician is bound, to give up, if need be, his life, in such way as it may be demanded of him. Two main points he has in his providing function to maintain: first, his engagements (faithfulness to engagements being the real root of all possibilities, in commerce); and, secondly, the perfectness and purity of the thing provided; so that, rather than fail in any engagement, or consent to any deterioration, adulteration, or unjust and exorbitant price of that which he provides, he is bound to meet fearlessly any form of distress, poverty, or labor, which may, through maintenance of these points, come upon him.

Again: in his office as governor of the men employed by him, the merchant or manufacturer is invested with a distinctly paternal authority and responsibility. In most cases, a youth entering a commercial establishment is withdrawn altogether from home influence; his master must become his father, else he has, for practical and constant help, no father at hand: in all cases the master's authority, together with the general tone and atmosphere of his business, and the character of the men with whom the youth is compelled in the course of it to associate, have more immediate and pressing weight than the home influence, and will usually neutralize it either for good or evil; so that the only means which the master has of doing justice to the men employed by him is to ask himself sternly whether he is dealing with such subordinate as he would with his own son, if compelled by circumstances to take such a position.

Supposing the captain of a frigate saw it right, or were by any chance obliged, to place his own son in the position of a common sailor; as he would then treat his son, he is bound always to treat every one of the men under him. So, also, supposing the master of a manufactory saw it right, or were by any chance obliged, to place his own son in the position of an ordinary workman; as he would then treat his son, he is bound always to treat every one of his men. This is the only effective, true, or practical RULE which can be given on this point of political economy.

And as the captain of a ship is bound to be the last man to leave his ship in case of wreck, and to share his last crust with the sailors in case of famine, so the manufacturer, in any commercial crisis or distress, is bound to take the suffering of it with his men, and even to take more of it for himself than he allows his men to feel; as a father would in a famine, shipwreck, or battle, sacrifice himself for his son.

All which sounds very strange: the only real strangeness in the matter being, nevertheless, that it should so sound. For all this is true, and that not partially nor theoretically, but everlastingly and practically; all other doctrine than this respecting matters political being false in premises, absurd in deduction, and impossible in practice, consistently with any progressive state of national life; all the life which we now possess as a nation showing itself in the resolute denial and scorn, by a few strong minds and faithful hearts, of the economic principles taught to our multitudes, which principles, so far as accepted, lead straight to national destruction. Respecting the modes and forms of destruction to which they lead, and, on the other hand, respecting the farther practical working of true polity, I hope to reason farther in a following paper.

THE VEINS OF WEALTH

[*Unto This Last,* Essay II.]

THE answer which would be made by any ordinary political economist to the statements contained in the preceding paper, is in few words as follows:—

"It is indeed true that certain advantages of a general nature may be obtained by the development of social affections. But political economists never professed, nor profess, to take advantages of a general nature into consideration. Our science is simply the science of getting rich. So far from being a fallacious or visionary one, it is found by experience to be practically effective. Persons who follow its precepts do actually become rich, and persons who disobey them become poor. Every capitalist of Europe has acquired his fortune by following the known laws of our science, and increases his capital daily by an adherence to them. It is vain to bring forward tricks of logic, against the force of accomplished facts. Every man of business knows by experience how money is made, and how it is lost."

Pardon me. Men of business do indeed know how they themselves made their money, or how, on occasion, they lost it. Playing a long-practiced game, they are familiar with the chances of its cards, and can rightly explain their losses and gains. But they neither know who keeps the bank of the gambling-house, nor what other games may be played with the same cards, nor what other losses and gains, far away among the dark streets, are essentially, though invisibly, dependent on theirs in the lighted rooms. They have learned a few, and only a few, of the laws of mercantile economy; but not one of those of political economy.

Primarily, which is very notable and curious, I observe that men of business rarely know the meaning of the word "rich." At least, if they know, they do not in their reasonings allow for the fact, that it is a relative word, implying its opposite "poor" as positively as the word "north" implies its opposite "south." Men nearly always speak and write as if riches were absolute, and it were possible, by following certain scientific precepts, for everybody to be rich. Whereas riches are a power like that of electricity, acting only through inequalities or negations of itself. The force of the guinea you have in your pocket depends wholly on the default of a guinea in your neighbor's pocket. If he did not want it, it would be of no use to you; the degree of power it possesses depends accurately upon the need or desire he has for it,—and the art of making yourself rich, in the ordinary mercantile economist's sense, is therefore equally and necessarily the art of keeping your neighbor poor.

I would not contend in this matter (and rarely in any matter) for the acceptance of terms. But I wish the reader clearly and deeply to understand the difference between the two economies, to which the terms "Political" and "Mercantile" might not unadvisably be attached.

Political economy (the economy of a State, or of citizens) consists simply in the production, preservation, and distribution, at fittest time and place, of useful or pleasurable things. The farmer who cuts his hay at the right time; the shipwright who drives his bolts well home in sound wood; the builder who lays good bricks in well-tempered mortar; the housewife who takes care of her furniture in the parlor, and guards against all waste in her kitchen; and the singer who rightly disciplines, and never overstrains her voice, are all political economists in the true and final sense: adding continually to the riches and well-being of the nation to which they belong.

But mercantile economy, the economy of "merces" or of "pay," signifies the accumulation, in the hands of individuals, of legal or moral claim upon, or power over, the labor of others; every such claim implying precisely as much poverty or debt on one side, as it implies riches or right on the other.

It does not, therefore, necessarily involve an addition to the actual property, or well-being of the State in which it exists. But since this commercial wealth, or power over labor, is nearly always convertible at once into real property, while real property is not always convertible at once into power over labor, the idea of riches among active men in civilized nations generally refers to commercial wealth; and in estimating their possessions, they rather calculate the value of their horses and fields by the number of guineas they could get for them, than the value of their guineas by the number of horses and fields they could buy with them.

There is, however, another reason for this habit of mind: namely, that an accumulation of real property is of little use to its owner, unless, together with it, he has commercial power over labor. Thus, suppose any person to be put in possession of a large estate of fruitful land, with rich beds of gold in its gravel; countless herds of cattle in its pastures; houses, and gardens, and store-houses full of useful stores: but suppose, after all, that he could get no servants? In order that he may be able to have servants, someone in the neighborhood must be

poor, and in want of his gold—or his corn. Assume that
no one is in want of either, and that no servants are to
be had. He must, therefore, bake his own bread, make
his own clothes, plough his own ground, and shepherd
his own flocks. His gold will be as useful to him as any
other yellow pebbles on his estate. His stores must rot,
for he cannot consume them. He can eat no more than
another man could eat, and wear no more than another
man could wear. He must lead a life of severe and common labor to procure even ordinary comforts; he will be
ultimately unable to keep either houses in repair, or fields
in cultivation; and forced to content himself with a poor
man's portion of cottage and garden, in the midst of a
desert of waste land, trampled by wild cattle, and encumbered by ruins of palaces, which he will hardly mock
at himself by calling "his own."

The most covetous of mankind would, with small exultation, I presume, accept riches of this kind on these
terms. What is really desired, under the name of riches,
is, essentially, power over men; in its simplest sense, the
power of obtaining for our own advantage the labor of
servant, tradesman, and artist; in wider sense, authority
of directing large masses of the nation to various ends
(good, trivial, or hurtful, according to the mind of the
rich person). And this power of wealth of course is
greater or less in direct proportion to the poverty of the
men over whom it is exercised, and in inverse proportion
to the number of persons who are as rich as ourselves,
and who are ready to give the same price for an article
of which the supply is limited. If the musician is poor,
he will sing for small pay, as long as there is only one
person who can pay him; but if there be two or three,
he will sing for the one who offers him most. And thus
the power of the riches of the patron (always imperfect
and doubtful, as we shall see presently even when most
authoritative) depends first on the poverty of the artist,
and then on the limitation of the number of equally
wealthy persons, who also want seats at the concert. So
that, as above stated, the art of becoming "rich," in the
common sense, is not absolutely nor finally the art of
accumulating much money for ourselves, but also of con-
triving that our neighbors shall have less. In accurate

terms, it is "the art of establishing the maximum inequality in our own favor."

Now, the establishment of such inequality cannot be shown in the abstract to be either advantageous or disadvantageous to the body of the nation. The rash and absurd assumption that such inequalities are necessarily advantageous, lies at the root of most of the popular fallacies on the subject of political economy. For the eternal and inevitable law in this matter is, that the beneficialness of the inequality depends, first, on the methods by which it was accomplished; and, secondly, on the purposes to which it is applied. Inequalities of wealth, unjustly established, have assuredly injured the nation in which they exist during their establishment; and, unjustly directed, injure it yet more during their existence. But inequalities of wealth, justly established, benefit the nation in the course of their establishment; and, nobly used, aid it yet more by their existence. That is to say, among every active and well-governed people, the various strength of individuals, tested by full exertion and specially applied to various need, issues in unequal, but harmonious results, receiving reward or authority according to its class and service;* while, in the inactive or ill-

---

* I have been naturally asked several times with respect to the sentence in the first of these papers, "the bad workmen unemployed," "But what are you to do with your bad unemployed workmen?" Well, it seems to me the question might have occurred to you before. Your housemaid's place is vacant—you give twenty pounds a year—two girls come for it, one neatly dressed, the other dirtily; one with good recommendations, the other with none. You do not, under these circumstances, usually ask the dirty one if she will come for fifteen pounds, or twelve; and, on her consenting, take her instead of the well-recommended one. Still less do you try to beat both down by making them bid against each other, till you can hire both, one at twelve pounds a year, and the other at eight. You simply take the one fittest for the place, and send away the other, not perhaps concerning yourself quite as much as you should with the question which you now impatiently put to me, "What is to become of her?" For, all that I advise you to do, is to deal with workmen as with servants; and verily the question is of weight: "Your bad workman, idler, and rogue—what are you to do with him?"

We will consider of this presently: remember that the administration of a complete system of national commerce and industry cannot be explained in full detail within the space of twelve pages. Meantime, consider whether, there being confessedly some difficulty in dealing with rogues and idlers, it may not be advisable to produce as few of them as possible. If you examine into the history of rogues, you will find they are as truly manufactured articles as anything else, and it is just because our present system of political economy gives so large a stimulus to that manufacture that you may know it to be a false one. We had

overned nation, the gradations of decay and the victories
f treason work out also their own rugged system of sub-
ection and success; and substitute, for the melodious in-
qualities of concurrent power, the iniquitous dominances
nd depressions of guilt and misfortune.

Thus the circulation of wealth in a nation resembles
hat of the blood in the natural body. There is one quick-
ess of the current which comes of cheerful emotion or
wholesome exercise; and another which comes of shame
r of fever. There is a flush of the body which is full
f warmth and life; and another which will pass into
utrefaction.

The analogy will hold down even to minute particulars.
'or as diseased local determination of the blood involves
epression of the general health of the system, all morbid
ocal action of riches will be found ultimately to involve
weakening of the resources of the body politic.

The mode in which this is produced may be at once
nderstood by examining one or two instances of the
evelopment of wealth in the simplest possible circum-
tances.

Suppose two sailors cast away on an uninhabited coast,
nd obliged to maintain themselves there by their own
abor for a series of years.

If they both kept their health, and worked steadily
nd in amity with each other, they might build them-
elves a convenient house, and in time come to possess
certain quantity of cultivated land, together with vari-
us stores laid up for future use. All these things would
e real riches or property; and, supposing the men both
o have worked equally hard, they would each have right
o equal share or use of it. Their political economy would
onsist merely in careful preservation and just division
f these possessions. Perhaps, however, after some time
ne or other might be dissatisfied with the results of their
ommon farming; and they might in consequence agree
o divide the land they' had brought under the spade into
qual shares, so that each might thenceforward work in
is own field, and live by it. Suppose that after this ar-

etter seek for a system which will develop honest men, than for one
which will deal cunningly with vagabonds. Let us reform our schools,
nd we shall find little reform needed in our prisons. [Ruskin's note.]

rangement had been made, one of them were to fall il
and be unable to work on his land at a critical time—
say of sowing or harvest.

He would naturally ask the other to sow or reap fo
him.

Then his companion might say, with perfect justice
"I will do this additional work for you; but if I do i
you must promise to do as much for me at another time
I will count how many hours I spend on your groun
and you shall give me a written promise to work for th
same number of hours on mine, whenever I need you
help, and you are able to give it."

Suppose the disabled man's sickness to continue, an
that under various circumstances, for several years, re
quiring the help of the other, he on each occasion gave
written pledge to work, as soon as he was able, at hi
companion's orders, for the same number of hours whic
the other had given up to him. What will the position
of the two men be when the invalid is able to resum
work?

Considered as a "Polis," or state, they will be poore
than they would have been otherwise: poorer by the with
drawal of what the sick man's labor would have produce
in the interval. His friend may perhaps have toiled wit
an energy quickened by the enlarged need, but in th
end, his own land and property must have suffered b
the withdrawal of so much of his time and thought fror
them; and the united property of the two men will b
certainly less than it would have been if both had re
mained in health and activity.

But the relations in which they stand to each othe
are also widely altered. The sick man has not onl
pledged his labor for some years, but will probably hav
exhausted his own share of the accumulated stores, an
will be in consequence for some time dependent on th
other for food, which he can only "pay" or reward hir
for by yet more deeply pledging his own labor.

Supposing the written promises to be held entirel
valid (among civilized nations their validity is secure
by legal measures*), the person who had hitherto worke

---

* The disputes which exist respecting the real nature of money aris
more from the disputants examining its functions on different side

for both might now, if he chose, rest altogether, and pass his time in idleness, not only forcing his companion to redeem all the engagements he had already entered into, but exacting from him pledges for further labor, to an arbitrary amount, for what food he had to advance to him.

There might not, from first to last, be the least illegality (in the ordinary sense of the word) in the arrangement; but if a stranger arrived on the coast at this advanced epoch of their political economy, he would find one man commercially Rich; the other commercially Poor. He would see, perhaps, with no small surprise, one passing his days in idleness; the other laboring for both, and living sparely, in the hope of recovering his independence at some distant period.

This is, of course, an example of one only out of many ways in which inequality of possession may be established between different persons, giving rise to the Mercantile forms of Riches and Poverty. In the instance before us, one of the men might from the first have deliberately chosen to be idle, and to put his life in pawn for present ease; or he might have mismanaged his land, and been compelled to have recourse to his neighbor for food and help, pledging his future labor for it. But what I want the reader to note especially is the fact, common to a large number of typical cases of this kind, that the establishment of the mercantile wealth which consists in a claim upon labor, signifies a political diminution of the real wealth which consists in substantial possessions.

Take another example, more consistent with the ordinary course of affairs of trade. Suppose that three men, instead of two, formed the little isolated republic, and found themselves obliged to separate, in order to farm

man from any real dissent of their opinions. All money, properly so called, is an acknowledgment of debt; but as such, it may either be considered to represent the labor and property of the creditor, or the idleness and penury of the debtor. The intricacy of the question has been much increased by the (hitherto necessary) use of marketable commodities, such as gold, silver, salt, shells, etc., to give intrinsic value — security to currency; but the final and best definition of money is that it is a documentary promise ratified and guaranteed by the nation to give or find a certain quantity of labor on demand. A man's labor for a day is a better standard of value than a measure of any produce, because no produce ever maintains a consistent rate of productibility. Ruskin's note.]

different pieces of land at some distance from each othe along the coast: each estate furnishing a distinct kine of produce, and each more or less in need of the ma terial raised on the other. Suppose that the third man in order to save the time of all three, undertakes simply to superintend the transference of commodities from on farm to the other; on condition of receiving some suffi ciently remunerative share of every parcel of goods con veyed, or of some other parcel received in exchange for it

If this carrier or messenger always brings to each estate from the other, what is chiefly wanted, at the right time the operations of the two farmers will go on prosperously and the largest possible result in produce, or wealth, wil be attained by the little community. But suppose no in tercourse between the land owners is possible, excep through the traveling agent; and that, after a time, thi agent, watching the course of each man's agriculture keeps back the articles with which he has been entrustec until there comes a period of extreme necessity for them on one side or other, and then exacts in exchange fo them all that the distressed farmer can spare of othe kinds of produce: it is easy to see that by ingeniously watching his opportunities, he might possess himsel regularly of the greater part of the superfluous produc of the two estates, and at last, in some year of severes trial or scarcity, purchase both for himself and main tain the former proprietors thenceforward as his laborer or his servants.

This would be a case of commercial wealth acquiree on the exactest principles of modern political economy But more distinctly even than in the former instance it is manifest in this that the wealth of the State, or o the three men considered as a society, is collectively les than it would have been had the merchant been conten with juster profit. The operations of the two agricul turists have been cramped to the utmost; and the con tinual limitations of the supply of things they wanted a critical times, together with the failure of courage con sequent on the prolongation of a struggle for mere ex istence, without any sense of permanent gain, must hav seriously diminished the effective results of their labor and the stores finally accumulated in the merchant' hands will not in any wise be of equivalent value to those which, had his dealings been honest, would have filled at once the granaries of the farmers and his own.

The whole question, therefore, respecting not only the advantage, but even the quantity, of national wealth, resolves itself finally into one of abstract justice. It is impossible to conclude, of any given mass of acquired wealth, merely by the fact of its existence, whether it signifies good or evil to the nation in the midst of which it exists. Its real value depends on the moral sign attached to it, just as sternly as that of a mathematical quantity depends on the algebraical sign attached to it. Any given accumulation of commercial wealth may be indicative, on the one hand, of faithful industries, progressive energies, and productive ingenuities: or, on the other, it may be indicative of mortal luxury, merciless tyranny, ruinous chicane. Some treasures are heavy with human tears, as an ill-stored harvest with untimely rain; and some gold is brighter in sunshine than it is in substance.

And these are not, observe, merely moral or pathetic attributes of riches, which the seeker of riches may, if he chooses, despise; they are, literally and sternly, material attributes of riches, depreciating or exalting, incalculably, the monetary signification of the sum in question. One mass of money is the outcome of action which has created, — another, of action which has annihilated, — ten times as much in the gathering of it; such and such strong hands have been paralyzed, as if they had been numbed by night-shade: so many strong men's courage broken, so many productive operations hindered; this and the other false direction given to labor, and lying image of prosperity set up, on Dura plains dug into seven-times-heated furnaces. That which seems to be wealth may in verity be only the gilded index of far-reaching ruin; a wrecker's handful of coin gleaned from the beach to which he has beguiled an argosy; a camp-follower's bundle of rags unwrapped from the breasts of goodly soldiers dead; the purchase-pieces of potter's fields, wherein shall be buried together the citizen and the stranger.

And therefore, the idea that directions can be given for the gaining of wealth, irrespectively of the considera-

tion of its moral sources, or that any general and technical law of purchase and gain can be set down for
national practice, is perhaps the most insolently futile
of all that ever beguiled men through their vices. So far
as I know, there is not in history record of anything so
disgraceful to the human intellect as the modern idea
that the commercial text, "Buy in the cheapest market
and sell in the dearest," represents, or under any circumstances could represent, an available principle of national
economy. Buy in the cheapest market?—yes; but what
made your market cheap? Charcoal may be cheap among
your roof timbers after a fire, and bricks may be cheap
in your streets after an earthquake; but fire and earthquake may not therefore be national benefits. Sell in
the dearest?—yes, truly; but what made your market
dear? You sold your bread well to-day: was it to a
dying man who gave his last coin for it, and will never
need bread more; or to a rich man who to-morrow will
buy your farm over your head; or to a soldier on his
way to pillage the bank in which you have put your
fortune?

None of these things you can know. One thing only
you can know: namely, whether this dealing of yours is
a just and faithful one, which is all you need concern
yourself about respecting it; sure thus to have done your
own part in bringing about ultimately in the world a
state of things which will not issue in pillage or in death.
And thus every question concerning these things merges
itself ultimately in the great question of justice, which,
the ground being thus far cleared for it, I will enter
upon in the next paper, leaving only, in this, three final
points for the reader's consideration.

It has been shown that the chief value and virtue of
money consists in its having power over human beings;
that, without this power, large material possessions are
useless, and to any person possessing such power, comparatively unnecessary. But power over human beings
is attainable by other means than by money. As I said
a few pages back, the money power is always imperfect
and doubtful; there are many things which cannot be
reached with it, others which cannot be retained by it.
Many joys may be given to men which cannot be bought

for gold, and many fidelities found in them which cannot be rewarded with it.

Trite enough,—the reader thinks. Yes: but it is not so trite,—I wish it were,—that in this moral power, quite inscrutable and immeasurable though it be, there is a monetary value just as real as that represented by more ponderous currencies. A man's hand may be full of invisible gold, and the wave of it, or the grasp, shall do more than another's with a shower of bullion. This invisible gold, also, does not necessarily diminish in spending. Political economists will do well some day to take heed of it, though they cannot take measure.

But farther. Since the essence of wealth consists in its authority over men, if the apparent or nominal wealth fail in this power, it fails in essence; in fact, ceases to be wealth at all. It does not appear lately in England, that our authority over men is absolute. The servants show some disposition to rush riotously upstairs, under an impression that their wages are not regularly paid. We should augur ill of any gentleman's property to whom this happened every other day in his drawing-room.

So, also, the power of our wealth seems limited as respects the comfort of the servants, no less than their quietude. The persons in the kitchen appear to be ill-dressed, squalid, half-starved. One cannot help imagining that the riches of the establishment must be of a very theoretical and documentary character.

Finally. Since the essence of wealth consists in power over men, will it not follow that the nobler and the more in number the persons are over whom it has power, the greater the wealth? Perhaps it may even appear, after some consideration, that the persons themselves *are* the wealth—that these pieces of gold with which we are in the habit of guiding them, are, in fact, nothing more than a kind of Byzantine harness or trappings, very glittering and beautiful in barbaric sight, wherewith we bridle the creatures; but that if these same living creatures could be guided without the fretting and jingling of the Byzants in their mouths and ears, they might themselves be more valuable than their bridles. In fact, it may be discovered that the true veins of wealth are purple—and not in Rock, but in Flesh—perhaps even

that the final outcome and consummation of all wealth
is in the producing as many as possible full-breathed,
bright-eyed, and happy-hearted human creatures. Our
modern wealth, I think, has rather a tendency the other
way;—most political economists appearing to consider
multitudes of human creatures not conducive to wealth,
or at best conducive to it only by remaining in a dim-
eyed and narrow-chested state of being.

Nevertheless, it is open, I repeat, to serious question,
which I leave to the reader's pondering, whether, among
national manufacturers, that of Souls of a good quality
may not at last turn out a quite leadingly lucrative one?
Nay, in some far-away and yet undreamed-of hour, I can
even imagine that England may cast all thoughts of
possessive wealth back to the barbaric nations among
whom they first arose; and that, while the sands of the
Indus and adamant of Golconda may yet stiffen the
housings of the charger, and flash from the turban of the
slave, she, as a Christian mother, may at last attain to
the virtues and the treasures of a Heathen one, and be
able to lead forth her Sons, saying,—

"These are MY Jewels."

TIME AND TIDE

By Weare and Tyne

Letter I

*The two kinds of Cooperation.—In its highest sense it
is not yet thought of*

DENMARK HILL, February 4, 1867.

MY DEAR FRIEND—You have now everything I have yet
published on political economy; but there are several
points in these books of mine which I intended to add
notes to, and it seems little likely I shall get that soon
done. So I think the best way of making up for the
want of these is to write you a few simple letters, which
you can read to other people, or send to be printed, if

you like, in any of your journals where you think they may be useful.

I especially want you, for one thing, to understand the sense in which the word "cooperation" is used in my books. You will find I am always pleading for it; and yet I don't at all mean the cooperation of partnership (as opposed to the system of wages) which is now so gradually extending itself among our great firms. I am glad to see it doing so, yet not altogether glad: for none of you who are engaged in the immediate struggle between the system of cooperation and the system of mastership know how much the dispute involves; and none of us know the results to which it may finally lead. For the alternative is not, in reality, only between two modes of conducting business—it is between two different states of society. It is not the question whether an amount of wages, no greater in the end than that at present received by the men, may be paid to them in a way which shall give them share in the risks, and interest in the prosperity, of the business. The question is, really, whether the profits which are at present taken, as his own right, by the person whose capital, or energy, or ingenuity, has made him head of the firm, are not in some proportion to be divided among the subordinates of it.

I do not wish, for the moment, to enter into any inquiry as to the just claims of capital, or as to the proportions in which profits ought to be, or are in actually existing firms, divided. I merely take the one assured and essential condition, that a somewhat larger income will be in cooperative firms secured to the subordinates, by the diminution of the income of the chief. And the general tendency of such a system is to increase the facilities of advancement among the subordinates; to stimulate their ambition; to enable them to lay by, if they are provident, more ample and more early provision for declining years; and to form in the end a vast class of persons wholly different from the existing operative:— members of society, possessing each a moderate competence; able to procure, therefore, not indeed many of the luxuries, but all the comforts of life; and to devote some leisure to the attainments of liberal education, and to the other objects of free life. On the other hand, by the exact sum which is divided among them, more than their present wages, the fortune of the man who, under the present system, takes all the profits of the business, will be diminished; and the acquirement of large private fortune by regular means, and all the conditions of life belonging to such fortune, will be rendered impossible in the manufacturing community.

Now, the magnitude of the social change hereby involved, and the consequent differences in the moral relations between individuals, have not as yet been thought of,—much less estimated,—by any of your writers on commercial subjects; and it is because I do not yet feel able to grapple with them that I have left untouched, in the books I send you, the question of cooperative labor. When I use the word "cooperation," it is not meant to refer to these new constitutions of firms at all. I use the word in a far wider sense, as opposed, not to masterhood, but to *competition*. I do not mean, for instance, by cooperation, that all the master bakers in a town are to give a share of their profits to the men who go out with the bread; but that the masters are not to try to undersell each other, nor seek each to get the other's business, but are all to form one society, selling to the public under a common law of severe penalty for unjust dealing, and at an established price. I do not mean that all bankers' clerks should be partners in the bank; but I do mean that all bankers should be members of a great national body, answerable as a society for all deposits; and that the private business of speculating with other people's money should take another name than that of "banking." And, for final instance, I mean by "cooperation" not only fellowships between trading *firms,* but between trading *nations;* so that it shall no more be thought (as it is now, with ludicrous and vain selfishness) an advantage for one nation to undersell another; and take its occupation away from it; but that the primal and eternal law of vital commerce shall be of all men understood—namely, that every nation is fitted by its character, and the nature of its territories, for some particular employments or manufacturers; and that it is the true interest of every other nation to encourage it in such specialty, and by no means to interfere with, but in all ways forward and protect, its efforts, ceasing all rivalship with it, so soon as it is strong enough to occupy its proper place. You see, therefore, that the idea of cooperation, in the sense in which I employ it, has hardly yet entered into the minds of political inquirers; and I will not pursue it at present; but return to that system which is beginning to obtain credence and practice among us. This, however, must be in a following letter.

. . . .

LETTER II

Cooperation, as hitherto understood, is perhaps not expedient

February 4, 1867.

LIMITING the inquiry, then, for the present, as proposed in the close of my last letter, to the form of cooperation which is now upon its trial in practice, I would beg of you to observe that the points at issue, in the comparison of this system with that of mastership, are by no means hitherto frankly stated; still less can they as yet be fairly brought to test. For all mastership is not alike in principle; there are just and unjust masterships; and while, on the one hand, there can be no question but that cooperation is better than unjust and tyrannous mastership, there is very great room for doubt whether it be better than a just and benignant mastership.

At present you—everyone of you—speak, and act, as if there were only one alternative; namely, between a system in which profits shall be divided in due proportion among all; and the present one, in which the workman is paid the least wages he will take, under the pressure of competition in the labor-market. But an intermediate method is conceivable; a method which appears to me more prudent, and in its ultimate results more just, than the cooperative one. An arrangement may be supposed, and I have good hope also may one day be effected, by which every subordinate shall be paid sufficient and regular wages, according to his rank; by which due provision shall be made out of the profits of the business for sick and superannuated workers; and by which the master, *being held responsible, as a minor king or governor, for the conduct as well as the comfort of all those under his rule,* shall, on that condition, be permitted to retain to his own use the surplus profits of the business which the fact of his being its master may be assumed to prove that he has organized by superior intellect and energy. And I think this principle of regular wage-paying, whether it be in the abstract more just, or not, is at all events the more prudent; for this reason mainly, that in spite of all the cant which is continually talked by cruel, foolish, or designing persons about "the duty of remaining content in the position in which Providence has placed you," there is a root of the very deepest and holiest truth in the saying, which gives to it such power as it still retains, even uttered by unkind and unwise lips, and received into doubtful and embittered hearts.

If, indeed, no effort be made to discover, in the course of their early training, for what services the youths of a nation are individually qualified; nor any care taken to place those who have unquestionably proved their fitness for certain functions, in the offices they could best fulfil —then, to call the confused wreck of social order and life brought about by malicious collision and competition an arrangement of Providence, is quite one of the most insolent and wicked ways in which it is possible to take the name of God in vain. But if, at the proper time, some earnest effort be made to place youths, according to their capacities, in the occupations for which they are fitted, I think the system of organization will be finally found the best, which gives the least encouragement to thoughts of any great future advance in social life.

The healthy sense of progress, which is necessary to the strength and happiness of men, does not consist in the anxiety of a struggle to attain higher place, or rank, but in gradually perfecting the manner, and accomplishing the ends, of the life which we have chosen, or which circumstances have determined for us. Thus, I think the object of a workman's ambition should not be to become a master; but to attain daily more subtle and ex

emplary skill in his own craft, to save from his wages
enough to enrich and complete his home gradually with
more delicate and substantial comforts; and to lay by
such store as shall be sufficient for the happy maintenance of his old age (rendering him independent of the
help provided for the sick and indigent by the arrangement presupposed), and sufficient also for the starting
of his children in a rank of life equal to his own. If his
wages are not enough to enable him to do this, they are
unjustly low; if they are once raised to this adequate
standard, I do not think that by the possible increase of
his gains under contingencies of trade, or by divisions
of profits with his master, he should be enticed into
feverish hope of an entire change of condition; and as
an almost necessary consequence, pass his days in an
anxious discontent with immediate circumstances, and a
comfortless scorn of his daily life, for which no subsequent success could indemnify him. And I am the more
confident in this belief, because, even supposing a gradual
rise in social rank possible for all well-conducted persons,
my experience does not lead me to think the elevation itself, when attained, would be conducive to their happiness.

The grounds of this opinion I will give you in a future
letter; in the present one, I must pass to a more important
point—namely, that if this stability of condition be indeed
desirable for those in whom existing circumstances might
seem to justify discontent, much more must it be good
and desirable for those who already possess everything
which can be conceived necessary to happiness. It is the
merest insolence of selfishness to preach contentment to a
laborer who gets thirty shillings a week, while we suppose
an active and plotting covetousness to be meritorious in a
man who has three thousand a year. In this, as in all
other points of mental discipline, it is the duty of the
upper classes to set an example to the lower; and to recommend and justify the restraint of the ambition of their
inferiors, chiefly by severe and timely limitation of their
own. And, without at present inquiring into the greater
or less convenience of the possible methods of accomplishing such an object (every detail in suggestions of this
kind necessarily furnishing separate matter of dispute),

I will merely state my long-fixed conviction, that one of
the most important conditions of a healthful system of
social economy would be the restraint of the properties
and incomes of the upper classes within certain fixed limits. The temptation to use every energy in the accumulation of wealth being thus removed, another, and a higher
ideal of the duties of advanced life would be necessarily
created in the national mind; by withdrawal of those who
had attained the prescribed limits of wealth from commercial competition, earlier worldly success, and earlier marriage, with all its beneficent moral results, would become
possible to the young; while the older men of active intellect, whose sagacity is now lost or warped in the furtherance of their own meanest interests, would be induced
unselfishly to occupy themselves in the superintendence of
public institutions, or furtherance of public advantage.
And out of this class it would be found natural and prudent always to choose the members of the legislative body
of the Commons; and to attach to the order also some
peculiar honors, in the possession of which such complacency would be felt as would more than replace the
unworthy satisfaction of being supposed richer than
others, which to many men is the principal charm of their
wealth. And although no law of this purport would ever
be imposed on themselves by the actual upper classes, there
is no hindrance to its being gradually brought into force
from beneath, without any violent or impatient proceed-
ings; and this I will endeavor to show you in my next
letter.

·   ·   ·   ·   ·   ·   ·   ·

LETTER XXI

*Of the Dignity of the Four Fine Arts; and of the
Proper System of Retail Trade.*

April 15, 1867.

I RETURN now to the part of the subject at which I was
interrupted—the inquiry as to the proper means of finding
persons willing to maintain themselves and others by degrading occupations.

That, on the whole, simply manual occupations *are* degradings, I suppose I may assume you to admit; at all events, the fact is so, and I suppose few general readers will have any doubt of it.*

Granting this, it follows as a direct consequence that it is the duty of all persons in higher stations of life, by every means in their power, to diminish their demand for work of such kind, *and to live with as little aid from the lower trades,* as they can possibly contrive.

I suppose you see that this conclusion is not a little at variance with received notions on political economy? It is popularly supposed that it benefits a nation to invent a want. But the fact is, that the true benefit is in *extinguishing* a want—in living with as few wants as possible.

I cannot tell you the contempt I feel for the common writers on political economy, in their stupefied missing of this first principal of all human economy—individual or political—to live, namely, with as few wants as possible, and to waste nothing of what is given you to supply them.

This ought to be the first lesson of every rich man's political code. "Sir," his tutor should early say to him, "you are so placed in society,—it may be for your misfortune, it *must* be for your trial—that you are likely to be maintained all your life by the labor of other men. You will have to make shoes for nobody, but some one will have to make a great many for you. You will have to dig ground for nobody, but some one will have to dig through every summer's hot day for you. You will build houses and make clothes for no one, but many a rough hand must knead clay, and many an elbow be crooked to the stitch, to keep that body of yours warm and fine. Now remember, whatever you and your work may be worth, the less your keep costs, the better. It does not cost money only. It costs degradation. You do not merely employ

---

* Many of my working readers have disputed this statement eagerly, feeling the good effect of work in themselves; but observe, I only say, *simply* or *totally* manual work; and that, alone, *is* degrading, though often in measure, refreshing, wholesome, and necessary. So it is highly necessary and wholesome to eat all day—if you can. A highly bred court lady, rightly interested in politics and literature, is a much finer type of the human creature than a servant-of-all-work, however clever and honest. [Ruskin's note.]

these people. You also *tread* upon them. It cannot be
helped;—you have your place, and they have theirs; but
see that you tread as lightly as possible, and on as few
as possible. What food, and clothes, and lodging, you
honestly need, for your health and peace, you may righteously take. See that you take the plainest you can serve
yourself with—that you waste or wear nothing vainly—
and that you employ no man in furnishing you with any
useless luxury."

That is the first lesson of Christian—or human—economy; and depend upon it, my friend, it is a sound one,
and has every voice and vote of the spirits of Heaven and
earth to back it, whatever views the Manchester men, or
any other manner of men, may take respecting "demand
and supply." Demand what you deserve, and you shall
be supplied with it, for your good. Demand what you
do *not* deserve, and you shall be supplied with something
which you have not demanded, and which Nature perceives that you deserve, quite to the contrary of your good.
That is the law of your existence, and if you do not make
it the law of your resolved acts, so much, precisely, the
worse for you and all connected with you.

Yet observe, though it is out of its proper place said
here, this law forbids no luxury which men are *not* degraded in providing. You may have Paul Veronese to
paint your ceiling, if you like, or Benvenuto Cellini to
make cups for you. But you must not employ a hundred
divers to find beads to stitch over your sleeve. (Did you
see the account of the sales of the Esterhazy jewels the
other day? *)

And the degree in which you recognize the difference

---

* The reference is to the *Times* of February 9, 1867, which gave an
account of the Esterhazy jewels. On the death of the last Prince
of the House, Paul, in 1866, the jewels had come into the hands of
his creditors, and were on view at the shop of a London jeweller.
"The jewelled suits of the Esterhazys," said the *Times*, "became the
talk of the courts of Europe. As the feudal proprietor of nearly
one-third of Hungary, the Prince Nicholas had no difficulty in qualify-
ing a taste which had become a mania. Every part of the equipment
of an officer's dress which should have been of metal was made of pure
brilliants. The gems were sewn over uniforms till the fabric was
literally stiff and cumbrous with the weight. The pearl suit is especially famous. The display is well worth seeing, not only for its
extraordinary value and splendor, but as a striking illustration of the
length to which personal display can rise even among men when once
the passion is indulged in." [Cook and Wedderburn's note.]

between these two kinds of services, is precisely what makes the difference between your being a civilized person or a barbarian. If you keep slaves to furnish forth your dress—to glut your stomach—sustain your indolence —or deck your pride, you are a barbarian. If you keep servants, properly cared for, to furnish you with what you verily want, and no more than that—you are a "civil" person—a person capable of the qualities of citizenship.

Now, farther, observe that in a truly civilized and disciplined state, no man would be allowed to meddle with any material who did not know how to make the best of it. In other words, the arts of working in wood, clay, stone, and metal, would all be *fine* arts (working in iron for machinery becoming an entirely distinct business). There would be no joiner's work, no smith's, no pottery nor stone-cutting, so debased in character as to be entirely unconnected with the finer branches of the same art; and to at least one of these finer branches (generally in metal-work) every painter and sculptor would be necessarily apprenticed during some years of his education. There would be room, in these four trades alone, for nearly every grade of practical intelligence and productive imagination.

But it should not be artists alone who are exercised early in these crafts. It would be part of my scheme of physical education that every youth in the state—from the King's son downward,—should learn to do something finely and thoroughly with his hand, so as to let him know what *touch* meant; and what stout craftsmanship meant; and to inform him of many things besides, which no man can learn but by some severely accurate discipline in doing. Let him once learn to take a straight shaving off a plank, or draw a fine curve without faltering, or lay a brick level in its mortar; and he has learned a multitude of other matters which no lips of man could ever teach him. He might choose his craft, but whatever it was, he should learn it to some sufficient degree of true dexterity: and the result would be, in after life, that among the middle classes a good deal of their house furniture would be made, and a good deal of rough work, more or less clumsily, but not ineffectively, got through, by the master himself and his sons, with much furtherance of their general health and peace of mind, and increase of innocent domestic pride and pleasure, and to the extinction of a great deal of vulgar upholstery and other mean handicraft.

Farther. A great deal of the vulgarity, and nearly all the vice, of retail commerce, involving the degradation of persons occupied in it, depends simply on the fact that their minds are always occupied by the vital (or rather mortal) question of profits. I should at once put an end to this source of baseness by making all retail dealers merely salaried officers in the employ of the trade guilds; the stewards, that is to say, of the salable properties of those guilds, and purveyors of such and such articles to a given number of families. A perfectly well-educated person might, without the least degradation, hold such an office as this, however poorly paid; and it would be precisely the fact of his being well educated which would enable him to fulfil his duties to the public without the stimulus of direct profit. Of course the current objection to such a system would be that no man, for a regularly paid salary, would take pains to please his customers; and the answer to that objection is, that if you can train a man to so much unselfishness as to offer himself fearlessly to the chance of being shot, in the course of his daily duty, you can most assuredly, if you make it also a point of honor with him, train him to the amount of self-denial involved in looking you out with care such a piece of cheese or bacon as you have asked for.

You see that I have already much diminished the number of employments involving degradation; and raised the character of many of those that are left. There remain to be considered the necessarily painful or mechanical works of mining, forging, and the like; the unclean, noisome, or paltry manufactures—the various kinds of transport—(by merchant shipping, etc.), and the conditions of menial service.

It will facilitate the examination of these if we put them for the moment aside, and pass to the other division of our dilemma, the question, namely, what kind of lives our gentlemen and ladies are to live, for whom all this hard work is to be done.

SHIELD AND APRON

[*Val D'Arno,* Lecture III.]

I LAID before you, in my last lecture, first lines of the chart of Italian history in the thirteenth century, which I hope gradually to fill with color, and enrich, to such degree as may be sufficient for all comfortable use. But I indicated, as the more special subject of our immediate study, the nascent power of liberal thought, and liberal art, over dead tradition and rude workmanship.

To-day I must ask you to examine in greater detail the exact relation of this liberal art to the illiberal elements which surrounded it.

You do not often hear me use that word "Liberal" in any favorable sense. I do so now, because I use it also in a very narrow and exact sense. I mean that the thirteenth century is, in Italy's year of life, her 17th of March. In the light of it, she assumes her toga virilis; and it is sacred to her god Liber.

To her god *Liber,*—observe; not Dionusos, still less Bacchus, but her own ancient and simple deity. And if you have read with some care the statement I gave you, with Carlyle's help, of the moment and manner of her change from savageness to dexterity, and from rudeness to refinement of life, you will hear, familiar as the lines are to you, the invocation in the first Georgic with a new sense of its meaning:

> "Vos, O clarrissima mundi
> Lumina, labentem cœlo quæ ducitis annum,
> Liber, et alma Ceres; vestro si munere tellus
> Chaoniam pingui glandem mutavit arista,
> Poculaque inventis Acheloia miscuit uvis. . . .
> Munera vestra cano." *

These gifts, innocent, rich, full of life, exquisitely beautiful in order and grace of growth, I have thought

---

* "O ye most radiant lights of the firmament, that guide through heaven the gliding year, O Liber and bounteous Ceres, if by your grace Earth changed Chaouia's acorn for the rich corn-ear, and blended draughts of Achelous with the new-found grapes, ... 'tis of your bounties I sing." (Virgil's *Georgics* I, 5-9, 12. Fairclough's translation.)

best to symbolize to you, in the series of types of the power of the Greek gods, placed in your Educational Series, by the blossom of the wild strawberry; which in rising from its trine cluster of trine leaves,—itself as beautiful as a white rose, and always single on its stalk, like an ear of corn, yet with a succeeding blossom at its side, and bearing a fruit which is as distinctly a group of seeds as an ear of corn itself, and yet is the pleasantest to taste of all the pleasant things prepared by nature for the food of men,—may accurately symbolize, and help you to remember, the conditions of this liberal and delightful, yet entirely modest and orderly, art, and thought.

You will find in the fourth of my inaugural lectures, at the 98th paragraph, this statement,—much denied by modern artists and authors, but nevertheless quite unexceptionally true,—that the entire vitality of art depends upon its having for object either to *state a true thing, or adorn a serviceable one.* The two functions of art in Italy, in this entirely liberal and virescent phase of it,—virgin art, we may call it, retaining the most literal sense of the words virga and virgo,—are to manifest the doctrines of a religion which now, for the first time, men had soul enough to understand; and to adorn edifices or dress, with which the completed politeness of daily life might be invested, its convenience completed, and its decorous and honorable pride satisfied.

That pride was, among the men who gave its character to the century, in honorableness of private conduct, and useful magnificence of public art. Not of private or domestic art; observe this very particularly.

"Such was the simplicity of private manners"—(I am now quoting Sismondi, but with the fullest ratification that my knowledge enables me to give),—"and the economy of the richest citizens, that if a city enjoyed repose only for a few years, it doubled its revenues, and found itself, in a sort, encumbered with its riches. The Pisans knew neither the luxury of the table, nor that of furniture, nor that of a number of servants; yet they were sovereigns of the whole of Sardinia, Corsica, and Elba, had colonies at St. Jean d'Acre and Constantinople, and their merchants in those cities carried on the most extended commerce with the Saracens and Greeks."

"And in that time"—(I now give you my own translation of Giovanni Villani),—"the citizens of Florence lived sober, and on coarse meats, and at little cost; and had many customs and playfulnesses which were blunt and rude; and they dressed themselves and their wives with coarse cloth; many wore merely skins, with no lining, and *all* had only leather buskins; and the Florentine ladies, plain shoes and stockings with no ornaments; and the best of them were content with a close gown of coarse scarlet of Cyprus, or camlet girded with an old-fashioned clasp-girdle; and a mantle over all, lined with vaire, with a hood above; and that, they threw over their heads. The women of lower rank were dressed in the same manner, with coarse green Cambray cloth; fifty pounds was the ordinary bride's dowry, and a hundred or a hundred and fifty would in those times have been held brilliant ("isfolgorata," dazzling, with sense of dissipation or extravagance); and most maidens were twenty or more before they married. Of such gross customs were then the Florentines; but of good faith, and loyal among themselves and in their state, and in their coarse life, and poverty, did more and braver things than are done in our days with more refinement and riches."

I detain you a moment at the words "scarlet of Cyprus, or camlet."

Observe that camelot (camelet) from χαμηλωτή, camel's skin, is a stuff made of silk and camel's hair originally, afterward of silk and wool. At Florence, the camel's hair would always have reference to the Baptist, who, as you know, in Lippi's picture, wears the camel's skin itself, made into a Florentine dress, such as Villani has just described, "col tassello sopra," with the hood above. Do you see how important the word "Capulet" is becoming to us, in its main idea?

Not in private nor domestic art, therefore, I repeat to you, but in useful magnificence of public art, these citizens expressed their pride:—and that public art divided itself into two branches—civil, occupied upon ethic subjects of sculpture and painting; and religious, occupied upon scriptural or traditional histories, in treatment of which, nevertheless, the nascent power and liberality of thought were apparent, not only in continual amplification and illustration of scriptural story by the artist's own invention, but in the acceptance of profane mythology, as part of the Scripture, or tradition, given by Divine inspiration.

Nevertheless, for the provision of things necessary in domestic life, there developed itself, together with the group of inventive artists exercising these nobler functions, a vast body of craftsmen, and, literally, manufacturers, workers by hand, who associated themselves, as chance, tradition, or the accessibility of material directed, in towns which thenceforward occupied a leading position in commerce, as producers of a staple of excellent or perhaps inimitable, quality; and the linen or cambric of Cambray, the lace of Mechlin, the wool of Worstead, and the steel of Milan, implied the tranquil and hereditary skill of multitudes, living in wealthy industry, and humble honor.

Among these artisans, the weaver, the ironsmith, the goldsmith, the carpenter, and the mason necessarily took the principal rank, and on their occupations the more refined arts were wholesomely based, so that the five businesses may be more completely expressed thus:—

> The weaver and embroiderer,
> The ironsmith and armorer,
> The goldsmith and jeweller,
> The carpenter and engineer,
> The stonecutter and painter.

You have only once to turn over the leaves of Leonardo's sketch-book, in the Ambrosian Library, to see how carpentry is connected with engineering,—the architect was always a stonecutter, and the stonecutter not often practically separate, as yet, from the painter, and never so in general conception of function. You recollect, at a much later period, Kent's description of Cornwall's steward:

"KENT. You cowardly rascal! — nature disclaims in thee, a tailor made thee!

CORNWALL. Thou art a strange fellow—a tailor make a man?

KENT. Ay, sir; a stonecutter, or a painter, could not have made him so ill; though they had been but two hours at the trade."

You may consider then this group of artisans with the merchants, as now forming in each town an important Tiers Etat, or Third State of the people, occupied in service, first, of the ecclesiastics, who in monastic bodies inhabited the cloisters round each church; and, secondly, of the knights, who, with their retainers, occupied, each family their own fort, in allied defense of their appertaining streets.

A Third Estate, indeed; but adverse alike to both the others, to Montague as to Capulet, when they become disturbers of the public peace; and having a pride of its own,—hereditary still, but consisting in the inheritance of skill and knowledge rather than of blood,—which expressed the sense of such inheritance by taking its name habitually from the master rather than the sire; and which, in its natural antagonism to dignities won only by violence, or recorded only by heraldry, you may think of generally as the race whose bearing is the Apron, instead of the Shield.

When, however, these two, or in perfect subdivision three, bodies of men, lived in harmony,—the knights remaining true to the State, the clergy to their faith, and the workmen to their craft,—conditions of national force were arrived at, under which all the great art of the Middle Ages was accomplished. The pride of the knights, the avarice of the priests, and the gradual abasement of character in the craftsman, changing him from a citizen able to wield either tools in peace or weapons in war, to a dull tradesman, forced to pay mercenary troops to defend his shop door, are the direct causes of common ruin toward the close of the sixteenth century.

But the deep underlying cause of the decline in national character itself, was the exhaustion of the Christian faith. None of its practical claims were avouched either by reason or experience; and the imagination grew weary of sustaining them in despite of both. Men could not, as their powers of reflection became developed, steadily conceive that the sins of a life might be done away with, by finishing it with Mary's name on the lips; nor could tradition of miracle forever resist the personal discovery, made by each rude disciple by himself, that he might pray to all the saints for a twelvemonth together, and yet not get what he asked for.

The Reformation succeeded in proclaiming that existing Christianity was a lie; but substituted no theory of it which could be more rationally or credibly sustained; and ever since, the religion of educated persons throughout Europe has been dishonest or ineffectual; it is only among the laboring peasantry that the grace of a pure Catholicism, and the patient simplicities of the Puritan, maintain their imaginative dignity, or assert their practical use.

The existence of the nobler arts, however, involves the harmonious life and vital faith of the three classes whom we have just distinguished; and that condition exists, more or less disturbed, indeed, by the vices inherent in each class, yet, on the whole, energetically and productively, during the twelfth, thirteenth, fourteenth, and fifteenth centuries. But our present subject being Architecture only, I will limit your attention altogether to the state of society in the great age of architecture, the thirteenth century. A great age in all ways; but most notably so in the correspondence it presented, up to a just and honorable point, with the utilitarian energy of our own days.

The increase of wealth, the safety of industry, and the conception of more convenient furniture of life, to which we must attribute the rise of the entire artist class, were accompanied, in that century, by much enlargement in the conception of useful public works; and—not by *private* enterprise,—that idle persons might get dividends out of the public pocket,—but by *public* enterprise,—each citizen paying down at once his share of what was necessary to accomplish the benefit to the State,—great architectural and engineering efforts were made for the common service. Common, observe; but not, in our present sense, republican. One of the most ludicrous sentences ever written in the blindness of party spirit is that of Sismondi, in which he declares, thinking of these public works only, that "the architecture of the thirteenth century is entirely republican." The architecture of the thirteenth century is, in the mass of it, simply baronial or ecclesiastical; it is of castles, palaces, or churches; but it is true that splendid

civic works were also accomplished by the vigor of the
newly risen popular power.

"The canal named Naviglio Grande, which brings the waters
of the Ticino to Milan, traversing a distance of thirty miles,
was undertaken in 1179, recommenced in 1257, and, soon after,
happily terminated; in it still consists the wealth of a vast
extent of Lombardy. At the same time the town of Milan
rebuilt its walls, which were three miles round, and had sixteen marble gates, of magnificence which might have graced
the capital of all Italy. The Genoese, in 1276 and 1283, built
their two splendid docks, and the great wall of their quay;
and in 1295 finished the noble aqueduct which brings pure and
abundant waters to their city from a great distance among
their mountains. There is not a single town in Italy which at
the same time did not undertake works of this kind; and while
these larger undertakings were in progress, stone bridges were
built across the rivers, the streets and piazzas were paved with
large slabs of stone, and every free government recognized the
duty of providing for the convenience of the citizens."

The necessary consequence of this enthusiasm in useful building, was the formation of a vast body of craftsmen and architects; corresponding in importance to that
which the railway, with its associated industry, has developed in modern times, but entirely different in personal
character, and relation to the body politic.

Their personal character was founded on the accurate
knowledge of their business in all respects; the ease and
pleasure of unaffected invention; and the true sense of
power to do everything better than it had ever been yet
done, coupled with general contentment in life, and in its
vigor and skill.

It is impossible to overrate the difference between such
a condition of mind, and that of the modern artist, who
either does not know his business at all, or knows it only
to recognize his own inferiority to every former workman of distinction.

Again: the political relation of these artificers to the
State was that of a cast entirely separate from the
noblesse; paid for their daily work what was just, and
competing with each other to supply the best article they
could for the money. And it is, again, impossible to overrate the difference between such a social condition, and
that of the artists of to-day, struggling to occupy a position

of equality in wealth with the noblesse,—paid irregular and monstrous prices by an entirely ignorant and selfish public; and competing with each other to supply the worst article they can for the money.

I never saw anything so impudent on the walls of any exhibition, in any country, as last year in London. It was a daub professing to be a "harmony in pink and white" (or some such nonsense); absolute rubbish, and which had taken about a quarter of an hour to scrawl or daub—it had no pretense to be called painting. The price asked for it was two hundred and fifty guineas.

In order to complete your broad view of the elements of social power in the thirteenth century, you have now farther to understand the position of the country people, who maintained by their labor these three classes, whose action you can discern, and whose history you can read; while, of those who maintained them, there is no history, except of the annual ravage of their fields by contending cities or nobles;—and, finally, that of the higher body of merchants, whose influence was already beginning to counterpoise the prestige of noblesse in Florence, and who themselves constituted no small portion of the noblesse of Venice.

The food-producing country was for the most part still possessed by the nobles; some by the ecclesiastics; but a portion, I do not know how large, was in the hands of peasant proprietors, of whom Sismondi gives this, to my mind, completely pleasant and satisfactory, though, to his, very painful, account:—

"They took no interest in public affairs; they had assemblies of their commune at the village in which the church of their parish was situated, and to which they retreated to defend themselves in case of war; they had also magistrates of their own choice; but all their interests appeared to them enclosed in the circle of their own commonalty; they did not meddle with general politics, and held it for their point of honor to remain faithful, through all revolutions, to the State of which they formed a, part, obeying, without hesitation, its chiefs, whoever they were, and by whatever title they occupied their places."

Of the inferior agricultural laborers, employed on the farms of the nobles and richer ecclesiastics, I find nowhere due notice, nor does any historian seriously examine their manner of life. Liable to every form of robbery and oppression, I yet regard their state as not only morally but physically happier than that of riotous soldiery, or the lower class of artisans, and as the safeguard of every civilized nation, through all its worst vicissitudes of folly and crime. Nature has mercifully appointed that seed must be sown, and sheep folded, whatever lances break, or religions fail; and at this hour, while the streets of Florence and Verona are full of idle politicians, loud of tongue, useless of hand and treacherous of heart, there still may be seen in their market-places, standing, each by his heap of pulse or maize, the gray-haired laborers, silent, serviceable, honorable, keeping faith, untouched by change, to their country and to Heaven.

It is extremely difficult to determine in what degree the feelings or intelligence of this class influenced the architectural design of the thirteenth century;—how far afield the cathedral tower was intended to give delight, and to what simplicity of rustic conception Quercia or Ghiberti appealed by the fascination of their Scripture history. You may at least conceive, at this date, a healthy animation in all men's minds, and the children of the vineyard and sheep-cote crowding the city on its festa days, and receiving impulse to busier, if not nobler, education in its splendor.

The great class of the merchants is more difficult to define; but you may regard them generally as the examples of whatever modes of life might be consistent with peace and justice, in the economy of transfer, as opposed to the military license of pillage.

They represent the gradual ascendency of foresight, prudence, and order in society, and the first ideas of advantageous national · intercourse. Their body is therefore composed of the most intelligent and temperate natures of the time,—uniting themselves, not directly for the purpose of making money, but to obtain stability for legal institutions, security of property, and pacific relations with neighboring states. Their guilds form the only representatives of true national council, unaffected, as the landed proprietors were, by merely local circumstances and accidents.

The strength of this order, when its own conduct was upright, and its opposition to the military body was not in avaricious cowardice, but in the resolve to compel justice and to secure peace, can only be understood by you after an examination of the great changes in the government of Florence during the thirteenth century, which, among other minor achievements interesting to us, led to that destruction of the Tower of the Death-watch, so ingeniously accomplished by Niccola Pisano. This change, and its results, will be the subject of my next lecture. I must to-day sum, and in some farther degree make clear, the facts already laid before you.

We have seen that the inhabitants of every great Italian state may be divided, and that very stringently, into the five classes of knights, priests, merchants, artists, and peasants. No distinction exists between artist and artisan, except that of higher genius or better conduct; the best artist is assuredly also the best artisan; and the simplest workman uses his invention and emotion as well as his fingers. The entire body of artists is under the orders (as shopmen are under the orders of their customers), of the knights, priests, and merchants,—the knights for the most part demanding only fine goldsmiths' work, stout armor, and rude architecture; the priests commanding both the finest architecture and painting, and the richest kinds of decorative dress and jewellery,—while the merchants directed works of public use, and were the best judges of artistic skill. The competition for the Baptistery gates of Florence is before the guild of merchants; nor is their award disputed, even in thought, by any of the candidates.

This is surely a fact to be taken much to heart by our present communities of Liverpool and Manchester. They probably suppose, in their modesty, that lords and clergymen are the proper judges of art, and merchants can only, in the modern phrase, "know what they like," or follow humbly the guidance of their golden-crested or flat-capped superiors. But in the great ages of art, neither knight nor pope shows signs of true power of criticism. The artists crouch before them, or quarrel with them, according to their own tempers. To the merchants they submit silently, as to just and capable judges. And look what men these are, who submit. Donatello, Ghiberti, Quercia, Luca! If men like these submit to the merchant, who shall rebel?

But the still franker, and surer, judgment of innocent pleasure was awarded them by all classes alike: and the interest of the public was the *final* rule of right,—that public being always eager to see, and earnest to learn. For the stories told by their artists formed, they fully believed, a Book of Life; and every man of real genius took up his function of illustrating the scheme of human morality and salvation, as naturally, and faithfully, as an English mother of to-day giving her children their first lessons in the Bible. In this endeavor to teach they almost unawares taught themselves; the question "How shall I represent this most clearly?" became to themselves, presently "How was this most likely to have happened?" and habits of fresh and accurate thought thus quickly enlivened the formalities of the Greek pictorial theology; formalities themselves beneficent, because restraining by their severity and mystery the wantonness of the newer life. Foolish modern critics have seen nothing in the Byzantine school but a barbarism to be conquered and forgotten. But that school brought to the art-scholars of the thirteenth century, laws which had been serviceable to Phidias, and symbols which had been beautiful to Homer; and methods and habits of pictorial scholarship which gave a refinement of manner to the work of the simplest craftsman, and became an education to the higher artists which no discipline of literature can now bestow, developed themselves in the effort to decipher, and the impulse to reinterpret, the Eleusinian divinity of Byzantine tradition.

The words I have just used, "pictorial scholarship," and "pictorial theology," remind me how strange it must appear to you that in this sketch of the intellectual state of Italy in the thirteenth century I have taken no note of literature itself, nor of the fine art of Music with which it was associated in minstrelsy. The corruption of the meaning of the word "clerk," from "a chosen person," to "a learned one," partly indicates the position of literature in the war between the golden crest and scarlet cap; but in the higher ranks, literature and music became the grace of the noble's life, or the occupation of the monk's, without forming any separate class, or exercising any materially visible political power. Masons or butchers might establish a government,—but never troubadours: and though a good knight held his education to be imperfect unless he could write a sonnet and sing it, he did not esteem his castle to be at the mercy of the "editor" of a manuscript. He might indeed owe his life to the fidelity of a minstrel, or be guided in his policy by the wit of a clown; but he was not the slave of sensual music, or vulgar literature, and never allowed his Saturday reviewer to appear at table without the cock's comb.

On the other hand, what was noblest in thought or saying was in those times as little attended to as it is now. I do not feel sure that, even in after-times, the poem of Dante has had any political effect on Italy; but at all events, in his life, even at Verona, where he was treated most kindly, he had not half so much influence with Can Grande as the rough Count of Castelbarco, not one of whose words was ever written, or now remains; and whose portrait, by no means that of a man of literary genius, almost disfigures, by its plainness, the otherwise grave and perfect beauty of his tomb.

THE WHITE-THORN BLOSSOM

[Fors Clavigera, Vol. I, Letter 5.]

"For lo, the winter is past,
The rain is over and gone,
The flowers appear on the earth,
The time of the singing of birds is come,

Arise, oh my fair one, my dove,
And come."

DENMARK HILL, 1st May, 1871.

MY FRIENDS—It has been asked of me, very justly, why I have hitherto written to you of things you were little likely to care for, in words which it was difficult for you to understand.

I have no fear but that you will one day understand all my poor words,—the saddest of them, perhaps, too well. But I have great fear that you may never come to understand these written above, which are part of a king's love-song, in one sweet May, of many long since gone.

I fear that for you the wild winter's rain may never pass, —the flowers never appear on the earth;—that for you no bird may ever sing;—for you no perfect Love arise, and fulfil your life in peace.

"And why not for us, as for others?" will you answer me so, and take my fear for you as an insult?

Nay, it is no insult;—nor am I happier than you. For me, the birds do not sing, nor ever will. But they would, for you, if you cared to have it so. When I told you that you would never understand that love-song, I meant only that you would not desire to understand it.

Are you again indignant with me? Do you think, though you should labor, and grieve, and be trodden down in dishonor all your days, at least you can keep that one joy of Love, and that one honor of Home? Had you, indeed, kept that, you had kept all. But no men yet, in the history of the race, have lost it so piteously. In many a country, and many an age, women have been compelled to labor for their husbands' wealth, or bread; but never until now were they so homeless as to say, like the poor Samaritan, "I have no husband." Women of every country and people have sustained without complaint the labor of fellowship: for the women of the latter days in England it has been reserved to claim the privilege of isolation.

This, then, is the end of your universal education and civilization, and contempt of the ignorance of the Middle Ages, and of their chivalry. Not only do you declare yourselves too indolent to labor for daughters and wives, and too poor to support them; but you have made the neglected and distracted creatures hold it for an honor to be independent of you, and shriek for some hold of the mattock for themselves. Believe it or not, as you may, there has not been so low a level of thought reached by any race, since they grew to be male and female out of star-fish, or chickweed, or whatever else they have been made from, by natural selection,—according to modern science.

That modern science also, Economic and of other kinds, has reached its climax at last. For it seems to be the appointed function of the nineteenth century to exhibit in

all things the elect pattern of perfect Folly, for a warning
to the farthest future. Thus the statement of principle
which I quoted to you in my last letter, from the circular
of the Emigration Society, that it is over-production which
is the cause of distress, is accurately the most Foolish
thing, not only hitherto ever said by men, but which it is
possible for men ever to say, respecting their own business.
It is a kind of opposite pole (or negative acme of mortal
stupidity) to Newton's discovery of gravitation as an acme
of mortal wisdom:—as no wise being on earth will ever
be able to make such another wise discovery, so no foolish
being on earth will ever be capable of saying such another
foolish thing, through all the ages.

And the same crisis has been exactly reached by our
natural science and by our art. It has several times
chanced to me, since I began these papers, to have the
exact thing shown or brought to me that I wanted for
illustration, just in time*—and it happened that on the
very day on which I published my last letter, I had to go
to the Kensington Museum; and there I saw the most perfectly and roundly ill-done thing which, as yet, in my
whole life, I ever saw produced by art. It had a tablet
in front of it, bearing this inscription:—

"Statue in black and white marble, a Newfoundland Dog
standing on a Serpent, which rests on a marble cushion, the
pedestal ornamented with pietra dura fruits in relief.—*English. Present Century. No. I.*"

It was so very right for me, the Kensington people having been good enough to number it "I.," the thing itself
being almost incredible in its one-ness; and, indeed, such
a punctual accent over the iota of Miscreation,—so absolutely and exquisitely miscreant, that I am not myself
capable of conceiving a Number two, or three, or any
rivalship or association with it whatsoever. The extremity
of its unvirtue consisted, observe, mainly in the quantity

* Here is another curious instance: I have but a minute ago finished
correcting these sheets, and take up the *Times* of this morning, April
21st, and find in it the suggestion by the Chancellor of the Exchequer
for the removal of exemption from taxation of Agricultural horses and
carts, in the very nick of time to connect it, as a proposal for economic
practice, with the statement of economic principle respecting Production, quoted on this page. [Ruskin's note.]

of instruction which was abused in it. It showed that the persons who produced it had seen everything, and practised everything; and misunderstood everything they saw, and misapplied everything they did. They had seen Roman work, and Florentine work, and Byzantine work, and Gothic work; and misunderstanding of everything had passed through them as the mud does through earthworms, and here at last was their worm-cast of a Production.

But the second chance that came to me that day, was more significant still. From the Kensington Museum I went to an afternoon tea, at a house where I was sure to meet some nice people. And among the first I met was an old friend who had been hearing some lectures on botany at the Kensington Museum, and been delighted by them. She is the kind of person who gets good out of everything, and she was quite right in being delighted; besides that, as I found by her account of them, the lectures were really interesting, and pleasantly given. She had expected botany to be dull, and had not found it so, and "had learned so much." On hearing this, I proceeded naturally to inquire what; for my idea of her was that before she went to the lectures at all, she had known more botany than she was likely to learn by them. So she told me that she had learned first of all that "there were seven sorts of leaves." Now I have always a great suspicion of the number Seven; because when I wrote the *Seven Lamps of Architecture,* it required all the ingenuity I was master of to prevent them from becoming Eight, or even Nine, on my hands. So I thought to myself that it would be very charming if there were only seven sorts of leaves; but that, perhaps, if one looked the woods and forests of the world carefully through, it was just possible that one might discover as many as eight sorts; and then where would my friend's new knowledge of Botany be? So I said, "That was very pretty; but what more?" Then my friend told me that she had no idea, before, that petals were leaves. On which, I thought to myself that it would not have been any great harm to her if she had remained under her old impression that petals were petals. But I said, "That was very pretty, too; and what more?" So then my friend told me that the lecturer said, "the object of his lectures would be entirely accomplished if he could convince his hearers that there was no such thing as a flower." Now, in that sentence you have the most perfect and admirable summary given you of the general temper and purposes of modern science. It gives lectures on Botany, of which the object is to show that there is no such thing as a flower; on Humanity, to show that there is no such thing as a Man; and on Theology, to show there is no such thing as a God. No such thing as a Man, but only a Mechanism; no such thing as a God, but only a series of forces. The two faiths are essentially one: if you feel yourself to be only a machine, constructed to be a Regulator of minor machinery, you will put your statue of such science on your Holborn Viaduct, and necessarily recognize only major machinery as regulating *you*.

I must explain the real meaning to you, however, of that saying of the Botanical lecturer, for it has a wide bearing. Some fifty years ago, the poet Goethe discovered that all the parts of plants had a kind of common nature, and would change into each other. Now this was a true discovery, and a notable one; and you will find that, in fact, all plants are composed of essentially two parts—the leaf and root—one loving the light, the other darkness; one liking to be clean, the other to be dirty; one liking to grow for the most part up, the other for the most part down; and each having faculties and purposes of its own. But the pure one which loves the light has, above all things, the purpose of being married to another leaf, and having child-leaves, and children's children of leaves, to make the earth fair forever. And when the leaves marry, they put on wedding-robes, and are more glorious than Solomon in all his glory, and they have feasts of honey, and we call them "Flowers."

In a certain sense, therefore, you see the lecturer was quite right. There are no such things as Flowers—there are only—gladdened Leaves. Nay, farther than this, there may be a dignity in the less happy, but unwithering leaf, which is, in some sort, better than the brief lily of its bloom;—which the great poets always knew,—well;— Chaucer, before Goethe; and the writer of the first Psalm, before Chaucer. The Botanical lecturer was, in a deeper sense than he knew, right.

But in the deepest sense of all, the Botanical lecturer was, to the extremity of wrongness, wrong; for leaf, and root, and fruit, exist, all of them, only—that there may be flowers. He disregarded the life and passion of the creature, which were its essence. Had he looked for these, he would have recognized that in the thought of Nature herself, there is, in a plant, nothing else but its flowers.

Now in exactly the sense that modern Science declares there is no such thing as a Flower, it has declared there is no such thing as a Man, but only a transitional form of Ascidians and apes. It may, or may not be true—it is not of the smallest consequence whether it be or not. The real fact is, that, rightly seen with human eyes, there is nothing else but man; that all animals and beings beside him are only made that they may change into him; that the world truly exists only in the presence of Man, acts only in the passion of Man. The essence of Light is in his eyes,—the centre of Force in his soul,—the pertinence of action in his deeds.

And all true science—which my Savoyard guide rightly scorned me when he thought I had not,—all true science is "savoir vivre." But all your modern science is the contrary of that. It is "savoir mourir."

And of its very discoveries, such as they are, it cannot make use.

That telegraphic signalling was a discovery; and conceivably, some day, may be a useful one. And there was some excuse for your being a little proud when, about last sixth of April (Cœur-de-Lion's death-day, and Albert Dürer's, you knotted a copper wire all the way to Bombay, and flashed a message along it, and back.

But what was the message, and what the answer? Is India the better for what you said to her? Are you the better for what she replied?

If not, you have only wasted an all-round-the-world's length of copper wire,—which is, indeed, about the sum of your doing. If you had had, perchance, two words of common-sense to say, though you had taken wearisome time and trouble to send them;—though you had written them slowly in gold, and sealed them with a hundred seals, and sent a squadron of ships of the line to carry the scroll, and the squadron had fought its way round the Cape of

Good Hope, through a year of storms, with loss of all its ships but one,—the two words of common-sense would have been worth the carriage, and more. But you have not anything like so much as that to say, either to India, or to any other place.

You think it a great triumph to make the sun draw brown landscapes for you. That was also a discovery, and some day may be useful. But the sun had drawn landscapes before for you, not in brown, but in green, and blue, and all imaginable colors, here in England. Not one of you ever looked at them then; not one of you cares for the loss of them now, when you have shut the sun out with smoke, so that he can draw nothing more, except brown blots through a hole in a box. There was a rocky valley between Buxton and Bakewell, once upon a time, divine as the Vale of Tempe; you might have seen the Gods there morning and evening—Apollo and all the sweet Muses of the light—walking in fair procession on the lawns of it, and to and fro among the pinnacles of its crags. You cared neither for Gods nor grass, but for cash (which you did not know the way to get); you thought you could get it by what the *Times* calls "Railroad Enterprise." You Enterprised a Railroad through the valley —you blasted its rocks away, heaped thousands of tons of shale into its lovely stream. The valley is gone, and the Gods with it; and now, every fool in Buxton can be at Bakewell in half-an-hour, and every fool in Bakewell at Buxton; which you think a lucrative process of exchange— you Fools Everywhere.

To talk at a distance, when you have nothing to say, though you were ever so near; to go fast from this place to that, with nothing to do either at one or the other: these are powers certainly. Much more, power of increased Production, if you, indeed, had got it, would be something to boast of. But are you so entirely sure that you *have* got it—that the mortal disease of plenty, and afflictive affluence of good things, are all you have to' dread?

Observe. A man and a woman, with their children, properly trained, are able easily to cultivate as much ground as will feed them; to build as much wall and roof as will lodge them, and to spin and weave as much cloth as will clothe them. They can all be perfectly happy and healthy in doing this. Supposing that they invent machinery which will build, plough, thresh, cook, and weave, and that they have none of these things any more to do, but may read, or play croquet, or cricket, all day long, I believe myself that they will neither be so good nor so happy as without the machines. But I waive my belief in this matter for the time. I will assume that they become more refined and moral persons, and that idleness is in future to be the mother of all good. But observe, I repeat, the power of your machine is only in enabling them to be idle. It will not enable them to live better than they did before, nor to live in greater numbers. Get your heads quite clear on this matter. Out of so much ground, only so much living is to be got, with or without machinery. You may set a million of steam-ploughs to work on an acre, if you like—out of that acre only a given number of grains of corn will grow, scratch or scorch it as you will. So that the question is not at all whether, by having more machines, more of you can live. No machines will increase the possibilities of life. They only increase the possibilities of idleness. Suppose, for instance, you could get the oxen in your plough driven by a goblin, who would ask for no pay, not even a cream bowl,—(you have nearly managed to get it driven by an iron goblin, as it is);—Well, your furrow will take no more seeds than if you had held the stilts yourself. But, instead of holding them, you sit, I presume, on a bank beside the field, under an eglantine;—watch the goblin at his work, and read poetry. Meantime, your wife in the house has also got a goblin to weave and wash for her. And she is lying on the sofa, reading poetry.

Now, as I said, I don't believe you would be happier so, but I am willing to believe it; only, since you are already such brave mechanists, show me at least one or two places where you *are* happier. Let me see one small example of approach to this seraphic condition. *I* can show *you* examples, millions of them, of happy people, made happy by their own industry. Farm after farm I can show you, in Bavaria, Switzerland, the Tyrol, and such other places, where men and women are perfectly happy and good, without any iron servants. Show me, therefore, some English family, with its fiery familiar, happier than these. Or bring me—for I am not inconvincible by any kind of evidence,—bring me the testimony of an English family or two to their increased felicity. Or if you cannot do so much as that, can you convince even themselves of it? They *are* perhaps happy, if only they knew how happy they were; Virgil thought so, long ago, of simple rustics; but you hear at present your steam-propelled rustics are crying out that they are anything else than happy, and that they regard their boasted progress "in the light of a monstrous Sham." I must tell you one little thing, however, which greatly perplexes my imagination of the relieved ploughman sitting under his rose bower, reading poetry. I have told it you before, indeed, but I forget where. There was really a great festivity, and expression of satisfaction in the new order of things, down in Cumberland, a little while ago; some first of May, I think it was, a country festival, such as the old heathens, who had no iron servants, used to keep with piping and dancing. So I thought, from the liberated country people—their work all done for them by goblins—we should have some extraordinary piping and dancing. But there was no dancing at all, and they could not even provide their own piping. They had their goblin to pipe for them. They walked in procession after their steam-plough, and their steam-plough whistled to them occasionally in the most melodious manner it could. Which seemed to me, indeed, a return to more than Arcadian simplicity; for in old Arcadia, ploughboys truly whistled as they went, for want of thought; whereas, here was verily a large company walking without thought, but not having any more even the capacity of doing their own whistling.

But next, as to the inside of the house. Before you got your power-looms, a woman could always make herself a chemise and petticoat of bright and pretty appearance. I have seen a Bavarian peasant-woman at church in Munich, looking a much grander creature, and more beautifully dressed, than any of the crossed and embroidered angels in Hess's high-art frescoes (which happened to be just above her, so that I could look from one to the other). Well, here you are, in England, served by household demons, with five hundred fingers, at least, weaving, for one that used to weave in the day of Minerva. You ought to be able to show me five hundred dresses for one that used to be; tidiness ought to have become five hundred-fold tidier; tapestry should be increased into cinque-cento-fold iridescence of tapestry. Not only your peasant-girl ought to be lying on the sofa reading poetry, but she ought to have in her wardrobe five hundred petticoats instead of one. Is that, indeed, your issue? or are you only on a curiously crooked way to it?

It is just possible, indeed, that you may not have been allowed to get the use of the goblin's work—that other people may have got the use of it, and you none; because, perhaps, you have not been able to evoke goblins wholly for your own personal service: but have been borrowing goblins from the capitalist, and paying interest, in the "position of William," on ghostly self-going planes; but suppose you had laid by capital enough, yourselves, to hire all the demons in the world,—nay,—all that are inside of it; are you quite sure you know what you might best set them to work at? and what "useful things" you should command them to make for you? I told you, last month, that no economist going (whether by steam or ghost) knew what are useful things and what are not. Very few of you know, yourselves, except by bitter experience of the want of them. And no demons, either of iron or spirit, can ever make them.

There are three Material things, not only useful, but essential to Life. No one "knows how to live" till he has got them.

These are, Pure Air, Water, and Earth.

There are three Immaterial things, not only useful, but essential to Life. No one knows how to live till he has got them.

These are, Admiration, Hope, and Love.

Admiration—the power of discerning and taking delight in what is beautiful in visible Form, and lovely in human Character; and, necessarily, striving to produce what is beautiful in form, and to become what is lovely in character.

Hope—the recognition, by true Foresight, of better things to be reached hereafter, whether by ourselves or others; necessarily issuing in the straightforward and undisappointable effort to advance, according to our proper power, the gaining of them.

Love, both of family and neighbor, faithful and satisfied.

These are the six chiefly useful things to be got by Political Economy, when it *has* become a science. I will briefly tell you what modern Political Economy—the great "savoir mourir"—is doing with them.

The first three, I said, are Pure Air, Water, and Earth.

Heaven gives you the main elements of these. You can destroy them at your pleasure, or increase, almost without limit, the available quantities of them.

You can vitiate the air by your manner of life, and of death, to any extent. You might easily vitiate it so as to bring such a pestilence on the globe as would end all of you. You, or your fellows, German and French, are at present busy in vitiating it to the best of your power in every direction; chiefly at this moment with corpses, and animal and vegetable ruin in war: changing men, horses, and garden-stuff into noxious gas. But everywhere, and all day long, you are vitiating it with foul chemical exhalations; and the horrible nests, which you call towns, are little more than laboratories for the distillation into heaven of venomous smokes and smells, mixed with effluvia from decaying animal matter, and infectious miasmata from purulent disease.

On the other hand, your power of purifying the air, by dealing properly and swiftly with all substances in corruption; by absolutely forbidding noxious manufactures; and by planting in all soils the trees which cleanse and invigorate earth and atmosphere,—is literally infinite. You might make every breath of air you draw, food.

Secondly, your power over the rain and river-waters of the earth is infinite. You can bring rain where you will, by planting wisely and tending carefully;—drought where you will, by ravage of woods and neglect of the soil. You might have the rivers of England as pure as the crystal of the rock; beautiful in falls, in lakes, in living pools; so full of fish that you might take them out with your hands instead of nets. Or you may do always as you have done now, turn every river of England into a common sewer, so that you cannot so much as baptize an English baby but with filth, unless you hold its face out in the rain; and even *that* falls dirty.

Then for the third, Earth,—meant to be nourishing for you, and blossoming. You have learned, about it, that there is no such thing as a flower; and as far as your scientific hands and scientific brains, inventive of explosive and deathful, instead of blossoming and life-giving, Dust, can contrive, you have turned the Mother-Earth, Demeter,*

---

* Read this, for instance, concerning the Gardens of Paris: one sentence in the letter is omitted; I will give it in full elsewhere, with its necessary comments:—

"To the Editor of the 'Times'

"5th April, 1871.

"SIR,—As the paragraph you quoted on Monday from the *Field* gives no idea of the destruction in the gardens round Paris, if you can spare me a very little space I will endeavor to supplement it.

"The public gardens in the interior of Paris, including the planting on the greater number of the Boulevards, are in a condition perfectly surprising when one considers the sufferings even well-to-do persons had to endure for want of fuel during the siege. Some of them, like the little oases in the centre of the Louvre, even look as pretty as ever. After a similar ordeal, it is probable we should not have a stick left in London, and the presence of the very handsome planes on the Boulevards, and large trees in the various squares and gardens, after the winter of 1870-71, is most creditable to the population. But when one goes beyond the Champs Elysées and toward the Bois, down the once beautiful Avenue de l'Impératrice, a sad scene of desolation presents itself. A year ago it was the finest avenue garden in existence; now a considerable part of the surface where troops were camped is about as filthy and as cheerless as Leicester Square or a sparsely furnished rubbish yard.

"The view into the once richly-wooded Bois from the huge and ugly banks of earth which now cross the noble roads leading into it is desolate indeed, the stump of the trees cut down over a large extent of its surface reminding one of the dreary scenes observable in many parts of Canada and the United States, where the stumps of the burnt or cutdown pines are allowed to rot away for years. The zone of the ruins round the vast belt of fortifications I need not speak of, nor of the other zone of destruction round each of the forts, as here houses and gardens and all have disappeared. But the destruction in the wide zone occupied by French and Prussian outposts is beyond description. I got to Paris the morning after the shooting of Generals Clément Thomas and Lecomte, and in consequence did not see so much of it as I otherwise might have done; but round the villages of Sceaux, Bourg-la-Reine, L'Hay, Vitry, and Villejuif, I saw an amount of havoc which the subscriptions to the French Horticultural Relief Fund will go but a very small way to repair. Notwithstanding all his revolutions and wars, the Frenchman usually found time to cultivate a few fruit trees, and the neighborhood of the villages above mentioned was only a few of many covered by nurseries of young trees. When I last visited Vitry, in the autumn of 1868, the fields and hill-sides around were everywhere covered with trees; now the view across them is only interrupted by stumps about a foot high. When at Vitry on the 28th of March, I found the once fine nursery of M. Honoré Dufresne deserted, and many acres once covered with large stock and specimens cleared to the ground. And so it was in numerous other cases. It may give some

into the Avenger-Earth, Tisiphone—with the voice of your brother's blood crying out of it, in one wild harmony round all its murderous sphere.

This is what you have done for the Three Material Useful Things.

Then for the Three Immaterial Useful Things. For Admiration, you have learned contempt and conceit. There is no lovely thing ever yet done by man that you care for, or can understand, but you are persuaded you are able to do much finer things yourselves. You gather, and exhibit together, as if equally instructive, what is infinitely bad, with what is infinitely good. You do not know which is which; you instinctively prefer the Bad, and do more of it. You instinctively hate the Good, and destroy it.*

Then, secondly, for Hope. You have not so much spirit of it in you as to begin any plan which will not pay until ten years; nor so much intelligence of it in you (either politicians or workmen) as to be able to form one clear idea of what you would like your country to become.

Then, thirdly, for Love. You were ordered by the

---

notion of the effect of the war on the gardens and nurseries around Paris, when I state that, according to returns made up just before my visit to Vitry and Villejuif, it was found that around these two villages alone 2,400,400 fruit and other trees were destroyed. As to the private gardens, I cannot give a better idea of them than by describing the materials composing the protecting bank of a battery near Sceaux. It was made up of mattresses, sofas, and almost every other large article of furniture, with the earth stowed between. There were, in addition, nearly forty orange and oleander tubs gathered from the little gardens in the neighborhood visible in various parts of this ugly bank. One nurseryman at Sceaux, M. Keteleer, lost 1500 vols. of books, which were not taken to Germany, but simply mutilated and thrown out of the doors to rot. . . . Multiply these few instances by the number of districts occupied by the belligerents during the war, and some idea of the effects of glory on gardening in France may be obtained.

W. ROBINSON." [Ruskin's note.]

* Last night (I am writing this on the 18th of April) I got a letter from Venice, bringing me the, I believe, too well-grounded, report that the Venetians have requested permission from the government of Italy to pull down their Ducal Palace, and "rebuild" it. Put up a horrible model of it, in its place, that is to say, for which their architects may charge a commission. Meantime, all their canals are choked with human dung, which they are too poor to cart away, but throw out at their windows.

And all the great thirteenth-century cathedrals in France have been destroyed, within my own memory, only that architects might charge commissions for putting up false models of them in their place. [Ruskin's note.]

Founder of your religion to love your neighbor as your-selves.

You have founded an entire Science of Political Economy, on what you have stated to be the constant instinct of man—the desire to defraud his neighbor.

And you have driven your women mad, so that they ask no more for Love, nor for fellowship with you; but stand against you, and ask for "justice."

Are there any of you who are tired of all this? Any of you, Landlords or Tenants? Employers or Workmen?

Are there any landlords,—any masters,—who would like better to be served by men than by iron devils?

Any tenants, any workmen, who can be true to their leaders and to each other? who can vow to work and to live faithfully, for the sake of the joy of their homes?

Will any such give the tenth of what they have, and of what they earn,—not to emigrate with, but to stay in England with; and do what is in their hands and hearts to make her a happy England?

I am not rich (as people now estimate riches), and great part of what I have is already engaged in maintaining art-workmen, or for other objects more or less of public utility. The tenth of whatever is left to me, estimated as accurately as I can (you shall see the accounts), I will make over to you in perpetuity, with the best security that English law can give, on Christmas Day of this year, with engagement to add the tithe of whatever I earn afterward. Who else will help, with little or much? the object of such fund being, to begin, and gradually—no matter how slowly—to increase, the buying and securing of land in England, which shall not be built upon, but cultivated by Englishmen, with their own hands, and such help of force as they can find in wind and wave.

I do not care with how many, or how few, this thing is begun, nor on what inconsiderable scale,—if it be but in two or three poor men's gardens. So much, at least, I can buy, myself, and give them. If no help come, I have done and said what I could, and there will be an end. If any help come to me, it is to be on the following conditions:—We will try to make some small piece of English ground, beautiful, peaceful, and fruitful. We will have no steam-engines upon it, and no railroads; we will have no un-tended or unthought-of creatures on it; none wretched, but the sick; none idle but the dead. We will have no liberty upon it; but instant obedience to known law, and appointed persons; no equality upon it; but recognition of every betterness that we can find, and reprobation of every worseness. When we want to go anywhere, we will go there quietly and safely, not at forty miles an hour in the risk of our lives; when we want to carry anything anywhere, we will carry it either on the backs of beasts, or on our own, or in carts, or boats; we will have plenty of flowers and vegetables in our gardens, plenty of corn and grass in our fields,—and few bricks. We will have some music and poetry; the children shall learn to dance to it and sing it;—perhaps some of the old people, in time, may also. We will have some art, moreover; we will at least try if, like the Greeks, we can't make some pots. The Greeks used to paint pictures of gods on their pots; we, probably, cannot do as much, but we may put some pictures of insects on them, and reptiles;—butterflies, and frogs, if nothing better. There was an excellent old potter in France who used to put frogs and vipers into his dishes, to the admiration of mankind; we can surely put something nicer than that. Little by little, some higher art and imagination may manifest themselves among us; and feeble rays of science may dawn for us. Botany, though too dull to dispute the existence of flowers; and history, though too simple to question the nativity of men;—nay —even perhaps an uncalculating and uncovetous wisdom, as of rude Magi, presenting, at such nativity, gifts of gold and frankincense.

Faithfully yours,

JOHN RUSKIN.

COMPANIONSHIP

[*Fors Clavigera,* Vol. VI, Letter 67.]

As I am now often asked, in private letters, the constitution of St. George's Company, and cannot, hitherto, refer, in answer, to any clear summary of it, I will try to write such a summary in this number of *Fors,* that it may henceforward be sent to inquirers as alone sufficiently explanatory.

The St. George's Company is a society established to carry out certain charitable objects, toward which it invites, and thankfully will receive, help from any persons caring to give it, either in money, labor, or any kind of gift. But the Company itself consists of persons who agree in certain general principles of action, and objects of pursuit, and who can, therefore, act together in effective and constant unison.

These objects of pursuit are, in brief terms, the health, wealth, and long life of the British nation: the Company having thus devoted itself, in the conviction that the British nation is at present unhealthy, poor, and likely to perish, as a power, from the face of the earth. They accordingly propose to themselves the general medicining, enriching, and preserving in political strength, of the population of these islands; they themselves numbering at present, in their ranks, about thirty persons—none of them rich, several of them sick, and the leader of them, at all events, not likely to live long.

Whether the nation be healthy, or in unwholesome degradation of body and mind; wealthy, or in continual and shameful distress; strong, or in rapid decline of political power and authority,—the reader will find debated throughout the various contents of the preceding five volumes of *Fors*. But there is one public fact, which cannot be debated—that the nation is in debt. And the St. George's Company do practically make it their *first*, though not their principal, object, to bring *that* state of things to an end; and to establish, instead of a National Debt, a National Store. (See the last line of the fifth page of the first letter of the series, published 1st January, 1871, and the eleventh, and twenty-seventh, letters, throughout.)

That very few readers of *this* page have any notion, at this moment, what a National Debt is, or can conceive what a National Store should be, is one of many evil consequences of the lies which, under the title of "Political Economy," have been taught by the ill-educated, and mostly dishonest, commercial men who at present govern the press of the country.

I have again and again stated the truth in both these matters, but must try once more to do it, emphatically and intelligibly.

A "civilized nation" in modern Europe consists, in broad terms, of (A) a mass of half-taught, discontented, and mostly penniless populace, calling itself the people; of (B) a thing which it calls a government, meaning an apparatus for collecting and spending money; and (C) a small number of capitalists, many of them rogues, and most of them stupid persons, who have no idea of any object of human existence other than money-making, gambling, or champagne-bibbing. A certain quantity of literary men, saying anything they can get paid to say,—of clergymen, saying anything they have been taught to say,—of natural philosophers, saying anything that comes into their heads,—and of nobility, saying nothing at all, combine in disguising the action, and perfecting the disorganization, of the mass; but with respect to practical business, the civilized nation consists broadly of mob, money-collecting machine and capitalist.

Now when the civilized mob wants to spend money for any profitless or mischievous purposes,—fireworks, illuminations, battles, driving about from place to place, or what not,—being itself penniless, it sets its money-collecting machine to borrow the sum needful for these amusements from the civilized capitalist.

The civilized capitalist lends the money, on condition that, through the money-collecting machine, he may tax the civilized mob thenceforward forever. The civilized mob spends the money forthwith, in gunpowder, infernal machines, masquerade dresses, new boulevards, or anything else it has set its idiotic mind on for the moment; and appoints its money-collecting machine to collect a daily tax from its children, and children's children, to be paid to the capitalists from whom it had received the accommodation, thenceforward forever.

That is the nature of a National Debt.

In order to understand that of a National Store, my readers must first consider what any store whatever, serviceable to human beings, consists of. A store properly means a collection of useful things. Literally, it signifies only a quantity,—or much of *anything*. But the heap of broken bottles which, I hear, is accumulating under the principal cliff of Snowdon, through the contributions of tourists from the summit, is not properly to be called a store; though a bin full of old wine is. Neither is a heap of cannon-balls a store; though a heap of potatoes is. Neither is a cellar full of gunpowder a store; though a cellar full of coals is. A store is, for squirrels, of nuts; for bees, of honey; for men, of food, clothes, fuel, or pretty things, such as toys or jewels,—and, for educated persons, of books and pictures.

And the possession of such a store by the nation would signify, that there were no taxes to pay; that everybody had clothes enough, and some stuff laid by for next year; that everybody had food enough, and plenty of salted pork, pickled walnuts, potted shrimps, or other conserves, in the cupboard; that everybody had jewels enough, and some of the biggest laid by, in treasuries and museums; and, of persons caring for such things, that everybody had as many books and pictures as they could read or look at; with quantities of the highest quality besides, in easily accessible public libraries and galleries.

Now the wretches who have, at present, the teaching of the people in their hands, through the public press, tell them that it is not "practical" to attempt to bring about this state of things;—and that their government, or money-collecting machine, must not buy wine, potatoes, jewels, or pictures for them; but *must* buy iron plates two feet thick, gunpowder, and red tape. And this popular instruction is given, you will find, in the end, by persons who know that they could not get a percentage themselves (without the public's coming to know it) on buying potatoes or pictures; but *can* get it, and a large one, on manufacturing iron, on committing wholesale murder, or on tying up papers with red tape.

Now the St. George's Company propose to themselves, —and, if the God they believe in, lives, will assuredly succeed in their proposition,—to put an end to this rascally and inhuman state of things, and bring about an honest and human state of them, instead. And they have already actually begun the accumulation of a National Store of good and useful things; by the collection and

administration of which, they are not themselves to de‐
rive any gain whatsoever, but the Nation only.

We are, therefore, at present, as I said at first, a com‐
pany established for a charitable purpose; the object of
charity being the entire body of the British nation, now
paying taxes to cheating capitalists. But we hope to in‐
clude, finally, in our ranks a large number of the people
themselves, and to make quite a different sort of people
of them, carrying out our company's laws, to the aboli‐
tion of many existing interests, and in abrogation of
many existing arrangements.

And the laws which we hope thus to see accepted are
none of them new; but have already been recommended
by all wise men, and practised by all truly prosperous
states; nor is there anything whatever new in the modes
of administration proposed;—and especially be it noted
there is nothing of the present leader's fancies, in any
part or character of the scheme—which is merely the ap‐
plication, to our nationally diseased thoughts and prac‐
tices, of the direct precepts of the true sages of past time
who are every one of them in harmony concerning all
that is necessary for men to do, feel, and know.

And we hope to establish these laws, not by violence
but by obeying them ourselves, to the extent of which
existing circumstances admit; and so gradually showing
the advantage of them, and making them acceptable to
others. Not that, for the enforcement of some of them
(the abolition of all manufactures that make the air un‐
wholesome, for instance), we shall hesitate to use the
strong hand, when once our hands are strong. But we
shall not begin by street riots to throw down our neigh‐
bor's chimneys, or break his machinery;—though what
we shall *end* in doing—God knows, not I,—but I have
my own thoughts concerning it; not at present needing
exposition.

The Companions, for the most part, will remain ex‐
actly in the condition of life they held before entering
the Society; but they will direct all their powers, and
some part of their revenues, in that condition, to the ad‐
vance of its interests. We hold it short-sighted and
ruinous policy to form separate institutions, or attempt
the sudden establishment of new systems of labor. Every

one of us must use the advantages he now possesses, whatever they may be, and contend with the difficulties arising out of his present position, gradually modifying it, as he can, into conformity with the laws which the Society desires may be ultimately observed by all its members.

The first of our conditions of Companionship is Honesty. We are a company of honest persons, vowing to have no fellowship with dishonest ones. Persons who do not know the meaning of the word "Honesty," or who would in anywise, for selfish convenience, tolerate any manner of cheating or lying, either in others or themselves, we class indiscriminately with the self-conscious rogues, for whom we have more respect; and our separation from all such is to be quite manifest and unmistakable. We do not go into monasteries,—we seek no freedom of conscience in foreign lands,—we profess no severities of asceticism at home. We simply refuse to have any dealings with rogues, whether at home or abroad.

I repeat, for this must be strictly understood, we are a company of honest persons; and will add to ourselves none but persons of that quality. We, for our own part, entirely decline to live by passing bad half-crowns, by selling bad goods, or by lying as to their relative quality. And we hold only such communication with persons guilty of such practices, as we should with any other manner of thieves or liars.

It will follow that anything gravely said by a Companion of St. George may be, without investigation, believed; and anything sold by one, without scrutiny, bought for what it is said to be,—of which recovery of old principles of human speech and commerce, no words can set forth the infinitude of beneficial consequences, when it is once brought about among a discernible and every day increasing body of persons.

The second condition of Companionship is the resolution, so far as we have ability, to earn our own living with our own hands; and not to allow, much less compel, other people to work for us: this duty being of double force,—first, as necessary to our own health and honor; but much more, as striking home at the ghastly universal crime of modern society,—stealing the laborer's bread from him (making him work, that is to say, for ours, as well as his own), and then abusing and despising him for the degradation of character which his perpetual toil involves; deliberately, in many cases, refusing to encourage him in economy, that we may have him at our mercy to grind in the mill; always selling as much gin and beer to him as we can persuade him to swill, at the rate of twentypence for twopence worth (see Letter 27), to fill our own pockets; and teaching him pious catechisms, that we may keep him our quiet slave.

We cannot, at present, all obey this great law concerning labor, however willing we may be; for we may not, in the condition of life in which we have been brought up, have been taught any manual labor by which we now could make a living. I myself, the present Master of the Society, cannot obey this, its second main law; but then I am only a makeshift Master, taking the place till somebody more fit for it be found. Sir Walter Scott's life, in the full strength of it at Ashestiel, and early at Abbotsford with his literary work done by ten, or at latest twelve in the morning; and the rest of the day spent in useful work with Tom Purdie in his woods, is a model of wise moral management of mind and body, for men of true literary power; but I had neither the country training of body, nor have the natural strength of brain, which can reach this ideal in anywise. Sir Walter wrote as a stream flows; but I do all my brain-work like a wrung sponge, and am tired out, and good for nothing, after it. Sir Walter was in the open air, farm-bred, and playing with lambs, while I was a poor little Cockney wretch, playing, in a dark London nursery, with a bunch of keys. I do the best I can, and know what ought to be: and that is all the Company really need of me. I would fain, at this moment, both for pleasure and duty's sake, be cutting the dead stems out of my wood, or learning to build a dry stone wall under my good mason, Mr. Usher, than writing these institutes of St. George; but the institutes are needed, and must be written by me, since there is nobody else to write them.

Anyone, therefore, may be a Companion of St. George who sincerely does what they can, to make themselves useful, and earn their daily bread by their own labor:

and some forms of intellectual or artistic labor, inconsistent (as a musician's) with other manual labor, are
accepted by the Society as useful; provided they be truly
undertaken for the good and help of all; and that the
intellectual laborer ask no more pay than any other workman. A scholar can generally live on less food than a
ploughman, and there is no conceivable reason why he
should have more. And if he be a false-hearted scholar,
or a bad painter or fiddler, there is infinite reason why
he should have less. My readers may have been surprised at the instant and eager assertion, as of a leading
principle, in the first of these letters (January '71), that
people cannot live by art. But I spoke swiftly, because
the attempt so to live is among the worst possible ways
they can take of injurious begging. There are a few, a
very few persons born in each generation, whose words
are worth hearing, whose art is worth seeing. These born
few will preach, or sing, or paint, in spite of you; they
will starve like grasshoppers, rather than stop singing;
and even if you don't choose to listen, it is charitable to
throw them some crumbs to keep them alive. But the
people who take to writing or painting as a means of
livelihood, because they think it genteel, are just by
so much more contemptible than common beggars, in that
they are noisy and offensive beggars. I am quite willing
to pay for keeping our poor vagabonds in the workhouse;
but not to pay them for grinding organs outside my door,
defacing the streets with bills and caricatures, tempting
young girls to read rubbishy novels, or deceiving the
whole nation to its ruin, in a thousand leagues square of
dirtily printed falsehood, every morning at breakfast.
Whatever in literature, art, or religion, is done for money,
is poisonous itself; and doubly deadly, in preventing the
hearing or seeing of the noble literature and art which
have been done for love and truth. If people cannot
make their bread by honest labor, let them at least make
no noise about the streets; but hold their tongues, and
hold out their idle hands humbly; and they shall be fed
kindly.

Then the third condition of Companionship is, that,
after we have done as much manual work as will earn
our food, we all of us discipline ourselves, our children,

and anyone else willing to be taught, in all the branches of honorable knowledge and graceful art attainable by us. Having honestly obtained our meat and drink, and having sufficiently eaten and drunken, we proceed, during the rest of the day, to seek after things better than meat and drink; and to provide for the nobler necessities of what, in ancient days, Englishmen used to call their souls.

To this end, we shall, as we increase in numbers, establish such churches and schools as may best guide religious feeling, and diffuse the love of sound learning and prudent art. And when I set myself first to the work of forming the Society, I was induced to do so chiefly by the consciousness that the balanced unison of artistic sensibility with scientific faculty, which enabled me at once to love Giotto, and learn from Galileo, gave me singular advantages for a work of this kind. More particularly, the course of study through which, after being trained in the severest schools of Protestant divinity, I became acquainted with the mythology of Greece, and legends of Rome, in their most vivid power over the believing minds of both nations, permits me now to accept with freedom and respect the concurrence of a wider range of persons holding different views on religious subjects, than any other scholar I know, at the present day, in England, would feel himself secure in the hope of reconciling to a common duty, and in uncontested elements of faith.

The scheme, and elementary means, of this common education, I am now occupied in arranging and choosing as I best may. In especial, I have set myself to write three grammars—of geology, botany, and zoology,—which will contain nothing but indisputable facts in those three branches of proper human learning; and which, if I live a little longer, will embrace as many facts as any ordinary schoolboy or schoolgirl need be taught. In these three grammars (*Deucalion, Proserpina,* and *Love's Meinie*) I shall accept every aid that sensible and earnest men of science can spare me, toward the task of popular education: and I hope to keep thankful records of the names of the persons who are making true discoveries in any of these sciences, and of the dates of such discovery,

which shall be unassailably trustworthy as far as they
extend. I hope also to be able to choose, and in some
degree provide, a body of popular literature of entirely
serviceable quality. Of some of the most precious books
needed, I am preparing, with the help of my friends,
new editions, for a common possession in all our school
libraries.

If I have powers fitted for this task (and I should not
have attempted it but in conviction that I have), they
are owing mainly to this one condition of my life, that,
from my youth up, I have been seeking the fame, and
honoring the work, of others;—never my own. I first
was driven into literature that I might defend the fame
of Turner; since that day I have been explaining the
power, or proclaiming the praise, of Tintoret,—of Luini,
—of Carpaccio,—of Botticelli,—of Carlyle;—never thinking for an instant of myself: and sacrificing what little
faculty, and large pleasure, I had in painting, either from
nature or noble art, that, if possible, I might bring others
to see what I rejoiced in, and understand what I had
deciphered. There has been no heroism in this, nor virtue;—but only, as far as I am myself concerned, quaint
ordering of Fate; but the result is, that I *have* at last
obtained an instinct of impartial and reverent judgment,
which sternly fits me for this final work, to which, if to
anything, I was appointed.

And for the right doing of it, and for all future work
of the same kind, requiring to be done for the Society
by other persons, it is absolutely needful that the person
charged with it should be implicitly trusted, and accurately obeyed by the Companions, in all matters necessary to the working of the Society. He cannot lose his
time in contention or persuasion; he must act undis-
turbedly, or his mind will not suffice for its toil; and
with concurrence of all the Society's power, or half their
power will be wasted, and the whole perverted, by hesitation, and opposition. His authority over them must
correspond precisely, in the war against the poverty and
vice of the State, to that of a Roman Dictator, in his
war against its external enemies.

Of a Roman *"Dictator,"* I say, observe; not a Roman
"Emperor." It is not the command of private will, but

the dictation of necessary law, which the Society obeys:
—only, the obedience must be absolute, and without question; faithful to the uttermost,—that is to say, trusting to the uttermost. The practice of faith and obedience to some of our fellow-creatures is the alphabet by which we learn the higher obedience to heaven; and it is not only needful to the prosperity of all noble united action, but essential to the happiness of all noble living spirits.

I have not, in my past letters, much noticed this condition of the Society's work; because its explanation will involve that of our religious creed to the full; and its enforcement must be in the very teeth of the mad-dog's creed of modernism, "I will not be dictated to," which contains the essence of all diabolical error. For, in sum, the moral scale is raised exactly according to the degree and motive of obedience. To be disobedient through temptation, is human sin, but to be disobedient for the sake of disobedience, fiendish sin. To be obedient for the sake of success in conduct, is human virtue; but to be obedient for the sake of obedience, angelic virtue.

The constitution of the Society is to be, therefore, that of an aristocracy electing an absolute chief (as the Senate of Rome their Dictator, or the Senate of Venice their Doge), who is to be entirely responsible for the conduct of the Society's affairs; to appoint its principal officers, and to grant or refuse admission to candidates for Companionship. But he is liable to deposition at any moment, by a vote of the majority of the Companions; and is to have no control over the property of the Society, but through the Trustees in whom that property is vested.

And now, for farther explanation of the details of our constitution and design, I must refer the reader to the *Fors* for March of this year; and, if he desires to pursue his inquiry, to the 8th, 9th, 11th, 17th, and 19th Letters of the previous series. These state clearly what we propose to do, and how: but for defence of our principles, the entire series of Letters must be studied; and that with quiet attention, for not a word of them has been written but with purpose. Some parts of the plan are confessedly unexplained, and others obscurely hinted at; nor do I choose to say how much of this indistinctness has been intentional. But I am well assured that if any patient and candid person cares to understand the book, and master its contents, he may do so with less pains than would be required for the reading of any ordinary philosophical treatise on equally important subjects.

Only readers should be clearly aware of one peculiarity in the manner of my writing in *Fors*, which might otherwise much mislead them:—namely, that if they will enclose in brackets with their pen, passages of evident irony, all the rest of the book is written with absolute seriousness and literalness of meaning. The violence, or grotesque aspect, of a statement may seem as if I were mocking; but this comes mainly of my endeavor to bring the absolute truth out into pure crystalline structure, unmodified by disguise of custom, or obscurity of language; for the result of that process is continually to reduce the facts into a form so contrary, if theoretical, to our ordinary impressions, and so contrary, if moral, to our ordinary practice, that the straightforward statement of them looks like a jest. But every such apparent jest will be found, if you think of it, a pure, very dreadful, and utterly imperious veracity.

With this understanding, the following series of aphorisms contain the gist of the book, and may serve to facilitate the arrangement of its incidental matter.

(1) Any form of government will work, provided the governors are real, and the people obey them; and none will work, if the governors are unreal, or the people disobedient. If you mean to have logs for kings, no quantity of liberty in choice of the wood will be of any profit to you:—nor will the wisest or best governor be able to serve you, if you mean to discuss his orders instead of obeying them. Read carefully on this matter Letter 13, §§ 7, 8.

(2) The first duty of government is to see that the people have food, fuel, and clothes. The second, that they have means of moral and intellectual education.

(3) Food, fuel, and clothes can only be got out of the ground, or sea, by muscular labor; and no man has any business to have any, unless he has done, if able, the muscular work necessary to produce his portion, or to render (as the labor of a surgeon or a physician renders) equivalent benefit to life. It indeed saves both toil and

time that one man should dig, another bake, and another
tan; but the digger, baker, and tanner are alike bound to
do their equal day's duty; and the business of the government is to see that they have done it, before it gives
any one of them their dinner.

(4) While the daily teaching of God's truth, doing of
His justice, and heroic bearing of His sword, are to be
required of every human soul according to its ability,
the mercenary professions of preaching, law-giving, and
fighting must be entirely abolished.

(5) Scholars, painters, and musicians may be advisedly
kept, on due pittance, to instruct or amuse the laborer
after, or at, his work; provided the duty be severely restricted to those who have high special gifts· of voice,
touch, and imagination,* and that the possessors of these
melodious lips, light-fingered hands, and lively brains, do
resolutely undergo the normal discipline necessary to insure their skill; the people whom they are to please,
understanding, always, that they cannot employ these
tricksy artists without working double-tides themselves, to
provide them with beef and ale.

(6) The duty of the government, as regards the distribution of its work, is to attend first to the wants of
the most necessitous; therefore, to take particular charge
of the back streets of every town; leaving the fine ones,
more or less, according to their finery, to take care of
themselves. And it is the duty of magistrates, and other
persons in authority, but especially of all bishops, to
know thoroughly the numbers, means of subsistence, and
modes of life of the poorest persons in the community,
and to be sure that *they* at least are virtuous and comfortable; for if poor persons be not virtuous, after all the
wholesome discipline of poverty, what must be the state
of the rich, under their perilous trials and temptations?—
but, on the other hand, if the poor are made comfortable
and good, the rich have a fair chance of entering the
kingdom of heaven also, if they choose to live honorably
and decently.

---

* Such limitation being secured by the severity of the required education in the public schools of art, and thought; and by the high
standard of examination fixed before granting license of exhibition, in
the public theatres, or picture galleries. [Ruskin's note.]

(7) Since all are to be made to labor for their living, and it is not possible to labor without materials and tools, these must be provided by the government, for all persons, in the necessary quantities. If bricks are to be made, clay and straw must be provided; if sheep are to be kept, grass; if coats are to be made, cloth; if oakum to be picked, oakum. All these raw materials, with the tools for working them, must be provided by the government, at first, free of cost to the laborer, the value of them being returned to them as the first-fruits of his toil; and no pawnbrokers or usurers may be allowed to live by lending sea to fishermen, air to fowlers, land to farmers, crooks to shepherds, or bellows to smiths.

(8) When the lands and seas belonging to any nation are all properly divided, cultivated, and fished, its population cannot be increased, except by importing food in exchange for useless articles,—that is to say, by living as the toy-manufacturers of some independent nation, which can both feed itself, and afford to buy toys besides. But no nation can long exist in this servile state. It must either emigrate, and form colonies to assist in cultivating the land which feeds it, or become entirely slavish and debased. The moment any nation begins to import food,* its political power and moral worth are ended.

(9) All the food, clothing, and fuel required by men, can be produced by the labor of their own arms on the earth and sea; all food is appointed to be so produced, and *must* be so produced, at their peril. If instead of taking the quantity of exercise made necessary to their bodies by God, in the work appointed by God, they take it in hunting or shooting, they become ignorant, irreligious, and finally insane, and seek to live by fighting as well as by hunting; whence the type of Nimrod, in the circle of the Hell-towers, which I desire you to study in Dante. If they do not take exercise at all, they become sensual, and insane in worse ways. *And it is phy-*

---

* It may always import such food as its climate cannot produce, in exchange for such food as it can; it may buy oranges with corn, or pepper with cheese. But not with articles that do not support life. Separate cities may honorably produce salable art; Limoges its enamel, Sheffield its whittle; but a *nation* must not live on enamel or whittles. [Ruskin's note. In memoranda for a projected index of *Fors*, Ruskin wrote that "the note needs expansion."]

sically impossible that true religious knowledge, or pure morality, should exist among any classes of a nation who do not work with their hands for their bread. Read Letter 11 carefully.

(10) The use of machinery* in agriculture throws a certain number of persons out of wholesome employment, who must thenceforward either do nothing, or mischief. The use of machinery in art destroys the national intellect; and, finally, renders all luxury impossible. All machinery needful in ordinary life to supplement human or animal labor may be moved by wind or water: while steam, or any modes of *heat-power,* may only be employed justifiably under extreme or special conditions of need; as for speed on main lines of communication, and for raising water from great depths, or other such work beyond human strength.

(11) No true luxury, wealth, or religion is possible to dirty persons; nor is it decent or human to attempt to compass any temporal prosperity whatever by the sacrifice of cleanliness. The speedy abolition of all abolishable filth is the first process of education;† the principles of which I state in the second group of aphorisms following.

(12) All education must be moral first; intellectual secondarily. Intellectual, before—(much more without) —moral education, is, in completeness, impossible; and in incompleteness, a calamity.

(13) Moral education begins in making the creature to be educated, clean, and obedient. This must be done thoroughly, and at any cost, and with any kind of compulsion rendered necessary by the nature of the animal, be it dog, child, or man.

(14) Moral education consists next in making the

---

* Foolish people are continually quibbling and stupefying themselves about the word "machine." Briefly, any instrument is a machine so far as its action is, in any particular, or moment, beyond the control of a human hand. A violin, a pencil, and a plough, are tools, not machines. A grinding organ, or a windmill, is a machine, not a tool: often the two are combined; thus a lathe is a machine, and the workman's chisel, used at it, a tool. [Ruskin's note.]

† The ghastly squalor of the once lovely fields of Dulwich, trampled into mud, and strewn with rags and paper by the filthy London population, bred in cigar smoke, which is attracted by the Crystal Palace, would alone neutralize all possible gentlemanly education in the district. [Ruskin's note.]

creature practically serviceable to other creatures, according to the nature and extent of its own capacities; taking care that these be healthily developed in such service. It may be a question how long, and to what extent, boys and girls of fine race may be allowed to run in the paddock before they are broken; but assuredly the sooner they are put to such work as they are able for, the better. Moral education is summed when the creature has been made to do its work with delight, and thoroughly; but this cannot be until some degree of intellectual education has been given also.

(15) Intellectual education consists in giving the creature the faculties of admiration, hope, and love.

These are to be taught by the study of beautiful Nature; the sight and history of noble persons; and the setting forth of noble objects of action.

(16) Since all noble persons hitherto existent in the world have trusted in the government of it by a supreme Spirit, and in that trust, or faith, have performed all their great actions, the history of these persons will finally mean the history of their faith; and the sum of intellectual education will be the separation of what is inhuman, in such faiths, and therefore perishing, from what is human, and, for human creatures, eternally true.

These sixteen aphorisms contain, as plainly as I can speak it, the substance of what I have hitherto taught, and am now purposed to enforce practice of, as far as I am able. It is no business of mine to think about possibilities;—any day, any moment, may raise up someone to take the carrying forward of the plan out of my hands, or to furnish me with larger means of prosecuting it; meantime, neither fastening nor slackening, I shall go on doing what I can, with the people, few or many, who are ready to help me.

Such help (to conclude with what simplest practical direction I can) may be given me by any persons interested in my plans, mainly by sending me money; secondly, by acting out as much as they agree with of the directions for private life given in *Fors;* and thirdly, by promulgating and recommending such principles. If they wish to do more than this, and to become actual members of the Company, they must write to me, giving

a short and clear account of their past lives, and present
circumstances. I then examine them on such points as
seem to me necessary; and if I accept them, I inscribe
their names in the roll, at Corpus Christi College, with
two of our masters for witnesses. This roll of the Company is written, hitherto, on the blank leaves of an
eleventh-century MS. of the Gospels, always kept in my
rooms; and would enable the Trustees, in case of my
death, at once to consult the Companions respecting the
disposition of the Society's property. As to the legal
tenure of that property, I have taken counsel with my
lawyer-friends till I am tired; and, as will be seen by
the statement in the second page of the Correspondence,
I purpose henceforward to leave all such legal arrangements to the discretion of the Companions themselves.

THE CATHOLIC PRAYER

[*Fors Clavigera*, Vol. V, Letter 58.]

"Deus, a quo sancta desideria, recta consilia, et justa sunt opera, da
servis tuis illam quam mundus dare non potest pacem, ut et corda
nostra mandatis tuis, et, hostium sublata formidine, tempora, sint tuâ
protectione tranquilla."

"God, from whom are all holy desires, right counsels, and just works,
give to Thy servants that peace which the world cannot, that both our
hearts, in Thy commandments, and our times, the fear of enemies being
taken away, may be calm under Thy guard."

THE adulteration of this great Catholic prayer in our
English church-service (as needless as it was senseless,
since the pure form of it contains nothing but absolutely
Christian prayer, and is as fit for the most stammering
Protestant lips as for Dante's), destroyed all the definite
meaning of it, and left merely the vague expression of
desire for peace, on quite unregarded terms. For of the
millions of people who utter the prayer at least weekly,
there is not one in a thousand who is ever taught, or can
for themselves find out, either what a holy desire means,
or a right counsel means, or a just work means,—or
what the world is, or what the peace is which it cannot
give. And half-an-hour after they have insulted God
by praying to Him in this deadest of all dead languages,
not understood of the people, they leave the church,

themselves pacified in their perennial determination to put no check on their natural covetousness; to act on their own opinions, be they right or wrong; to do whatever they can make money by, be it just or unjust; and to thrust themselves, with the utmost of their soul and strength, to the highest, by them attainable, pinnacle of the most bedrummed and betrumpeted booth in the Fair of the World.

The prayer, in its pure text, is essentially, indeed, a monastic one; but it is written for the great Monastery of the Servants of God, whom the world hates. It cannot be uttered with honesty but by these; nor can it ever be answered but with the peace bequeathed to these, "not as the world giveth."

Of which peace, the nature is not to be without war, but undisturbed in the midst of war; and not without enemies, but without fear of them. It is a peace without pain, because desiring only what is holy; without anxiety, because it thinks only what is right; without disappointment, because a just work is always successful; without sorrow, because "great peace have they which love Thy Law, and nothing shall offend them"; and without terror, because the God of all battles is its Guard.

So far as any living souls in the England of this day can use, understandingly, the words of this collect, they are already, consciously or not, companions of all good laborers in the vineyard of God. For those who use it reverently, yet have never set themselves to find out what the commandments of God are, nor how lovable they are, nor how far, instead of those commandments, the laws of the world are the only code they care for, nor how far they still think their own thoughts and speak their own words, it is assuredly time to search out these things. And I believe that, after having searched them out, no sincerely good and religious person would find, whatever his own particular form of belief might be, anything which he could reasonably refuse, or which he ought in anywise to fear to profess before all men, in the following statement of creed and resolution, which must be written with their own hand, and signed, with the solemnity of a vow, by every person received into the St. George's Company.

I. I trust in the Living God, Father Almighty, Maker of heaven and earth, and of all things and creatures visible and invisible.

I trust in the kindness of His law, and the goodness of His work.

And I will strive to love Him, and keep His law and see His work, while I live.

II. I trust in the nobleness of human nature, in the majesty of its faculties, the fulness of its mercy, and the joy of its love.

And I will strive to love my neighbor as myself, and, even when I cannot, will act as if I did.

III. I will labor, with such strength and opportunity as God gives me, for my own daily bread; and all that my hand finds to do, I will do with my might.

IV. I will not deceive, or cause to be deceived, any human being for my gain or pleasure; nor hurt, or cause to be hurt, any human being for my gain or pleasure; nor rob, or cause to be robbed, any human being for my gain or pleasure.

V. I will not kill nor hurt any living creature needlessly, nor destroy any beautiful thing, but will strive to save and comfort all gentle life, and guard and perfect all natural beauty, upon the earth.

VI. I will strive to raise my own body and soul daily into higher powers of duty and happiness; not in rivalship or contention with others, but for the help, delight, and honor of others, and for the joy and peace of my own life.

VII. I will obey all the laws of my country faithfully; and the orders of its monarch, and of all persons appointed to be in authority under its monarch, so far as such laws or commands are consistent with what I suppose to be the law of God; and when they are not, or seem in anywise to need change, I will oppose them loyally and deliberately, not with malicious, concealed, or disorderly violence.

VIII. And with the same faithfulness, and under the limits of the same obedience, which I render to the laws of my country, and the commands of its rulers, I will obey the laws of the Society called of St. George, into which I am this day received; and the orders of its masters, and of all persons appointed to be in authority under its masters, so long as I remain a Companion, called of St. George

The Mystery of Life and Its Arts

[*Sesame and Lilies,* Lecture III.]

WHEN I accepted the privilege of addressing you to-day, I was not aware of a restriction with respect to the topics of discussion which may be brought before this Society*—a restriction which, though entirely wise and right under the circumstances contemplated in its introduction, would necessarily have disabled me, thinking as I think, from preparing any lecture for you on the subject of art in a form which might be permanently useful. Pardon me, therefore, in so far as I must transgress such limitation; for indeed my infringement will be of the letter—not of the spirit—of your commands. In whatever I may say touching the religion which has been the foundation of art, or the policy which has contributed to its power, if I offend one, I shall offend all; for I shall take no note of any separations in creeds, or antagonisms in parties: neither do I fear that ultimately I shall offend any, by proving—or at least stating as capable of positive proof—the connection of all that is best in the crafts and arts of man, with the simplicity of his faith, and the sincerity of his patriotism.

But I speak to you under another disadvantage, by which I am checked in frankness of utterance, not here only, but everywhere: namely, that I am never fully aware how far my audiences are disposed to give me credit for real knowledge of my subject, or how far they grant me attention only because I have been sometimes thought an ingenious or pleasant essayist upon it. For I have had what, in many respects, I boldly call the misfortune, to set my words sometimes prettily together; not without a foolish vanity in the poor knack that I had of doing so: until I was heavily punished for this pride, by finding that many people thought of the words only, and cared nothing for their meaning. Happily, therefore, the power of using such pleasant language—if indeed it ever were mine—is passing away from me; and whatever I am now

---

* That no reference should be made to religious questions. [Ruskin's note.] The address was given before the Royal College of Science, Dublin, 1868.

able to say at all, I find myself forced to say with great plainness. For my thoughts have changed also, as my words have; and whereas in earlier life, what little influence I obtained was due perhaps chiefly to the enthusiasm with which I was able to dwell on the beauty of the physical clouds, and of their colors in the sky; so all the influence I now desire to retain must be due to the earnestness with which I am endeavoring to trace the form and beauty of another kind of cloud than those; the bright cloud of which it is written—"What is your life? It is even as a vapor that appeareth for a little time, and then vanisheth away."

I suppose few people reach the middle or latter period of their age, without having, at some moment of change or disappointment, felt the truth of those bitter words; and been startled by the fading of the sunshine from the cloud of their life into the sudden agony of the knowledge that the fabric of it was as fragile as a dream, and the endurance of it as transient as the dew. But it is not always that, even at such times of melancholy surprise, we can enter into any true perception that this human life shares in the nature of it, not only the evanescence, but the mystery of the cloud; that its avenues are wreathed in darkness, and its forms and courses no less fantastic, than spectral and obscure; so that not only in the vanity which we cannot grasp, but in the shadow which we cannot pierce, it is true of this cloudy life of ours, that "man walketh in a vain shadow, and disquieteth himself in vain."

And least of all, whatever may have been the eagerness of our passions, or the height of our pride, are we able to understand in its depth the third and most solemn character in which our life is like those clouds of heaven; that to it belongs not only their transience, not only their mystery, but also their power; that in the cloud of the human soul there is a fire stronger than the lightning, and a grace more precious than the rain; and that though of the good and evil it shall one day be said alike, that the place that knew them knows them no more, there is an infinite separation between those whose brief presence had there been a blessing, like the mist of Eden that went up from the earth to water the garden, and those whose place knew them only as a drifting and changeful shade, of whom the heavenly sentence is, that they are "wells without water; clouds that are carried with a tempest, to whom the mist of darkness is reserved forever."

To those among us, however, who have lived long enough to form some just estimate of the rate of the changes which are, hour by hour in accelerating catastrophe, manifesting themselves in the laws, the arts, and the creeds of men, it seems to me, that now at least, if never at any former time, the thoughts of the true nature of our life, and of its powers and responsibilities, should present themselves with absolute sadness and sternness. And although I know that this feeling is much deepened in my own mind by disappointment, which, by chance, has attended the greater number of my cherished purposes, I do not for that reason distrust the feeling itself, though I am on my guard against an exaggerated degree of it: nay, I rather believe that in periods of new effort and violent change, disappointment is a wholesome medicine; and that in the secret of it, as in the twilight so beloved by Titian, we may see the colors of things with deeper truth than in the most dazzling sunshine. And because these truths about the works of men, which I want to bring to-day before you, are most of them sad ones, though at the same time helpful; and because also I believe that your kind Irish hearts will answer more gladly to the truthful expression of a personal feeling, than to the exposition of an abstract principle, I will permit myself so much unreserved speaking of my own causes of regret, as may enable you to make just allowance for what, according to your sympathies, you will call either the bitterness, or the insight, of a mind which has surrendered its best hopes, and been foiled in its favorite aims.

I spent the ten strongest years of my life (from twenty to thirty), in endeavoring to show the excellence of the work of the man whom I believed, and rightly believed, to be the greatest painter of the schools of England since Reynolds. I had then perfect faith in the power of every great truth of beauty to prevail ultimately, and take its right place in usefulness and honor; and I strove to bring the painter's work into this due place, while the painter was yet alive. But he knew, better than I, the uselessness of talking about what people could not see for themselves. He always discouraged me scornfully, even when he thanked me—and he died before even the superficial effect of my work was visible. I went on, however, thinking I could at least be of use to the public, if not to him, in proving his power. My books got talked about a little. The prices of modern pictures, generally, rose, and I was beginning to take some pleasure in a sense of gradual victory, when, fortunately or unfortunately, an opportunity of perfect trial undeceived me at once, and forever. The Trustees of the National Gallery commissioned me to arrange the Turner drawings there, and permitted me to prepare three hundred examples of his studies from nature, for exhibition at Kensington. At Kensington they were, and are, placed for exhibition; but they are not exhibited, for the room in which they hang is always empty.

Well—this showed me at once, that those ten years of my life had been, in their chief purpose, lost. For that, I did not so much care; I had, at least, learned my own business thoroughly, and should be able, as I fondly supposed, after such a lesson, now to use my knowledge, with better effect. But what I did care for was the—to me frightful—discovery, that the most splendid genius in the arts might be permitted by Providence to labor and perish uselessly; that in the very fineness of it there might be something rendering it invisible to ordinary eyes; but that, with this strange excellence, faults might be mingled which would be as deadly as its virtues were vain; that the glory of it was perishable, as well as invisible, and the gift and grace of it might be to us as snow in summer and as rain in harvest.

That was the first mystery of life to me. But, while my best energy was given to the study of painting, I had put collateral effort, more prudent if less enthusiastic, into that of architecture; and in this I could not complain of meeting with no sympathy. Among several personal reasons which caused me to desire that I might give this, my closing lecture on the subject of art here, in Ireland, one of the chief was, that in reading it, I should stand near the beautiful building,—the engineer's school of your college,—which was the first realization I had the joy to see, of the principles I had, until then, been endeavoring to teach! but which, alas, is now, to me, no more than the richly canopied monument of one of the most earnest souls that ever gave itself to the arts, and one of my truest and most loving friends, Benjamin Woodward. Nor was it here in Ireland only that I received the help of Irish sympathy and genius. When to another friend, Sir Thomas Deane, with Mr. Woodward, was entrusted the building of the museum at Oxford, the best details of the work were executed by sculptors who had been born and trained here; and the first window of the façade of the building, in which was inaugurated the study of natural science in England, in true fellowship with literature, was carved from my design by an Irish sculptor.

You may perhaps think that no man ought to speak of disappointment, to whom, even in one branch of labor, so much success was granted. Had Mr. Woodward now been beside me, I had not so spoken; but his gentle and passionate spirit was cut off from the fulfilment of its purposes, and the work we did together is now become vain. It may not be so in future; but the architecture we endeavored to introduce is inconsistent alike with the reckless luxury, the deforming mechanism, and the squalid misery of modern cities; among the formative fashions of the day, aided, especially in England, by ecclesiastical sentiment, it indeed obtained notoriety; and sometimes behind an engine furnace, or a railroad bank, you may detect the pathetic discord of its momentary grace, and, with toil, decipher its floral carvings choked with soot. I felt answerable to the schools I loved, only for their injury. I perceived that this new portion of my strength had also been spent in vain; and from amidst streets of iron, and palaces of crystal, shrank back at last to the carving of the mountain and color of the flower.

And still I could tell of failure, and failure repeated, as years went on; but I have trespassed enough on your patience to show you, in part, the causes of my discouragement. Now let me more deliberately tell you its results. You know there is a tendency in the minds of

many men, when they are heavily disappointed in the
main purposes of their life, to feel, and perhaps in warning, perhaps in mockery, to declare, that life itself is a
vanity. Because it has disappointed them, they think
its nature is of disappointment always, or at best, of
pleasure that can be grasped by imagination only; that
the cloud of it has no strength nor fire within; but is a
painted cloud only, to be delighted in, yet despised. You
know how beautifully Pope has expressed this particular
phase of thought:—

> "Meanwhile opinion gilds, with varying rays,
> These painted clouds that beautify our days;
> Each want of happiness by hope supplied,
> And each vacuity of sense, by pride.
> Hope builds as fast as Knowledge can destroy;
> In Folly's cup, still laughs the bubble joy.
> One pleasure past, another still we gain,
> And not a vanity is given in vain."

But the effect of failure upon my own mind has been
just the reverse of this. The more that my life disappointed me, the more solemn and wonderful it became to
me. It seemed, contrarily to Pope's saying, that the
vanity of it *was* indeed given in vain; but that there
was something behind the veil of it, which was not
vanity. It became to me not a painted cloud, but a terrible and impenetrable one: not a mirage, which vanished as I drew near, but a pillar of darkness, to which
I was forbidden to draw near. For I saw that both my
own failure, and such success in petty things as in its
poor triumph seemed to me worse than failure, came
from the want of sufficiently earnest effort to understand
the whole law and meaning of existence, and to bring it
to noble and due end; as, on the other hand, I saw more
and more clearly that all enduring success in the arts,
or in any other occupation, had come from the ruling of
lower purposes, not by a conviction of their nothingness,
but by a solemn faith in the advancing power of human
nature, or in the promise, however dimly apprehended,
that the mortal part of it would one day be swallowed
up in immortality; and that, indeed, the arts themselves
never had reached any vital strength or honor, but in

the effort to proclaim this immortality, and in the service either of great and just religion, or of some unselfish patriotism, and law of such national life as must be the foundation of religion.

Nothing that I have ever said is more true or necessary—nothing has been more misunderstood or misapplied—than my strong assertion that the arts can never be right themselves, unless their motive is right. It is misunderstood this way: weak painters, who have never learned their business, and cannot lay a true line, continually come to me, crying out—"Look at this picture of mine; it *must* be good, I had such a lovely motive. I have put my whole heart into it, and taken years to think over its treatment." Well, the only answer for these people is—if one had the cruelty to make it—"Sir, you cannot think over *anything* in any number of years,—you haven't the head to do it; and though you had fine motives, strong enough to make you burn yourself in a slow fire, if only first you could paint a picture, you can't paint one, nor half an inch of one; you haven't the hand to do it."

But, far more decisively we have to say to the men who *do* know their business, or may know it if they choose—"Sir, you have this gift, and a mighty one; see that you serve your nation faithfully with it. It is a greater trust than ships and armies: you might cast *them* away, if you were their captain, with less treason to your people than in casting your own glorious power away, and serving the devil with it instead of men. Ships and armies you may replace if they are lost, but a great intellect, once abused, is a curse to the earth forever."

This, then, I meant by saying that the arts must have noble motive. This also I said respecting them, that they never had prospered, nor could prosper, but when they had such true purpose, and were devoted to the proclamation of divine truth or law. And yet I saw also that they had always failed in this proclamation—that poetry, and sculpture, and painting, though only great when they strove to teach us something about the gods, never had taught us anything trustworthy about the gods, but had always betrayed their trust in the crisis of it, and, with their powers at the full reach, became ministers to pride and to lust. And I felt also, with increasing amazement, the unconquerable apathy in ourselves and hearers, no less than in these the teachers; and that while the wisdom and rightness of every act and art of life could only be consistent with a right understanding of the ends of life, we were all plunged as in a languid dream—our hearts fat, and our eyes heavy, and our ears closed, lest the inspiration of hand or voice should reach us—lest we should see with our eyes, and understand with our hearts, and be healed.

This intense apathy in all of us is the first great mystery of life; it stands in the way of every perception, every virtue. There is no making ourselves feel enough astonishment at it. That the occupations or pastimes of life should have no motive, is understandable; but— That life itself should have no motive—that we neither care to find out what it may lead to, nor to guard against its being forever taken away from us—here is a mystery indeed. For just suppose I were able to call at this moment to anyone in this audience by name, and to tell him positively that I knew a large estate had been lately left to him on some curious conditions; but that though I knew it was large, I did not know how large, nor even where it was—whether in the East Indies or the West, or in England, or at the Antipodes. I only knew it was a vast estate, and that there was a chance of his losing it altogether if he did not soon find out on what terms it had been left to him. Suppose I were able to say this positively to any single man in this audience, and he knew that I did not speak without warrant, do you think that he would rest content with that vague knowledge, if it were anywise possible to obtain more? Would he not give every energy to find some trace of the facts, and never rest till he had ascertained where this place was, and what it was like? And suppose he were a young man, and all he could discover by his best endeavor was that the estate was never to be his at all, unless he persevered, during certain years of probation, in an orderly and industrious life; but that, according to the rightness of his conduct, the portion of the estate assigned to him would be greater or less, so that it literally depended on his behavior from day to day whether he got ten thousand

a year, or thirty thousand a year, or nothing whatever—
would you not think it strange if the youth never troubled
himself to satisfy the conditions in any way, nor ever to
know what was required of him, but lived exactly as he
chose, and never inquired whether his chances of the
estate were increasing or passing away? Well, you know
that this is actually and literally so with the greater
number of the educated persons now living in Christian
countries. Nearly every man and woman in any company such as this, outwardly professes to believe—and a
large number unquestionably think they believe—much
more than this; not only that a quite unlimited estate
is in prospect for them if they please the Holder of it,
but that the infinite contrary of such a possession—an
estate of perpetual misery—is in store for them if they
displease this great Land-Holder, this great Heaven-
Holder. And yet there is not one in a thousand of these
human souls that cares to think, for ten minutes of the
day, where this estate is or how beautiful it is, or what
kind of life they are to lead in it, or what kind of life
they must lead to obtain it.

You fancy that you care to know this: so little do you
care that, probably, at this moment many of you are
displeased with me for talking of the matter! You came
to hear about the Art of this world, not about the Life
of the next, and you are provoked with me for talking of
what you can hear any Sunday in church. But do not
be afraid. I will tell you something before you go about
pictures, and carvings, and pottery, and what else you
would like better to hear of than the other world. Nay,
perhaps you say, "We want you to talk of pictures and
pottery, because we are sure that you know something of
them, and you know nothing of the other world." Well
—I don't. That is quite true. But the very strangeness
and mystery of which I urge you to take notice, is in
this—that I do not;—nor you either. Can you answer a
single bold question unflinchingly about that other world?
—Are you sure there is a heaven? Sure there is a hell?
Sure that men are dropping before your faces through
the pavements of these streets into eternal life, or sure
that they are not? Sure that at your own death you are
going to be delivered from all sorrow, to be endowed

with all virtue, to be gifted with all felicity, and raised into perpetual companionship with a King, compared to whom the kings of the earth are as grasshoppers, and the nations as the dust of His feet? Are you sure of this? or, if not sure, do any of us so much as care to make it sure? and, if not, how can anything that we do be right—how can anything we think be wise? what honor can there be in the arts that amuse us, or what profit in the possessions that please?

Is not this a mystery of life?

But farther, you may, perhaps, think it a beneficent ordinance for the generality of men that they do not, with earnestness or anxiety, dwell on such questions of the future because the business of the day could not be done if this kind of thought were taken by all of us for the morrow. Be it so: but at least we might anticipate that the greatest and wisest of us, who were evidently the appointed teachers of the rest, would set themselves apart to seek out whatever could be surely known of the future destinies of their race; and to teach this in no rhetorical or ambiguous manner, but in the plainest and most severely earnest words.

Now, the highest representatives of men who have thus endeavored, during the Christian era, to search out these deep things, and relate them, are Dante and Milton. There are none who for earnestness of thought, for mastery of word, can be classed with these. I am not at present, mind you, speaking of persons set apart in any priestly or pastoral office, to deliver creeds to us, or doctrines; but of men who try to discover and set forth, as far as by human intellect is possible, the facts of the other world. Divines may perhaps teach us how to arrive there, but only these two poets have in any powerful manner striven to discover, or in any definite words professed to tell, what we shall see and become there; or how those upper and nether worlds are, and have been, inhabited.

And what have they told us? Milton's account of the most important event in his whole system of the universe, the fall of the angels, is evidently unbelievable to himself; and the more so, that it is wholly founded on, and in a great part spoiled and degraded from, Hesiod's account of the decisive war of the younger gods with the Titans. The rest of his poem is a picturesque drama, in which every artifice of invention is visibly and consciously employed; not a single fact being, for an instant, conceived as tenable by any living faith. Dante's conception is far more intense, and, by himself, for the time, not to be escaped from; it is indeed a vision, but a vision only, and that one of the wildest that ever entranced a soul— a dream in which every grotesque type or phantasy of heathen tradition is renewed, and adorned; and the destinies of the Christian Church, under their most sacred symbols, become literally subordinate to the praise, and are only to be understood by the aid, of one dear Florentine maiden.

I tell you truly that, as I strive more with this strange lethargy and trance in myself, and awake to the meaning and power of life, it seems daily more amazing to me that men such as these should dare to play with the most precious truths (or the most deadly untruths), by which the whole human race listening to them could be informed, or deceived;—all the world their audiences forever, with pleased ear, and passionate heart;—and yet, to this submissive infinitude of souls, and evermore succeeding and succeeding multitude, hungry for bread of life, they do but play upon sweetly modulated pipes; with pompous nomenclature adorn the councils of hell; touch a troubadour's guitar to the courses of the sun; and fill the openings of eternity, before which prophets have veiled their faces, and which angels desire to look into, with idle puppets of their scholastic imagination, and melancholy lights of frantic faith in their lost mortal love.

Is not this a mystery of life?

But more. We have to remember that these two great teachers were both of them warped in their temper, and thwarted in their search for truth. They were men of intellectual war, unable, through darkness of controversy, or stress of personal grief, to discern where their own ambition modified their utterances of the moral law; or their own agony mingled with their anger at its violation. But greater men than these have been—innocent-hearted—too great for contest. Men, like Homer and Shakespeare, of so unrecognized personality, that it disappears in future ages, and becomes ghostly, like the tradition of a lost heathen god. Men, therefore, to whose unoffended, uncondemning sight, the whole of human nature reveals itself in a pathetic weakness, with which they will not strive; or in mournful and transitory strength, which they dare not praise. And all Pagan and Christian Civilization thus becomes subject to them. It does not matter how little, or how much, any of us have read, either of Homer or Shakespeare; everything round us, in substance, or in thought, has been moulded by them. All Greek gentlemen were educated under Homer. All Roman gentlemen, by Greek literature. All Italian, and French, and English gentlemen, by Roman literature, and by its principles. Of the scope of Shakespeare, I will say only, that the intellectual measure of every man since born, in the domains of creative thought, may be assigned to him, according to the degree in which he has been taught by Shakespeare. Well, what do these two men, centres of mortal intelligence, deliver to us of conviction respecting what it most behooves that intelligence to grasp? What is their hope—their crown of rejoicing? what manner of exhortation have they for us, or of rebuke? what lies next their own hearts, and dictates their undying words? Have they any peace to promise to our unrest—any redemption to our misery?

Take Homer first, and think if there is any sadder image of human fate than the great Homeric story. The main features in the character of Achilles are its intense desire of justice, and its tenderness of affection. And in that bitter song of the *Iliad,* this man, though aided continually by the wisest of the gods, and burning with the desire of justice in his heart, becomes yet, through ill-governed passion, the most unjust of men: and, full of the deepest tenderness in his heart, becomes yet, through ill-governed passion, the most cruel of men. Intense alike in love and in friendship, he loses, first his mistress, and then his friend; for the sake of the one, he surrenders to death the armies of his own land; for the sake of the other, he surrenders all. Will a man lay down his life for his friend? Yea—even for his *dead* friend, this Achilles, though goddess-born, and goddess-taught, gives up his kingdom, his country, and his life—casts alike the innocent and guilty, with himself, into one gulf of slaughter, and dies at last by the hand of the basest of his adversaries.

Is not this a mystery of life?

But what, then, is the message to us of our own poet, and searcher of hearts, after fifteen hundred years of Christian faith have been numbered over the graves of men? Are his words more cheerful than the Heathen's —is his hope more near—his trust more sure—his reading of fate more happy? Ah, no! He differs from the Heathen poet chiefly in this—that he recognizes, for deliverance, no gods nigh at hand; and that, by petty chance — by momentary folly — by broken message — by fool's tyranny—or traitor's snare, the strongest and most righteous are brought to their ruin, and perish without word of hope. He indeed, as part of his rendering of character, ascribes the power and modesty of habitual devotion to the gentle and the just. The death-bed of Katharine is bright with visions of angels; and the great soldier-king, standing by his few dead, acknowledges the presence of the Hand that can save alike by many or by few. But observe that from those who with deepest spirit, meditate, and with deepest passion, mourn, there are no such words as these; nor in their hearts are any such consolations. Instead of the perpetual sense of the helpful presence of the Deity, which, through all heathen tradition, is the source of heroic strength, in battle, in exile, and in the valley of the shadow of death, we find only in the great Christian poet, the consciousness of a moral law, through which "the gods are just, and of our pleasant vices make instruments to scourge us"; and of the resolved arbitration of the destinies, that conclude into precision of doom what we feebly and blindly began; and force us, when our indiscretion serves us, and our deepest plots do pall, to the confession, that "there's a divinity that shapes our ends, rough hew them how we will."

Is not this a mystery of life?

Be it so, then. About this human life that is to be, or that is, the wise religious men tell us nothing that we can trust; and the wise contemplative men, nothing that can give us peace. But there is yet a third class, to

whom we may turn—the wise practical men. We have
sat at the feet of the poets who sang of heaven, and they
have told us their dreams. We have listened to the poets
who sang of earth, and they have chanted to us dirges
and words of despair. But there is one class of men
more:—men, not capable of vision, nor sensitive to sorrow, but firm of purpose—practised in business; learned
in all that can be (by handling,) known. Men, whose
hearts and hopes are wholly in this present world, from
whom, therefore, we may surely learn, at least, how, at
present, conveniently to live in it. What will *they* say
to us, or show us by example? These kings—these coun-
cillors—these statesmen and builders of kingdoms—these
capitalists and men of business, who weigh the earth, and
the dust of it, in a balance. They know the world, surely;
and what is the mystery of life to us, is none to them.
They can surely show us how to live, while we live, and
to gather out of the present world what is best.

I think I can best tell you their answer, by telling you
a dream I had once. For though I am no poet, I have
dreams sometimes:—I dreamed I was at a child's May-
day party, in which every means of entertainment had
been provided for them, by a wise and kind host. It was
in a stately house, with beautiful gardens attached to it;
and the children had been set free in the rooms and gardens, with no care whatever but how to pass their afternoon rejoicingly. They did not, indeed, know much
about what was to happen next day; and some of them, I
thought, were a little frightened, because there was a
chance of their being sent to a new school where there
were examinations; but they kept the thoughts of that
out of their heads as well as they could, and resolved to
enjoy themselves. The house, I said, was in a beautiful
garden, and in the garden were all kinds of flowers; sweet,
grassy banks for rest; and smooth lawns for play; and
pleasant streams and woods; and rocky places for climbing. And the children were happy for a little while,
but presently they separated themselves into parties; and
then each party declared it would have a piece of the
garden for its own, and that none of the others should
have anything to do with that piece. Next, they quar-
relled violently which pieces they would have; and at last

the boys took up the thing, as boys should do, "practically," and fought in the flower-beds till there was hardly a flower left standing; then they trampled down each other's bits of the garden out of spite; and the girls cried till they could cry no more; and so they all lay down at last breathless in the ruin, and waited for the time when they were to be taken home in the evening.*

Meanwhile, the children in the house had been making themselves happy also in their manner. For them, there had been provided every kind of indoor pleasure: there was music for them to dance to; and the library was open, with all manner of amusing books; and there was a museum full of the most curious shells, and animals, and birds; and there was a workshop, with lathes and carpenter's tools, for the ingenious boys; and there were pretty fantastic dresses, for the girls to dress in; and there were microscopes, and kaleidoscopes; and whatever toys a child could fancy; and a table, in the dining-room, loaded with everything nice to eat.

But, in the midst of all this, it struck two or three of the more "practical" children, that they would like some of the brass-headed nails that studded the chairs; and so they set to work to pull them out. Presently, the others, who were reading, or looking at shells, took a fancy to do the like; and, in a little while, all the children, nearly, were spraining their fingers, in pulling out brass-headed nails. With all that they could pull out, they were not satisfied; and then, everybody wanted some of somebody else's. And at last, the really practical and sensible ones declared, that nothing was of any real consequence, that afternoon, except to get plenty of brass-headed nails; and that the books, and the cakes, and the microscopes were of no use at all in themselves, but only, if they could be exchanged for nail-heads. And at last they began to fight for nail-heads, as the others fought for the bits of garden. Only here and there, a despised one shrank away into a corner, and tried to get a little quiet with a book, in the midst of the noise; but all the

---

* I have sometimes been asked what this means. I intended it to set forth the wisdom of men in war contending for kingdoms, and what follows to set forth their wisdom in peace, contending for wealth. [Ruskin's note.]

practical ones thought of nothing else but counting nail-heads all the afternoon—even though they knew they would not be allowed to carry so much as one brass knob away with them. But no—it was—"who has most nails? I have a hundred, and you have fifty; or, I have a thousand, and you have two. I must have as many as you before I leave the house, or I cannot possibly go home in peace." At last, they made so much noise that I awoke, and thought to myself, "What a false dream that is, of *children!*" The child is the father of the man; and wiser. Children never do such foolish things. Only men do.

But there is yet one last class of persons to be interrogated. The wise religious men we have asked in vain; the wise contemplative men, in vain; the wise worldly men, in vain. But there is another group yet. In the midst of this vanity of empty religion—of tragic contemplation—of wrathful and wretched ambition, and dispute for dust, there is yet one great group of persons, by whom all these disputers live—the persons who have determined, or have had it by a beneficent Providence determined for them, that they will do something useful; that whatever may be prepared for them hereafter, or happen to them here, they will, at least, deserve the food that God gives them by winning it honorably: and that, however fallen from the purity, or far from the peace, of Eden, they will carry out the duty of human dominion, though they have lost its felicity; and dress and keep the wilderness, though they no more can dress or keep the garden.

These,—hewers of wood, and drawers of water,—these, bent under burdens, or torn of scourges—these, that dig and weave—that plant and build; workers in wood, and in marble, and in iron—by whom all food, clothing, habitation, furniture, and means of delight are produced, for themselves, and for all men besides; men, whose deeds are good, though their words may be few; men, whose lives are serviceable, be they never so short, and worthy of honor, be they never so humble;—from these, surely, at least, we may receive some clear message of teaching; and pierce, for an instant, into the mystery of life, and of its arts.

Yes; from these, at last, we do receive a lesson. But I grieve to say, or rather—for that is the deeper truth of the matter—I rejoice to say—this message of theirs can only be received by joining them—not by thinking about them.

You sent for me to talk to you of art; and I have obeyed you in coming. But the main thing I have to tell you is,—that art must not be talked about. The fact that there is talk about it at all, signifies that it is ill done, or cannot be done. No true painter ever speaks, or ever has spoken, much of his art. The greatest speak nothing. Even Reynolds is no exception, for he wrote of all that he could not himself do, and was utterly silent respecting all that he himself did.

The moment a man can really do his work he becomes speechless about it. All words become idle to him— all theories.

Does a bird need to theorize about building its nest, or boast of it when built? All good work is essentially done that way—without hesitation, without difficulty, without boasting; and in the doers of the best, there is an inner and involuntary power which approximates literally to the instinct of an animal—nay, I am certain that in the most perfect human artists, reason does *not* supersede instinct, but is added to an instinct as much more divine than that of the lower animals as the human body is more beautiful than theirs; that a great singer sings not with less instinct than the nightingale, but with more—only more various, applicable, and governable; that a great architect does not build with less instinct than the beaver or the bee, but with more—with an innate cunning of proportion that embraces all beauty, and a divine ingenuity of skill that improvises all construction. But be that as it may—be the instinct less or more than that of inferior animals—like or unlike theirs, still the human art is dependent on that first, and then upon an amount of practice, of science,—and of imagination disciplined by thought, which the true possessor of it knows to be incommunicable, and the true critic of it, inexplicable, except through long process of laborious years. That journey of life's conquest, in which hills over hills, and Alps on Alps arose, and sank,—do you think you can make another trace it painlessly by talking? Why, you cannot even carry us up an Alp, by talking. You can guide us up it, step by step, no otherwise—even so, best silently. You girls, who have been among the hills, know how the bad guide chatters and gesticulates, and it is "Put your foot here"; and "Mind how you balance yourself there"; but the good guide walks on quietly, without a word, only with his eyes on you when need is, and his arm like an iron bar, if need be.

In that slow way, also, art can be taught—if you have faith in your guide, and will let his arm be to you as an iron bar when need is. But in what teacher of art have you such faith? Certainly not in me; for, as I told you at first, I know well enough it is only because you think I can talk, not because you think I know my business, that you let me speak to you at all. If I were to tell you anything that seemed to you strange you would not believe it, and yet it would only be in telling you strange things that I could be of use to you. I could be of great use to you—infinite use—with brief saying, if you would believe it; but you would not, just because the thing that would be of real use would displease you. You are all wild, for instance, with admiration of Gustave Doré. Well, suppose I were to tell you, in the strongest terms I could use, that Gustave Doré's art was bad—bad, not in weakness, — not in failure, — but bad with dreadful power—the power of the Furies and the Harpies mingled, enraging, and polluting; that so long as you looked at it, no perception of pure or beautiful art was possible for you. Suppose I were to tell you that! What would be the use? Would you look at Gustave Doré less? Rather, more, I fancy. On the other hand, I could soon put you into good humor with me, if I chose. I know well enough what you like, and how to praise it to your better liking. I could talk to you about moonlight, and twilight, and spring flowers, and autumn leaves, and the Madonnas of Raphael—how motherly! and the Sibyls of Michael Angelo—how majestic! and the Saints of Angelico—how pious! and the Cherubs of Correggio—how delicious! Old as I am, I could play you a tune on the harp yet, that you would dance to. But neither you nor

I should be a bit the better or wiser; or, if we were, our increased wisdom could be of no practical effect. For, indeed, the arts, as regards teachableness, differ from the sciences also in this, that their power is founded not merely on facts which can be communicated, but on dispositions which require to be created. Art is neither to be achieved by effort of thinking, nor explained by accuracy of speaking. It is the instinctive and necessary result of power, which can only be developed through the mind of successive generations, and which finally burst into life under social conditions as slow of growth as the faculties they regulate. Whole æras of mighty history are summed, and the passions of dead myriads are concentrated, in the existence of a noble art; and if that noble art were among us, we should feel it and rejoice; not caring in the least to hear lectures on it; and since it is not among us, be assured we have to go back to the root of it, or, at least, to the place where the stock of it is yet alive, and the branches began to die.

And now, may I have your pardon for pointing out, partly with reference to matters which are at this time of greater moment than the arts—that if we undertook such recession to the vital germ of national arts that have decayed, we should find a more singular arrest of their power in Ireland than in any other European country? For in the eighth century Ireland possessed a school of art in her manuscripts and sculpture, which, in many of its qualities—apparently in all essential qualities of decorative invention—was quite without rival; seeming as if it might have advanced to the highest triumphs in architecture and in painting. But there was one fatal flaw in its nature, by which it was stayed, and stayed with a conspicuousness of pause to which there is no parallel: so that, long ago, in tracing the progress of European schools from infancy to strength, I chose for the students of Kensington, in a lecture since published, two characteristic examples of early art, of equal skill; but in the one case, skill which was progressive—in the other, skill which was at pause. In the one case, it was work receptive of correction—hungry for correction; and in the other, work which inherently rejected correction. I chose for them a corrigible Eve, and an incorrigible Angel, and

I grieve to say that the incorrigible Angel was also an Irish Angel!

And the fatal difference lay wholly in this. In both pieces of art there was an equal falling short of the needs of fact; but the Lombardic Eve knew she was in the wrong, and the Irish Angel thought himself all right. The eager Lombardic sculptor, though firmly insisting on his childish idea, yet showed in the irregular broken touches of the features, and the imperfect struggle for softer lines in the form, a perception of beauty and law that he could not render; there was the strain of effort, under conscious imperfection, in every line. But the Irish missal-painter had drawn his angel with no sense of failure, in happy complacency, and put red dots into the palm of each hand, and rounded the eyes into perfect circles, and, I regret to say, left the mouth out altogether, with perfect satisfaction to himself.

May I without offence ask you to consider whether this mode of arrest in ancient Irish art may not be indicative of points of character which even yet, in some measure, arrest your national power? I have seen much of Irish character, and have watched it closely, for I have also much loved it. And I think the form of failure to which it is most liable is this,—that being generous-hearted, and wholly intending always to do right, it does not attend to the external laws of right, but thinks it must necessarily do right because it means to do so, and therefore does wrong without finding it out; and then, when the consequences of its wrong come upon it, or upon others connected with it, it cannot conceive that the wrong is in any wise of its causing or of its doing, but flies into wrath, and a strange agony of desire for justice, as feeling itself wholly innocent, which leads it farther astray, until there is nothing that it is not capable of doing with a good conscience.

But mind, I do not mean to say that, in past or present relations between Ireland and England, you have been wrong, and we right. Far from that, I believe that in all great questions of principle, and in all details of administration of law, you have been usually right, and we wrong; sometimes in misunderstanding you, sometimes in resolute iniquity to you. Nevertheless, in all disputes between states, though the stronger is nearly always mainly in the wrong, the weaker is often so in a minor degree; and I think we sometimes admit the possibility of our being in error, and you never do.

And now, returning to the broader question, what these arts and labors of life have to teach us of its mystery, this is the first of their lessons—that the more beautiful the art, the more it is essentially the work of people who *feel themselves wrong:*—who are striving for the fulfilment of a law, and the grasp of a loveliness, which they have not yet attained, which they feel even farther and farther from attaining the more they strive for it. And yet, in still deeper sense, it is the work of people who know also that they are right. The very sense of inevitable error from their purpose marks the perfectness of that purpose, and the continued sense of failure arises from the continued opening of the eyes more clearly to all the sacredest laws of truth.

This is one lesson. The second is a very plain, and greatly precious one: namely—that whenever the arts and labors of life are fulfilled in this spirit of striving against misrule, and doing whatever we have to do, honorably and perfectly, they invariably bring happiness, as much as seems possible to the nature of man. In all other paths by which that happiness is pursued there is disappointment, or destruction: for ambition and for passion there is no rest—no fruition; the fairest pleasures of youth perish in a darkness greater than their past light: and the loftiest and purest love too often does but inflame the cloud of life with endless fire of pain. But, ascending from lowest to highest, through every scale of human industry, that industry worthily followed, gives peace. Ask the laborer in the field, at the forge, or in the mine; ask the patient, delicate-fingered artisan, or the strong-armed, fiery-hearted worker in bronze, and in marble, and with the colors of light; and none of these, who are true workmen, will ever tell you, that they have found the law of heaven an unkind one—that in the sweat of their face they should eat bread, till they return to the ground; nor that they ever found it an unrewarded obedience, if, indeed, it was rendered faithfully to the command—"Whatsoever thy hand findeth to do—do it with thy might."

These are the two great and constant lessons which our laborers teach us of the mystery of life. But there is another, and a sadder one, which they cannot teach us, which we must read on their tombstones.

"Do it with thy might." There have been myriads upon myriads of human creatures who have obeyed this law—who have put every breath and nerve of their being into its toil—who have devoted every hour, and exhausted every faculty — who have bequeathed their unaccomplished thoughts at death—who, being dead, have yet spoken, by majesty of memory, and strength of example. And, at last, what has all this "Might" of humanity accomplished, in six thousand years of labor and sorrow? What has it *done?* Take the three chief occupations and arts of men, one by one, and count their achievements. Begin with the first—the lord of them all—Agriculture. Six thousand years have passed since we were set to till the ground, from which we were taken. How much of it is tilled? How much of that which is, wisely or well? In the very centre and chief garden of Europe—where the two forms of parent Christianity have had their fortresses—where the noble Catholics of the Forest Cantons, and the noble Protestants of the Vaudois valleys, have maintained, for dateless ages, their faiths and liberties—there the unchecked Alpine rivers yet run wild in devastation; and the marshes, which a few hundred men could redeem with a year's labor, still blast their helpless inhabitants into fevered idiotism. That is so, in the centre of Europe! While, on the near coast of Africa, once the Garden of the Hesperides, an Arab woman, but a few sunsets since, ate her child, for famine. And, with all the treasures of the East at our feet, we, in our own dominion, could not find a few grains of rice, for a people that asked of us no more; but stood by, and saw five hundred thousand of them perish of hunger.

Then, after agriculture, the art of kings, take the next head of human arts—Weaving; the art of queens, honored of all noble Heathen women, in the person of their virgin goddess—honored of all Hebrew women, by the word of their wisest king—"She layeth her hands to the spindle, and her hands hold the distaff; she stretcheth out her hand to the poor. She is not afraid of the snow for her household, for all her household are clothed with scarlet. She maketh herself covering of tapestry; her clothing is silk and purple. She maketh fine linen, and selleth it, and delivereth girdles to the merchant." What have we done in all these thousands of years with this bright art of Greek maid and Christian matron? Six thousand years of weaving, and have we learned to weave? Might not every naked wall have been purple with tapestry, and every feeble breast fenced with sweet colors from the cold? What have we done? Our fingers are too few, it seems, to twist together some poor covering for our bodies. We set our streams to work for us, and choke the air with fire, to turn our spinning-wheels—and, —*are we yet clothed?* Are not the streets of the capitals of Europe foul with sale of cast clouts and rotten rags? Is not the beauty of your sweet children left in wretchedness of disgrace, while, with better honor, nature clothes the brood of the bird in its nest, and the suckling of the wolf in her den? And does not every winter's snow robe what you have not robed, and shroud what you have not shrouded; and every winter's wind bear up to heaven its wasted souls, to witness against you hereafter, by the voice of their Christ,—"I was naked, and ye clothed me not"?

Lastly — take the Art of Building — the strongest—proudest—most orderly—most enduring of the arts of man; that of which the produce is in the surest manner accumulative, and need not perish, or be replaced; but if once well done, will stand more strongly than the unbalanced rocks—more prevalently than the crumbling hills. The art which is associated with all civic pride and sacred principle; with which men record their power —satisfy their enthusiasm—make sure their defence—define and make dear their habitation. And in six thousand years of building, what have we done? Of the greater part of all that skill and strength, *no* vestige is left, but fallen stones, that encumber the fields and impede the streams. But, from this waste of disorder, and of time, and of rage, what *is* left to us? Constructive and progressive creatures that we are, with ruling brains, and forming hands, capable of fellowship, and thirsting for fame, can we not contend, in comfort, with the insects of the forest, or, in achievement, with the worm of the sea? The white surf rages in vain against the ramparts built by poor atoms of scarcely nascent life; but only ridges of formless ruin mark the places where once dwelt our noblest multitudes. The ant and the moth have cells for each of their young, but our little ones lie in festering heaps, in homes that consume them like graves; and night by night, from the corners of our streets, rises up the cry of the homeless—"I was a stranger, and ye took me not in."

Must it be always thus? Is our life forever to be without profit—without possession? Shall the strength of its generations be as barren as death; or cast away their labor, as the wild fig-tree casts her untimely figs? Is it all a dream then—the desire of the eyes and the pride of life—or, if it be, might we not live in nobler dream than this? The poets and prophets, the wise men, and the scribes, though they have told us nothing about a life to come, have told us much about the life that is now. They have had—they also,—their dreams, and we have laughed at them. They have dreamed of mercy, and of justice; they have dreamed of peace and good-will; they have dreamed of labor undisappointed, and of rest undisturbed; they have dreamed of fulness in harvest, and overflowing in store; they have dreamed of wisdom in council, and of providence in law; of gladness of parents, and strength of children, and glory of gray hairs. And at these visions of theirs we have mocked, and held them for idle and vain, unreal and unaccomplishable. What have we accomplished with our realities? Is this what has come of our worldly wisdom, tried against their folly? this, our mightiest possible, against their impotent ideal? or, have we only wandered among the spectra of a baser felicity, and chased phantoms of the tombs, instead of visions of the Almighty; and walked after the imaginations of our evil hearts, instead of after the counsels of Eternity, until our lives—not in the likeness of the cloud of heaven, but of the smoke of hell—have become "as a vapor, that appeareth for a little time, and then vanisheth away"?

Does it vanish then? Are you sure of that?—sure, that the nothingness of the grave will be a rest from this troubled nothingness; and that the coiling shadow, which disquiets itself in vain, cannot change into the smoke of the torment that ascends forever? Will any answer that they *are* sure of it, and that there is no fear, nor hope, nor desire, nor labor, whither they go? Be it so: will you not, then, make as sure of the Life that now is, as you are of the Death that is to come? Your hearts are wholly in this world—will you not give them to it wisely, as well as perfectly? And see, first of all, that you *have* hearts, and sound hearts, too, to give. Because you have no heaven to look for, is that any reason that you should remain ignorant of this wonderful and infinite earth, which is firmly and instantly given you in possession? Although your days are numbered, and the following darkness sure, is it necessary that you should share the degradation of the brute, because you are condemned to its mortality; or live the life of the moth, and of the worm, because you are to companion them in the dust? Not so; we may have but a few thousands of days to spend, perhaps hundreds only—perhaps tens; nay, the longest of our time and best, looked back on, will be but as a moment, as the twinkling of an eye; still we are men, not insects; we are living spirits, not passing clouds. "He maketh the winds His messengers; the momentary fire, His minister;" and shall we do less than *these?* Let us do the work of men while we bear the form of them; and, as we snatch our narrow portion of time out of Eternity, snatch also our narrow inheritance of passion out of Immortality—even though our lives *be* as a vapor, that appeareth for a little time, and then vanisheth away.

But there are some of you who believe not this—who think this cloud of life has no such close—that it is to float, revealed and illumined, upon the floor of heaven, in the day when He cometh with clouds, and every eye shall see Him. Some day, you believe, within these five, or ten, or twenty years, for every one of us the judgment will be set, and the books opened. If that be true, far more than that must be true. Is there but one day of judgment? Why, for us every day is a day of judgment—every day is a Dies Iræ, and writes its irrevocable ver-

dict in the flame of its West. Think you that judgment
waits till the doors of the grave are opened? It waits at
the doors of your houses—it waits at the corners of your
streets; we are in the midst of judgment—the insects
that we crush are our judges—the moments we fret away
are our judges—the elements that feed us, judge, as they
minister—and the pleasures that deceive us, judge, as
they indulge. Let us, for our lives, do the work of Men
while we bear the form of them, if indeed those lives are
Not as a vapor, and do *Not* vanish away.

"The work of men"—and what is that? Well, we may
any of us know very quickly, on the condition of being
wholly ready to do it. But many of us are for the most
part thinking, not of what we are to do, but of what we
are to get; and the best of us are sunk into the sin of
Ananias, and it is a mortal one—we want to keep back
part of the price; and we continually talk of taking up
our cross, as if the only harm in a cross was the *weight*
of it—as if it was only a thing to be carried, instead of
to be—crucified upon. "They that are His have crucified the flesh, with the affections and lusts." Does that
mean, think you, that in time of national distress, of religious trial, of crisis for every interest and hope of humanity—none of us will cease jesting, none cease idling,
none put themselves to any wholesome work, none take so
much as a tag of lace off their footmen's coats, to save
the world? Or does it rather mean, that they are ready
to leave houses, lands, and kindreds—yes, and life, if
need be? Life!—some of us are ready enough to throw
that away, joyless as we have made it. But *"station* in
Life"—how many of us are ready to quit *that?* Is it not
always the great objection, where there is question of
finding something useful to do—"We cannot leave our
stations in Life"?

Those of us who really cannot—that is to say, who can
only maintain themselves by continuing in some business
or salaried office, have already something to do; and all
that they have to see to is, that they do it honestly and
with all their might. But with most people who use that
apology, "remaining in the station of life to which Providence has called them" means keeping all the carriages,
and all the footmen and large houses they can possibly

pay for; and, once for all, I say that if ever Providence *did* put them into stations of that sort—which is not at all a matter of certainty—Providence is just now very distinctly calling them out again. Levi's station in life was the receipt of custom; and Peter's, the shore of Galilee; and Paul's, the ante-chambers of the High Priest,—which "station in life" each had to leave, with brief notice.

And, whatever our station in life may be, at this crisis, those of us who mean to fulfil our duty ought first to live on as little as we can; and, secondly, to do all the wholesome work for it we can, and to spend all we can spare in doing all the sure good we can.

And sure good is, first in feeding people, then in dressing people, then in lodging people, and lastly in rightly pleasing people, with arts, or sciences, or any other subject of thought.

I say first in feeding; and, once for all, do not let yourselves be deceived by any of the common talk of "indiscriminate charity." The order to us is not to feed the deserving hungry, nor the industrious hungry, nor the amiable and well-intentioned hungry, but simply to feed the hungry. It is quite true, infallibly true, that if any man will not work, neither should he eat—think of that, and every time you sit down to your dinner, ladies and gentlemen, say solemnly, before you ask a blessing, "How much work have I done to-day for my dinner?" But the proper way to enforce that order on those below you, as well as on yourselves, is not to leave vagabonds and honest people to starve together, but very distinctly to discern and seize your vagabond; and shut your vagabond up out of honest people's way, and very sternly then see that, until he has worked, he does *not* eat. But the first thing is to be sure you have the food to give; and, therefore, to enforce the organization of vast activities in agriculture and in commerce, for the production of the wholesomest food, and proper storing and distribution of it, so that no famine shall any more be possible among civilized beings. There is plenty of work in this business alone, and at once, for any number of people who like to engage in it.

Secondly, dressing people—that is to say, urging everyone within reach of your influence to be always neat and clean, and giving them means of being so. In so far as they absolutely refuse, you must give up the effort with respect to them, only taking care that no children within your sphere of influence shall any more be brought up with such habits; and that every person who is willing to dress with propriety shall have encouragement to do so. And the first absolutely necessary step toward this is the gradual adoption of a consistent dress for different ranks of persons, so that their rank shall be known by their dress; and the restriction of the changes of fashion within certain limits. All which appears for the present quite impossible; but it is only so far even difficult as it is difficult to conquer our vanity, frivolity, and desire to appear what we are not. And it is not, nor ever shall be, creed of mine, that these mean and shallow vices are unconquerable by Christian women.

And then, thirdly, lodging people, which you may think should have been put first, but I put it third, because we must feed and clothe people where we find them, and lodge them afterward. And providing lodgment for them means a great deal of vigorous legislation, and cutting down of vested interests that stand in the way, and after that, or before that, so far as we can get it, thorough sanitary and remedial action in the houses that we have; and then the building of more, strongly, beautifully, and in groups of limited extent, kept in proportion to their streams, and walled round, so that there may be no festering and wretched suburb anywhere, but clean and busy street within, and the open country without, with a belt of beautiful garden and orchard round the walls, so that from any part of the city perfectly fresh air and grass, and sight of far horizon, might be reachable in a few minutes' walk. This the final aim; but in immediate action every minor and possible good to be instantly done, when, and as, we can; roofs mended that have holes in them—fences patched that have gaps in them—walls buttressed that totter—and floors propped that shake; cleanliness and order enforced with our own hands and eyes, till we are breathless, every day. And all the fine arts will healthily follow. I myself have washed a flight of stone stairs all down, with bucket and broom, in a Savoy inn, where they hadn't washed their stairs since they first went up them; and I never made a better sketch than that afternoon.

These, then, are the three first needs of civilized life; and the law for every Christian man and woman is, that they shall be in direct service toward one of these three needs, as far as is consistent with their own special occupation, and if they have no special business, then wholly in one of these services. And out of such exertion in plain duty all other good will come; for in this direct contention with material evil, you will find out the real nature of all evil; you will discern by the various kinds of resistance, what is really the fault and main antagonism to good; also you will find the most unexpected helps and profound lessons given, and truths will come thus down to us which the speculation of all our lives would never have raised us up to. You will find nearly every educational problem solved, as soon as you truly want to do something; everybody will become of use in their own fittest way, and will learn what is best for them to know in that use. Competitive examination will then, and not till then, be wholesome, because it will be daily, and calm, and in practice; and on these familiar arts, and minute, but certain and serviceable knowledges, will be surely edified and sustained the greater arts and splendid theoretical sciences.

But much more than this. On such holy and simple practice will be founded, indeed, at last, an infallible religion. The greatest of all the mysteries of life, and the most terrible, is the corruption of even the sincerest religion, which is not daily founded on rational, effective, humble, and helpful action. Helpful action, observe! for there is just one law, which, obeyed, keeps all religions pure—forgotten, makes them all false. Whenever in any religious faith, dark or bright, we allow our minds to dwell upon the points in which we differ from other people, we are wrong, and in the devil's power. That is the essence of the Pharisee's thanksgiving—"Lord, I thank Thee that I am not as other men are." At every moment of our lives we should be trying to find out, not in what we differ from other people, but in what we agree with them; and the moment we find we can agree as to anything that should be done, kind or good (and who but fools couldn't?) then do it; push at it together: you can't quarrel in a side-by-side push; but the moment that even the best men stop pushing, and begin talking, they mistake their pugnacity for piety, and it's all over. I will not speak of the crimes which in past times have been committed in the name of Christ, nor of the follies which are at this hour held to be consistent with obedience to Him; but I *will* speak of the morbid corruption and waste of vital power in religious sentiment, by which the pure strength of that which should be the guiding soul of every nation, the splendor of its youthful manhood, and spotless light of its maidenhood, is averted or cast away. You may see continually girls who have never been taught to do a single useful thing thoroughly; who cannot sew, who cannot cook, who cannot cast an account, nor prepare a medicine, whose whole life has been passed either in play or in pride; you will find girls like these, when they are earnest-hearted, cast all their innate passion of religious spirit, which was meant by God to support them through the irksomeness of daily toil, into grievous and vain meditation over the meaning of the great Book, of which no syllable was ever yet to be understood but through a deed; all the instinctive wisdom and mercy of their womanhood made vain, and the glory of their pure consciences warped into fruitless agony concerning questions which the laws of common serviceable life would have either solved for them in an instant, or kept out of their way. Give such a girl any true work that will make her active in the dawn, and weary at night, with the consciousness that her fellow-creatures have indeed been the better for her day, and the powerless sorrow of her enthusiasm will transform itself into a majesty of radiant and beneficent peace.

So with our youths. We once taught them to make Latin verses, and called them educated; now we teach them to leap and to row, to hit a ball with a bat, and call them educated. Can they plough, can they sow, can they plant at the right time, or build with a steady hand? Is it the effort of their lives to be chaste, knightly, faithful, holy in thought, lovely in word and deed? Indeed it is, with some, nay, with many, and the strength of England is in them, and the hope; but we have to turn their courage from the toil of war to the toil of mercy; and their intellect from dispute of words to discernment of things; and their knighthood from the errantry of adventure to the state and fidelity of a kingly power. And then, indeed, shall abide, for them and for us, an incorruptible felicity, and an infallible religion; shall abide for us Faith, no more to be assailed by temptation, no more to be defended by wrath and by fear;—shall abide with us Hope, no more to be quenched by the years that overwhelm, or made ashamed by the shadows that betray: —shall abide for us, and with us, the greatest of these; the abiding will, the abiding name of our Father. For the greatest of these is Charity.